YU-GI-OH!: MILLENNIUM WORLD VOL. 2
The SHONEN JUMP Manga Edition

STORY AND ART BY
KAZUKI TAKAHASHI

Translation & English Adaptation/Anita Sengupta
Touch-up Art & Lettering/Kelle Han
Additional Touch-up/Josh Simpson
Design/Sean Lee
Editor/Jason Thompson

Managing Editor/Elizabeth Kawasaki
Director of Production/Noboru Watanabe
Vice President of Publishing/Alvin Lu
Vice President & Editor in Chief/Yumi Hoashi
Sr. Director of Acquisitions/Rika Inouye
Vice President of Sales & Marketing/Liza Coppola
Publisher/Hyoe Narita

In the original Japanese edition, YU-GI-OH!, YU-GI-OH!: DUELIST, and YU-GI-OH!: MILLENNIUM WORLD are known collectively as YU-GI-OH!. The English YU-GI-OH!: MILLENNIUM WORLD was originally volumes 32–38 of the Japanese YU-GI-OH!.

Printed in the U.S.A.

Published by VIZ Media, LLC
P.O. Box 77010
San Francisco, CA 94107

10 9 8 7 6 5 4 3 2
First printing, November 2005
Second printing, May 2010

viz media
www.viz.com

RATED T FOR TEEN

PARENTAL ADVISORY
YU-GI-OH!: MILLENNIUM WORLD is rated T for Teen and is recommended for ages 13 and up. It contains fantasy violence and alcohol usage.
ratings.viz.com

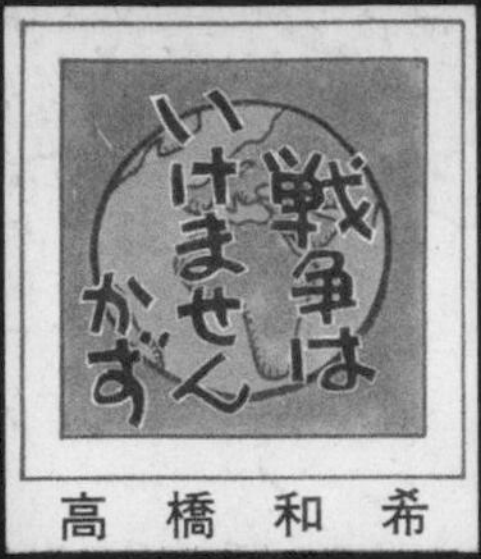
戦争はいけませんかず
高橋和希

WAR IS BAD! - KAZU

ON MARCH 20, 2003, A WAR BEGAN ON THE OTHER SIDE OF THE PLANET. NO MATTER WHAT THE REASON, I THINK KILLING AND WOUNDING PEOPLE IS UNFORGIVABLE. IN THE DISTANT FUTURE, WHEN WE ARE LONG GONE, I HOPE THAT EVERYONE CAN LIVE TOGETHER IN HARMONY WITHOUT RACES OR BORDERS.

—KAZUKI TAKAHASHI, 2003

Artist/author Kazuki Takahashi first tried to break into the manga business in 1982, but success eluded him until **Yu-Gi-Oh!** debuted in the Japanese **Weekly Shonen Jump** magazine in 1996. **Yu-Gi-Oh!**'s themes of friendship and fighting, together with Takahashi's weird and wonderful art, soon became enormously successful, spawning a real-world card game, video games, and two anime series. A lifelong gamer, Takahashi enjoys Shogi (Japanese chess), Mahjong, card games, and tabletop RPGs, among other games.

SHONEN JUMP MANGA

Yu-Gi-Oh!
Millennium World

Vol. 2
MAGICIAN'S GENESIS
STORY AND ART BY
KAZUKI TAKAHASHI

THE MAIN CHARACTERS

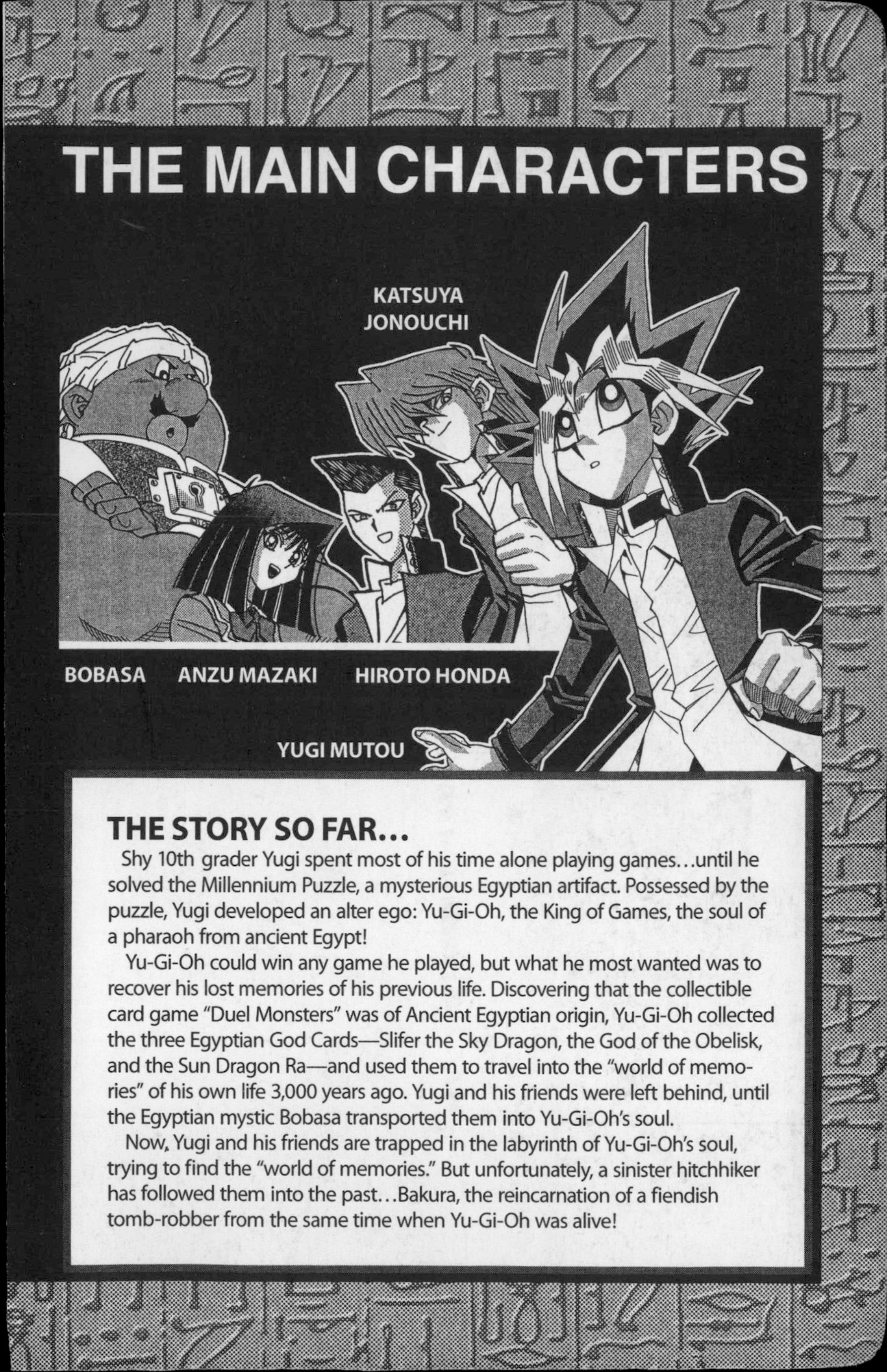
KATSUYA JONOUCHI
BOBASA
ANZU MAZAKI
HIROTO HONDA
YUGI MUTOU

THE STORY SO FAR...

Shy 10th grader Yugi spent most of his time alone playing games...until he solved the Millennium Puzzle, a mysterious Egyptian artifact. Possessed by the puzzle, Yugi developed an alter ego: Yu-Gi-Oh, the King of Games, the soul of a pharaoh from ancient Egypt!

Yu-Gi-Oh could win any game he played, but what he most wanted was to recover his lost memories of his previous life. Discovering that the collectible card game "Duel Monsters" was of Ancient Egyptian origin, Yu-Gi-Oh collected the three Egyptian God Cards—Slifer the Sky Dragon, the God of the Obelisk, and the Sun Dragon Ra—and used them to travel into the "world of memories" of his own life 3,000 years ago. Yugi and his friends were left behind, until the Egyptian mystic Bobasa transported them into Yu-Gi-Oh's soul.

Now, Yugi and his friends are trapped in the labyrinth of Yu-Gi-Oh's soul, trying to find the "world of memories." But unfortunately, a sinister hitchhiker has followed them into the past...Bakura, the reincarnation of a fiendish tomb-robber from the same time when Yu-Gi-Oh was alive!

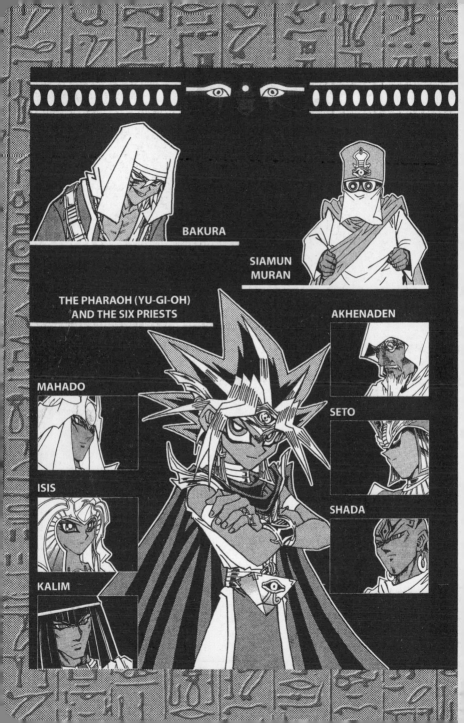

BAKURA

SIAMUN MURAN

THE PHARAOH (YU-GI-OH) AND THE SIX PRIESTS

AKHENADEN

MAHADO

SETO

ISIS

SHADA

KALIM

Yu-Gi-Oh!
Millennium World

Vol. 2

CONTENTS

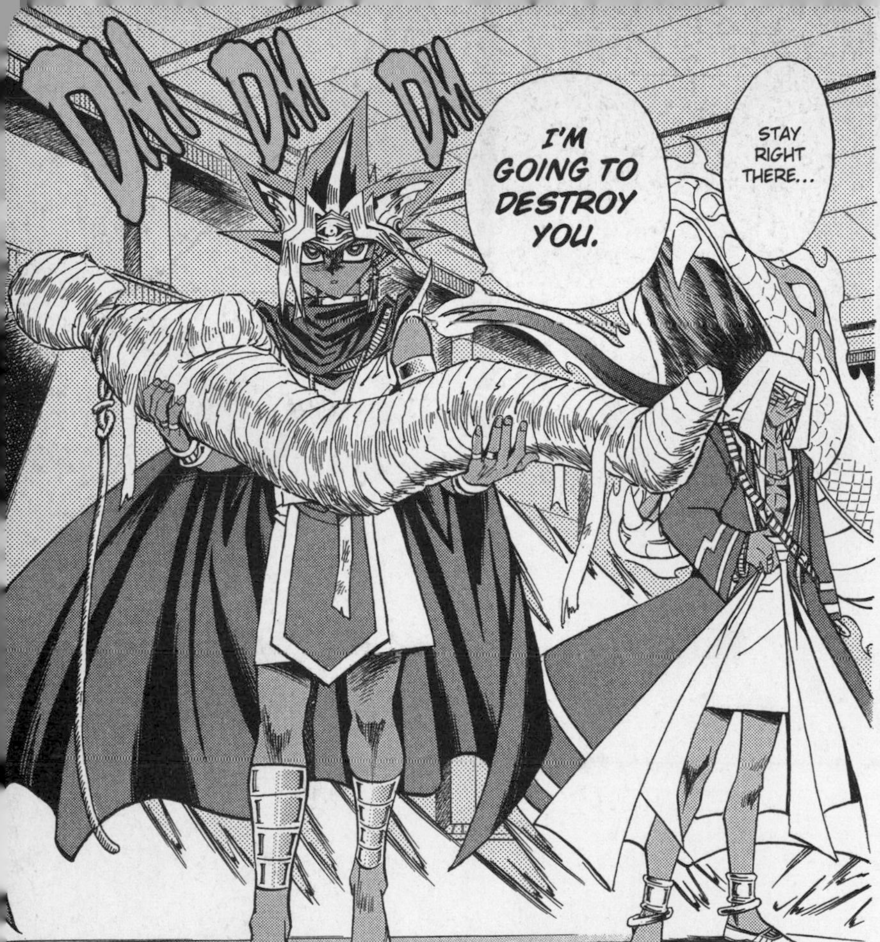
STAY RIGHT THERE...
I'M GOING TO DESTROY YOU.
DM DM DM

Duel 10: In the Name of the Gods

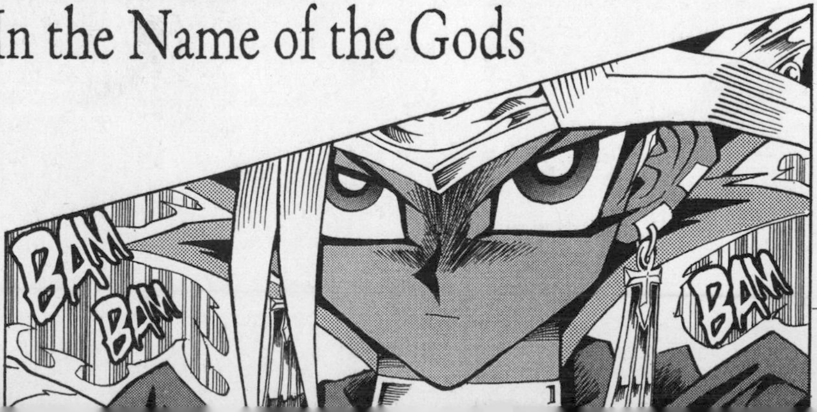
BAM
BAM BAM

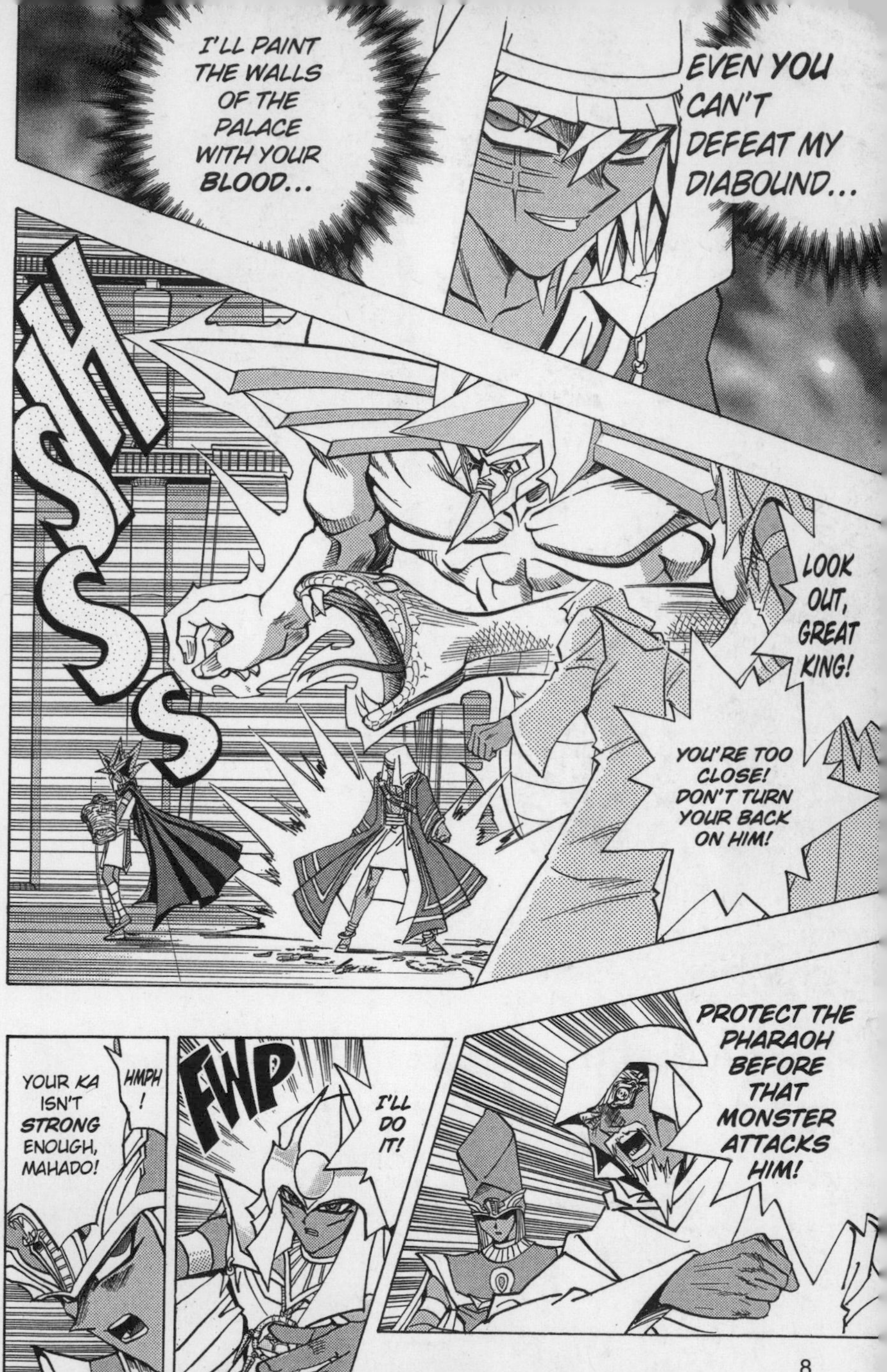
EVEN YOU CAN'T DEFEAT MY DIABOUND...
I'LL PAINT THE WALLS OF THE PALACE WITH YOUR BLOOD...
LOOK OUT, GREAT KING!
YOU'RE TOO CLOSE! DON'T TURN YOUR BACK ON HIM!
SSSHH
PROTECT THE PHARAOH BEFORE THAT MONSTER ATTACKS HIM!
I'LL DO IT!
FWP
HMPH!
YOUR KA ISN'T STRONG ENOUGH, MAHADO!

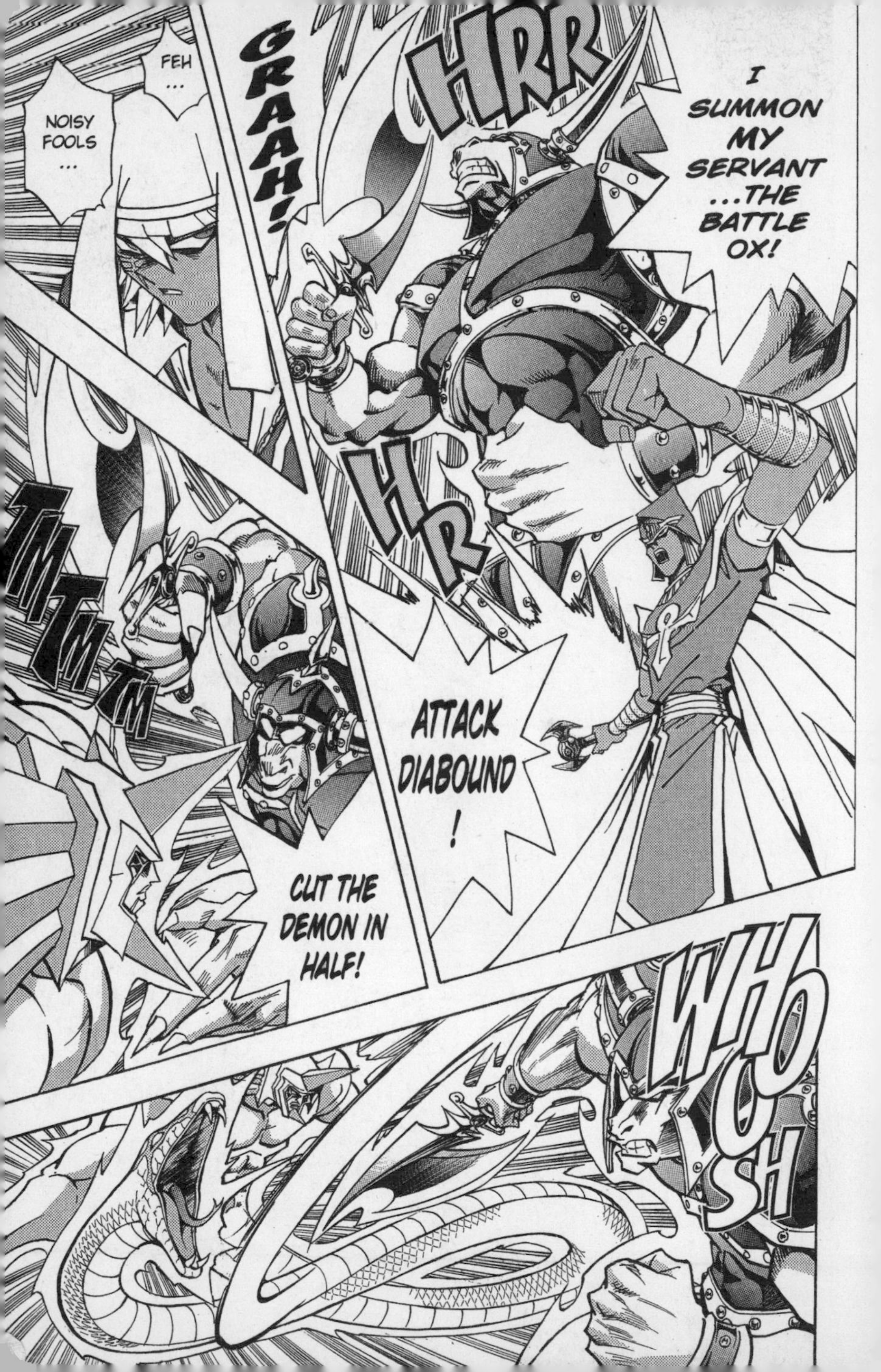
I SUMMON MY SERVANT ...THE BATTLE OX!
HRR
GRAAH!
HRR
FEH ...
NOISY FOOLS ...
ATTACK DIABOUND !
TMTMTM
CUT THE DEMON IN HALF!
WHOOSH

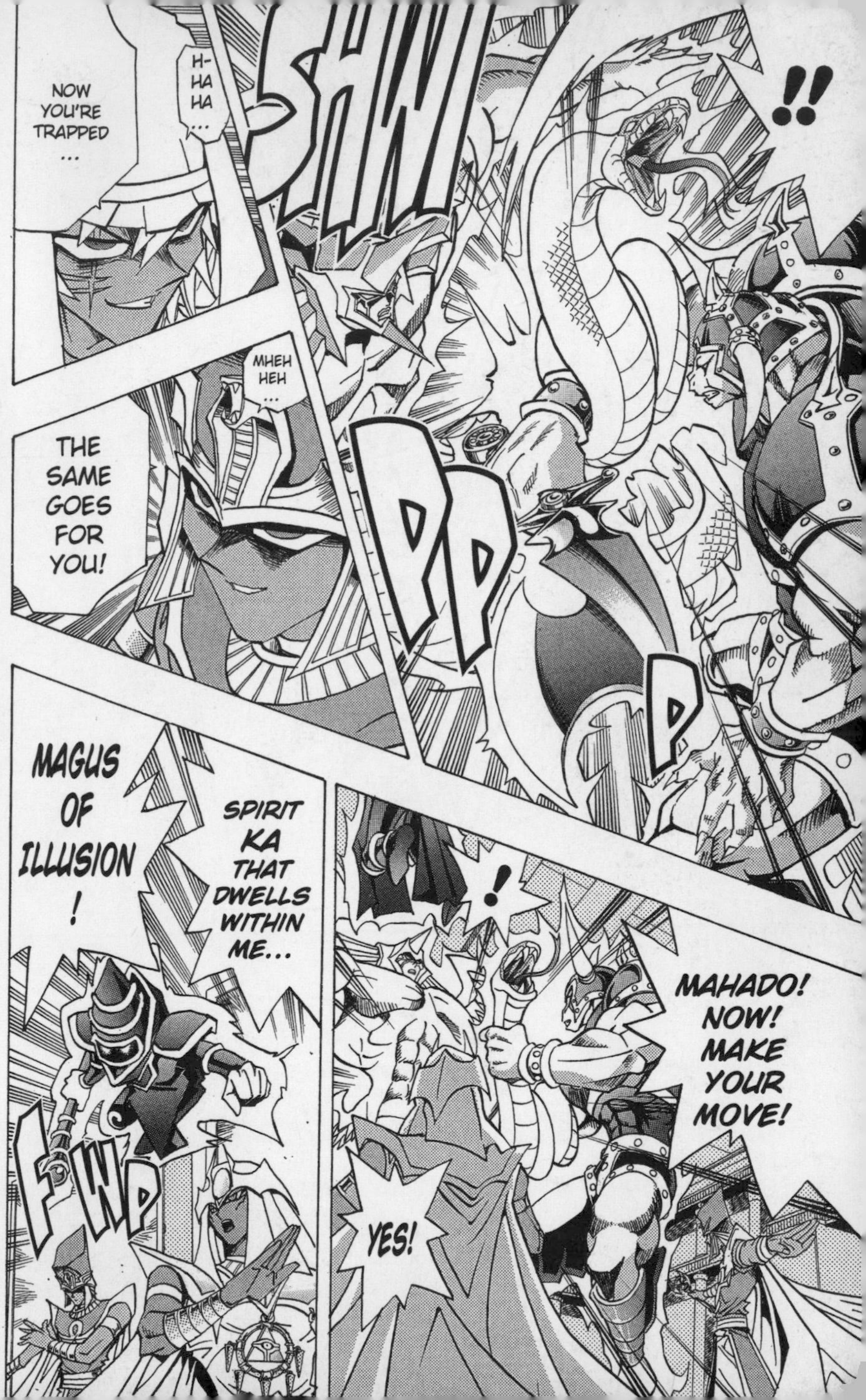
SHIN
!!
DP
D
H-HA HA...
NOW YOU'RE TRAPPED...
MHEH HEH...
THE SAME GOES FOR YOU!
!
MAHADO! NOW! MAKE YOUR MOVE!
YES!
SPIRIT KA THAT DWELLS WITHIN ME...
MAGUS OF ILLUSION!
FWP

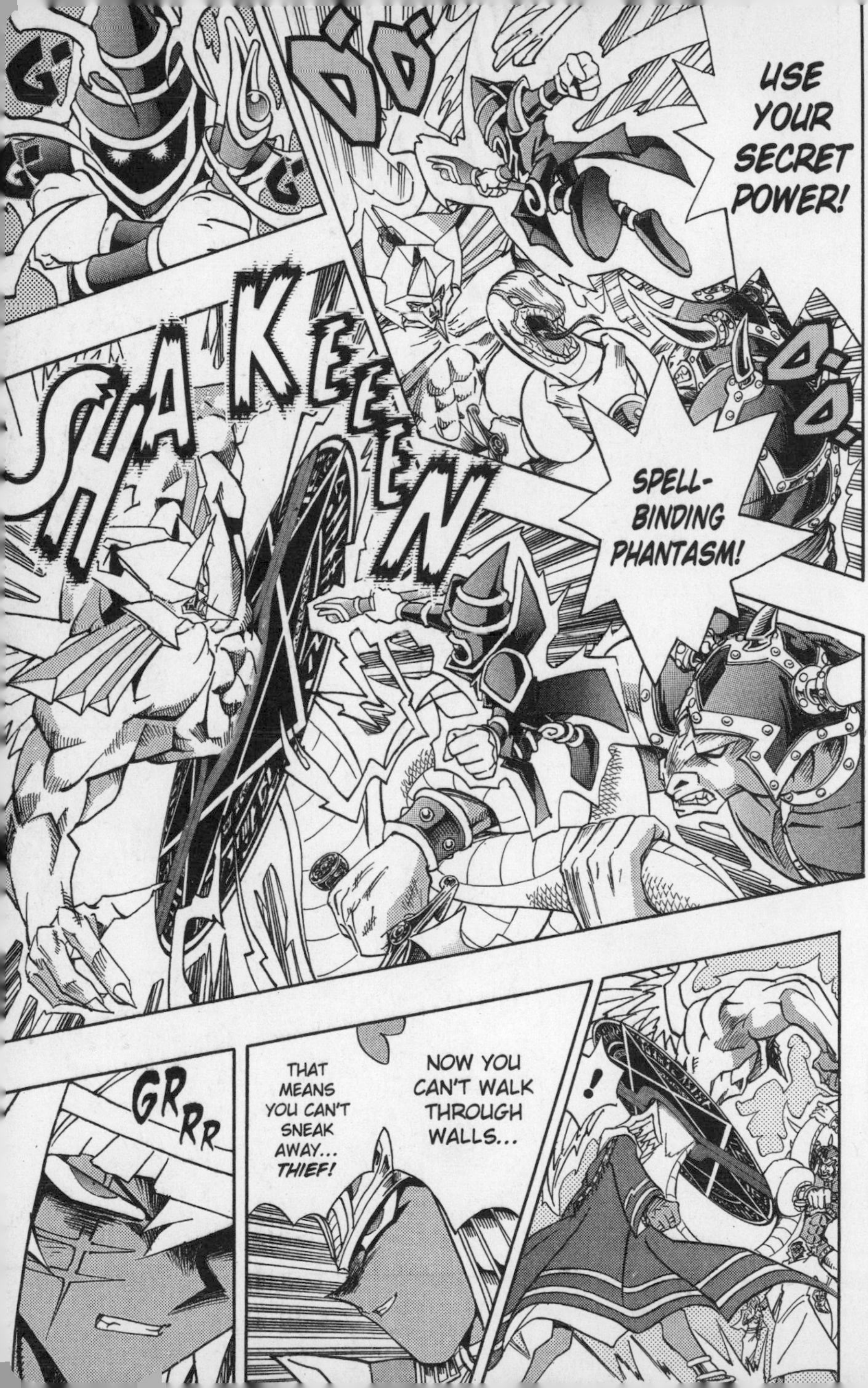
USE YOUR SECRET POWER!
SPELL-BINDING PHANTASM!
SHAKEEEN
!
NOW YOU CAN'T WALK THROUGH WALLS...
THAT MEANS YOU CAN'T SNEAK AWAY... THIEF!
GRRR

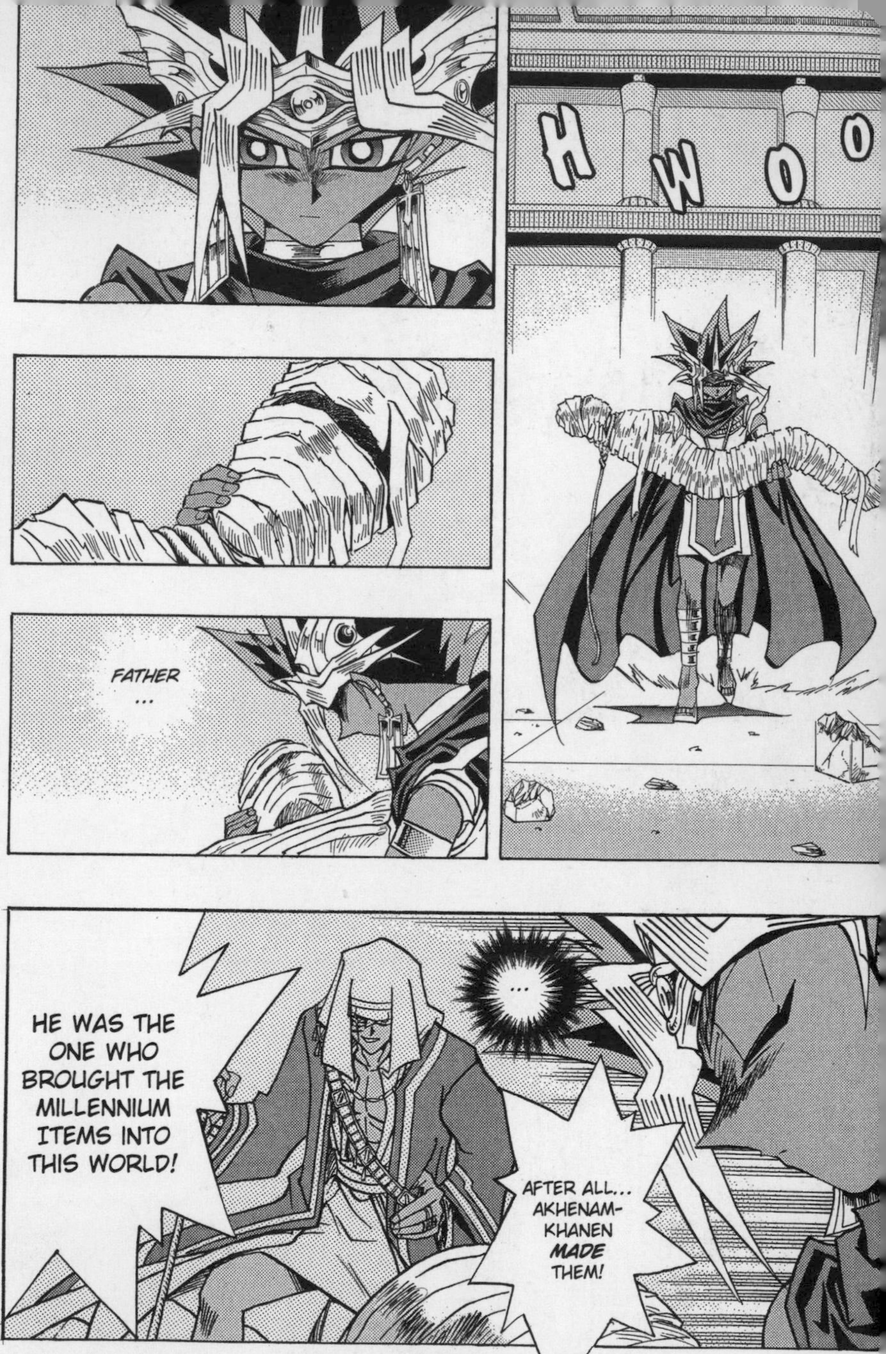
HWOO
FATHER ...
...
HE WAS THE ONE WHO BROUGHT THE MILLENNIUM ITEMS INTO THIS WORLD!
AFTER ALL... AKHENAMKHANEN *MADE* THEM!

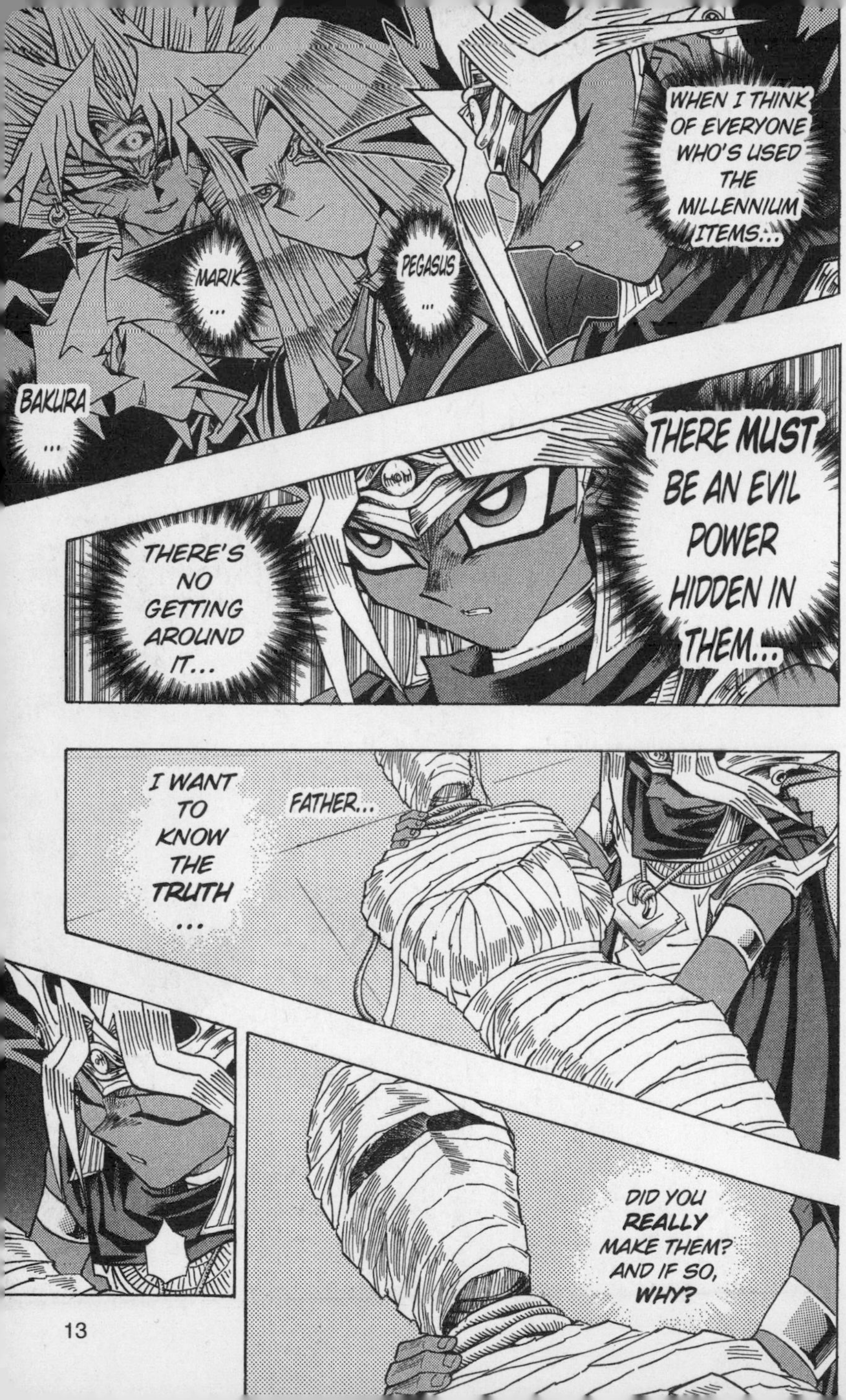
WHEN I THINK OF EVERYONE WHO'S USED THE MILLENNIUM ITEMS...
PEGASUS ...
MARIK ...
BAKURA ...
THERE MUST BE AN EVIL POWER HIDDEN IN THEM...
THERE'S NO GETTING AROUND IT...
FATHER...
I WANT TO KNOW THE TRUTH ...
DID YOU REALLY MAKE THEM? AND IF SO, WHY?

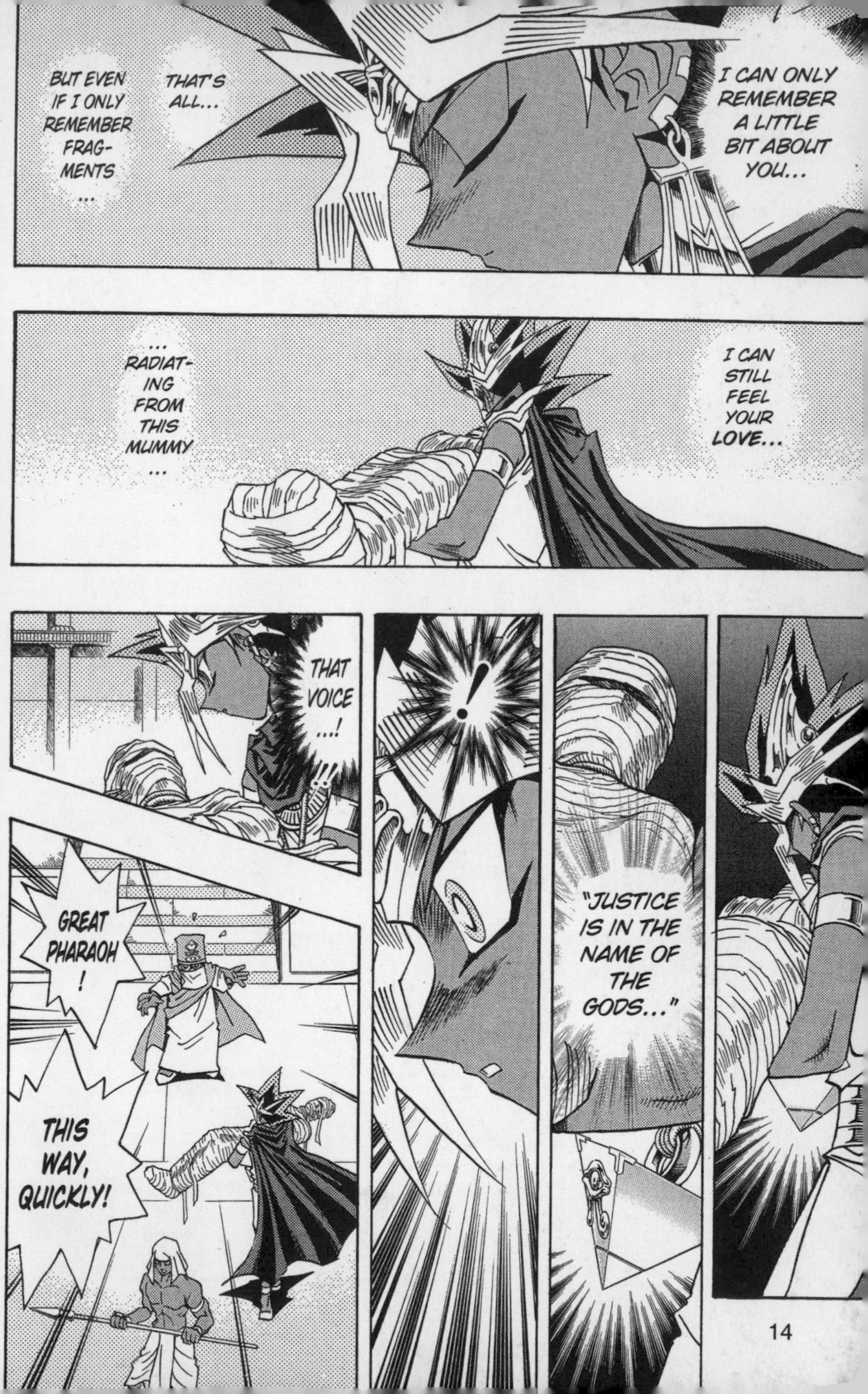
I CAN ONLY REMEMBER A LITTLE BIT ABOUT YOU...
THAT'S ALL...
BUT EVEN IF I ONLY REMEMBER FRAG-MENTS...
I CAN STILL FEEL YOUR LOVE...
...RADIAT-ING FROM THIS MUMMY...
"JUSTICE IS IN THE NAME OF THE GODS..."
!
THAT VOICE...!
GREAT PHARAOH!
THIS WAY, QUICKLY!

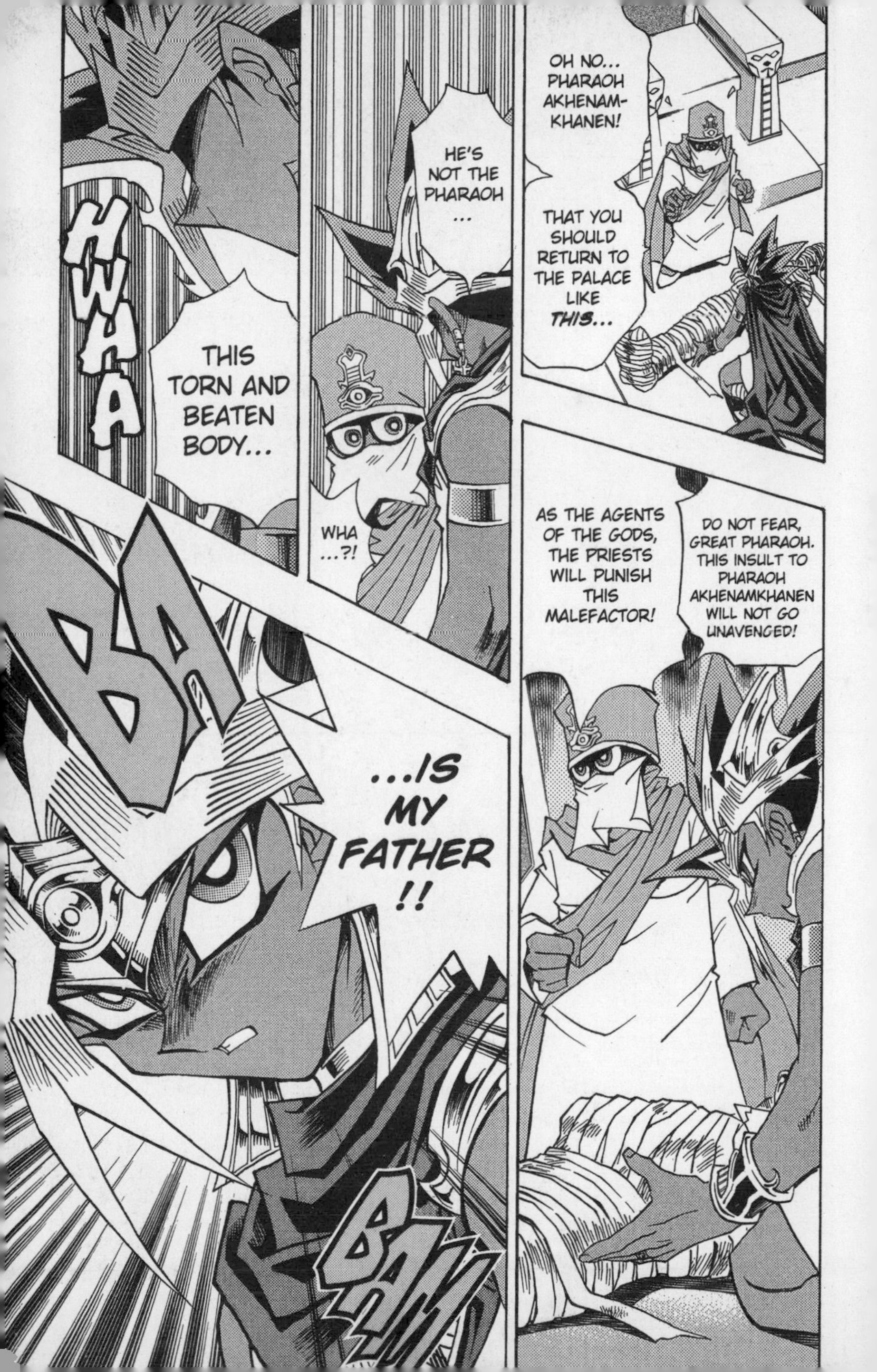
OH NO... PHARAOH AKHENAM-KHANEN!
THAT YOU SHOULD RETURN TO THE PALACE LIKE *THIS*...
DO NOT FEAR, GREAT PHARAOH. THIS INSULT TO PHARAOH AKHENAMKHANEN WILL NOT GO UNAVENGED!
AS THE AGENTS OF THE GODS, THE PRIESTS WILL PUNISH THIS MALEFACTOR!
HE'S NOT THE PHARAOH ...
WHA ...?!
HWHA
THIS TORN AND BEATEN BODY...
BAM
...IS MY FATHER !!
BAM

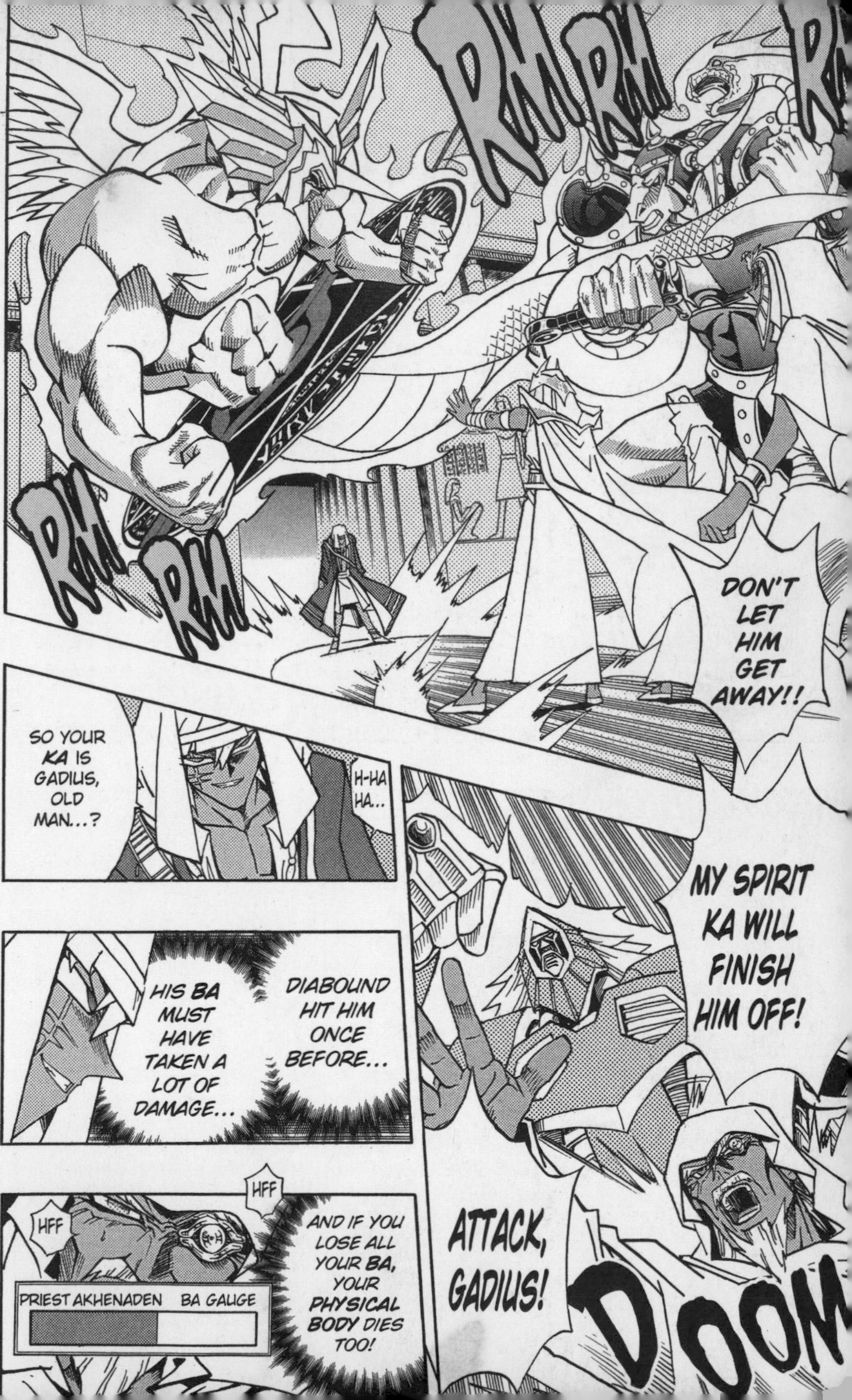

DON'T LET HIM GET AWAY!!
MY SPIRIT KA WILL FINISH HIM OFF!
ATTACK, GADIUS!
DOOM
SO YOUR KA IS GADIUS, OLD MAN...?
H-HA HA...
DIABOUND HIT HIM ONCE BEFORE...
HIS BA MUST HAVE TAKEN A LOT OF DAMAGE...
HFF
HFF
AND IF YOU LOSE ALL YOUR BA, YOUR PHYSICAL BODY DIES TOO!
PRIEST AKHENADEN BA GAUGE

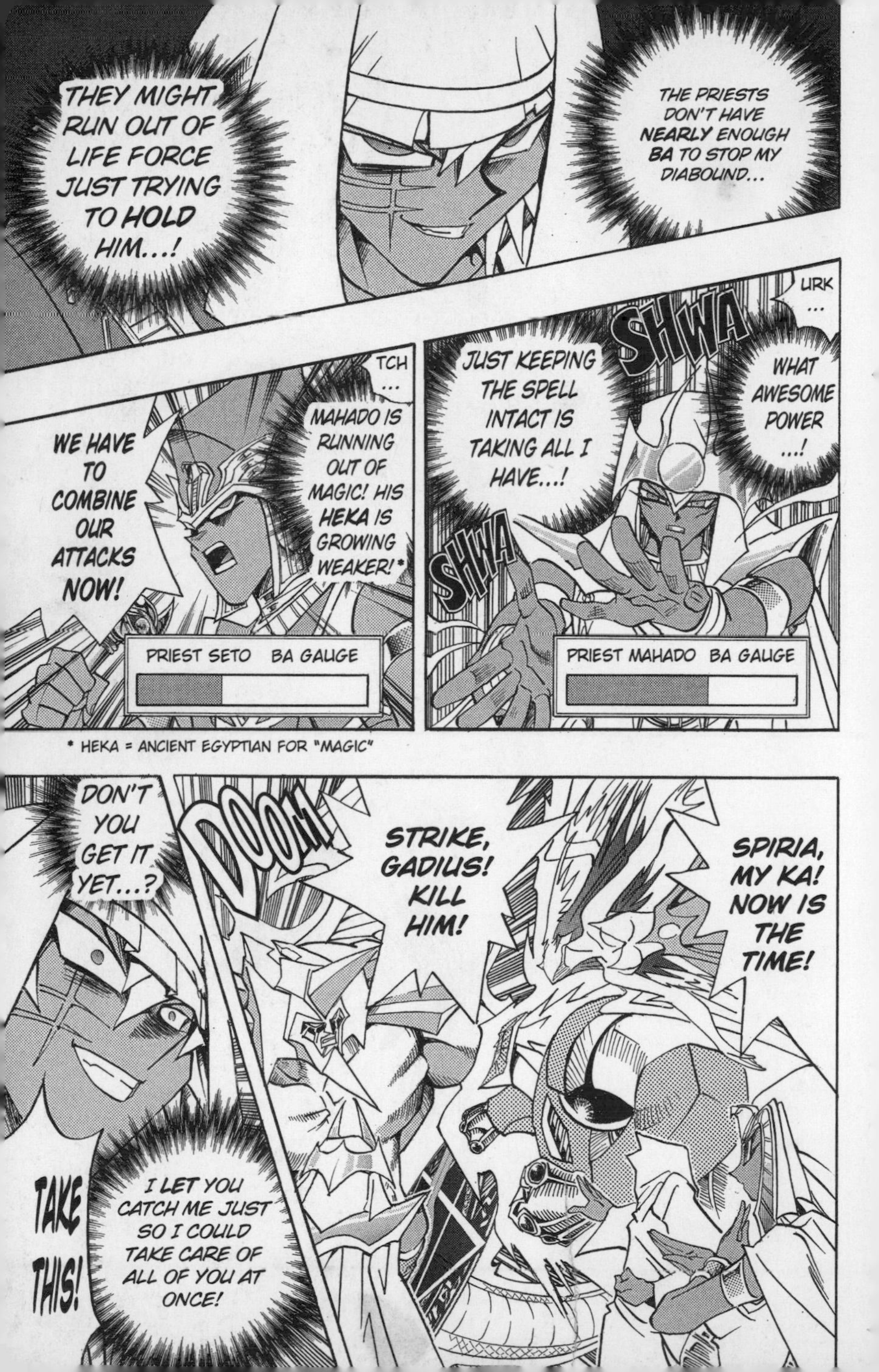
THE PRIESTS DON'T HAVE NEARLY ENOUGH BA TO STOP MY DIABOUND...
THEY MIGHT RUN OUT OF LIFE FORCE JUST TRYING TO HOLD HIM...!
URK...
SHWA
WHAT AWESOME POWER...!
JUST KEEPING THE SPELL INTACT IS TAKING ALL I HAVE...!
SHWA
PRIEST MAHADO BA GAUGE
TCH...
MAHADO IS RUNNING OUT OF MAGIC! HIS HEKA IS GROWING WEAKER!*
WE HAVE TO COMBINE OUR ATTACKS NOW!
PRIEST SETO BA GAUGE
SPIRIA, MY KA! NOW IS THE TIME!
STRIKE, GADIUS! KILL HIM!
DOOM
DON'T YOU GET IT YET...?
TAKE THIS!
I LET YOU CATCH ME JUST SO I COULD TAKE CARE OF ALL OF YOU AT ONCE!

* HEKA = ANCIENT EGYPTIAN FOR "MAGIC"

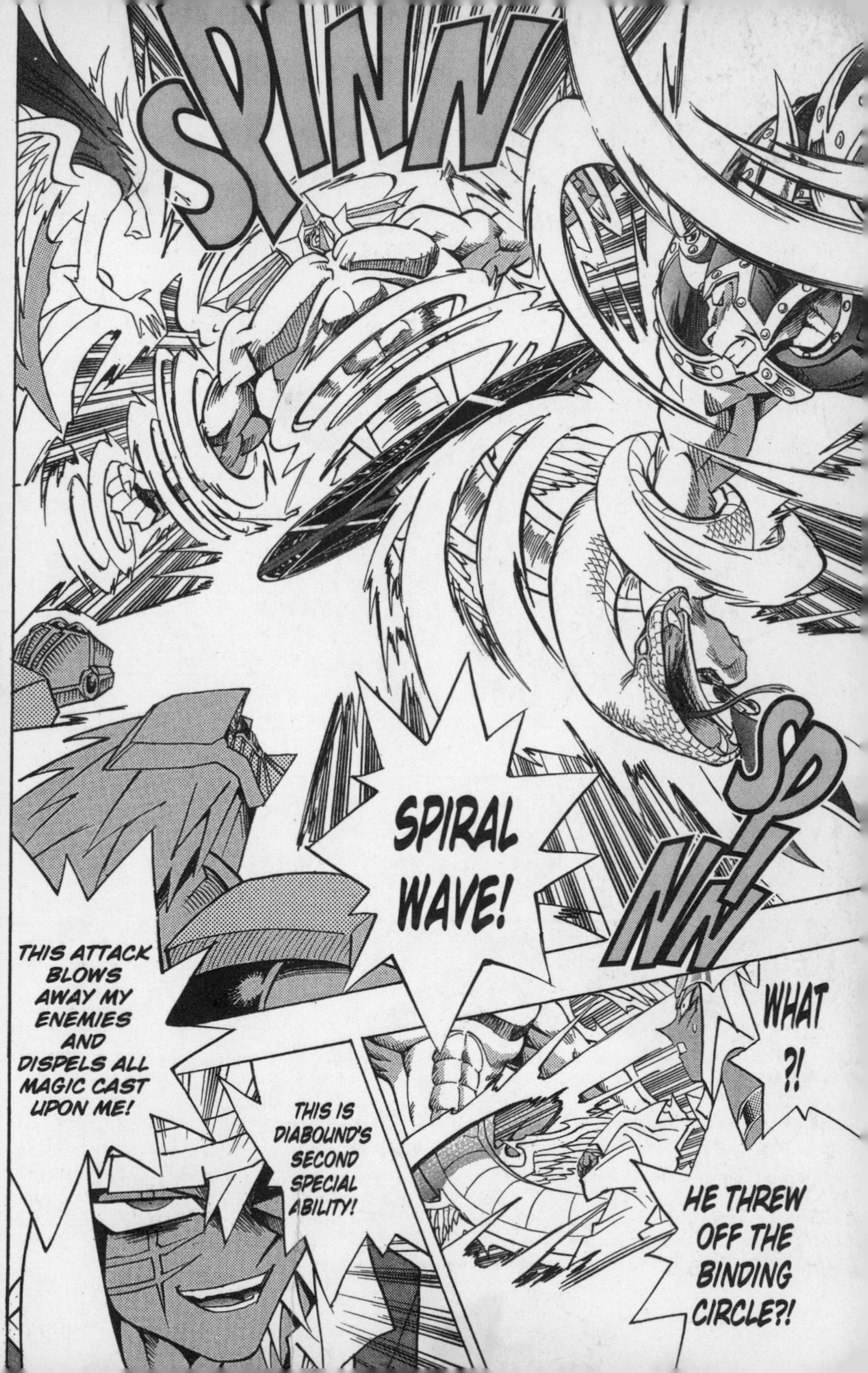
SPINN
SPIRAL WAVE!
SNN
WHAT ?!
HE THREW OFF THE BINDING CIRCLE?!
THIS ATTACK BLOWS AWAY MY ENEMIES AND DISPELS ALL MAGIC CAST UPON ME!
THIS IS DIABOUND'S SECOND SPECIAL ABILITY!

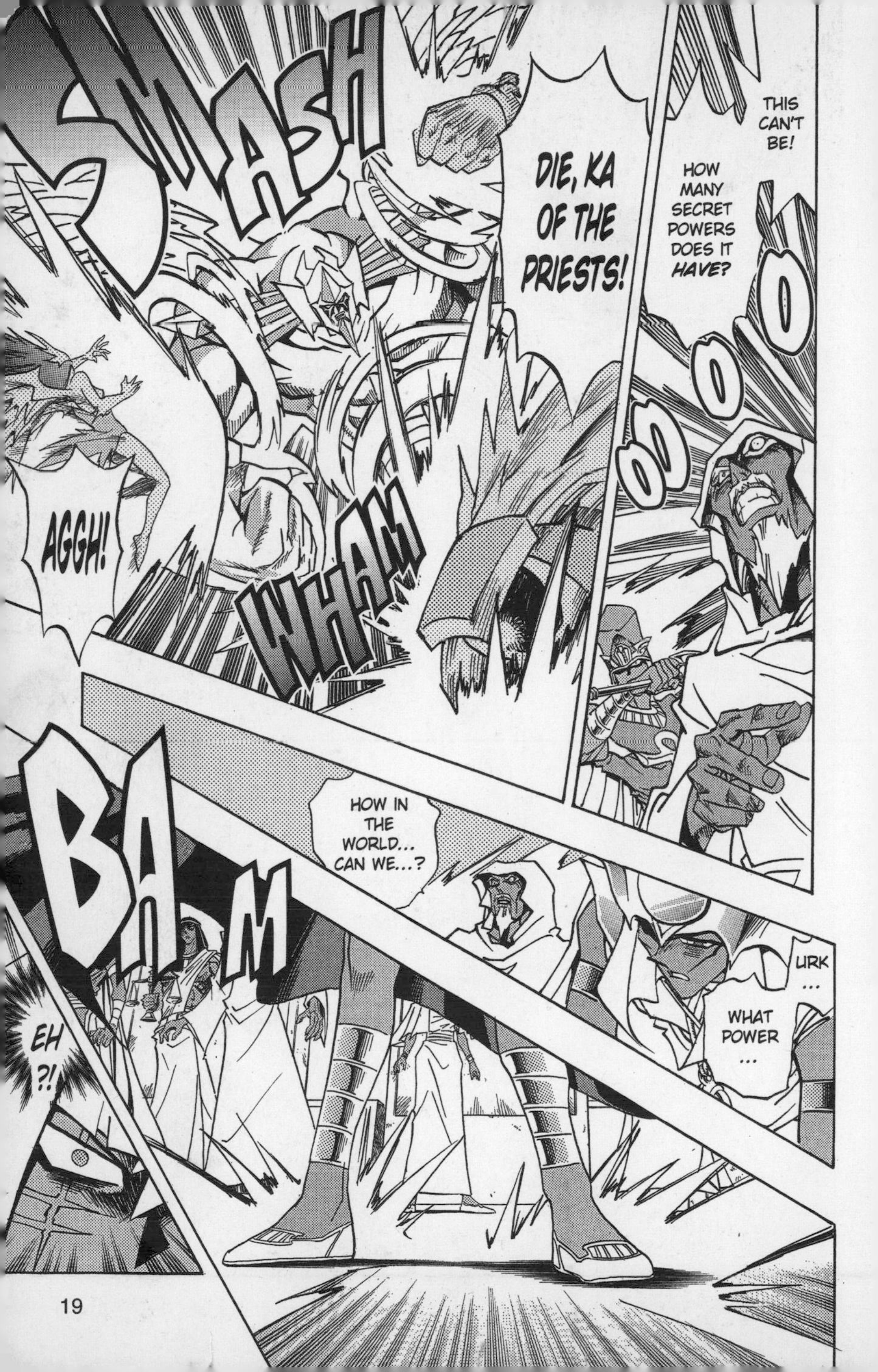
THIS CAN'T BE!
HOW MANY SECRET POWERS DOES IT *HAVE?*
DIE, KA OF THE PRIESTS!
SMASH
AGGH!
WHAM
HOW IN THE WORLD... CAN WE...?
URK ... WHAT POWER ...
BAM
EH ?!

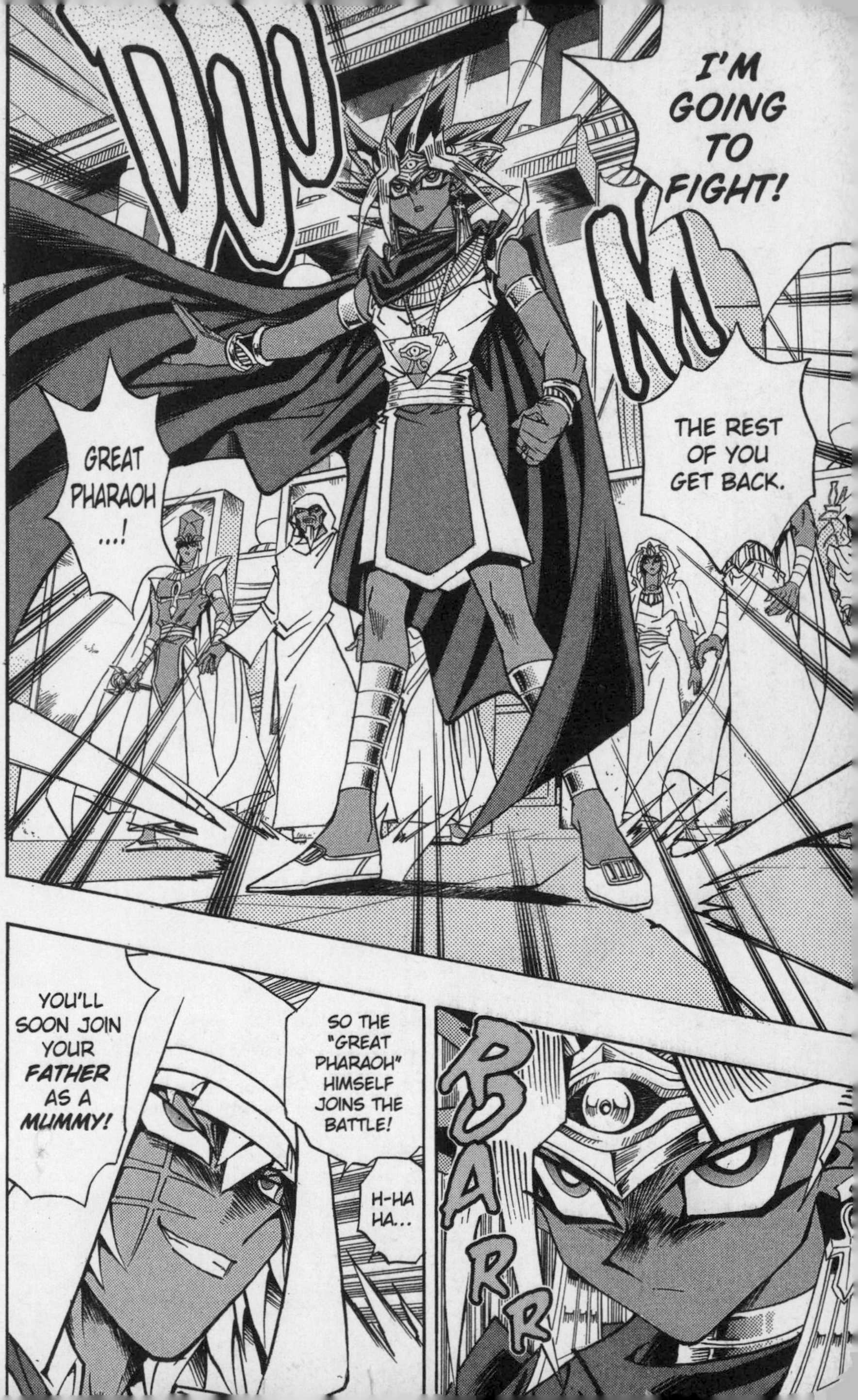
I'M GOING TO FIGHT!
DOOOM
THE REST OF YOU GET BACK.
GREAT PHARAOH ...!
ROARR
SO THE "GREAT PHARAOH" HIMSELF JOINS THE BATTLE!
H-HA HA...
YOU'LL SOON JOIN YOUR FATHER AS A MUMMY!

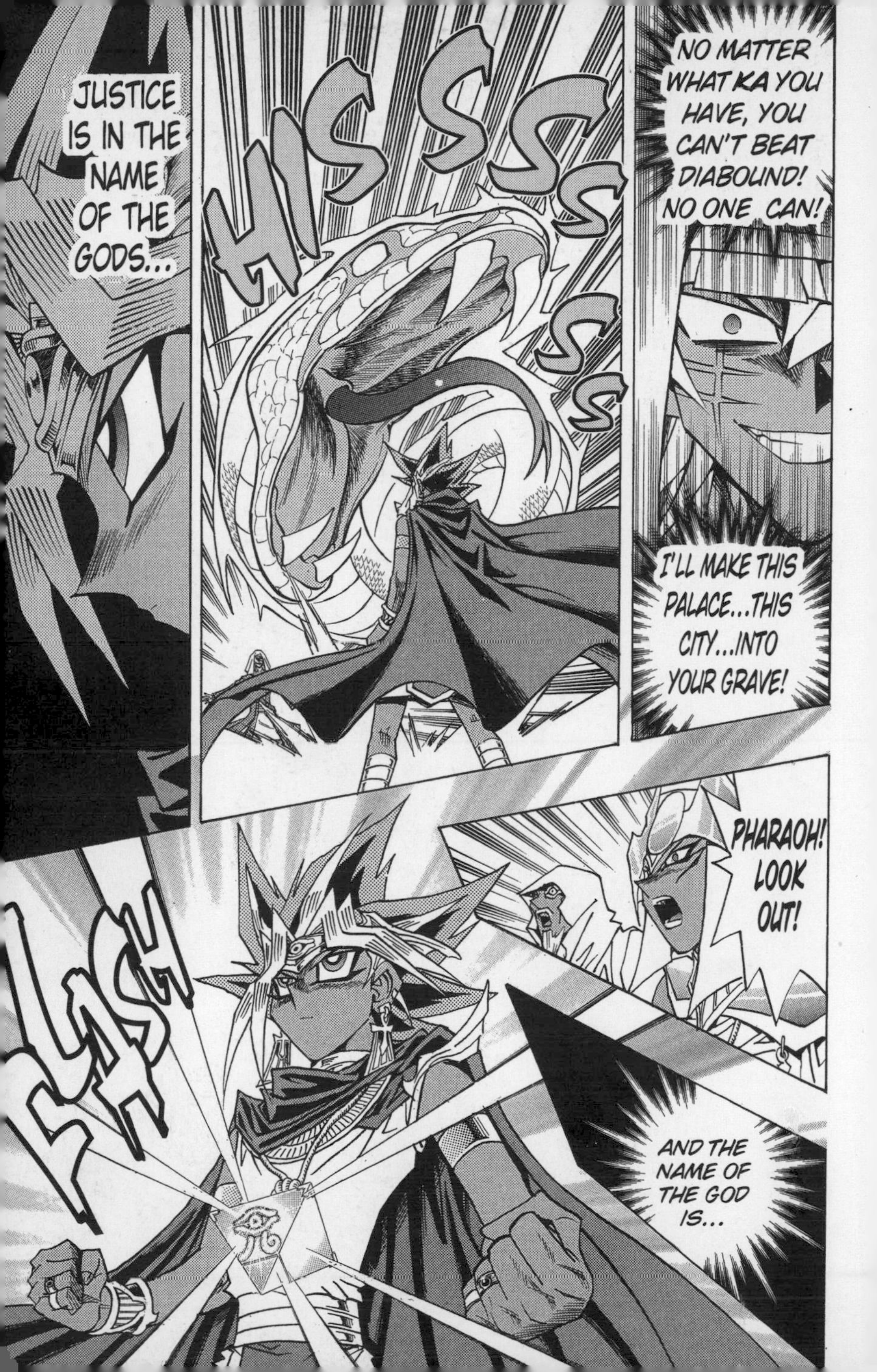
NO MATTER WHAT KA YOU HAVE, YOU CAN'T BEAT DIABOUND! NO ONE CAN!
I'LL MAKE THIS PALACE...THIS CITY...INTO YOUR GRAVE!
HISSSSSS
JUSTICE IS IN THE NAME OF THE GODS...
PHARAOH! LOOK OUT!
AND THE NAME OF THE GOD IS...

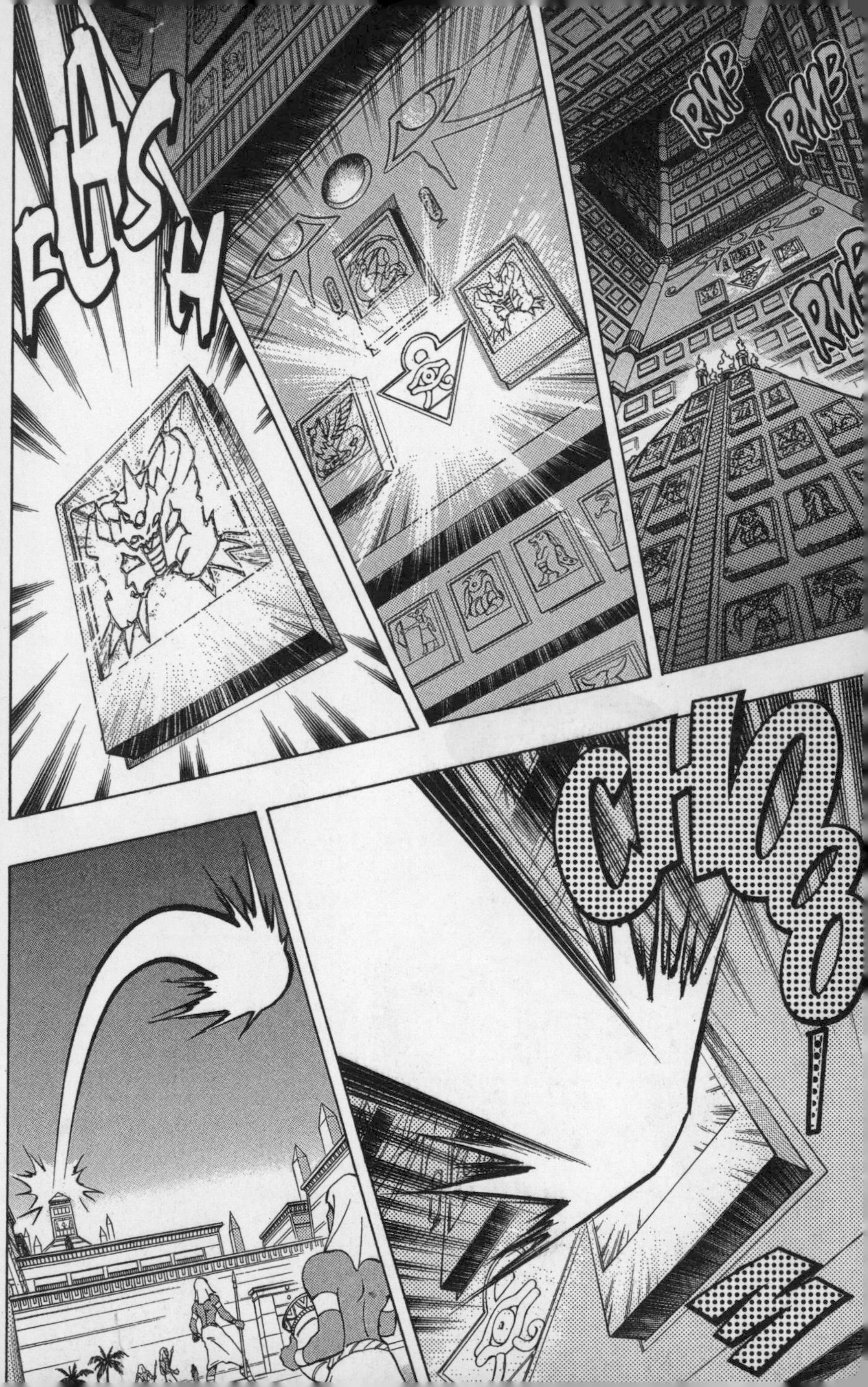
RMB RMB
RMB
FLASH
CHOOO!

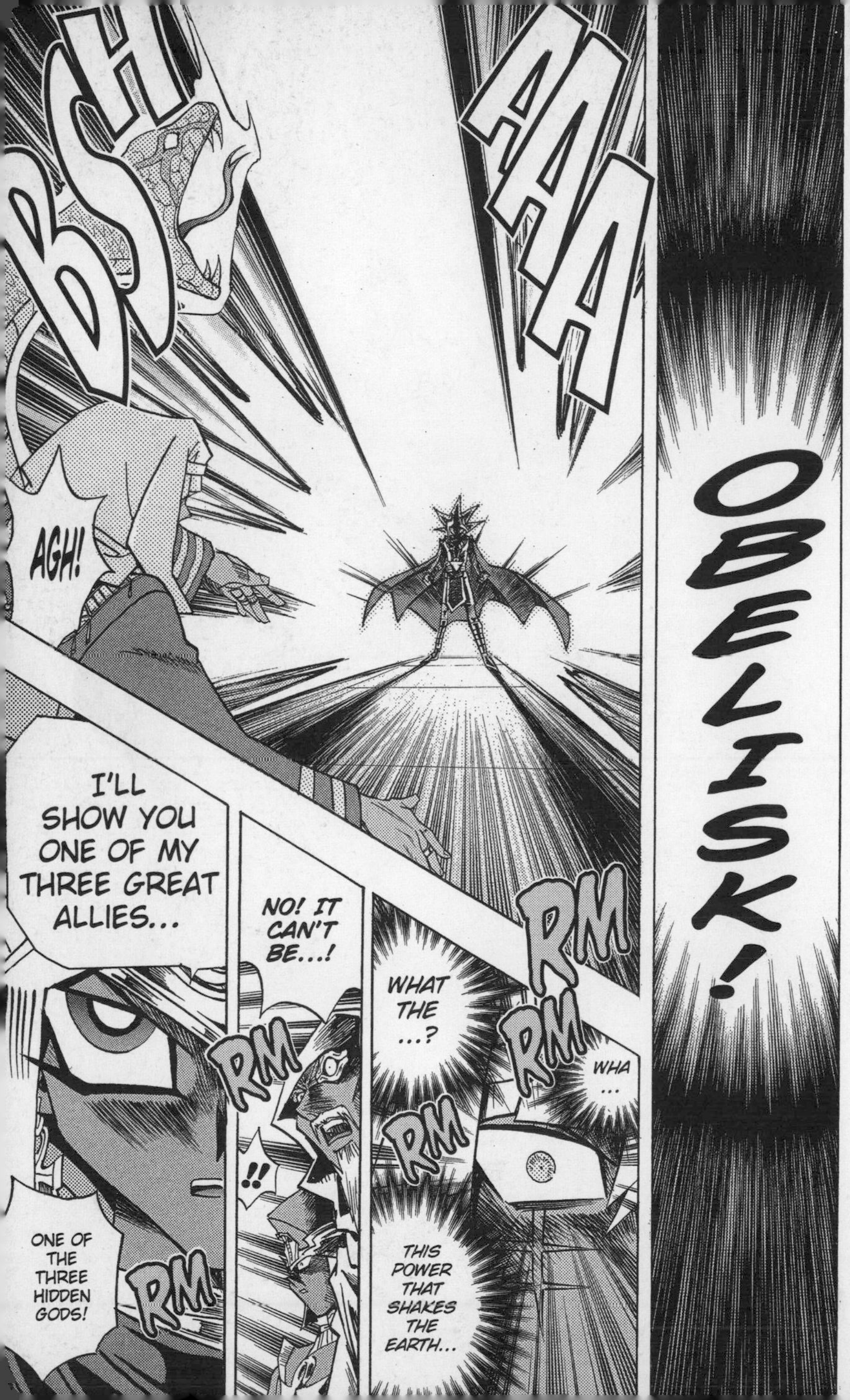
OBELISK!
AAA
BSCH
AGH!
RM
RM
WHA...
WHAT THE...?
RM
RM
THIS POWER THAT SHAKES THE EARTH...
NO! IT CAN'T BE...!
RM
!!
I'LL SHOW YOU ONE OF MY THREE GREAT ALLIES...
ONE OF THE THREE HIDDEN GODS!
RM

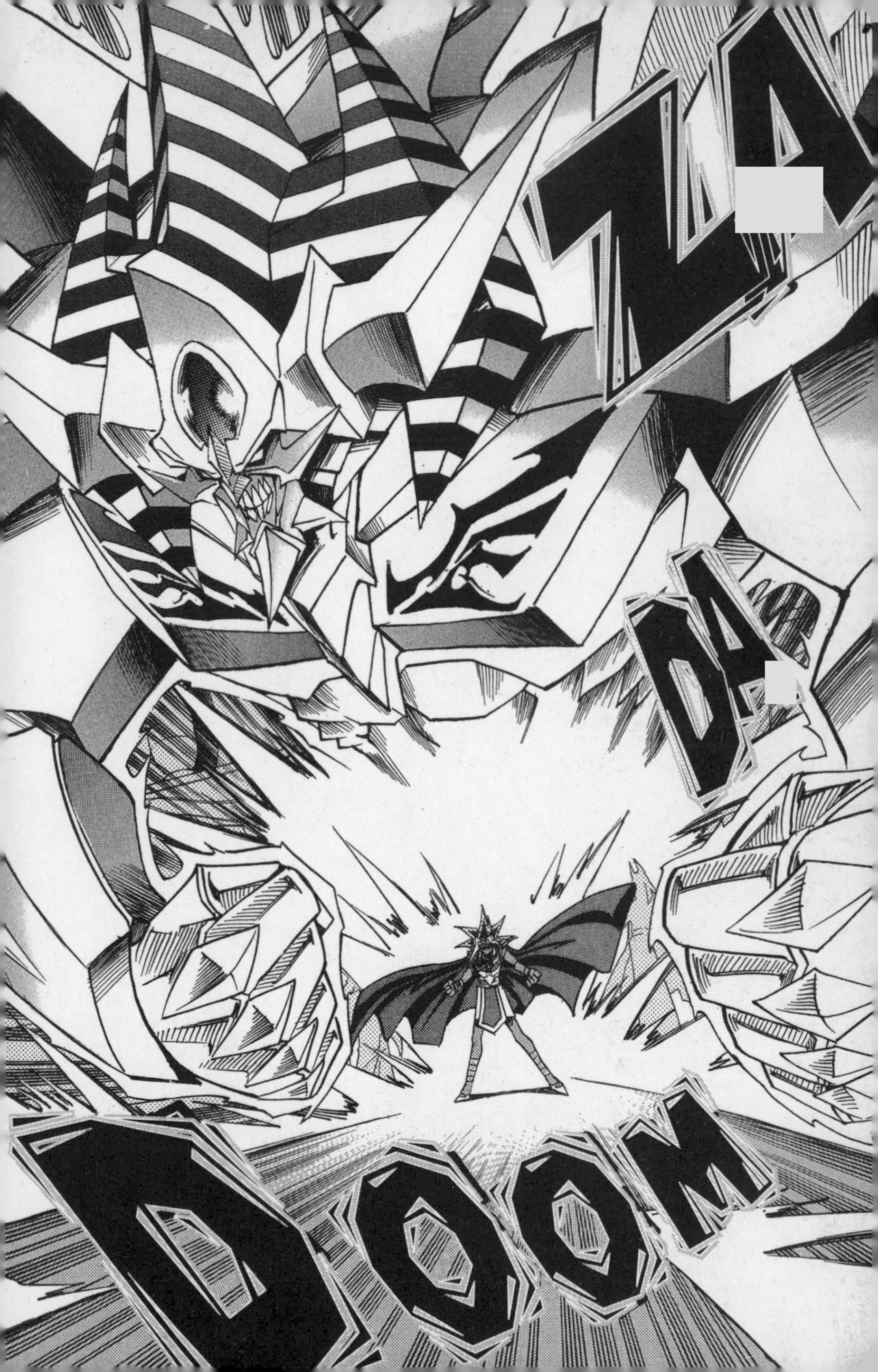
ZA
DA
DOOM

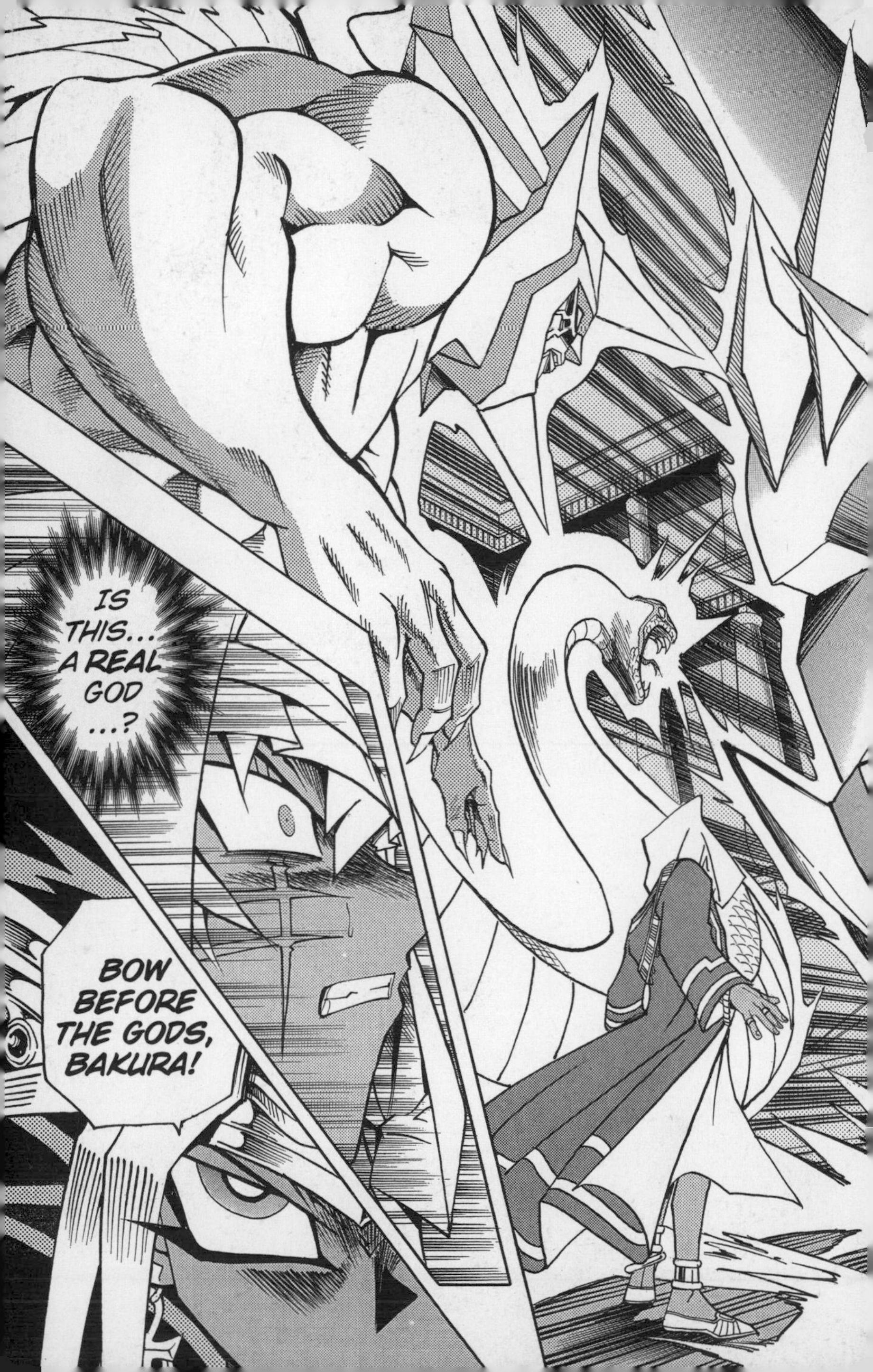
IS THIS... A REAL GOD ...?
BOW BEFORE THE GODS, BAKURA!

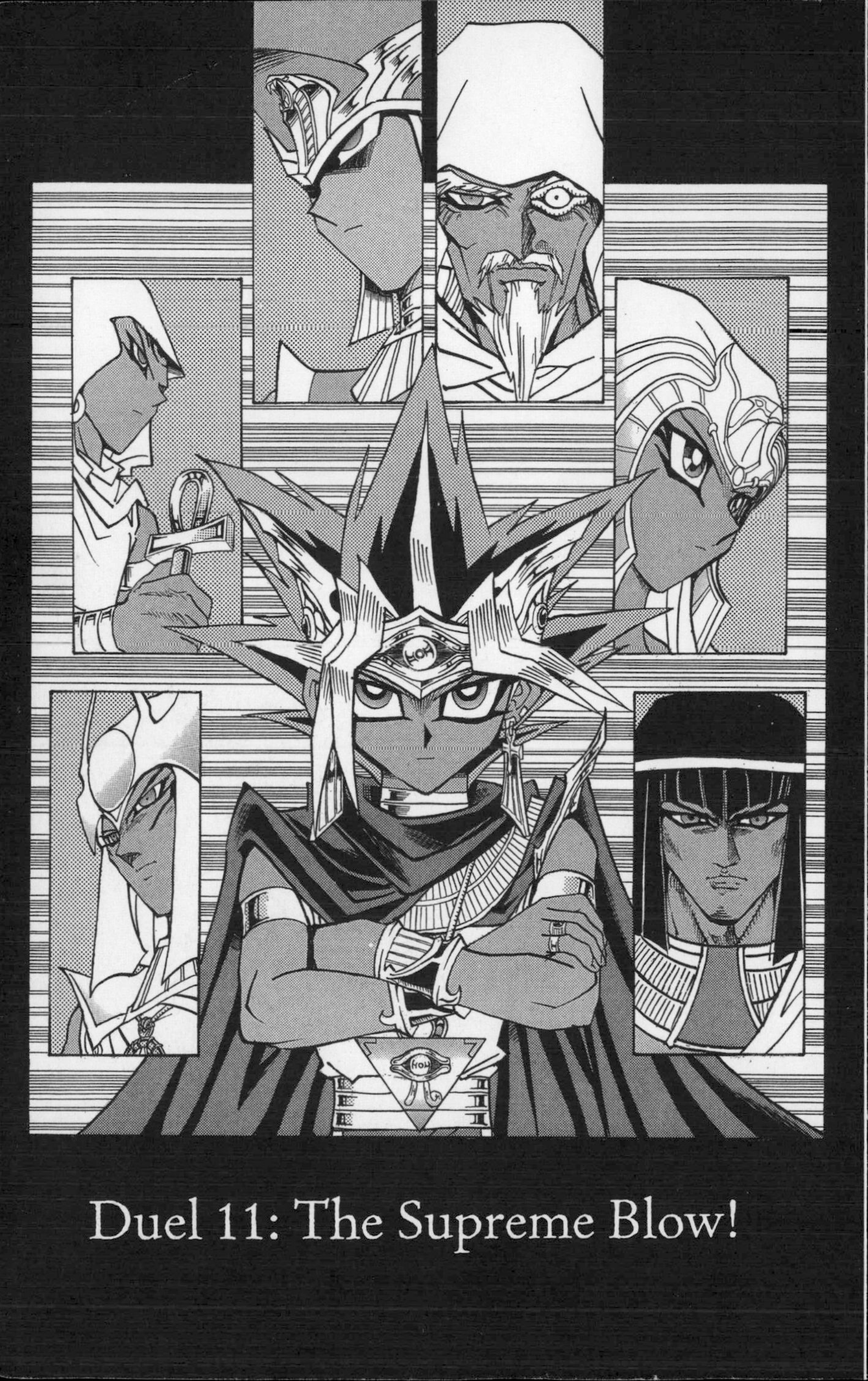

Duel 11: The Supreme Blow!

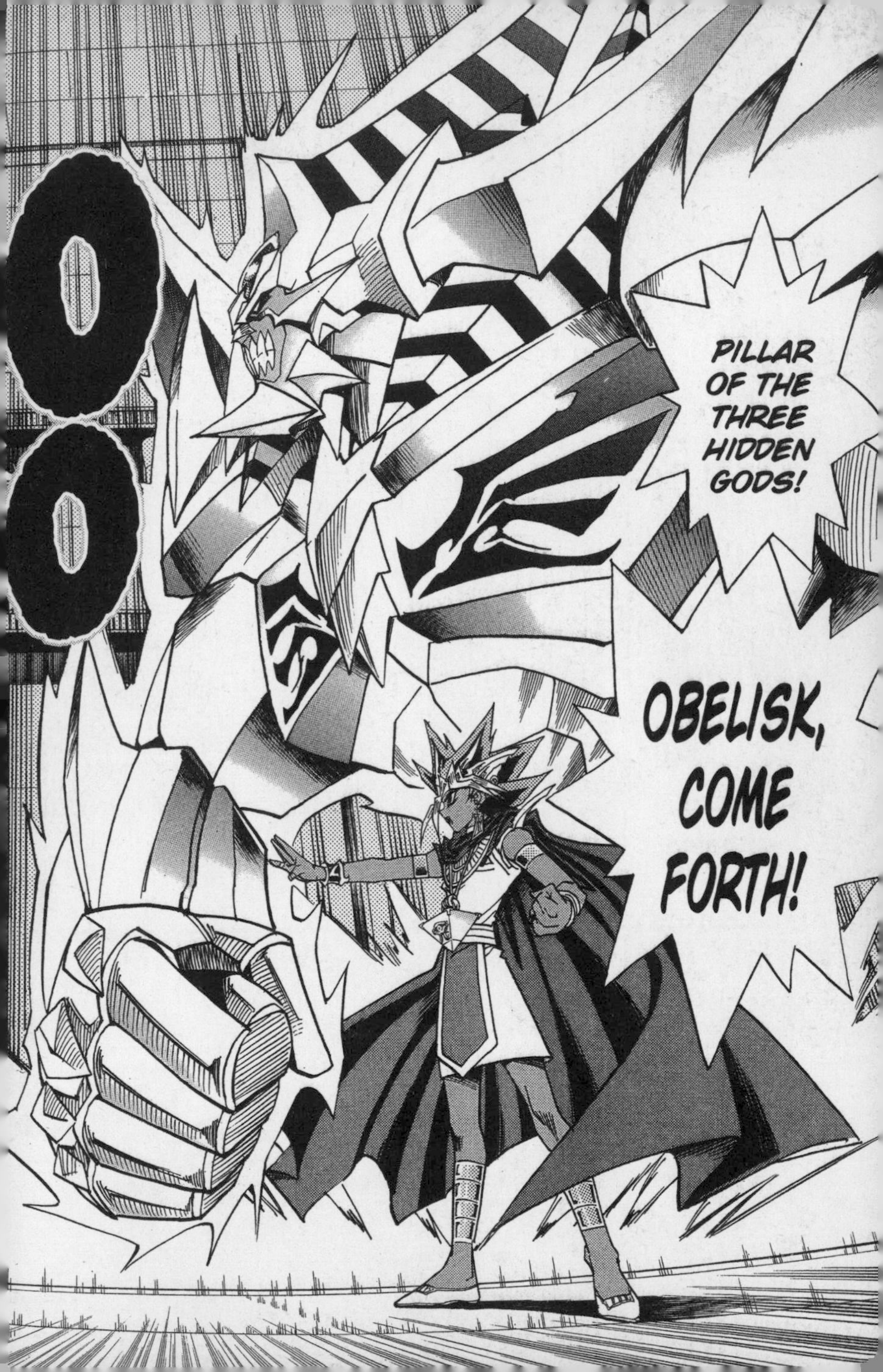
PILLAR OF THE THREE HIDDEN GODS!
OBELISK, COME FORTH!
OO

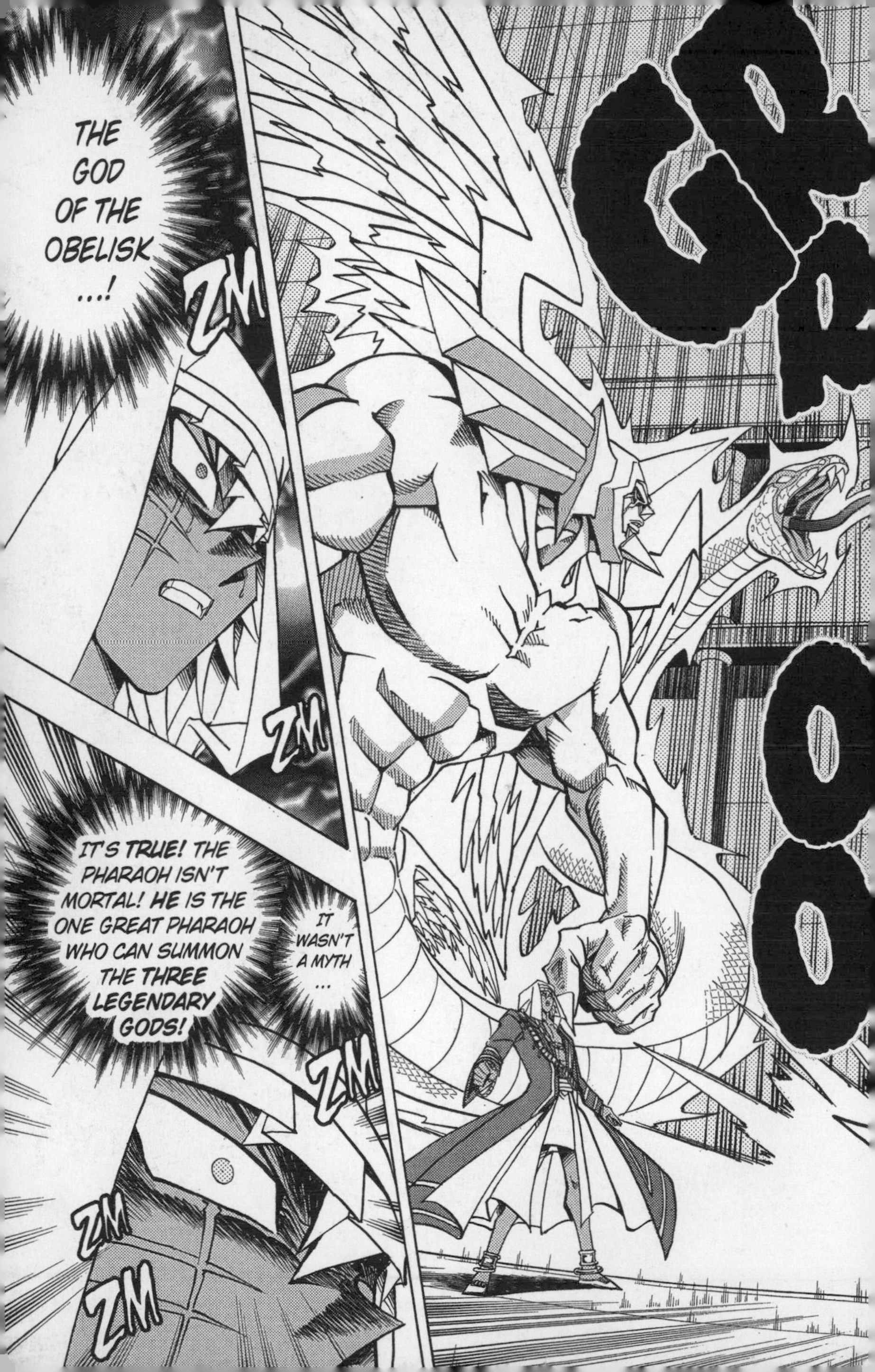
THE GOD OF THE OBELISK ...!
ZM
ZM
IT WASN'T A MYTH ...
IT'S TRUE! THE PHARAOH ISN'T MORTAL! HE IS THE ONE GREAT PHARAOH WHO CAN SUMMON THE THREE LEGENDARY GODS!
ZM
ZM
ZM

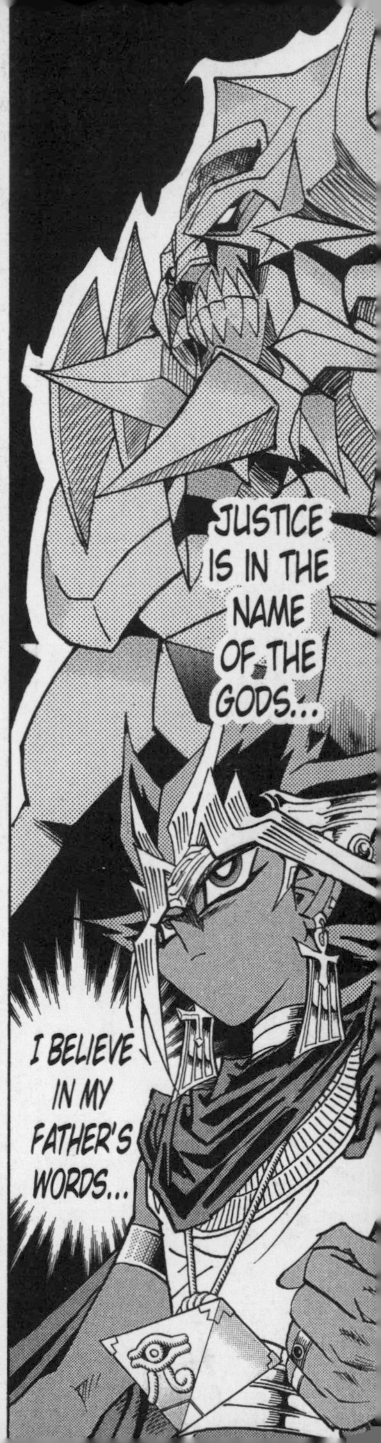
JUSTICE IS IN THE NAME OF THE GODS...
I BELIEVE IN MY FATHER'S WORDS...

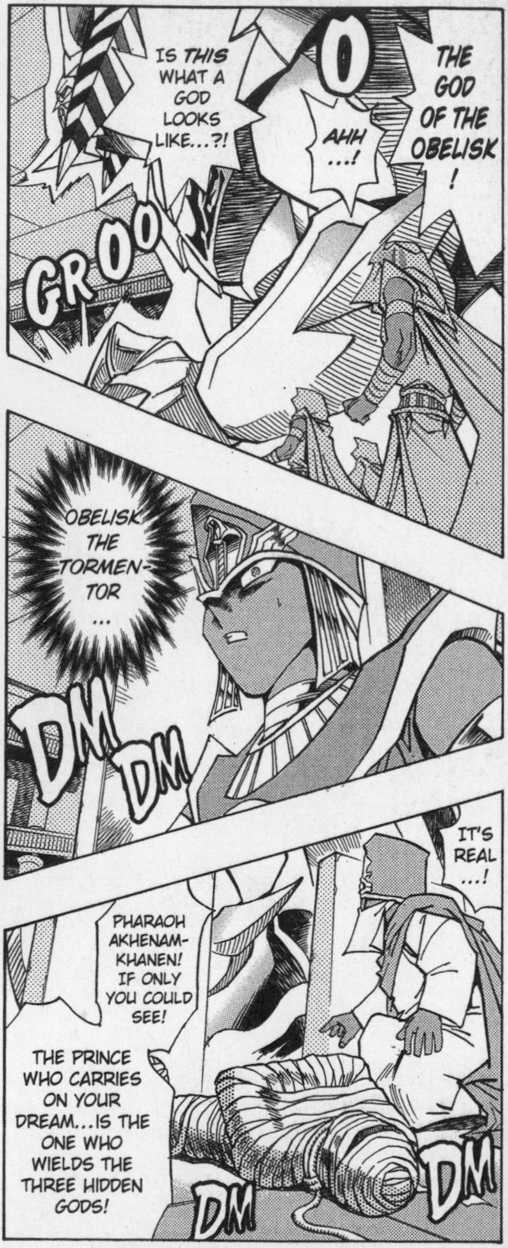
THE GOD OF THE OBELISK!
AHH...!
IS *THIS* WHAT A GOD LOOKS LIKE...?!
GROOO
OBELISK THE TORMENTOR...
DM DM
IT'S REAL...!
PHARAOH AKHENAMKHANEN! IF ONLY YOU COULD SEE!
THE PRINCE WHO CARRIES ON YOUR DREAM...IS THE ONE WHO WIELDS THE THREE HIDDEN GODS!
DM DM

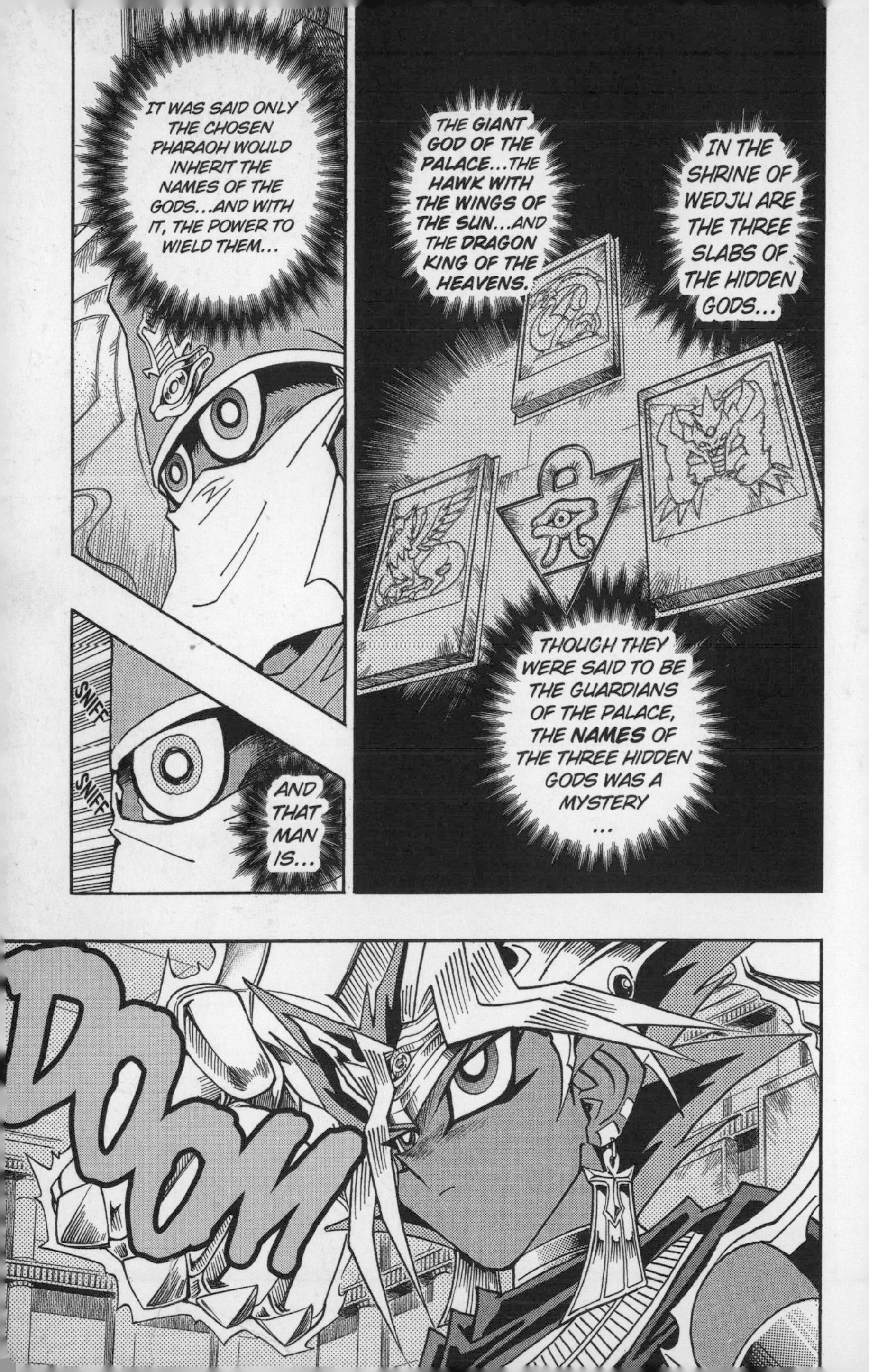

IN THE SHRINE OF WEDJU ARE THE THREE SLABS OF THE HIDDEN GODS...
THE GIANT GOD OF THE PALACE...THE HAWK WITH THE WINGS OF THE SUN...AND THE DRAGON KING OF THE HEAVENS.
THOUGH THEY WERE SAID TO BE THE GUARDIANS OF THE PALACE, THE NAMES OF THE THREE HIDDEN GODS WAS A MYSTERY ...
IT WAS SAID ONLY THE CHOSEN PHARAOH WOULD INHERIT THE NAMES OF THE GODS...AND WITH IT, THE POWER TO WIELD THEM...
SNIFF
SNIFF
AND THAT MAN IS...
DOOM

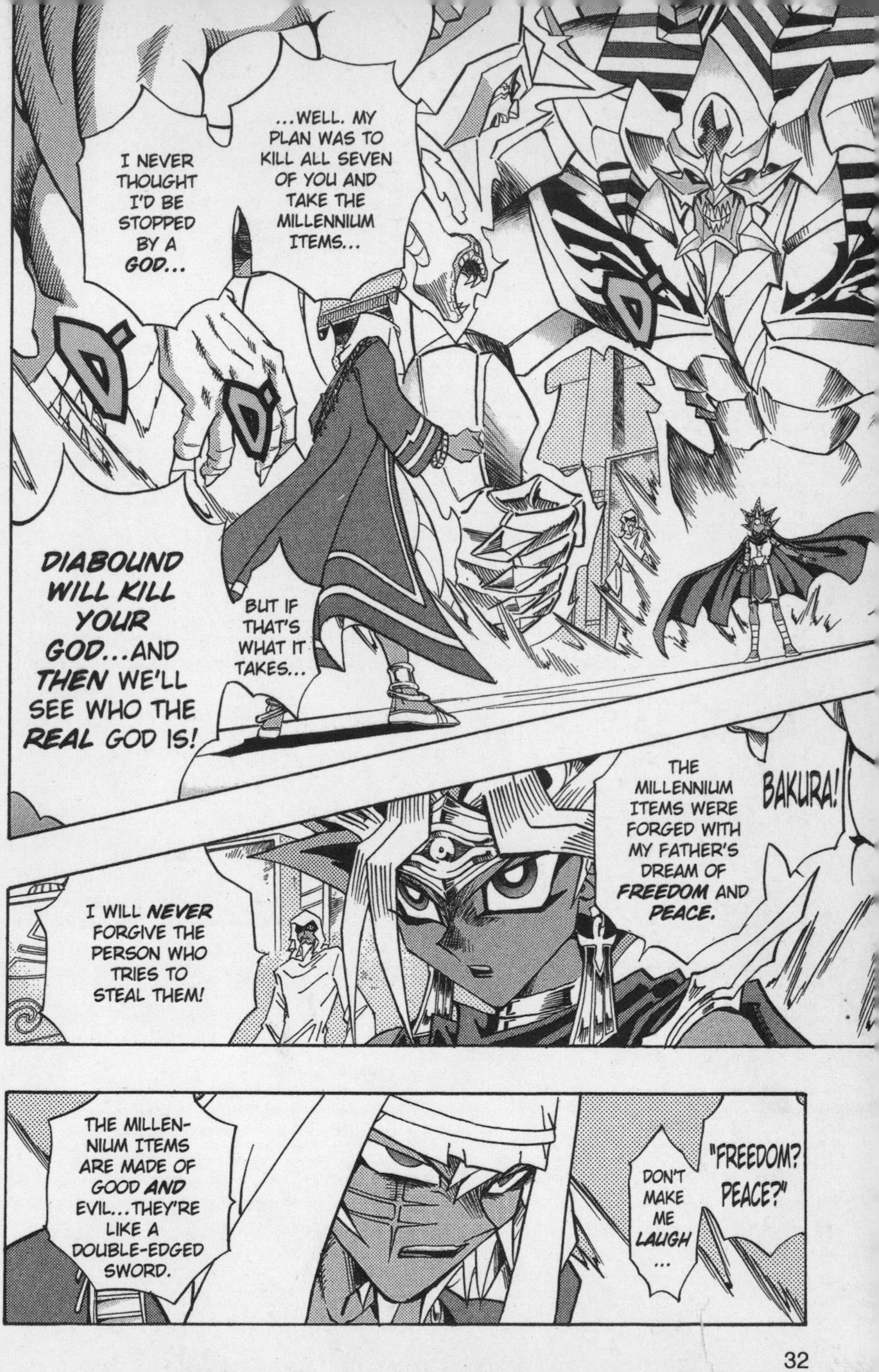
...WELL. MY PLAN WAS TO KILL ALL SEVEN OF YOU AND TAKE THE MILLENNIUM ITEMS...
I NEVER THOUGHT I'D BE STOPPED BY A *GOD*...
BUT IF THAT'S WHAT IT TAKES...
DIABOUND WILL KILL YOUR GOD...AND ***THEN*** WE'LL SEE WHO THE ***REAL*** GOD IS!
BAKURA!
THE MILLENNIUM ITEMS WERE FORGED WITH MY FATHER'S DREAM OF ***FREEDOM*** AND ***PEACE.***
I WILL ***NEVER*** FORGIVE THE PERSON WHO TRIES TO STEAL THEM!
"FREEDOM? PEACE?"
DON'T MAKE ME ***LAUGH***...
THE MILLENNIUM ITEMS ARE MADE OF GOOD ***AND*** EVIL...THEY'RE LIKE A DOUBLE-EDGED SWORD.

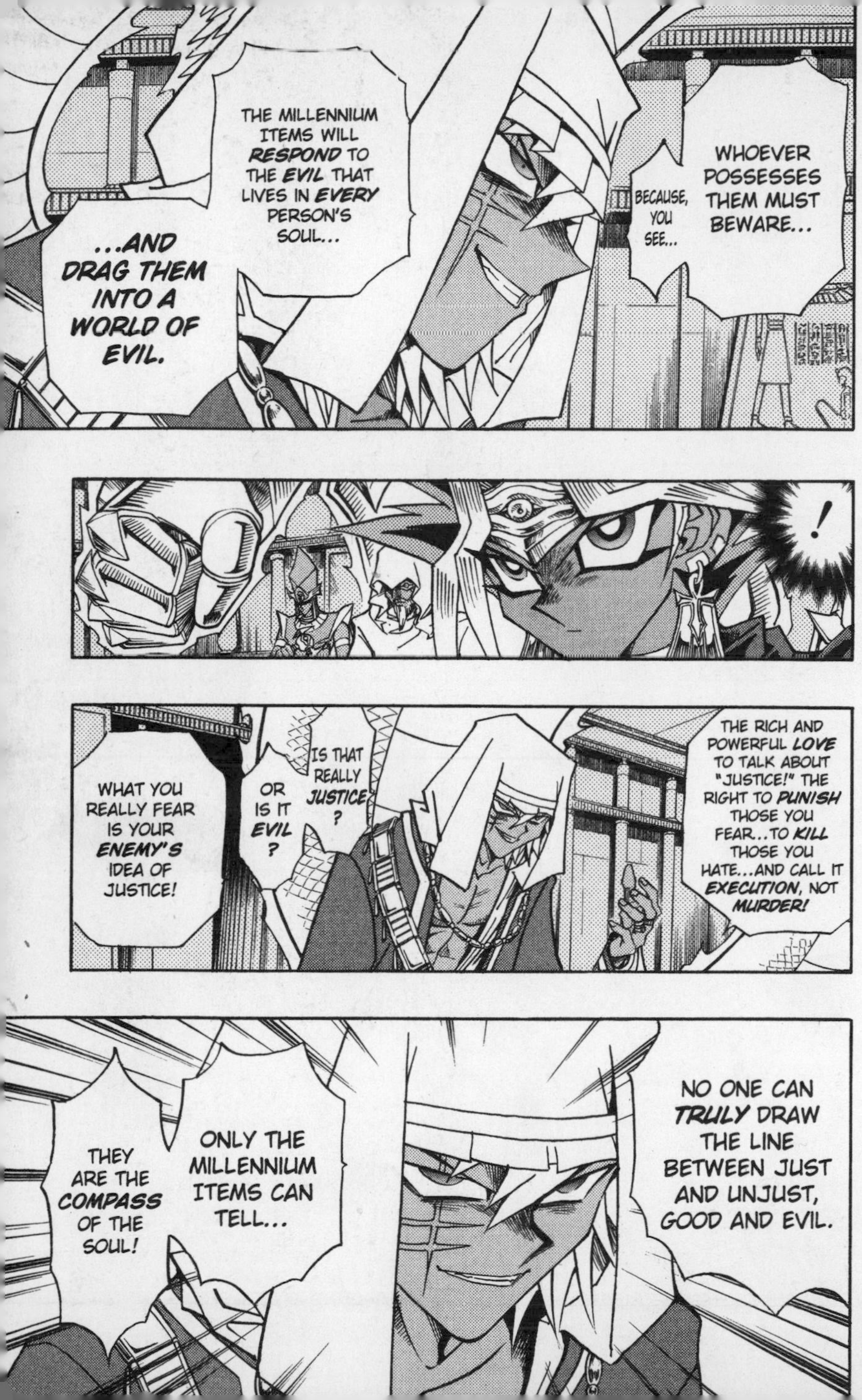
WHOEVER POSSESSES THEM MUST BEWARE...
BECAUSE, YOU SEE...
THE MILLENNIUM ITEMS WILL RESPOND TO THE EVIL THAT LIVES IN EVERY PERSON'S SOUL...
...AND DRAG THEM INTO A WORLD OF EVIL.
!
THE RICH AND POWERFUL LOVE TO TALK ABOUT "JUSTICE!" THE RIGHT TO PUNISH THOSE YOU FEAR...TO KILL THOSE YOU HATE...AND CALL IT EXECUTION, NOT MURDER!
IS THAT REALLY JUSTICE?
OR IS IT EVIL?
WHAT YOU REALLY FEAR IS YOUR ENEMY'S IDEA OF JUSTICE!
NO ONE CAN TRULY DRAW THE LINE BETWEEN JUST AND UNJUST, GOOD AND EVIL.
ONLY THE MILLENNIUM ITEMS CAN TELL...
THEY ARE THE COMPASS OF THE SOUL!

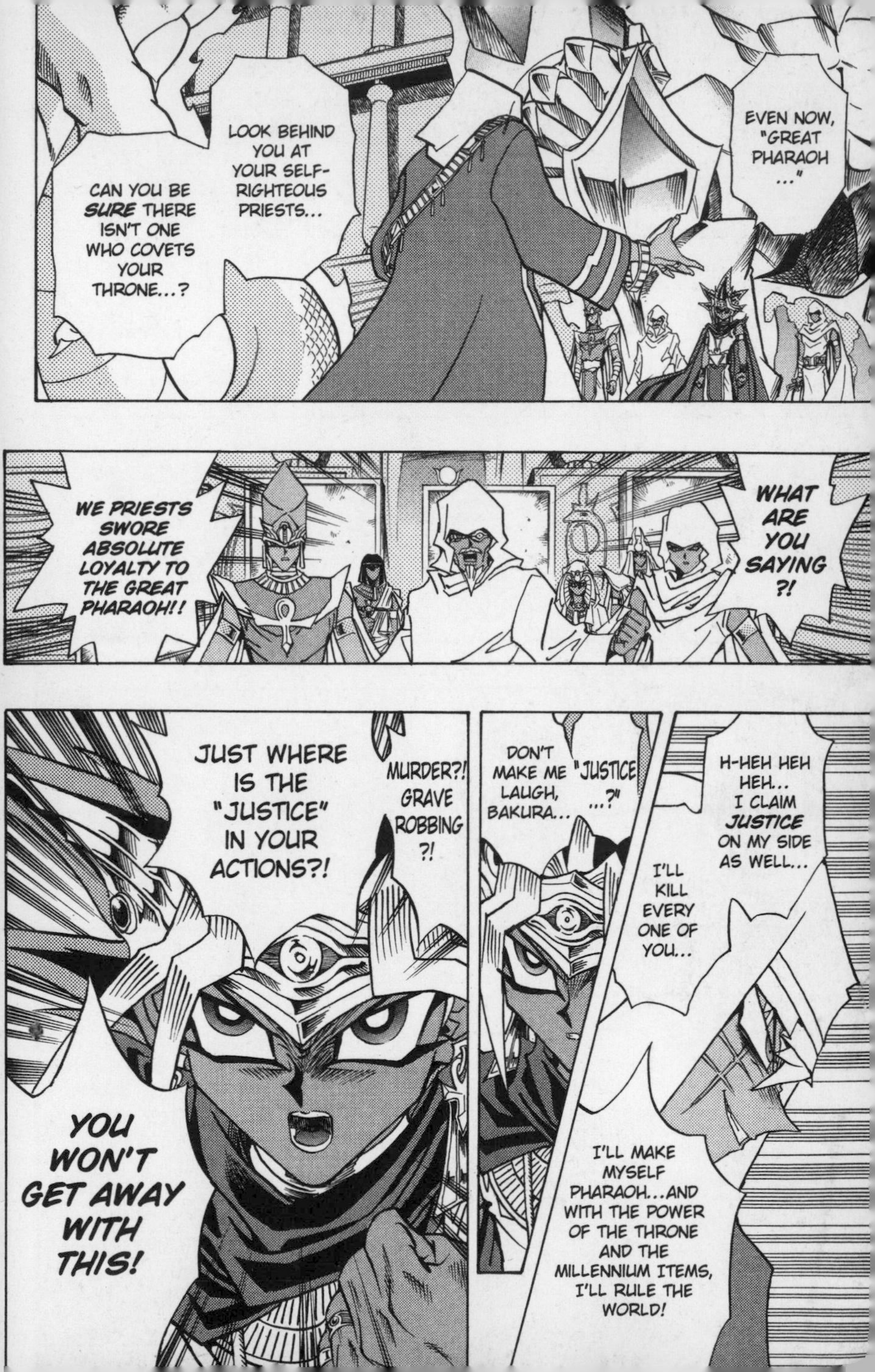
EVEN NOW, "GREAT PHARAOH..."
LOOK BEHIND YOU AT YOUR SELF-RIGHTEOUS PRIESTS...
CAN YOU BE *SURE* THERE ISN'T ONE WHO COVETS YOUR THRONE...?
WHAT ARE YOU SAYING?!
WE PRIESTS SWORE ABSOLUTE LOYALTY TO THE GREAT PHARAOH!!
H-HEH HEH HEH... I CLAIM *JUSTICE* ON MY SIDE AS WELL...
I'LL KILL EVERY ONE OF YOU...
I'LL MAKE MYSELF PHARAOH...AND WITH THE POWER OF THE THRONE AND THE MILLENNIUM ITEMS, I'LL RULE THE WORLD!
"JUSTICE...?"
DON'T MAKE ME LAUGH, BAKURA...
MURDER?! GRAVE ROBBING?!
JUST WHERE IS THE "JUSTICE" IN YOUR ACTIONS?!
YOU WON'T GET AWAY WITH THIS!

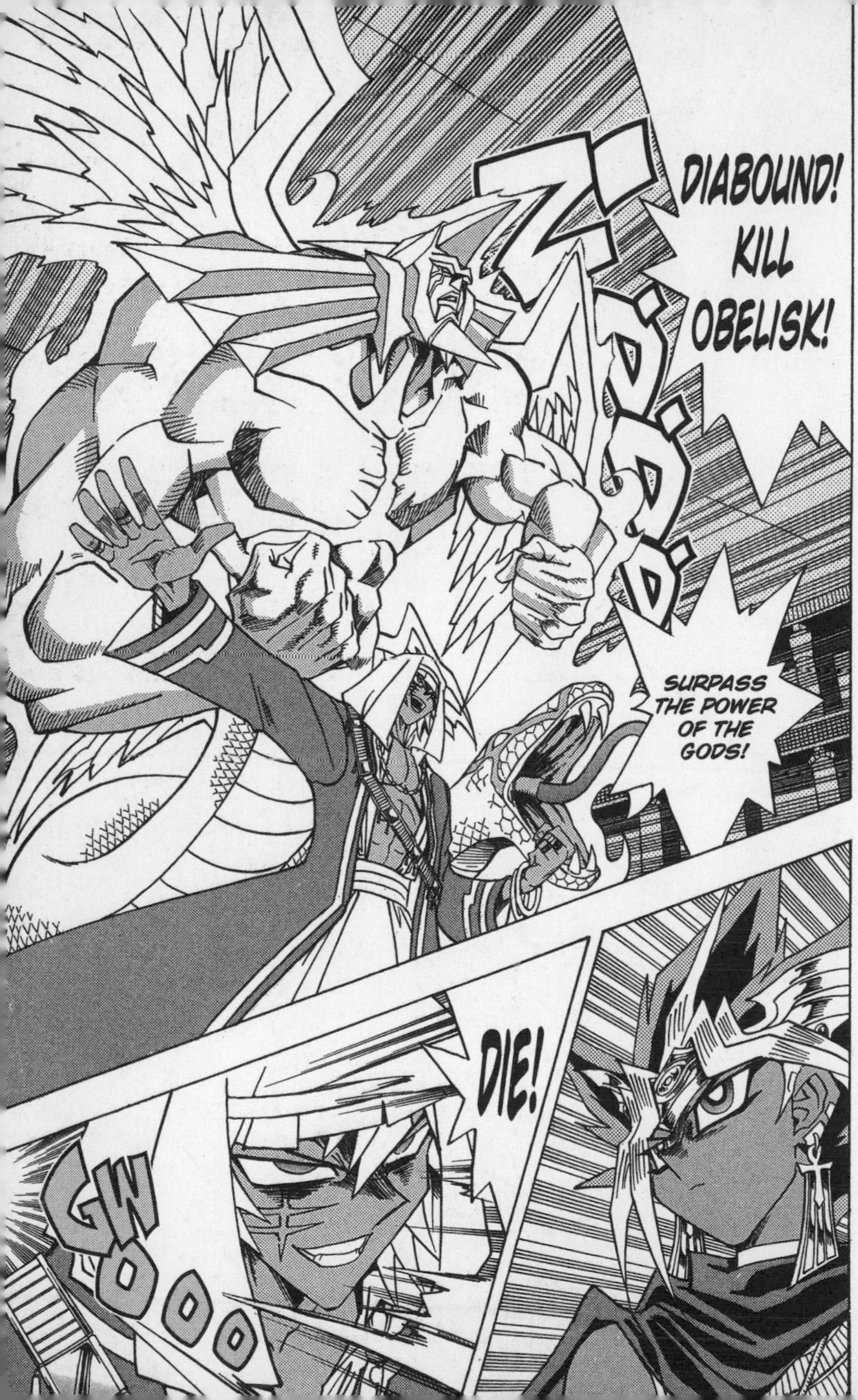
DIABOUND! KILL OBELISK!
SURPASS THE POWER OF THE GODS!
DIE!

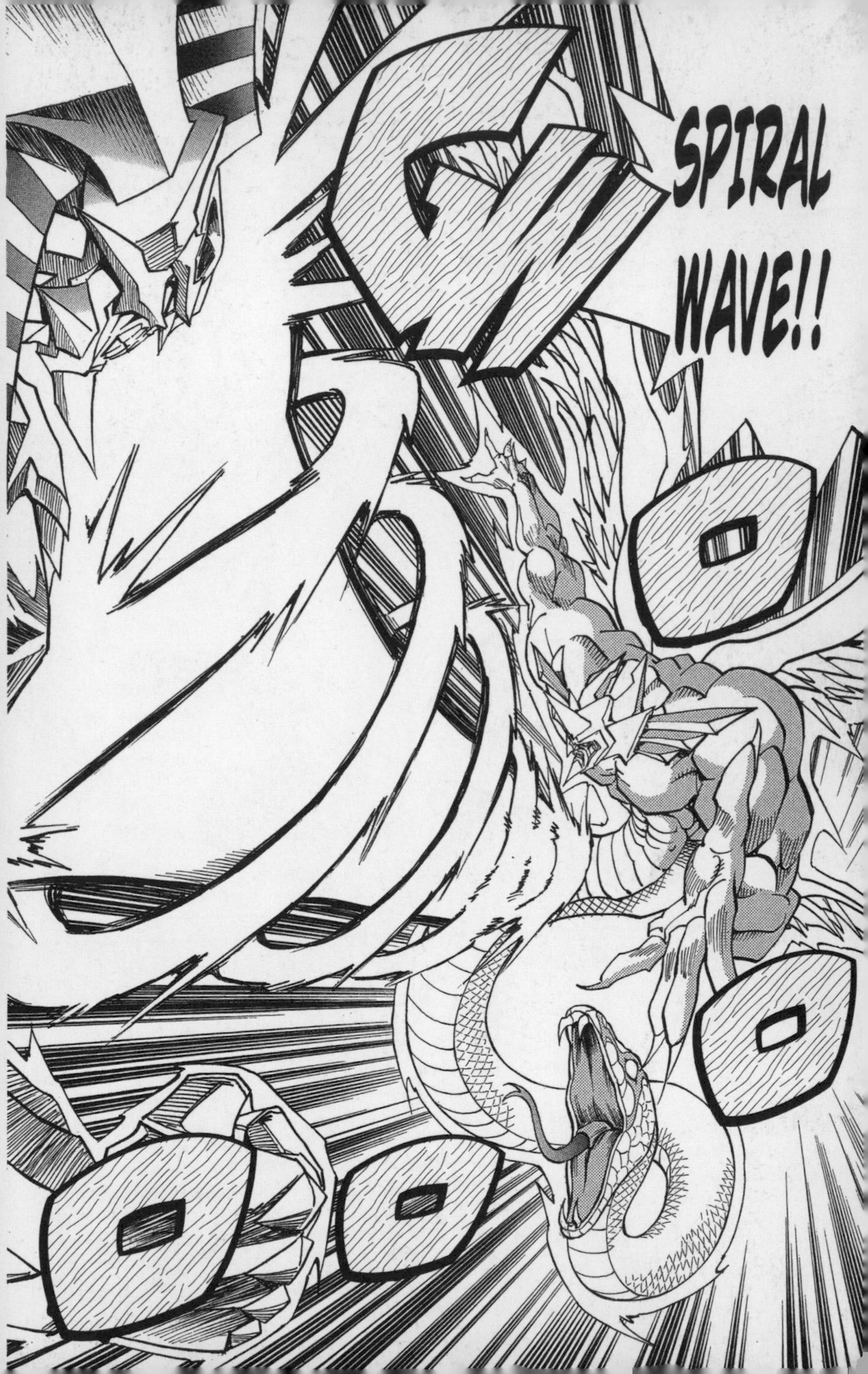
SPIRAL WAVE!!

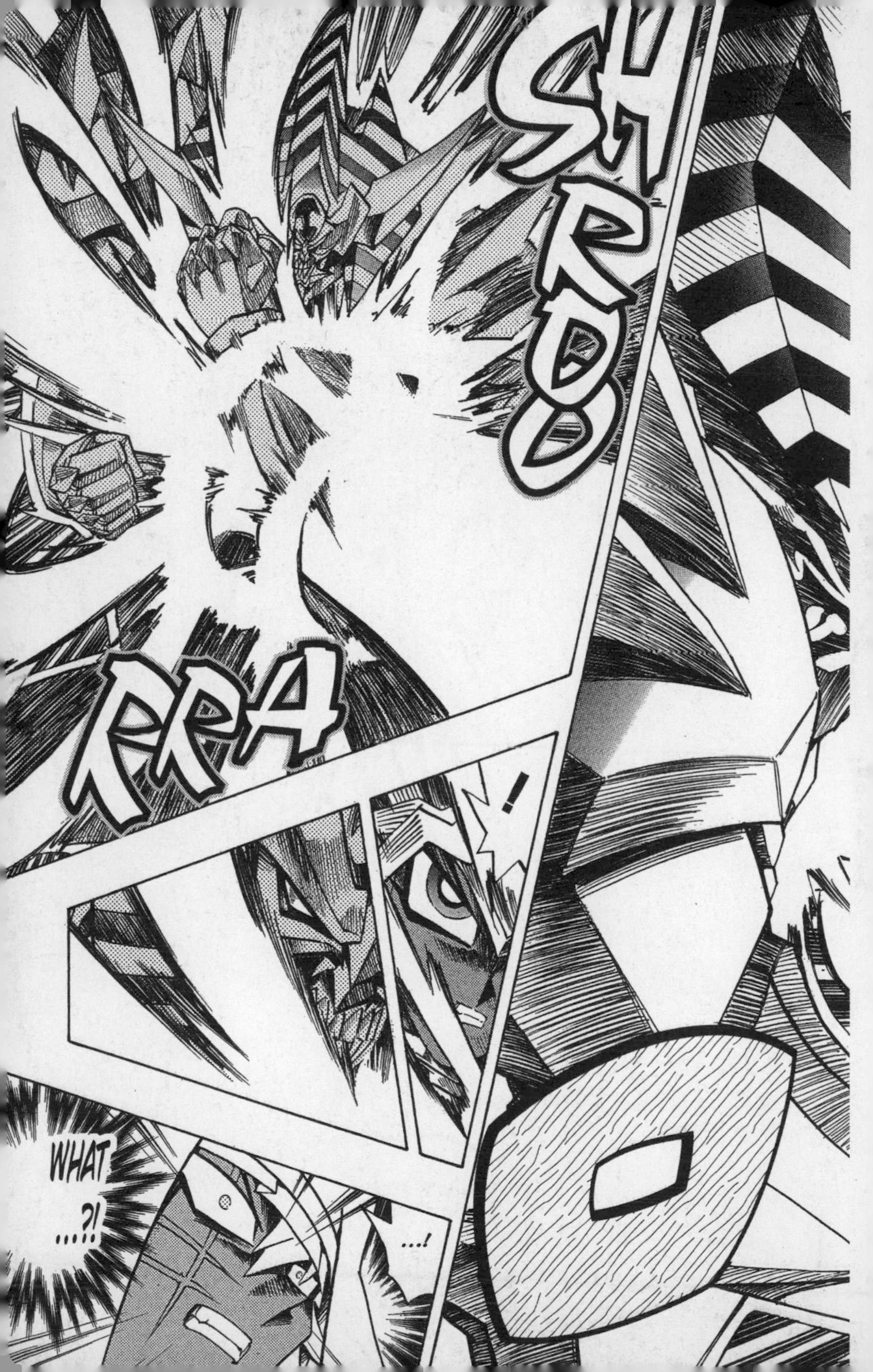
SHRDOO
RRA
!
...!
WHAT ...?!

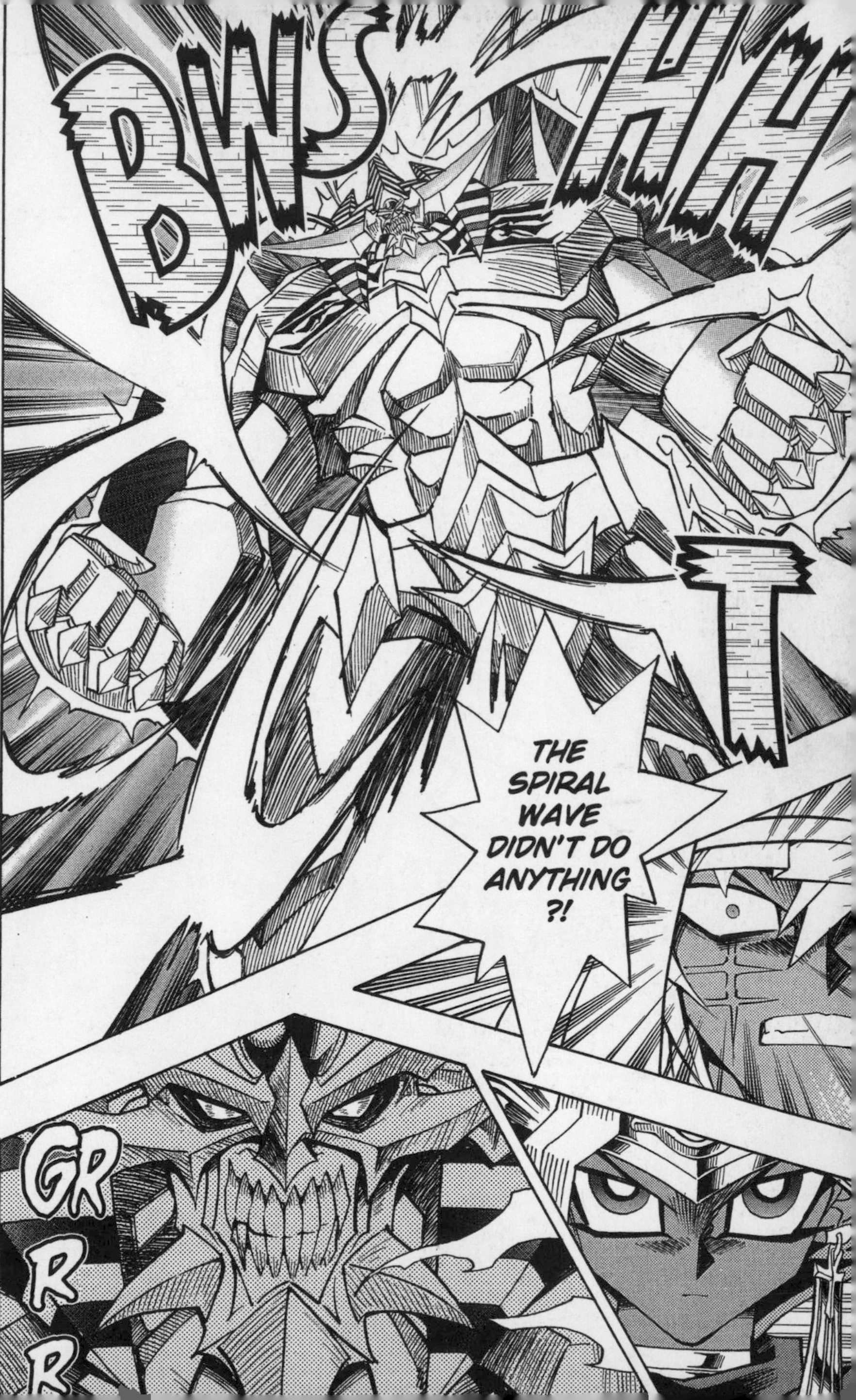
BWSHHT
THE SPIRAL WAVE DIDN'T DO ANYTHING ?!
GRRR

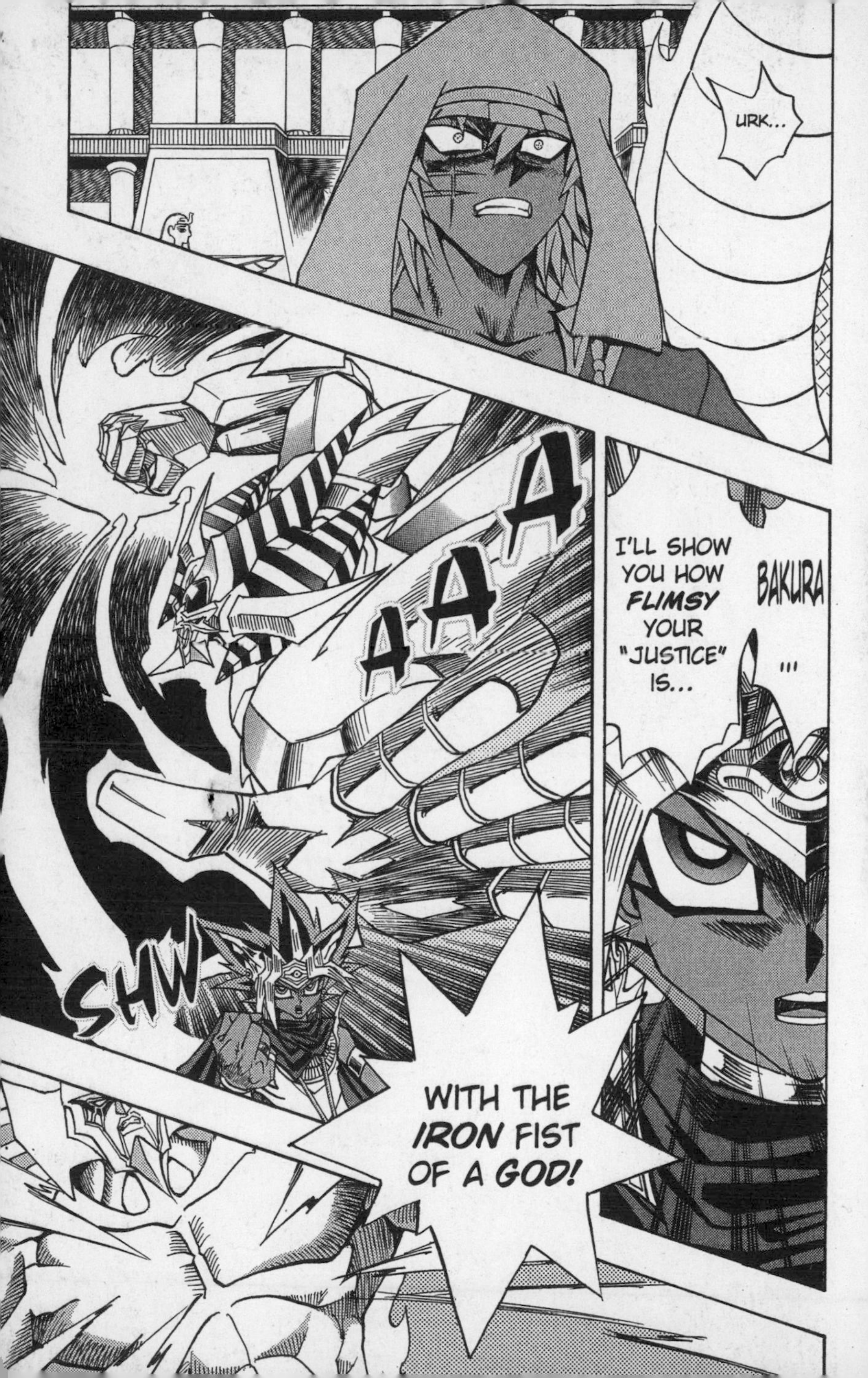
URK...
BAKURA...
I'LL SHOW YOU HOW FLIMSY YOUR "JUSTICE" IS...
WITH THE IRON FIST OF A GOD!
AAAA
SHW

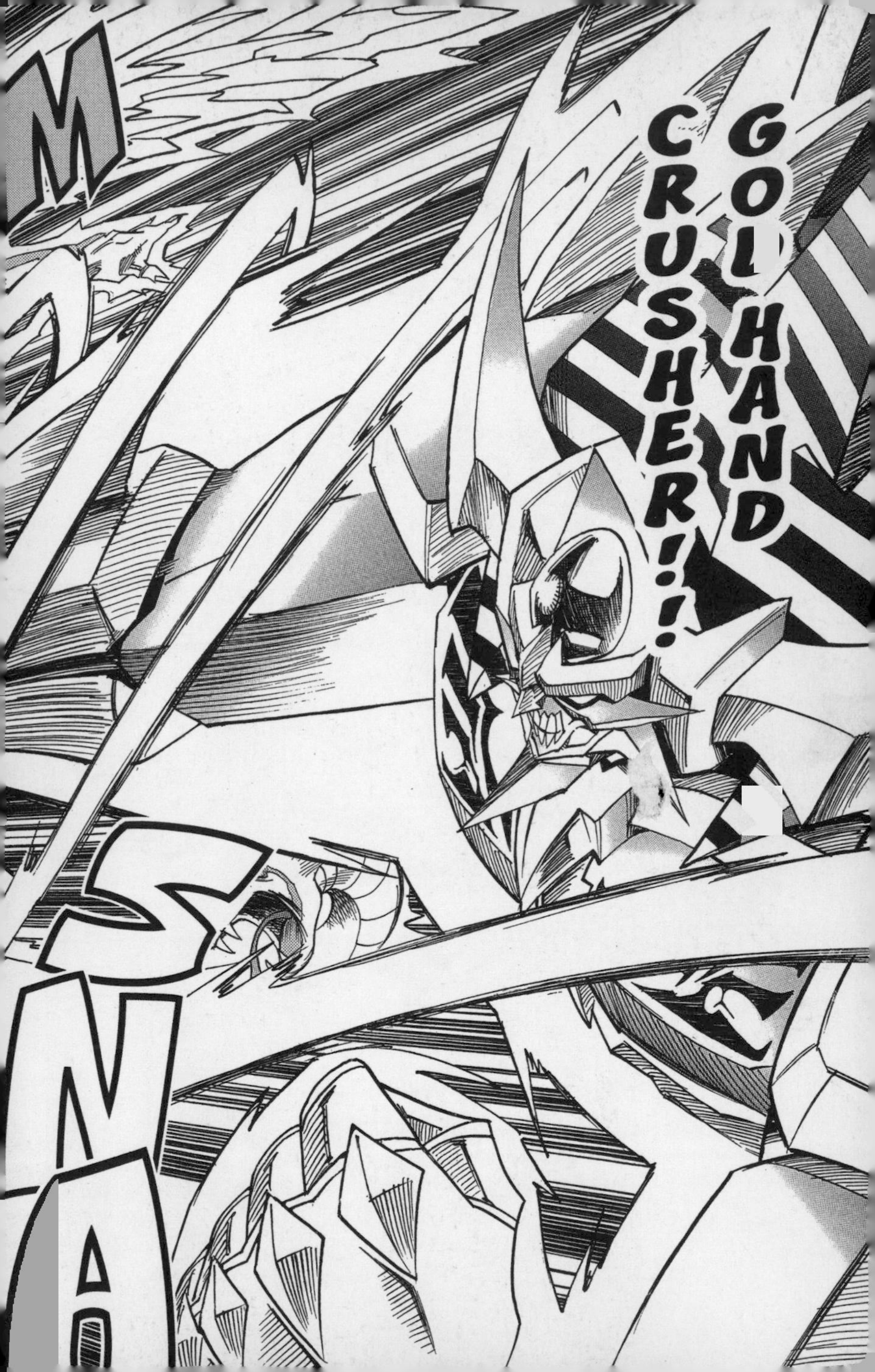
GOD HAND
CRUSHER!!!
M
SNA

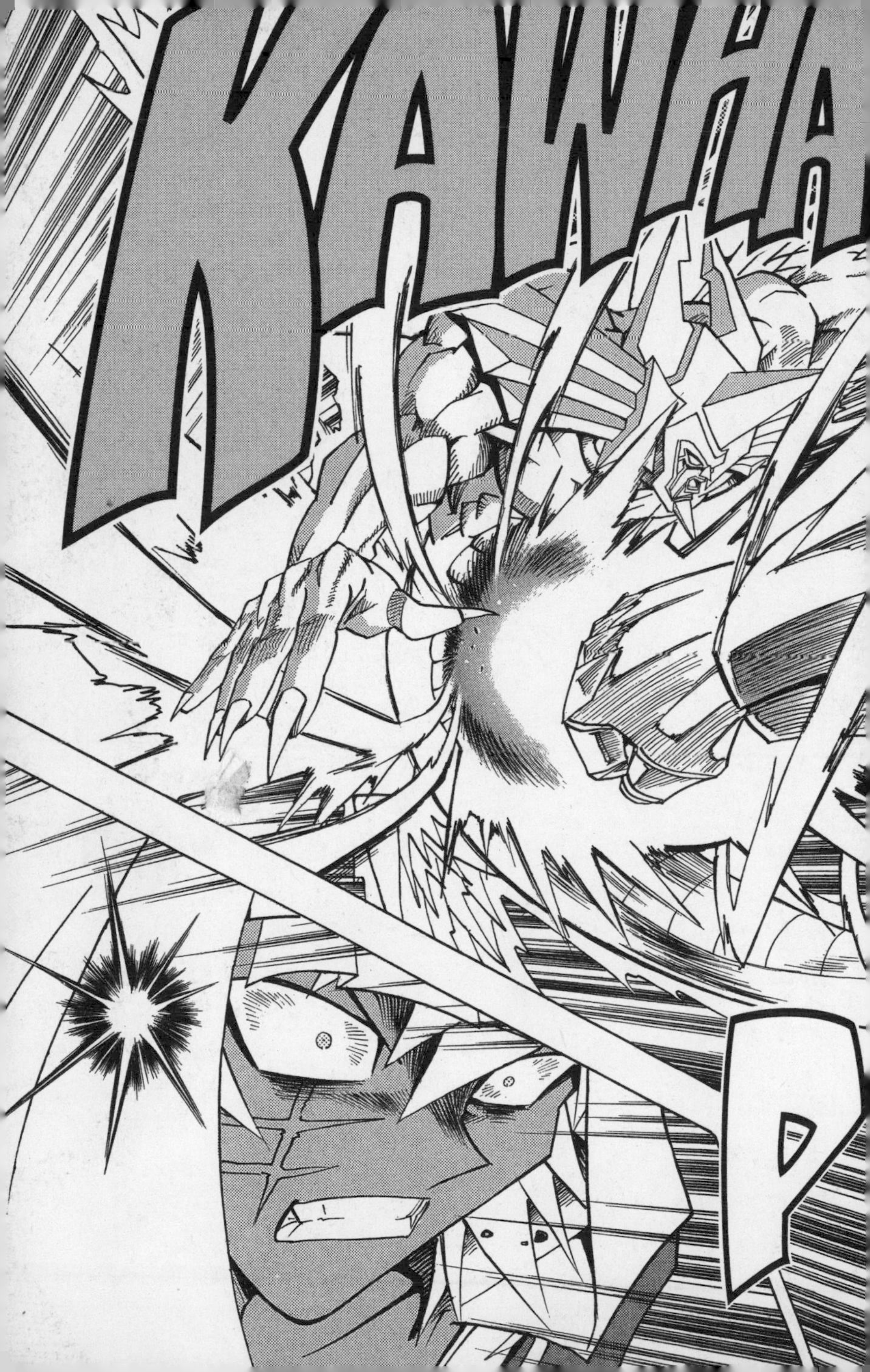

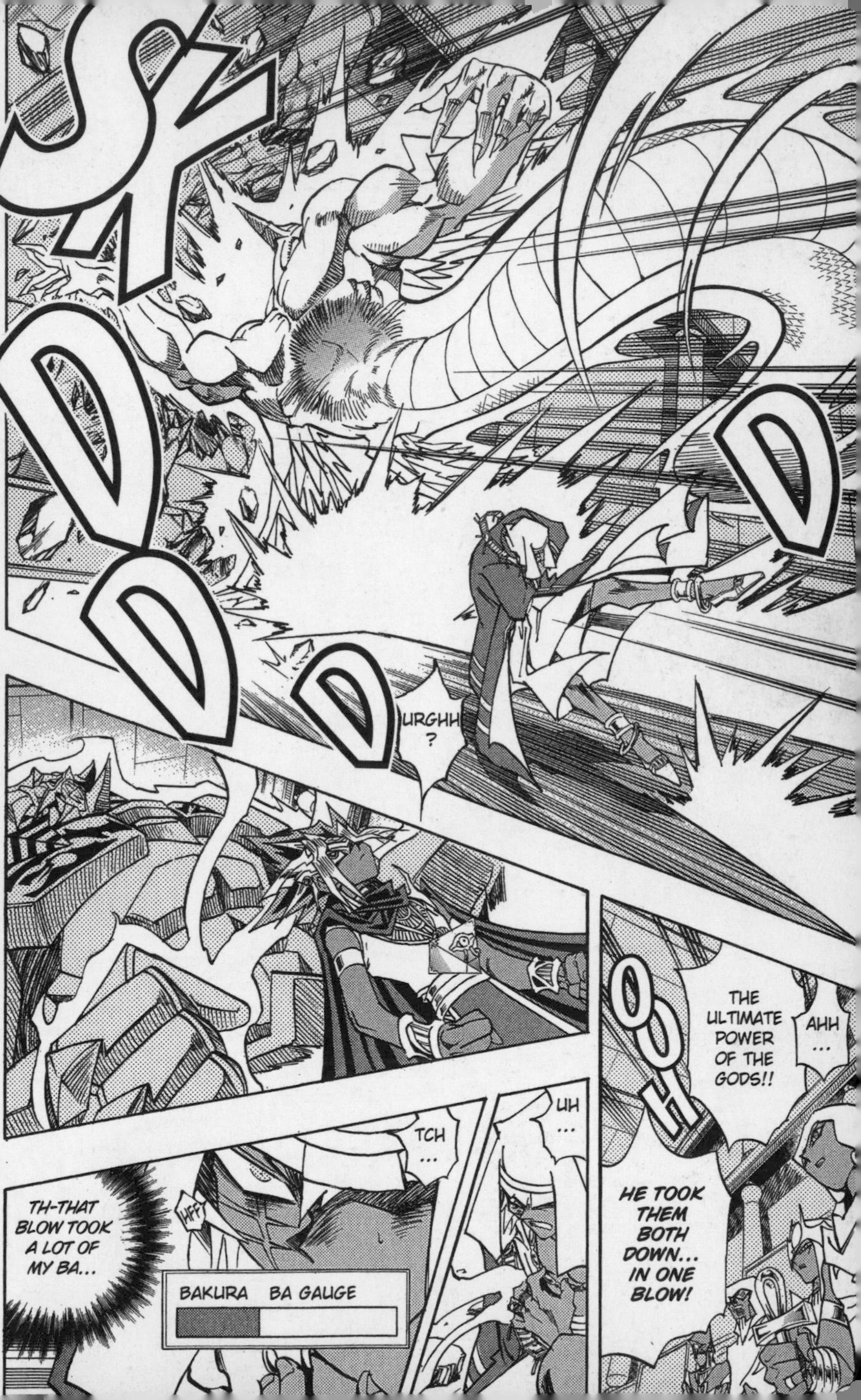
URGHH
?
THE ULTIMATE POWER OF THE GODS!!
AHH
...
HE TOOK THEM BOTH DOWN... IN ONE BLOW!
UH
...
TCH
...
HFF
TH-THAT BLOW TOOK A LOT OF MY BA...
BAKURA BA GAUGE

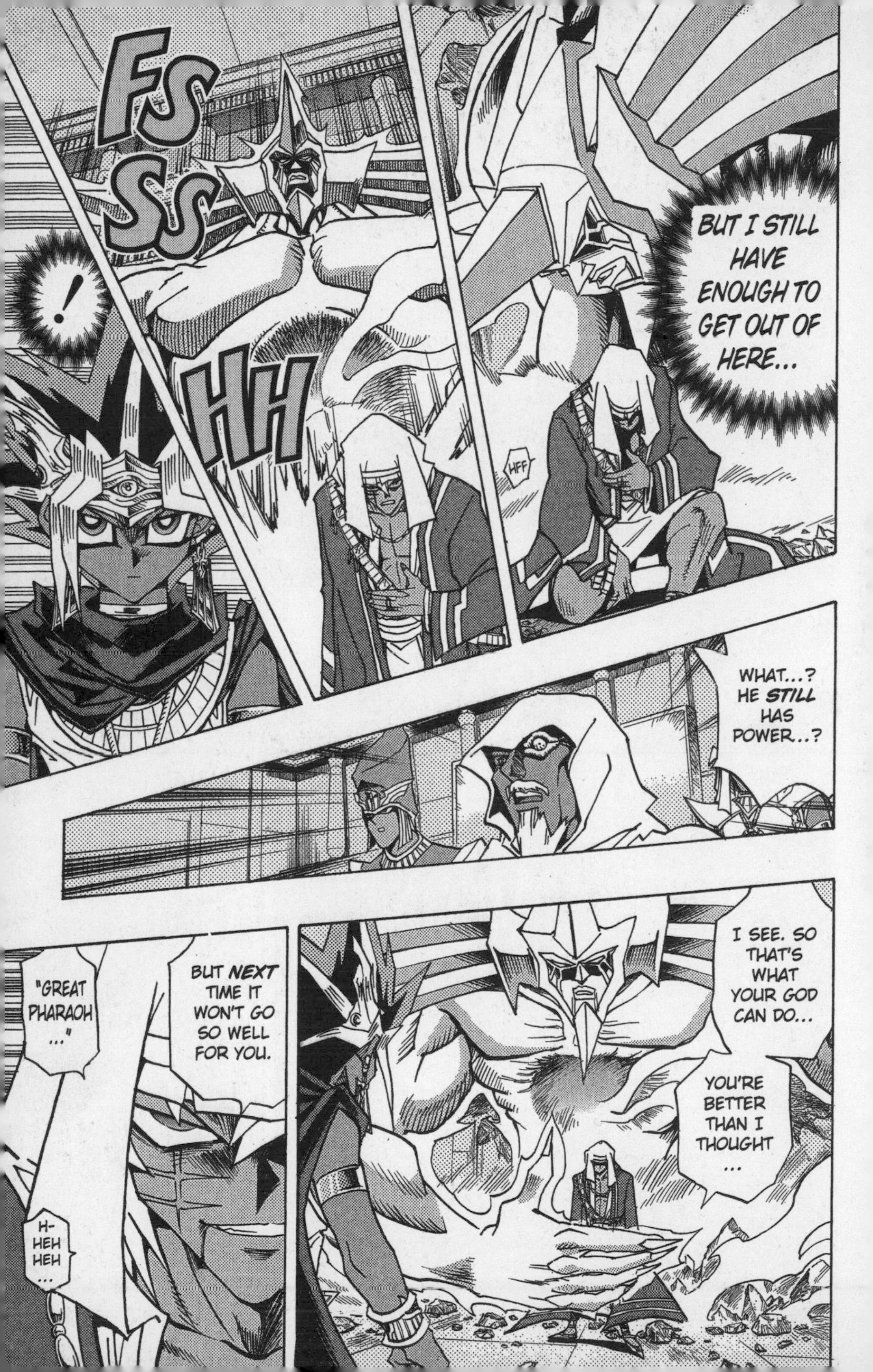
BUT I STILL HAVE ENOUGH TO GET OUT OF HERE...
HFF
FSSSHH
!
WHAT...? HE STILL HAS POWER...?
I SEE. SO THAT'S WHAT YOUR GOD CAN DO...
YOU'RE BETTER THAN I THOUGHT...
BUT NEXT TIME IT WON'T GO SO WELL FOR YOU.
"GREAT PHARAOH..."
H-HEH HEH...

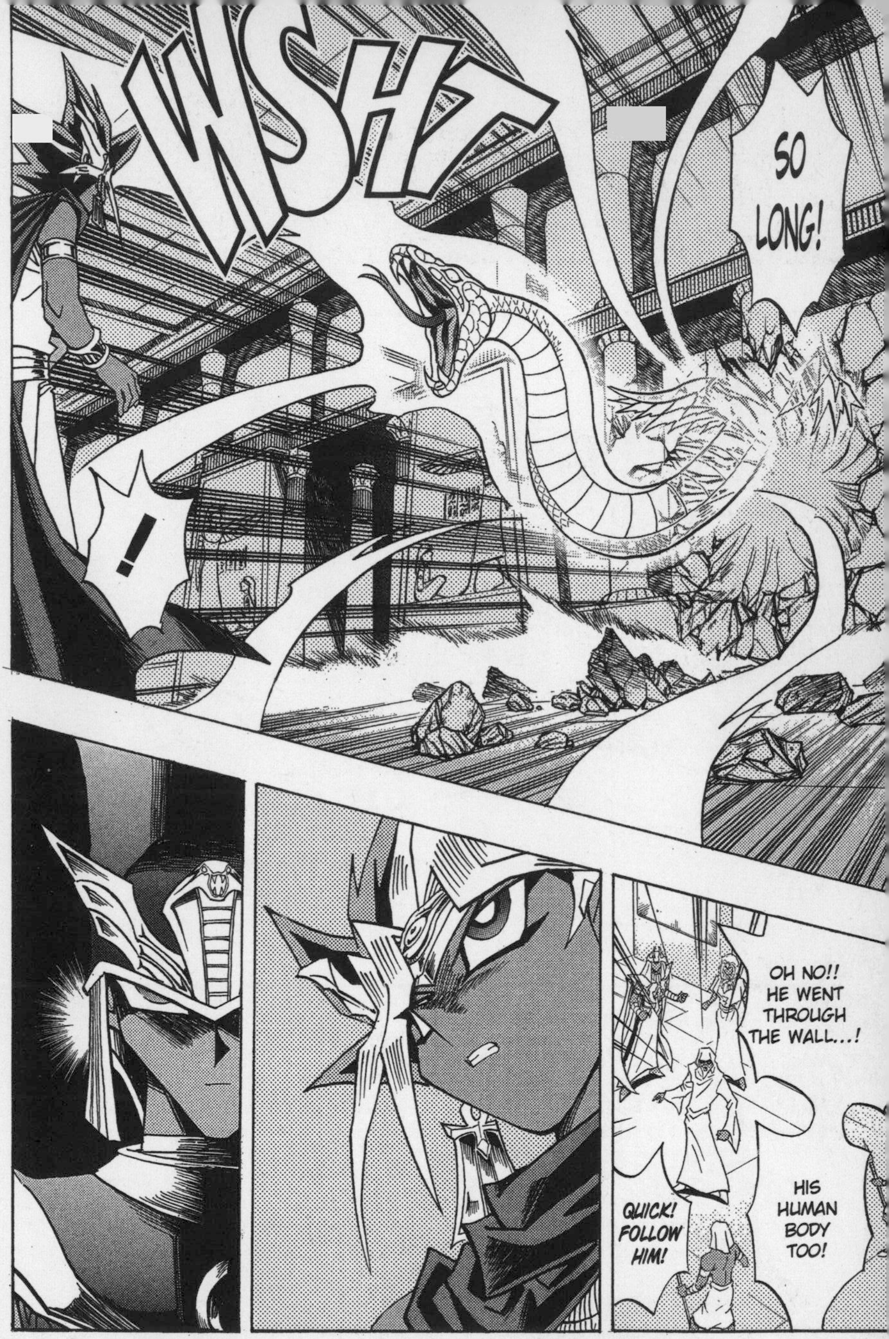
SO LONG!
WSHT
!
OH NO!! HE WENT THROUGH THE WALL...!
HIS HUMAN BODY TOO!
QUICK! FOLLOW HIM!

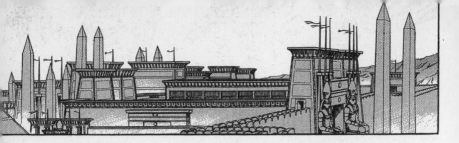

THIS IS THE PRELUDE TO THE *FALL* OF YOUR DYNASTY...

H-HEH HEH...

JUST YOU WAIT...

ONE THIEF WILL START A WAR!

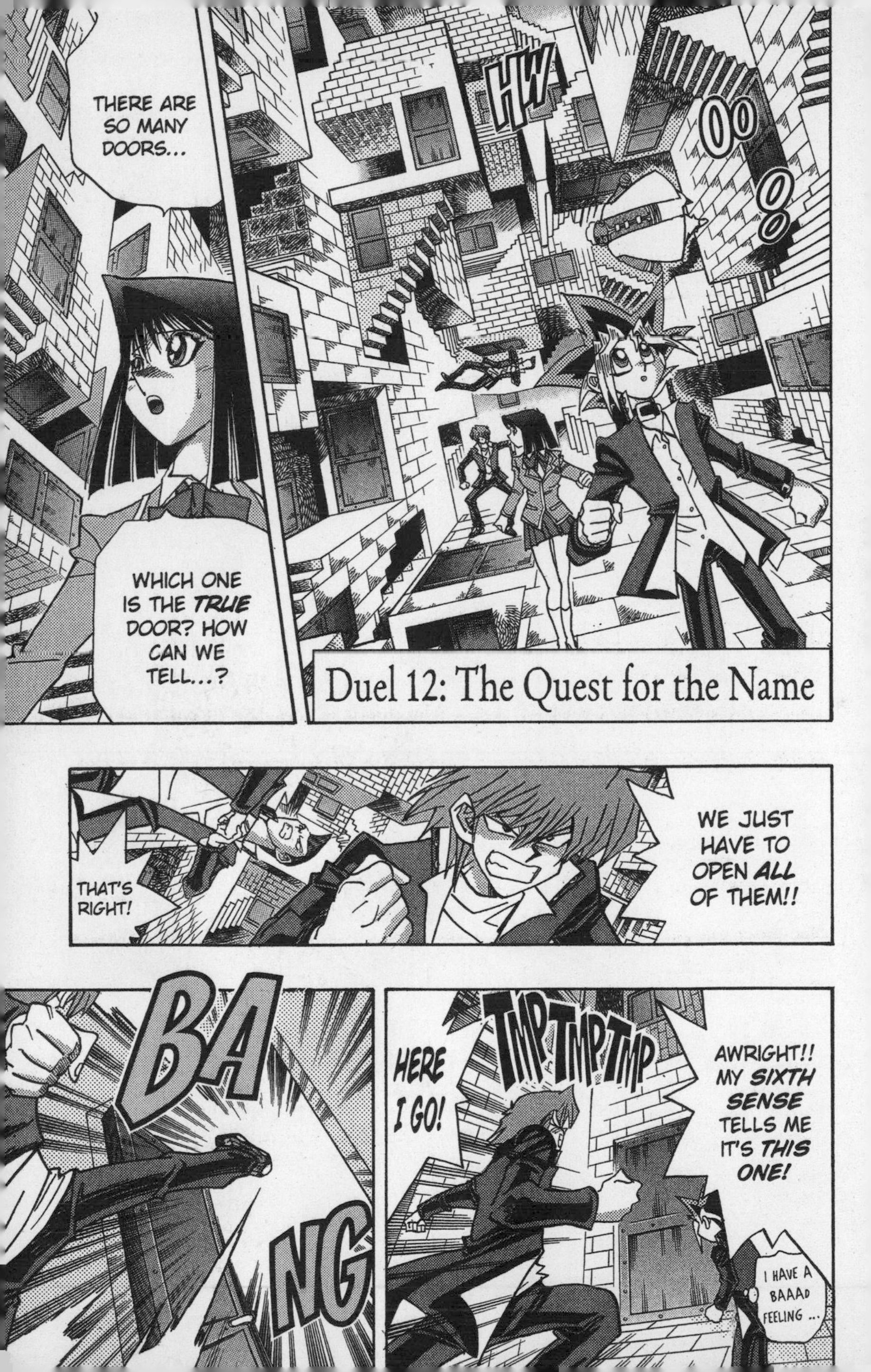
HWOOOOO
Duel 12: The Quest for the Name
THERE ARE SO MANY DOORS...
WHICH ONE IS THE TRUE DOOR? HOW CAN WE TELL...?
WE JUST HAVE TO OPEN ALL OF THEM!!
THAT'S RIGHT!
AWRIGHT!! MY SIXTH SENSE TELLS ME IT'S THIS ONE!
TMPTMPTMP
HERE I GO!
I HAVE A BAAAD FEELING...
BANG

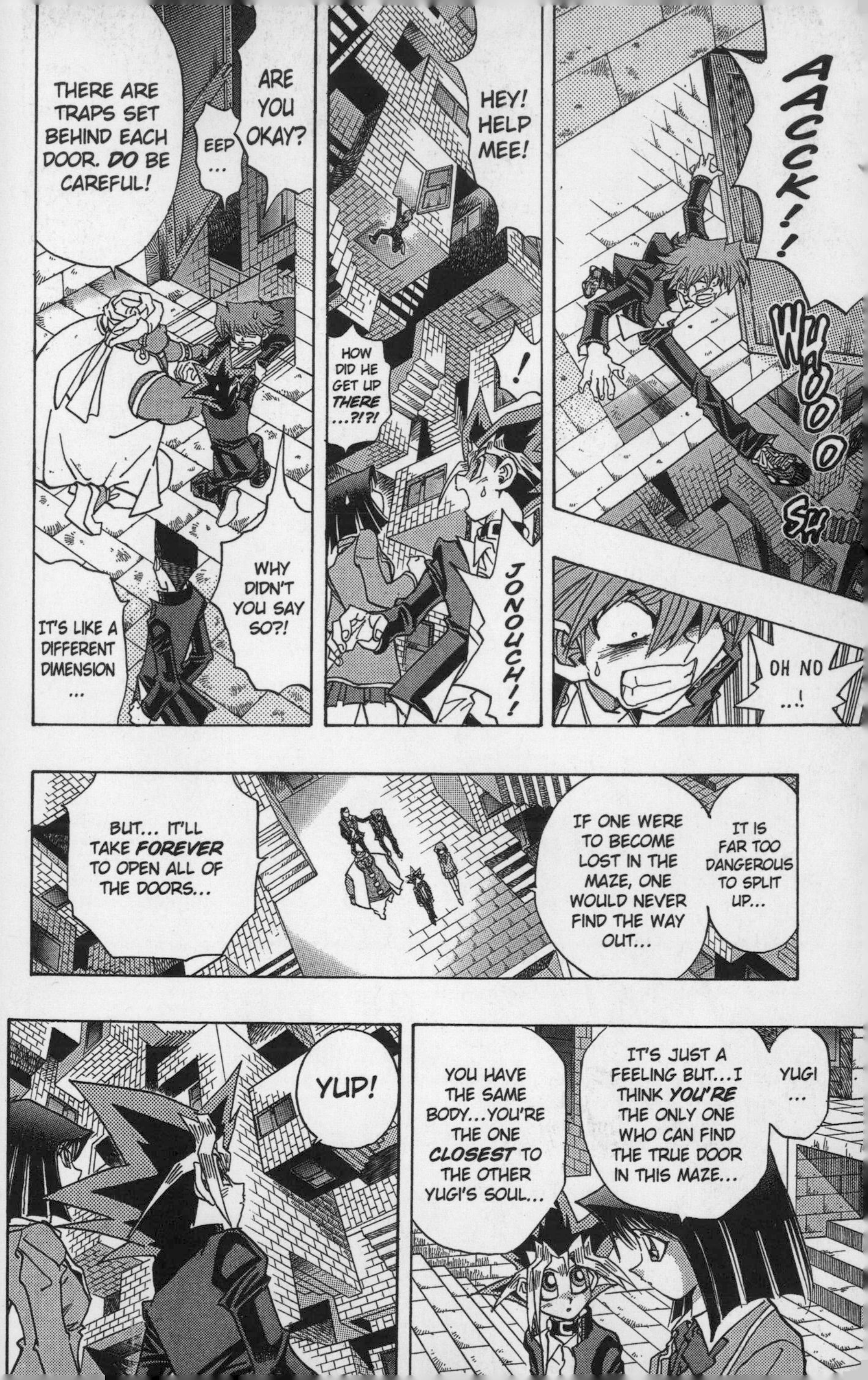
AACCK!!
WHOOOO
SH
OH NO ...!
HEY! HELP MEE!
!
HOW DID HE GET UP THERE ...?!?!
JONOUCHI!!
ARE YOU OKAY?
EEP ...
THERE ARE TRAPS SET BEHIND EACH DOOR. DO BE CAREFUL!
WHY DIDN'T YOU SAY SO?!
IT'S LIKE A DIFFERENT DIMENSION ...
IT IS FAR TOO DANGEROUS TO SPLIT UP...
IF ONE WERE TO BECOME LOST IN THE MAZE, ONE WOULD NEVER FIND THE WAY OUT...
BUT... IT'LL TAKE FOREVER TO OPEN ALL OF THE DOORS...
YUGI ...
IT'S JUST A FEELING BUT...I THINK YOU'RE THE ONLY ONE WHO CAN FIND THE TRUE DOOR IN THIS MAZE...
YOU HAVE THE SAME BODY...YOU'RE THE ONE CLOSEST TO THE OTHER YUGI'S SOUL...
YUP!

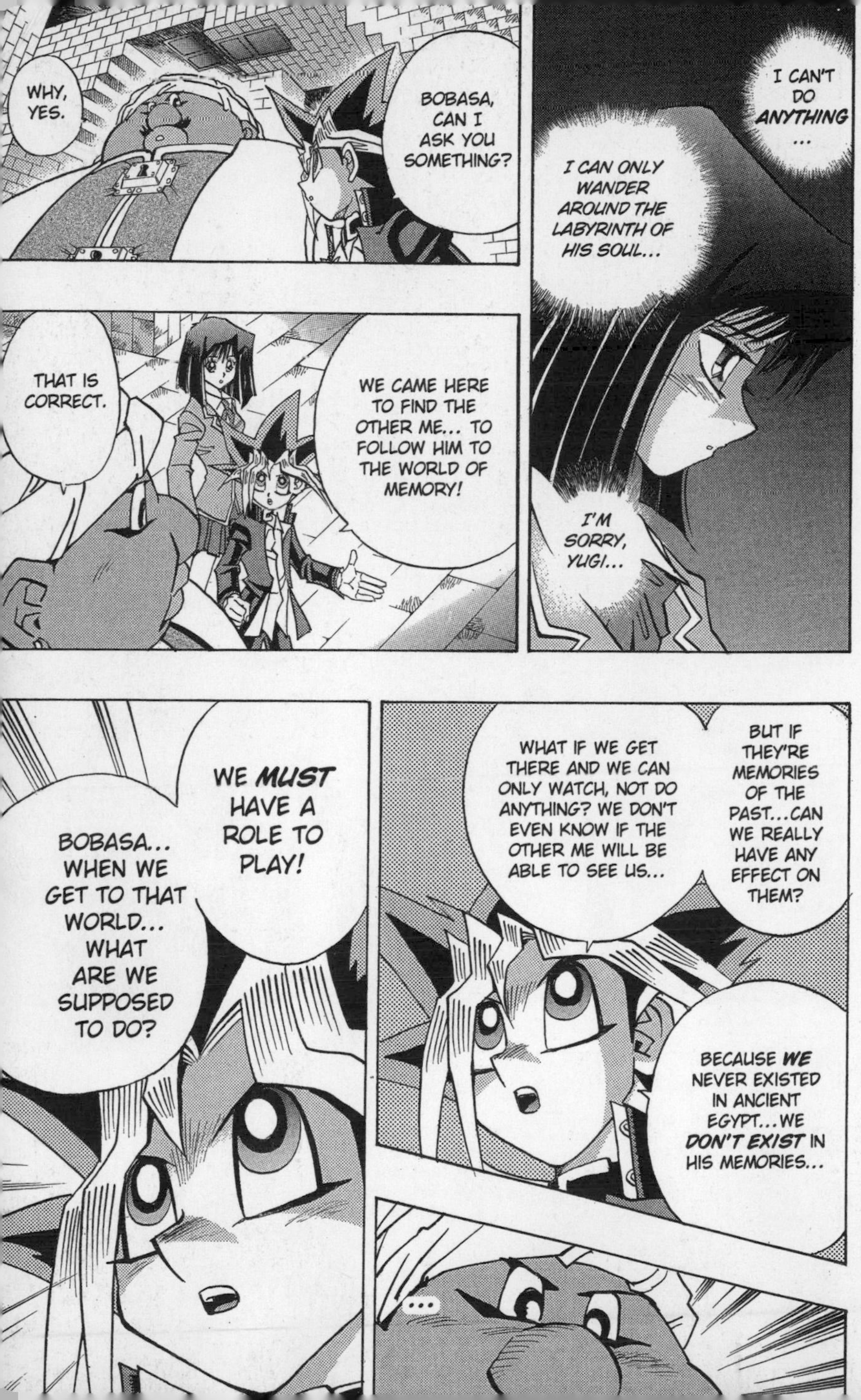
I CAN'T DO ANYTHING...
I CAN ONLY WANDER AROUND THE LABYRINTH OF HIS SOUL...
I'M SORRY, YUGI...
BOBASA, CAN I ASK YOU SOMETHING?
WHY, YES.
WE CAME HERE TO FIND THE OTHER ME... TO FOLLOW HIM TO THE WORLD OF MEMORY!
THAT IS CORRECT.
BUT IF THEY'RE MEMORIES OF THE PAST...CAN WE REALLY HAVE ANY EFFECT ON THEM?
WHAT IF WE GET THERE AND WE CAN ONLY WATCH, NOT DO ANYTHING? WE DON'T EVEN KNOW IF THE OTHER ME WILL BE ABLE TO SEE US...
BECAUSE WE NEVER EXISTED IN ANCIENT EGYPT...WE DON'T EXIST IN HIS MEMORIES...
...
WE MUST HAVE A ROLE TO PLAY!
BOBASA... WHEN WE GET TO THAT WORLD... WHAT ARE WE SUPPOSED TO DO?

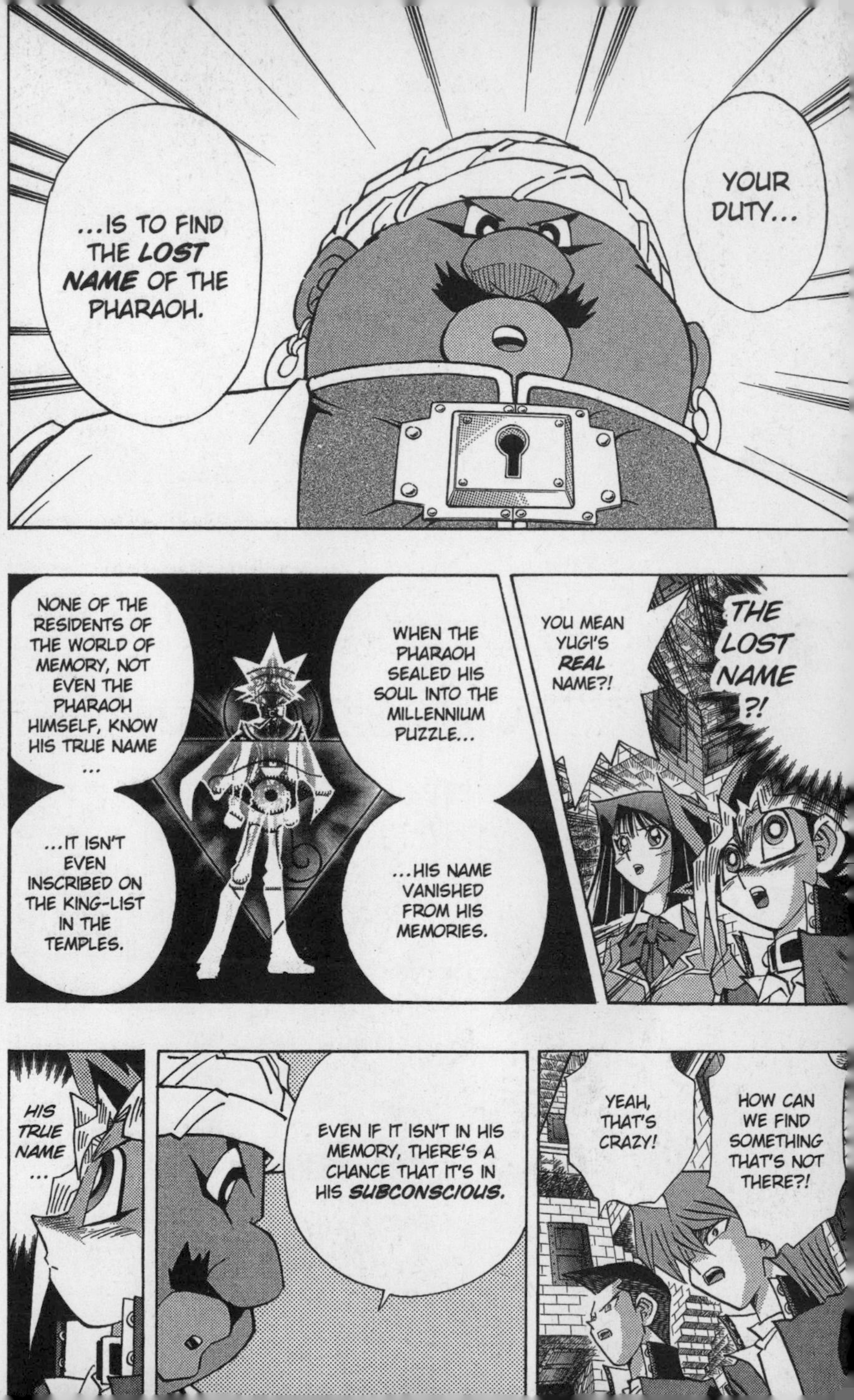
YOUR DUTY...
...IS TO FIND THE LOST NAME OF THE PHARAOH.
THE LOST NAME?!
YOU MEAN YUGI'S REAL NAME?!
WHEN THE PHARAOH SEALED HIS SOUL INTO THE MILLENNIUM PUZZLE...
...HIS NAME VANISHED FROM HIS MEMORIES.
NONE OF THE RESIDENTS OF THE WORLD OF MEMORY, NOT EVEN THE PHARAOH HIMSELF, KNOW HIS TRUE NAME...
...IT ISN'T EVEN INSCRIBED ON THE KING-LIST IN THE TEMPLES.
HOW CAN WE FIND SOMETHING THAT'S NOT THERE?!
YEAH, THAT'S CRAZY!
EVEN IF IT ISN'T IN HIS MEMORY, THERE'S A CHANCE THAT IT'S IN HIS SUBCONSCIOUS.
HIS TRUE NAME...

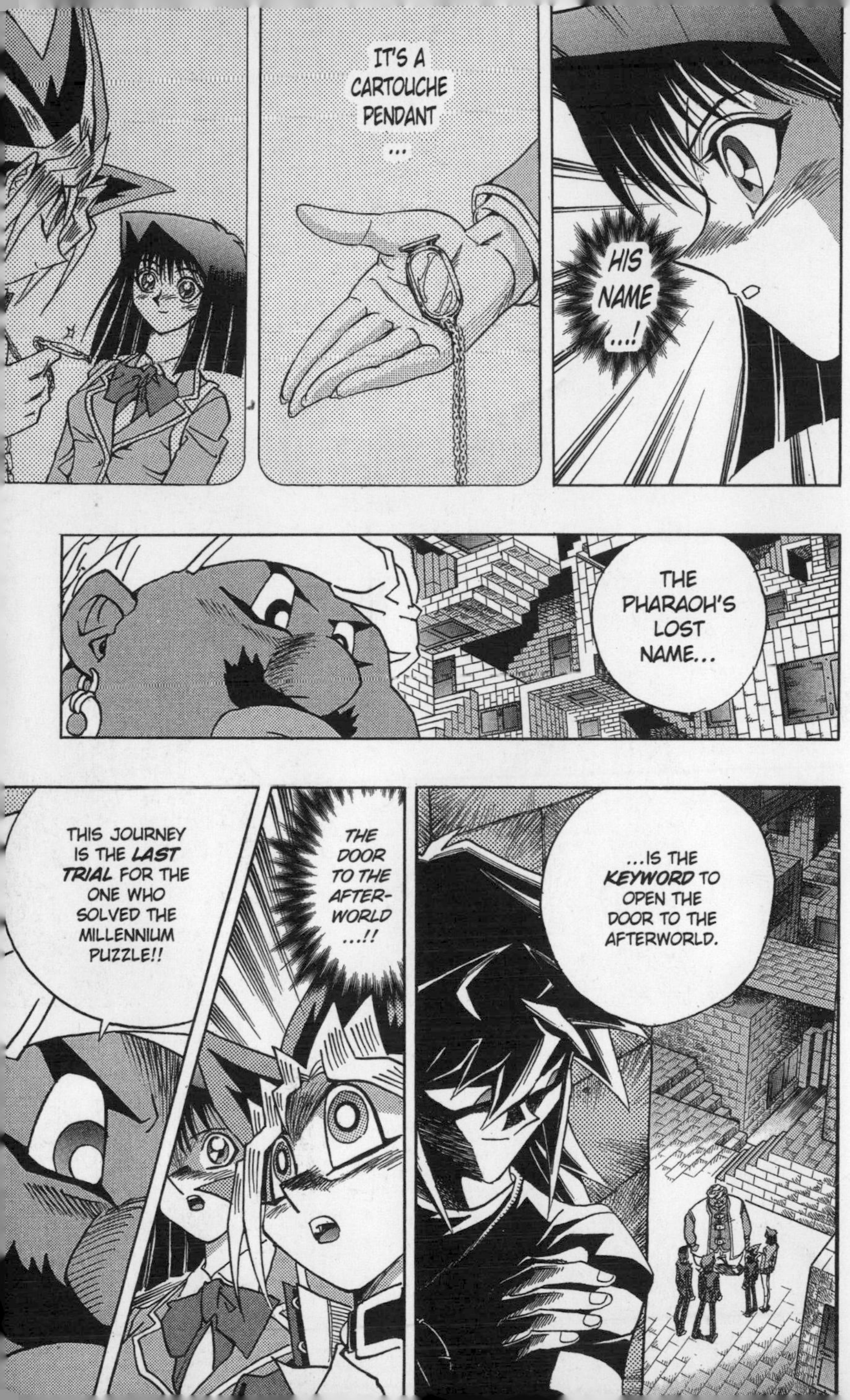
HIS NAME ...!
IT'S A CARTOUCHE PENDANT ...
THE PHARAOH'S LOST NAME...
...IS THE **KEYWORD** TO OPEN THE DOOR TO THE AFTERWORLD.
THE DOOR TO THE AFTER-WORLD ...!!
THIS JOURNEY IS THE **LAST TRIAL** FOR THE ONE WHO SOLVED THE MILLENNIUM PUZZLE!!

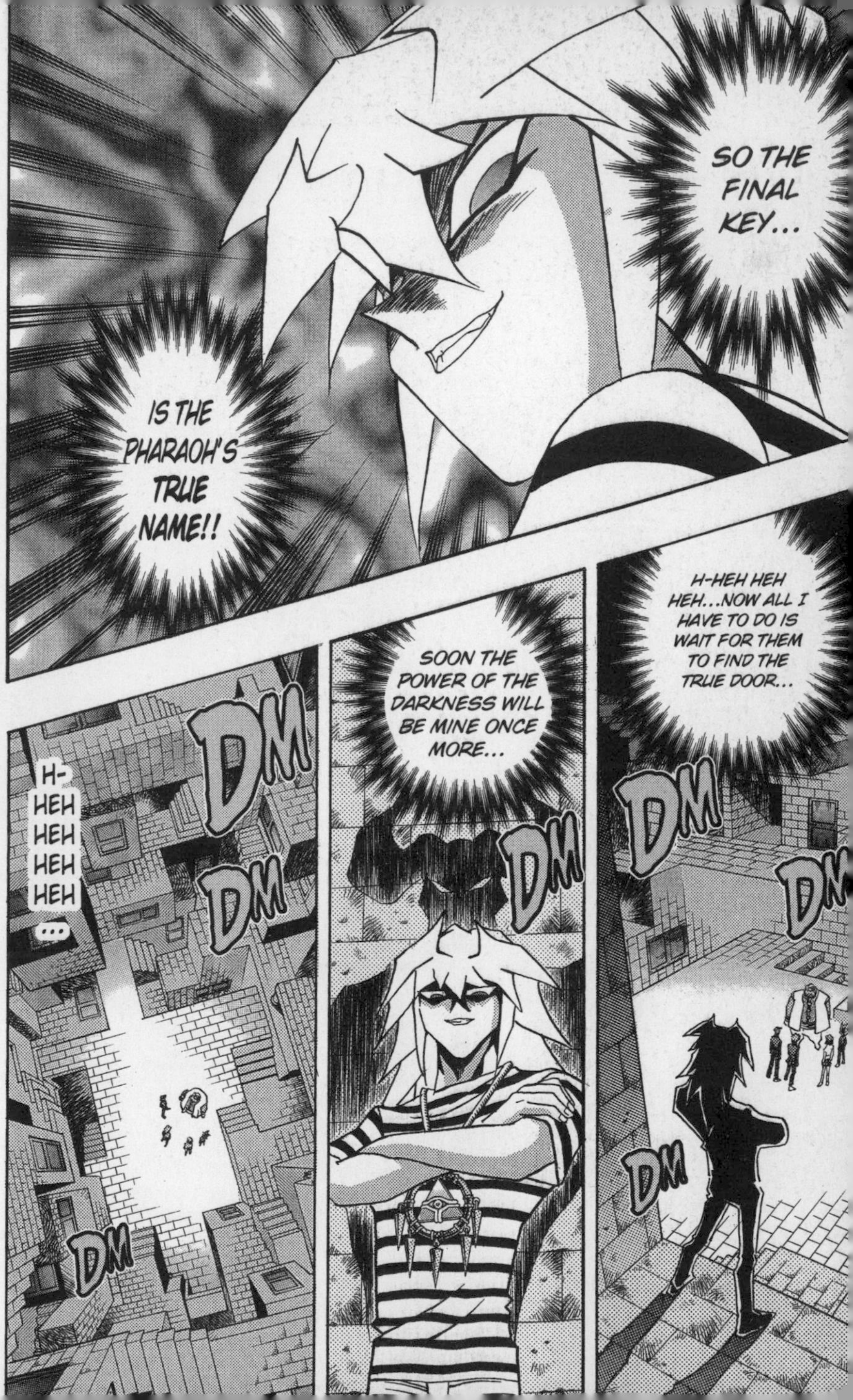
SO THE FINAL KEY...
IS THE PHARAOH'S TRUE NAME!!
H-HEH HEH HEH...NOW ALL I HAVE TO DO IS WAIT FOR THEM TO FIND THE TRUE DOOR...
DM
DM
DM
SOON THE POWER OF THE DARKNESS WILL BE MINE ONCE MORE...
DM
DM
H-HEH HEH HEH HEH...
DM
DM
DM

Duel 12: The Quest for the Name

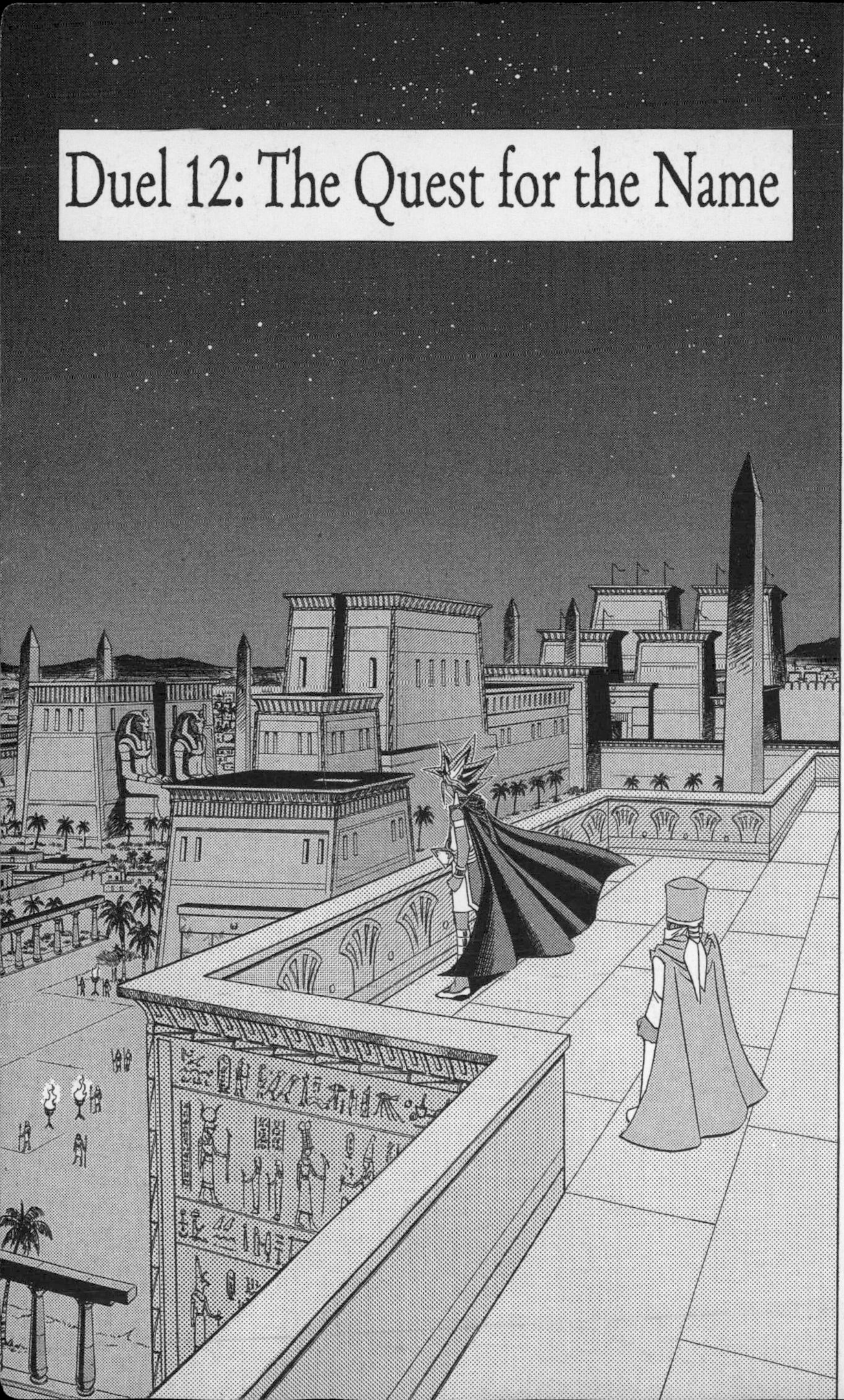

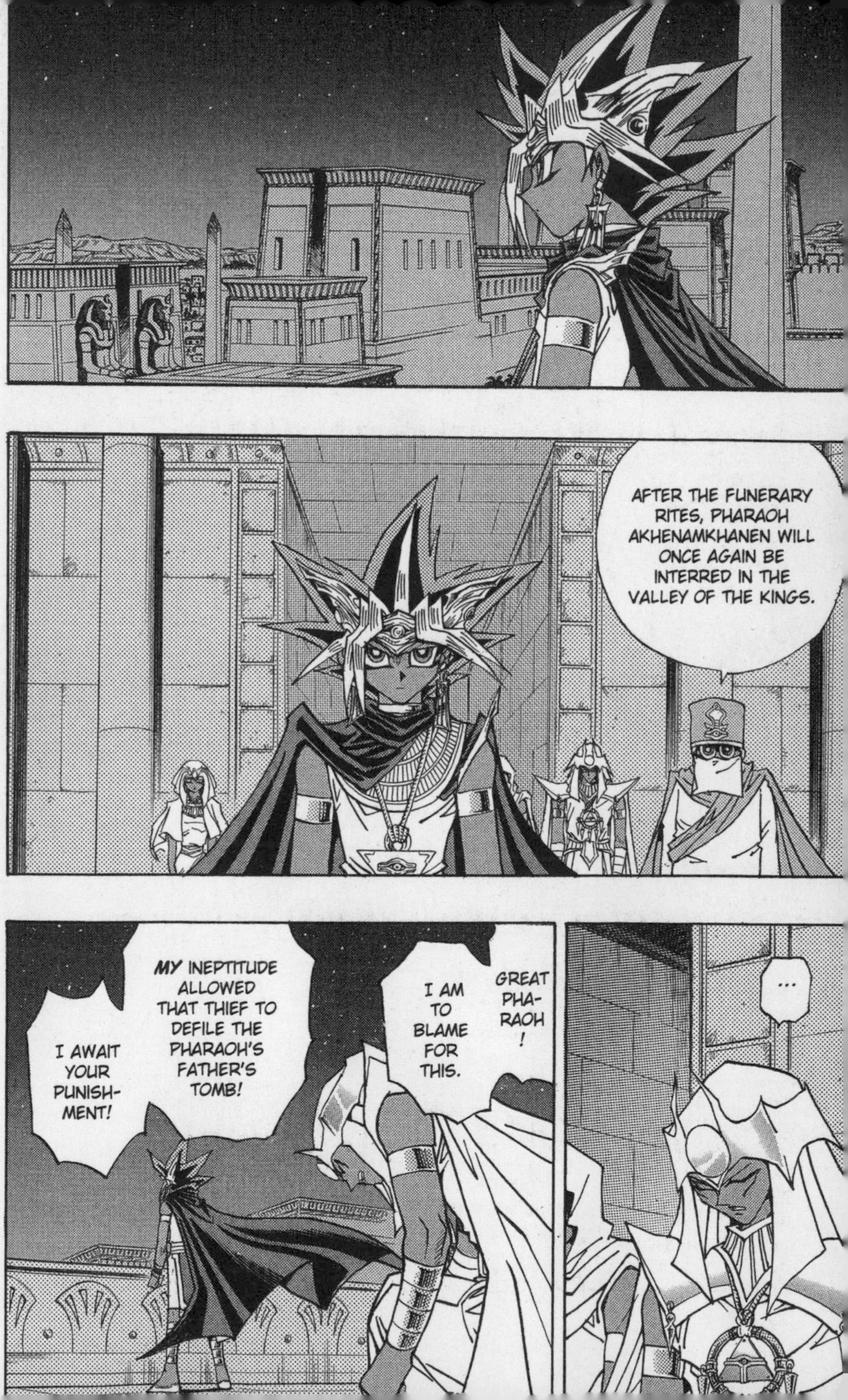
AFTER THE FUNERARY RITES, PHARAOH AKHENAMKHANEN WILL ONCE AGAIN BE INTERRED IN THE VALLEY OF THE KINGS.
...
GREAT PHARAOH!
I AM TO BLAME FOR THIS.
MY INEPTITUDE ALLOWED THAT THIEF TO DEFILE THE PHARAOH'S FATHER'S TOMB!
I AWAIT YOUR PUNISHMENT!

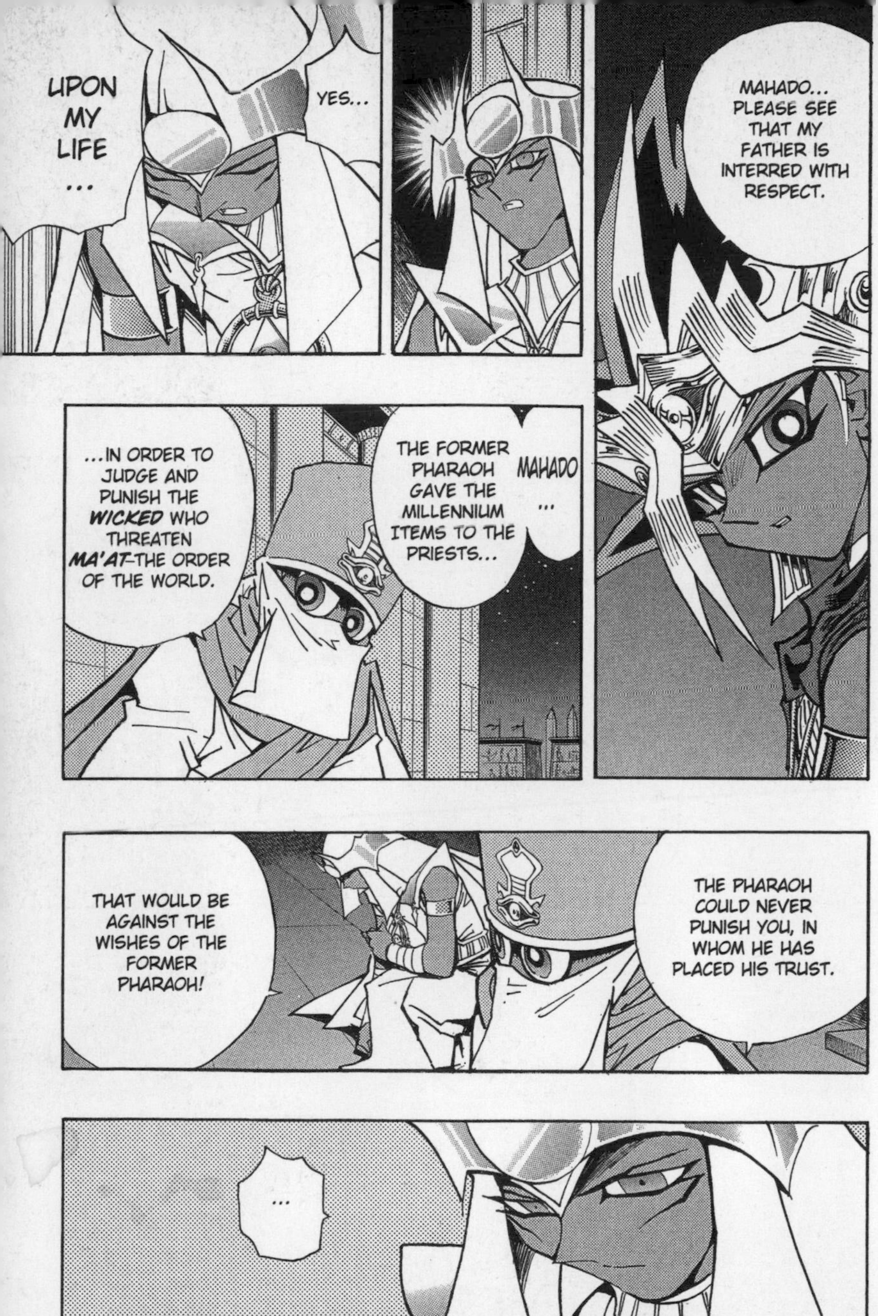

MAHADO... PLEASE SEE THAT MY FATHER IS INTERRED WITH RESPECT.
YES...
UPON MY LIFE...
MAHADO...
THE FORMER PHARAOH GAVE THE MILLENNIUM ITEMS TO THE PRIESTS...
...IN ORDER TO JUDGE AND PUNISH THE *WICKED* WHO THREATEN *MA'AT*—THE ORDER OF THE WORLD.
THE PHARAOH COULD NEVER PUNISH YOU, IN WHOM HE HAS PLACED HIS TRUST.
THAT WOULD BE AGAINST THE WISHES OF THE FORMER PHARAOH!
...

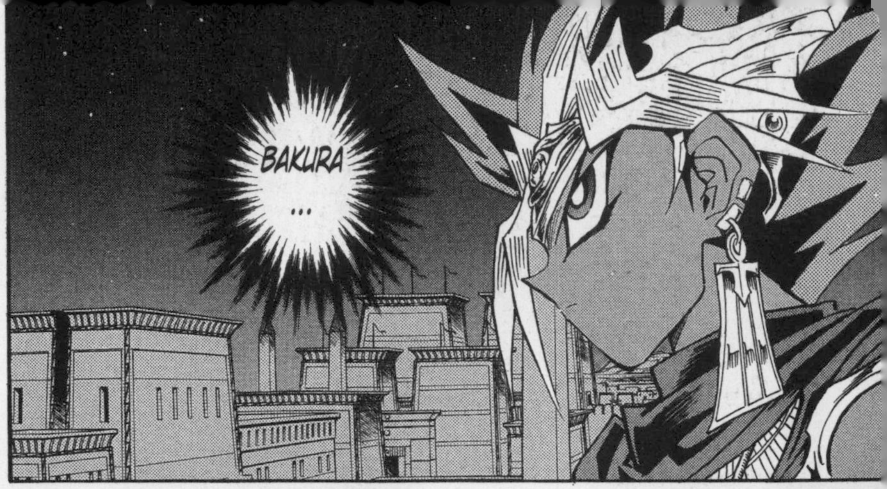
BAKURA
...
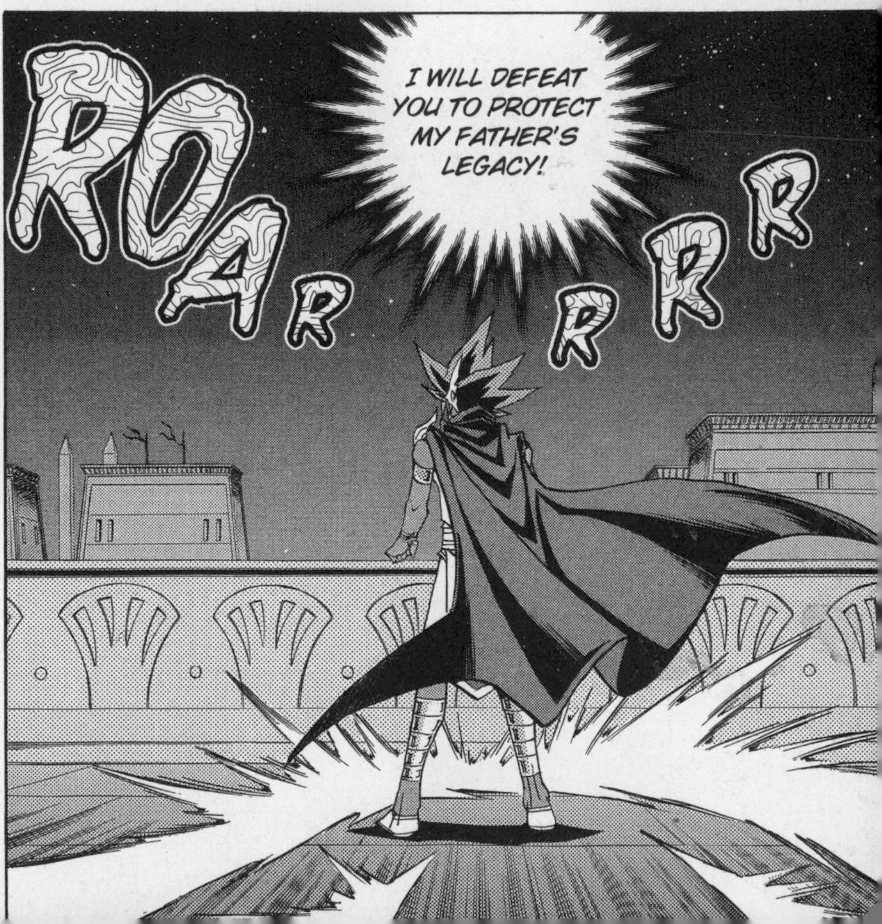
I WILL DEFEAT YOU TO PROTECT MY FATHER'S LEGACY!
ROARRRR

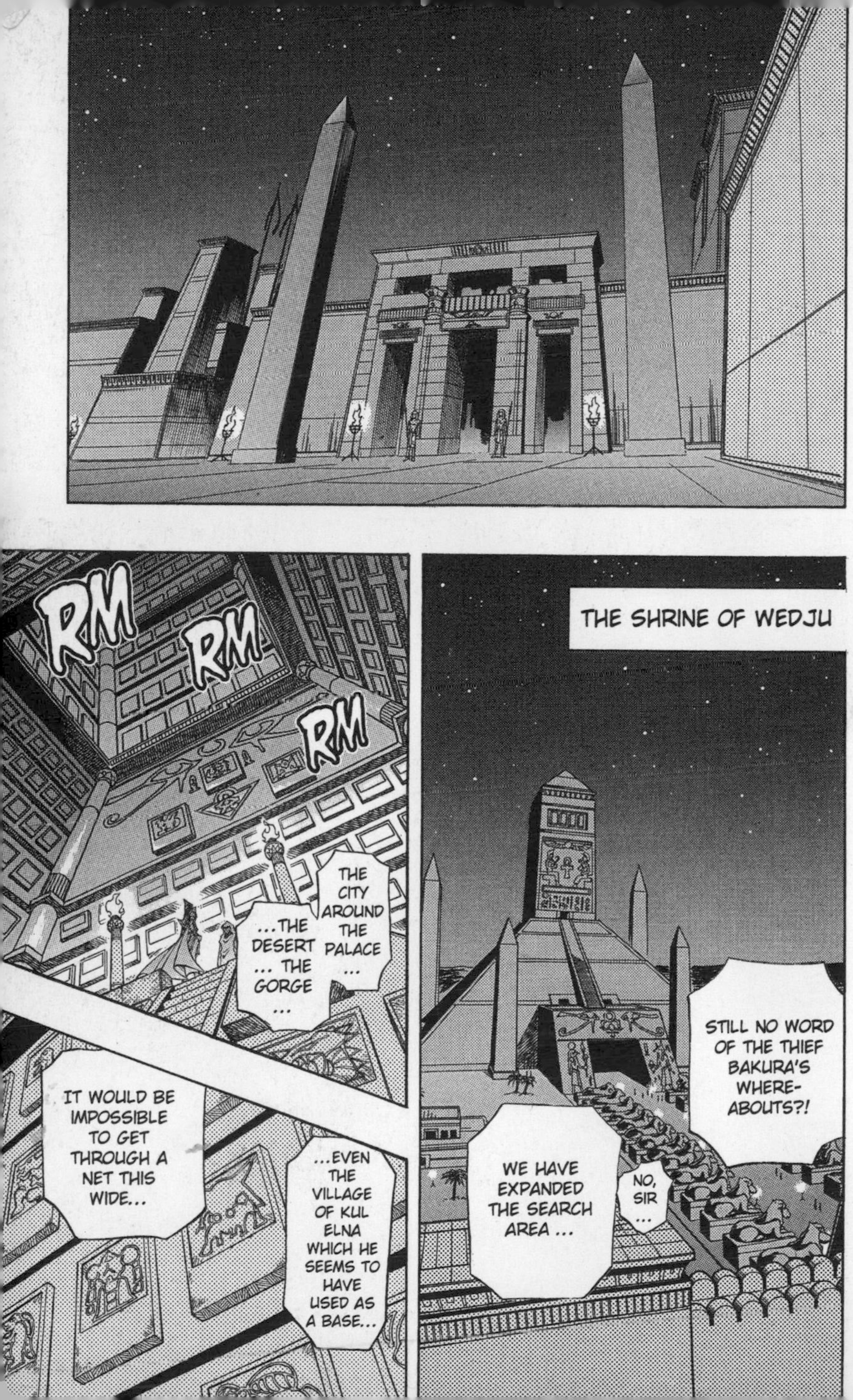
THE SHRINE OF WEDJU
STILL NO WORD OF THE THIEF BAKURA'S WHERE-ABOUTS?!
NO, SIR ...
WE HAVE EXPANDED THE SEARCH AREA ...
RM RM RM
THE CITY AROUND THE PALACE ...
...THE DESERT ... THE GORGE ...
...EVEN THE VILLAGE OF KUL ELNA WHICH HE SEEMS TO HAVE USED AS A BASE...
IT WOULD BE IMPOSSIBLE TO GET THROUGH A NET THIS WIDE...

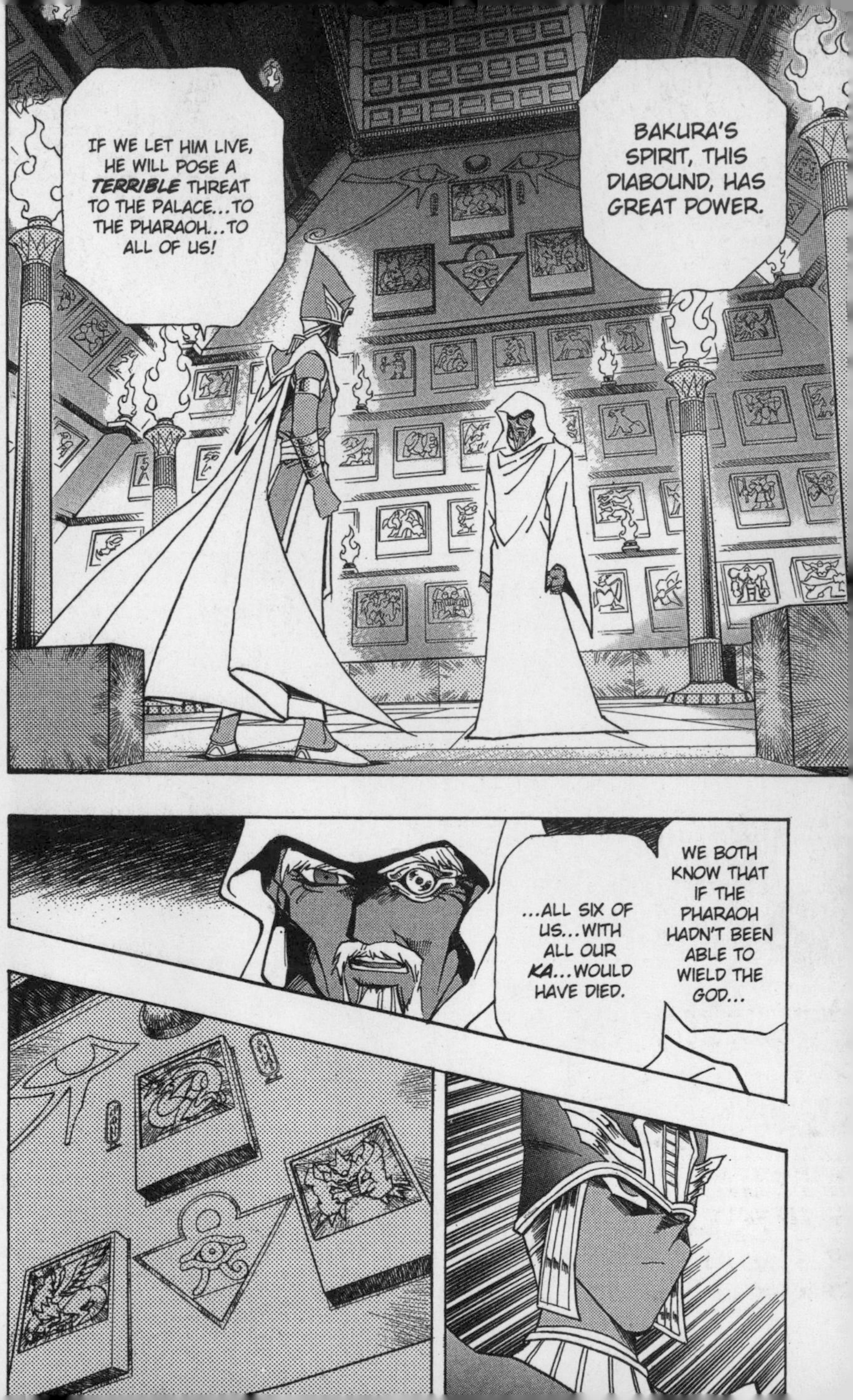
BAKURA'S SPIRIT, THIS DIABOUND, HAS GREAT POWER.
IF WE LET HIM LIVE, HE WILL POSE A *TERRIBLE* THREAT TO THE PALACE...TO THE PHARAOH...TO ALL OF US!
WE BOTH KNOW THAT IF THE PHARAOH HADN'T BEEN ABLE TO WIELD THE GOD...
...ALL SIX OF US...WITH ALL OUR *KA*...WOULD HAVE DIED.

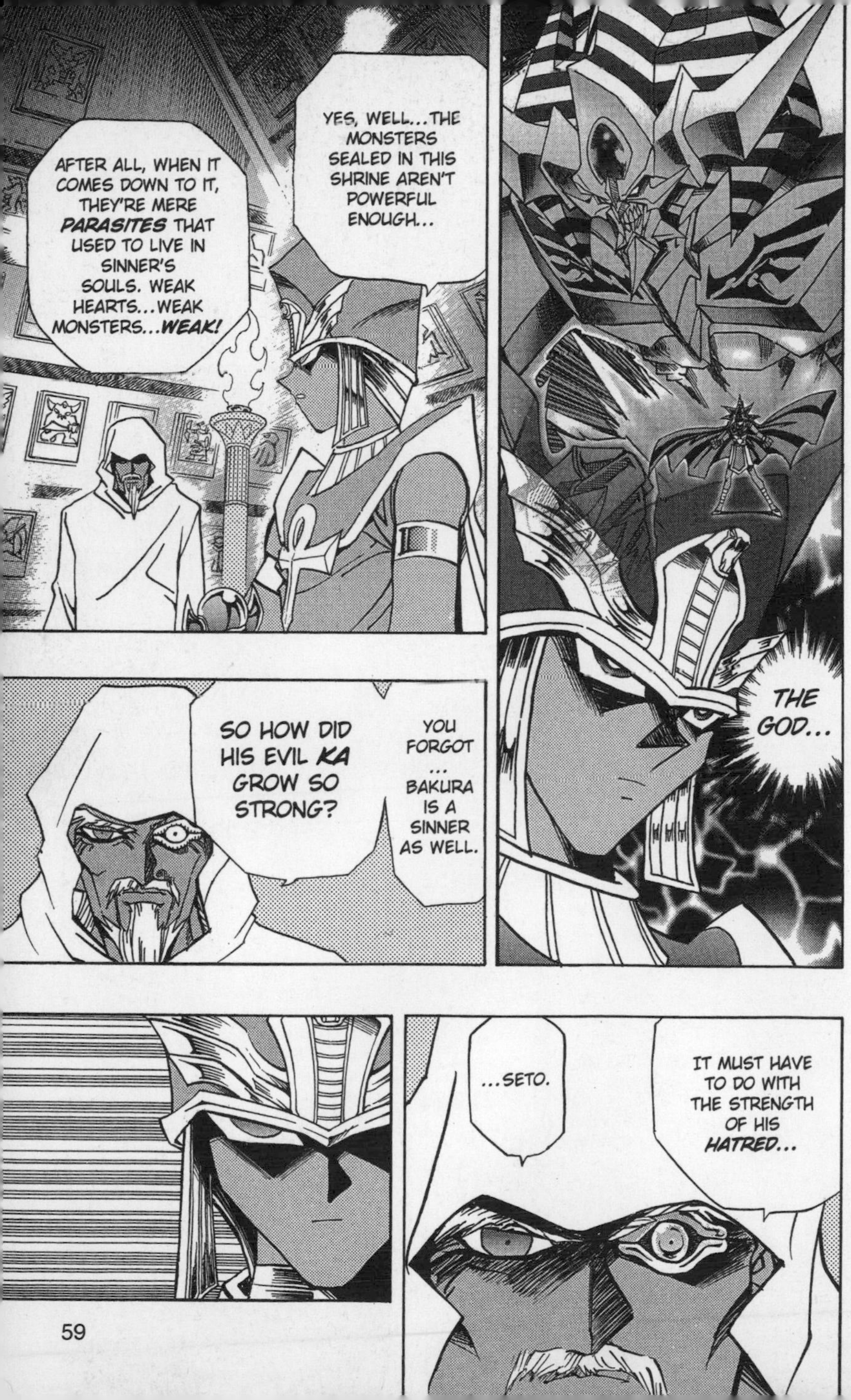
THE GOD...
YES, WELL...THE MONSTERS SEALED IN THIS SHRINE AREN'T POWERFUL ENOUGH...
AFTER ALL, WHEN IT COMES DOWN TO IT, THEY'RE MERE **PARASITES** THAT USED TO LIVE IN SINNER'S SOULS. WEAK HEARTS...WEAK MONSTERS...**WEAK!**
YOU FORGOT ... BAKURA IS A SINNER AS WELL.
SO HOW DID HIS EVIL **KA** GROW SO STRONG?
IT MUST HAVE TO DO WITH THE STRENGTH OF HIS **HATRED...**
...SETO.

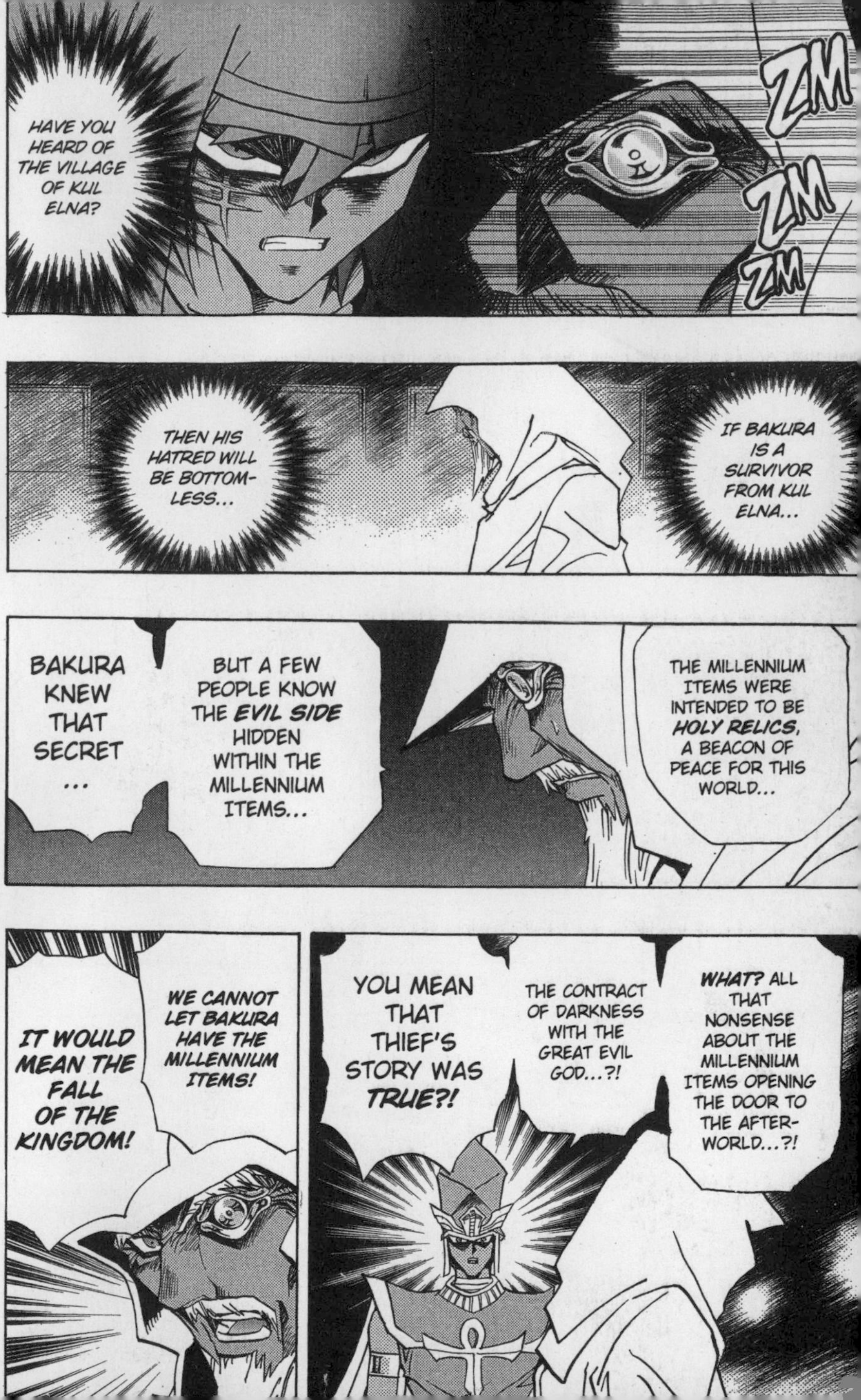
ZM
ZM
ZM
HAVE YOU HEARD OF THE VILLAGE OF KUL ELNA?
IF BAKURA IS A SURVIVOR FROM KUL ELNA...
THEN HIS HATRED WILL BE BOTTOM-LESS...
THE MILLENNIUM ITEMS WERE INTENDED TO BE HOLY RELICS, A BEACON OF PEACE FOR THIS WORLD...
BUT A FEW PEOPLE KNOW THE EVIL SIDE HIDDEN WITHIN THE MILLENNIUM ITEMS...
BAKURA KNEW THAT SECRET...
WHAT? ALL THAT NONSENSE ABOUT THE MILLENNIUM ITEMS OPENING THE DOOR TO THE AFTER-WORLD...?!
THE CONTRACT OF DARKNESS WITH THE GREAT EVIL GOD...?!
YOU MEAN THAT THIEF'S STORY WAS TRUE?!
WE CANNOT LET BAKURA HAVE THE MILLENNIUM ITEMS!
IT WOULD MEAN THE FALL OF THE KINGDOM!

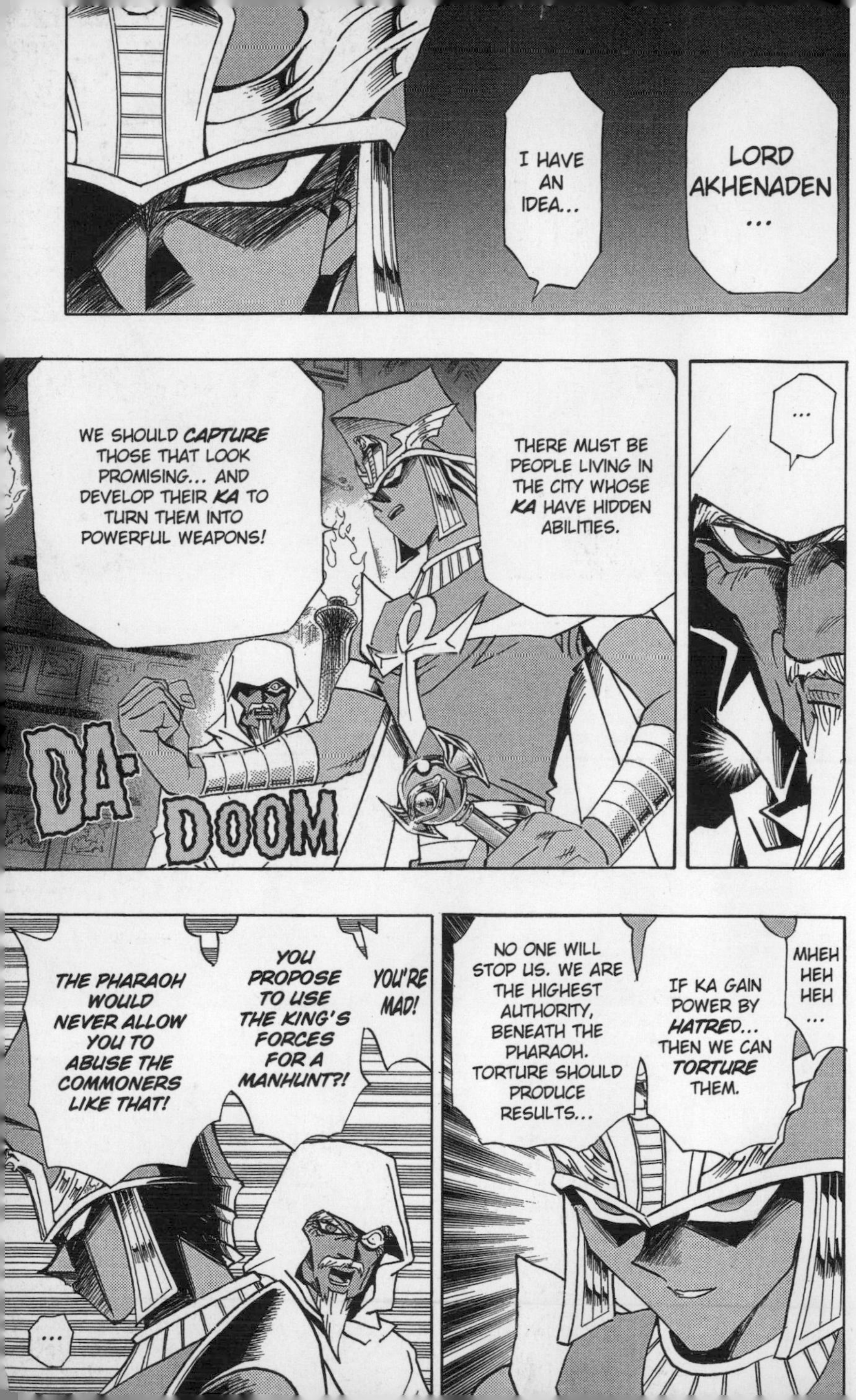
LORD AKHENADEN ...
I HAVE AN IDEA...
...
THERE MUST BE PEOPLE LIVING IN THE CITY WHOSE KA HAVE HIDDEN ABILITIES.
WE SHOULD CAPTURE THOSE THAT LOOK PROMISING... AND DEVELOP THEIR KA TO TURN THEM INTO POWERFUL WEAPONS!
DA-DOOM
MHEH HEH HEH ...
IF KA GAIN POWER BY HATRED... THEN WE CAN TORTURE THEM.
NO ONE WILL STOP US. WE ARE THE HIGHEST AUTHORITY, BENEATH THE PHARAOH. TORTURE SHOULD PRODUCE RESULTS...
YOU'RE MAD!
YOU PROPOSE TO USE THE KING'S FORCES FOR A MANHUNT?!
THE PHARAOH WOULD NEVER ALLOW YOU TO ABUSE THE COMMONERS LIKE THAT!
...

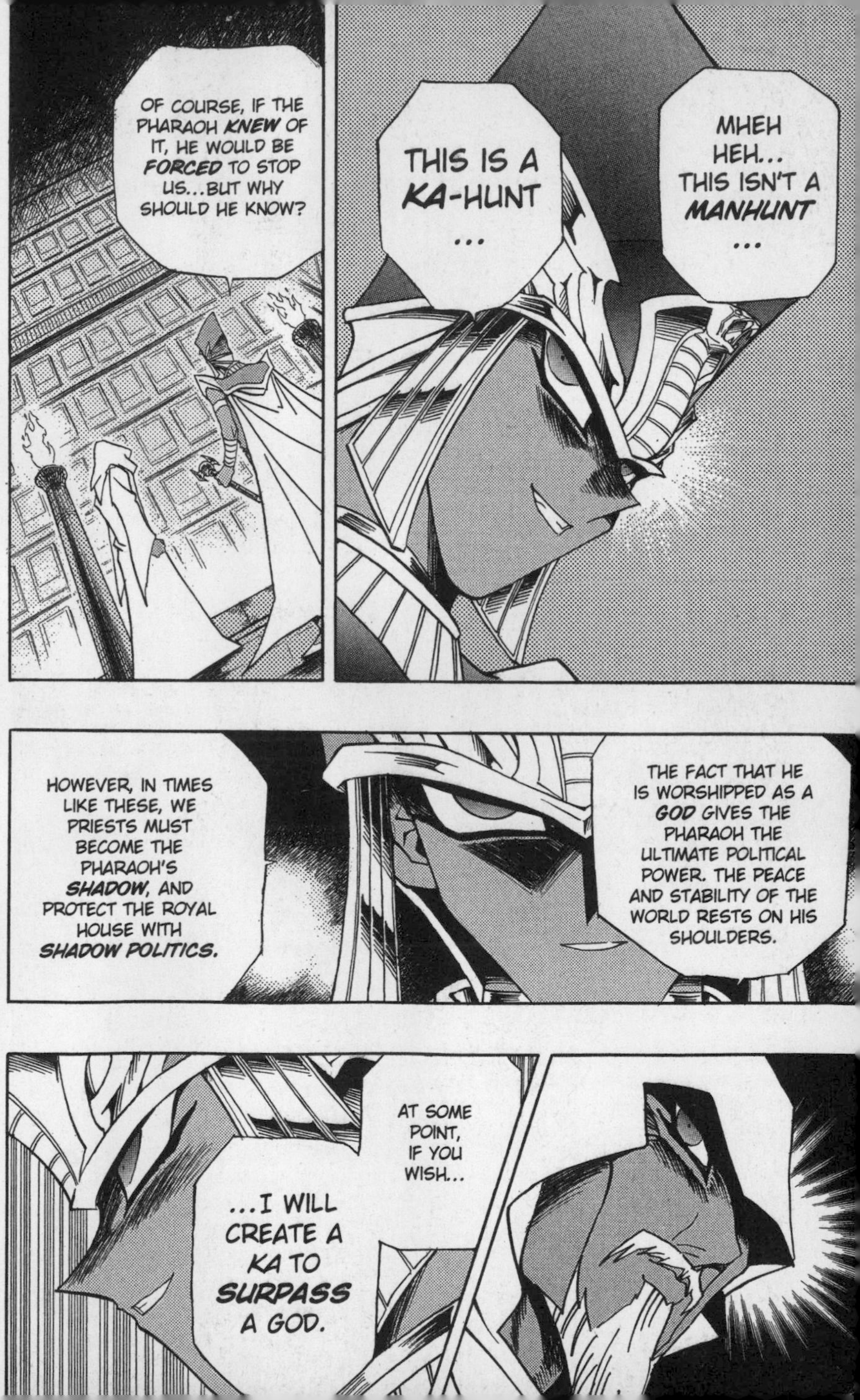
MHEH HEH... THIS ISN'T A MANHUNT ...
THIS IS A KA-HUNT ...
OF COURSE, IF THE PHARAOH KNEW OF IT, HE WOULD BE FORCED TO STOP US...BUT WHY SHOULD HE KNOW?
THE FACT THAT HE IS WORSHIPPED AS A GOD GIVES THE PHARAOH THE ULTIMATE POLITICAL POWER. THE PEACE AND STABILITY OF THE WORLD RESTS ON HIS SHOULDERS.
HOWEVER, IN TIMES LIKE THESE, WE PRIESTS MUST BECOME THE PHARAOH'S SHADOW, AND PROTECT THE ROYAL HOUSE WITH SHADOW POLITICS.
AT SOME POINT, IF YOU WISH...
...I WILL CREATE A KA TO SURPASS A GOD.

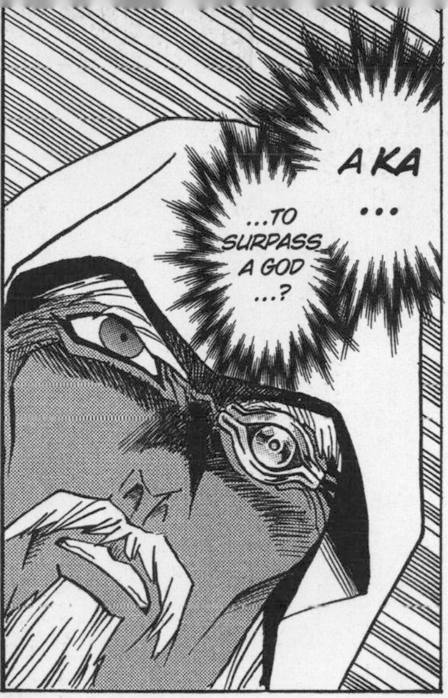
A KA . . .
...TO SURPASS A GOD ...?

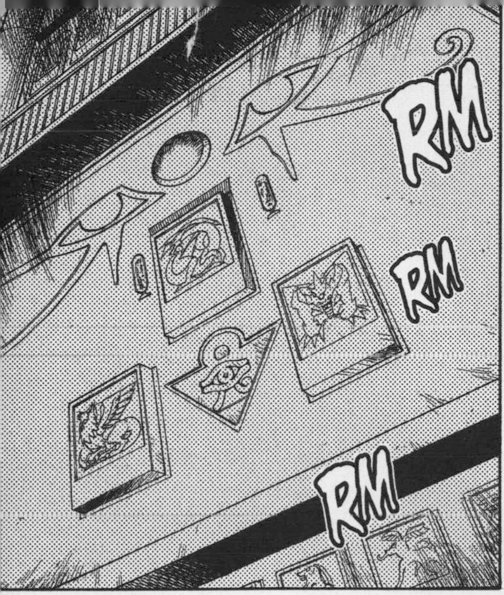
RM
RM
RM

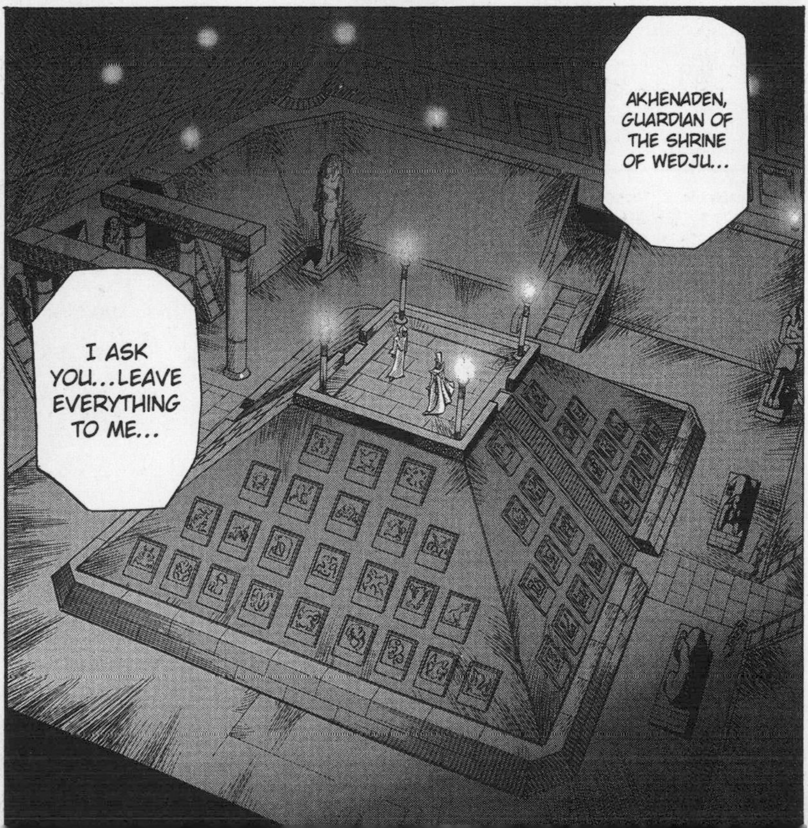
AKHENADEN, GUARDIAN OF THE SHRINE OF WEDJU...
I ASK YOU...LEAVE EVERYTHING TO ME...

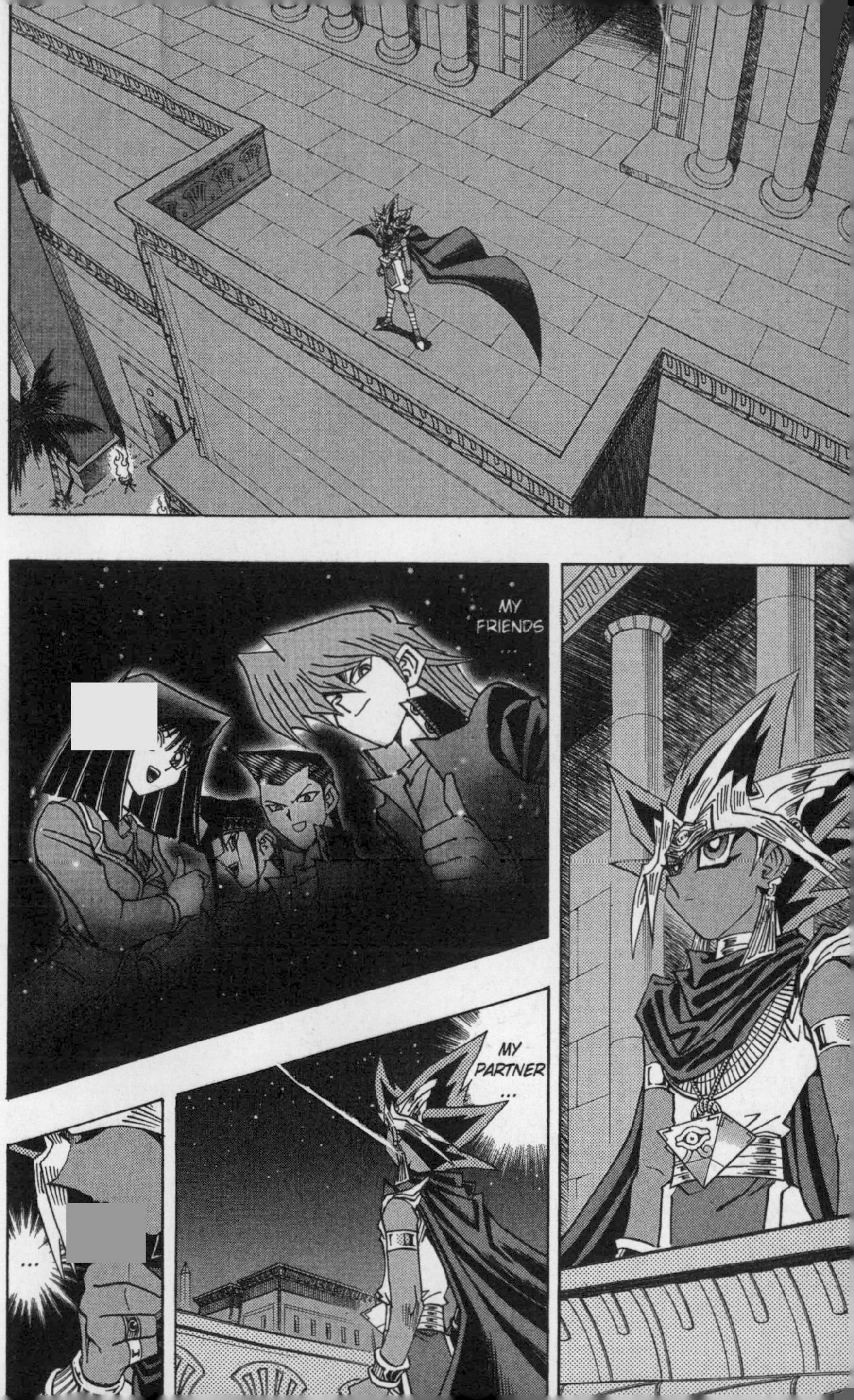
MY FRIENDS ...
MY PARTNER ...
...

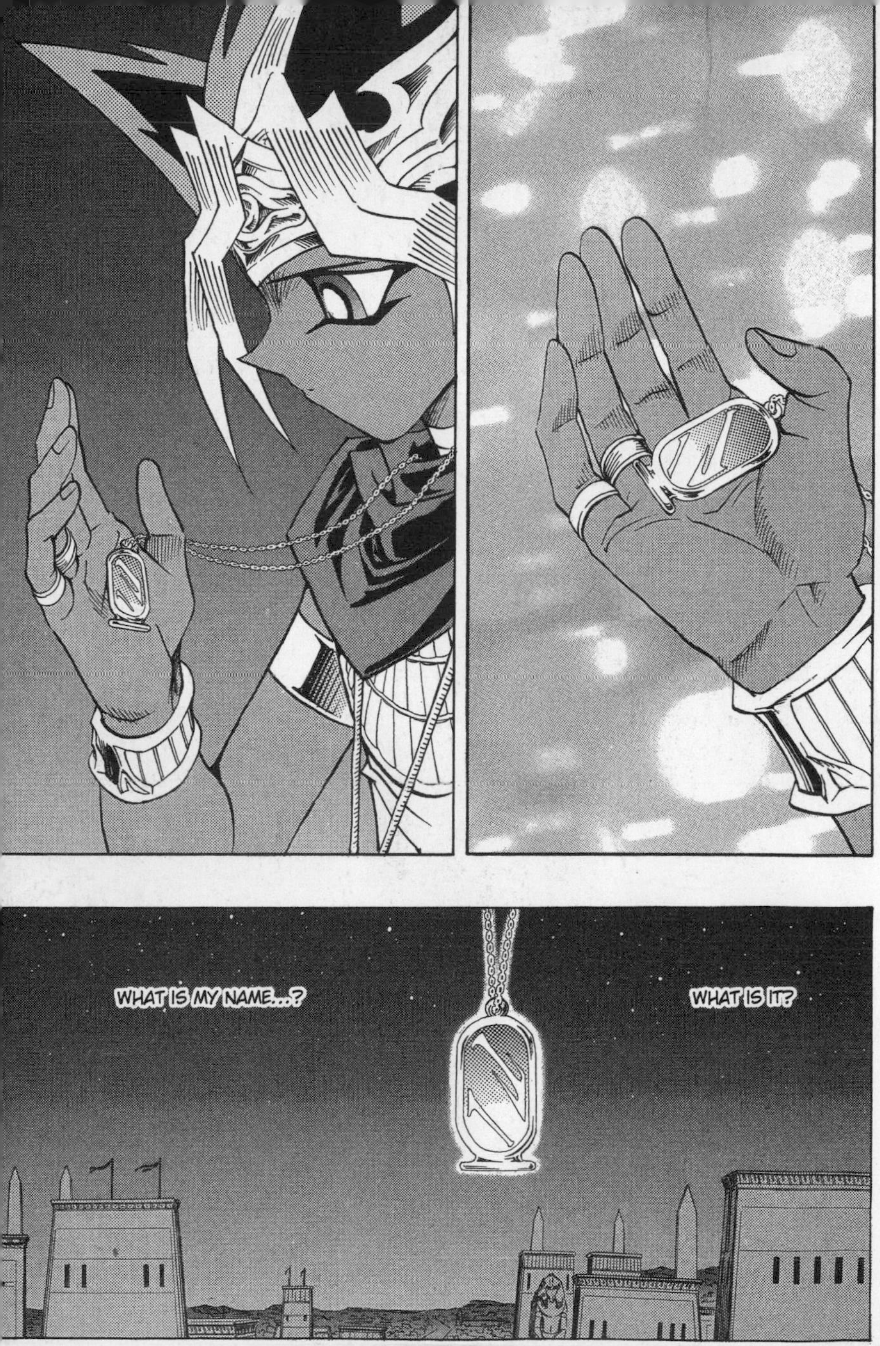
WHAT IS IT?
WHAT IS MY NAME...?

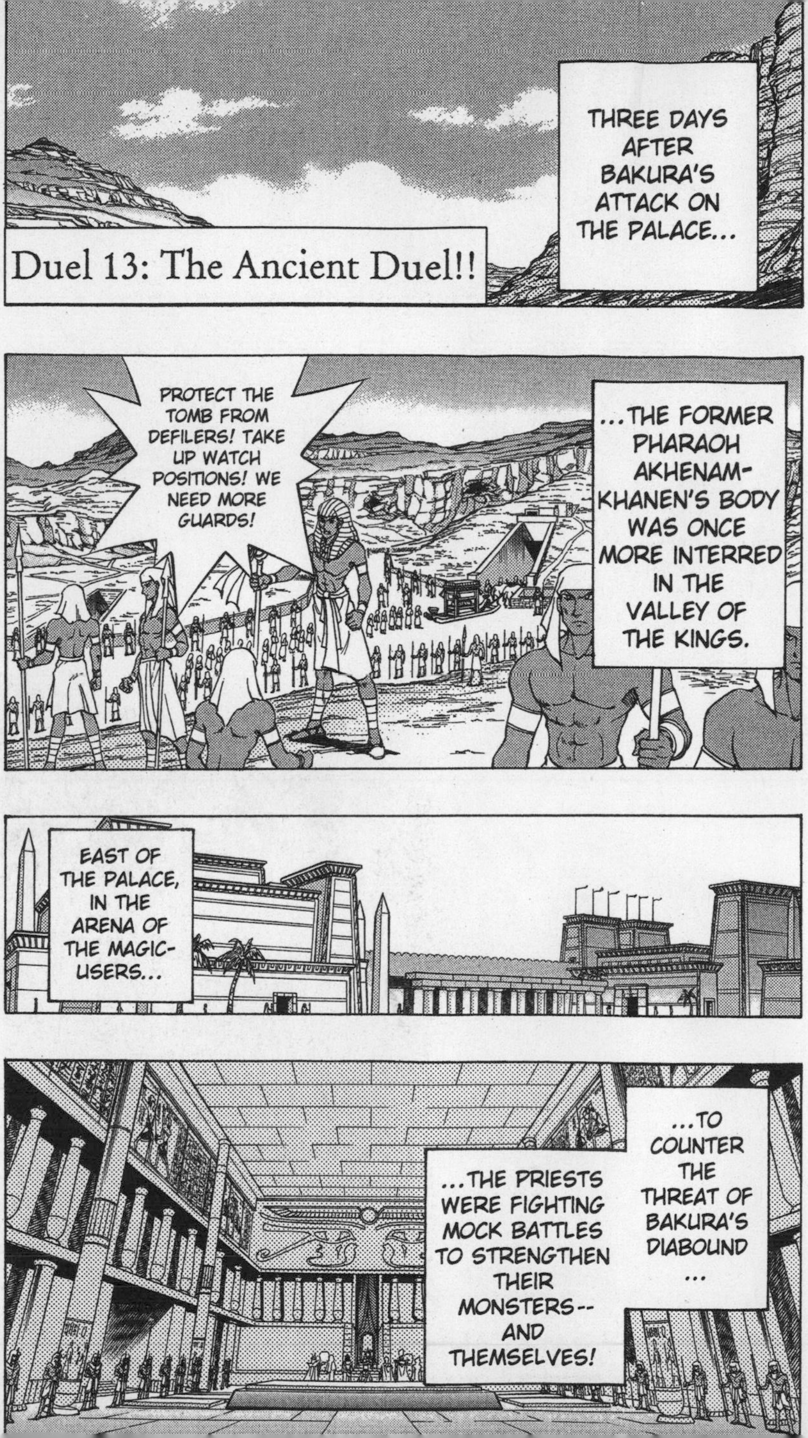
THREE DAYS AFTER BAKURA'S ATTACK ON THE PALACE...
Duel 13: The Ancient Duel!!
...THE FORMER PHARAOH AKHENAM-KHANEN'S BODY WAS ONCE MORE INTERRED IN THE VALLEY OF THE KINGS.
PROTECT THE TOMB FROM DEFILERS! TAKE UP WATCH POSITIONS! WE NEED MORE GUARDS!
EAST OF THE PALACE, IN THE ARENA OF THE MAGIC-USERS...
...TO COUNTER THE THREAT OF BAKURA'S DIABOUND ...
...THE PRIESTS WERE FIGHTING MOCK BATTLES TO STRENGTHEN THEIR MONSTERS-- AND THEMSELVES!

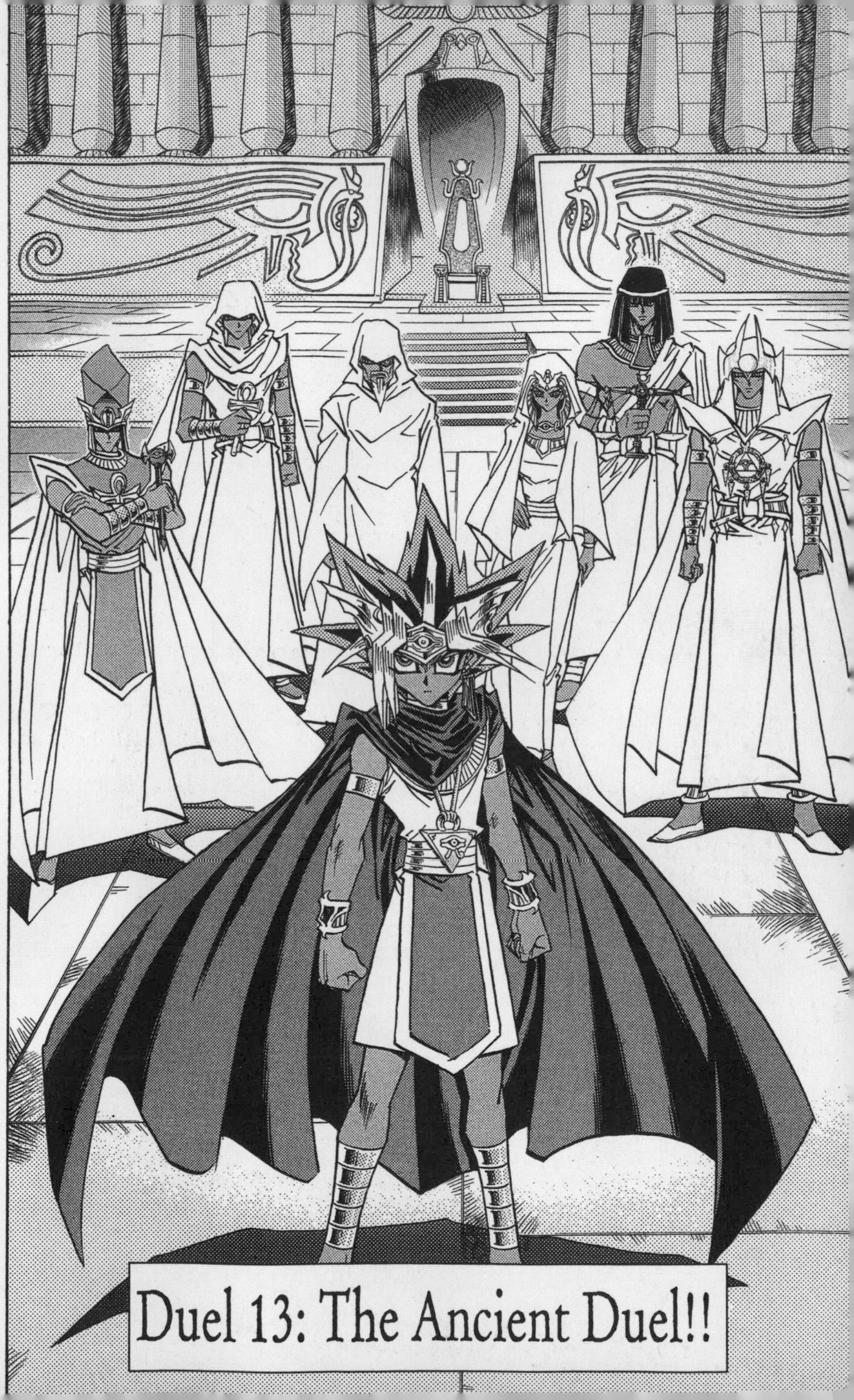
Duel 13: The Ancient Duel!!

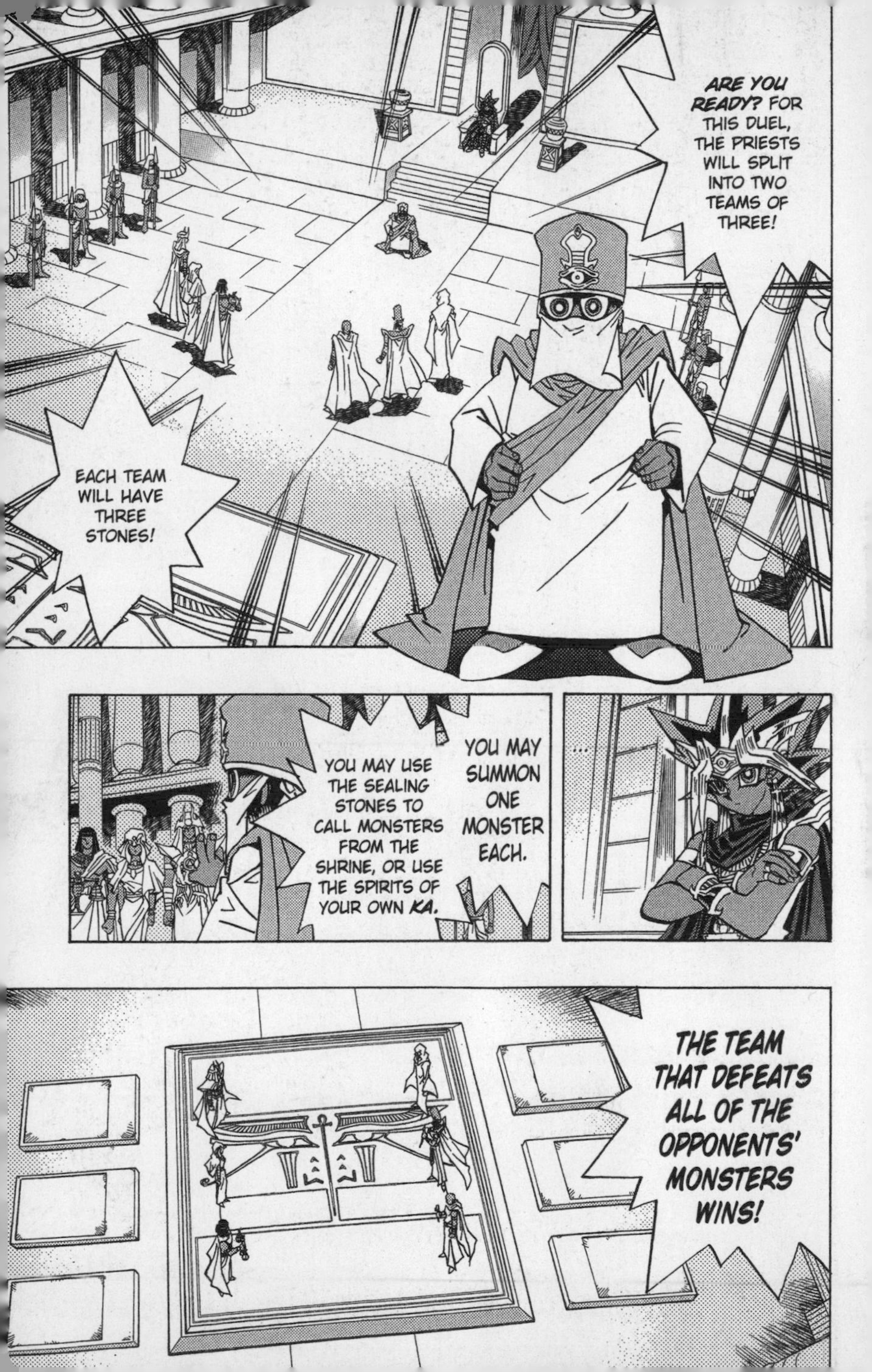
ARE YOU READY? FOR THIS DUEL, THE PRIESTS WILL SPLIT INTO TWO TEAMS OF THREE!
EACH TEAM WILL HAVE THREE STONES!
...
YOU MAY SUMMON ONE MONSTER EACH.
YOU MAY USE THE SEALING STONES TO CALL MONSTERS FROM THE SHRINE, OR USE THE SPIRITS OF YOUR OWN KA.
THE TEAM THAT DEFEATS ALL OF THE OPPONENTS' MONSTERS WINS!

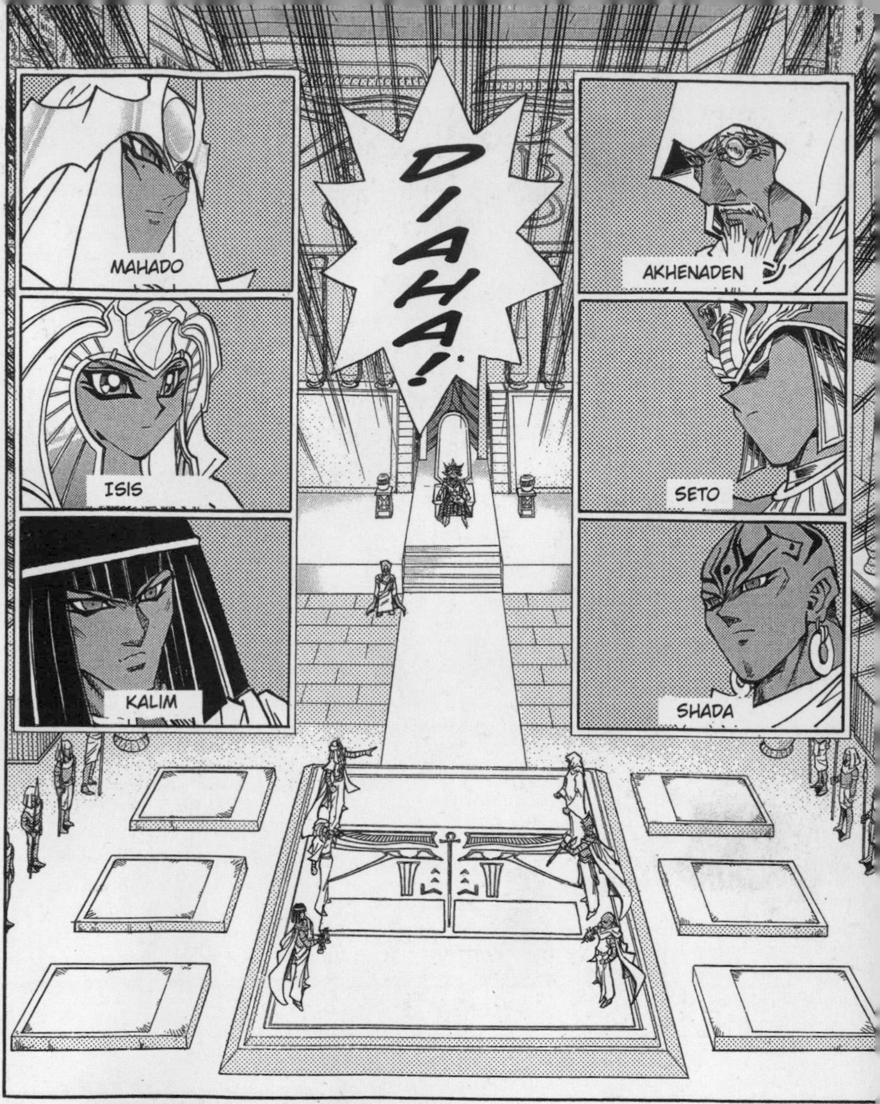
DIAHA!*
AKHENADEN
SETO
SHADA
MAHADO
ISIS
KALIM

*DIAHA = EGYPTIAN FOR "DUEL START"

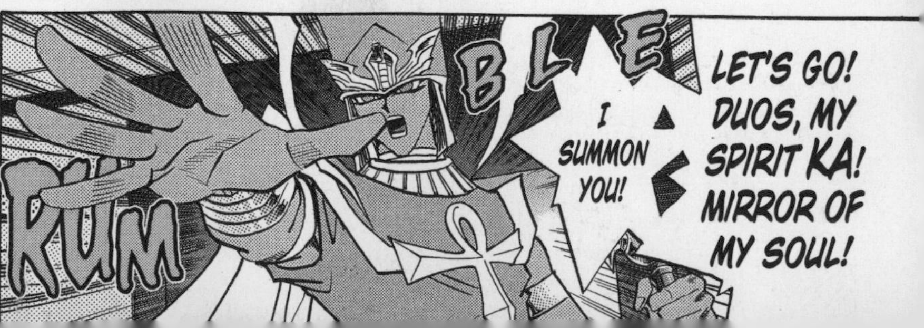
LET'S GO! DUOS, MY SPIRIT KA! MIRROR OF MY SOUL!
I SUMMON YOU!
RUMBLE

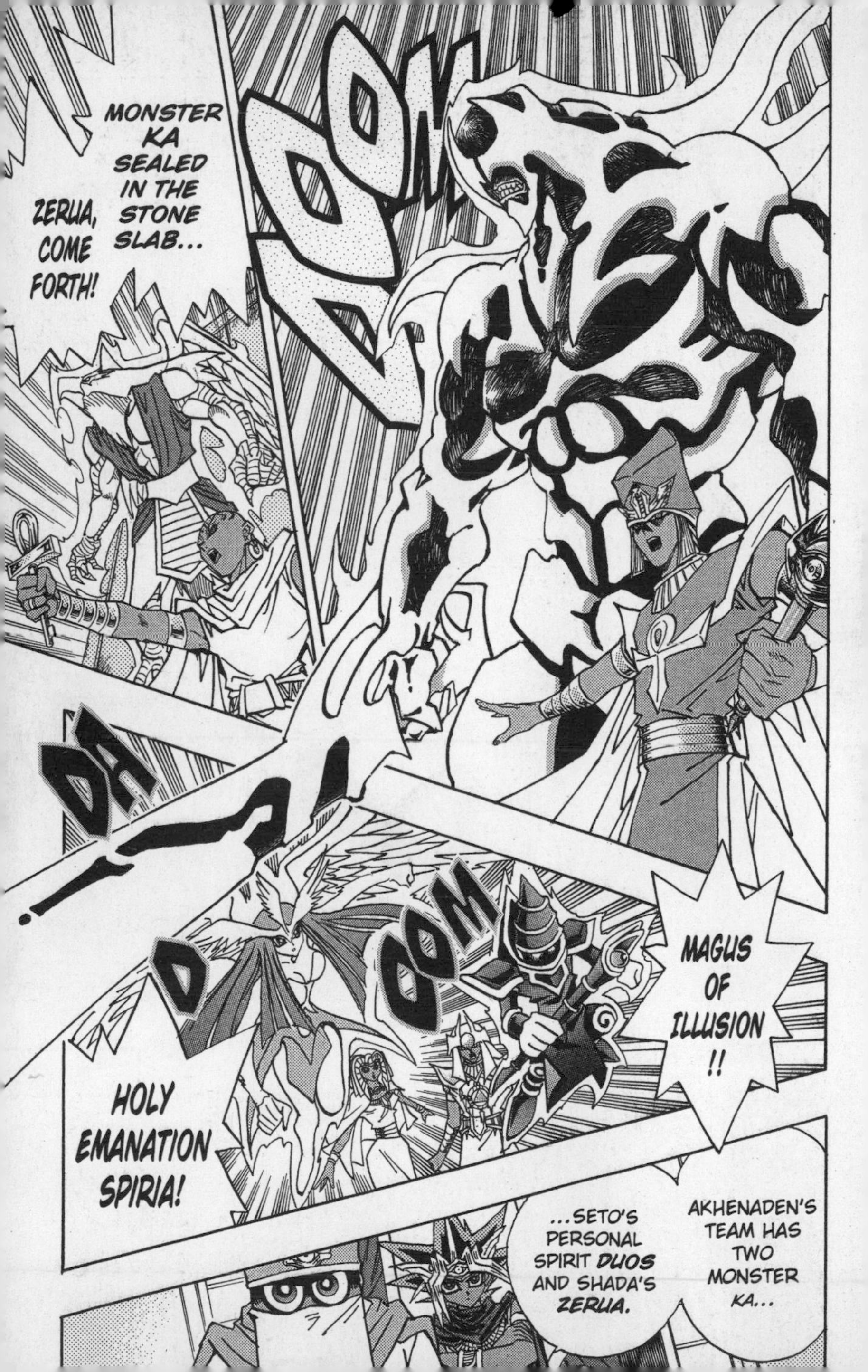
MONSTER KA SEALED IN THE STONE SLAB...
ZERUA, COME FORTH!
MAGUS OF ILLUSION !!
HOLY EMANATION SPIRIA!
AKHENADEN'S TEAM HAS TWO MONSTER KA...
...SETO'S PERSONAL SPIRIT *DUOS* AND SHADA'S *ZERUA*.

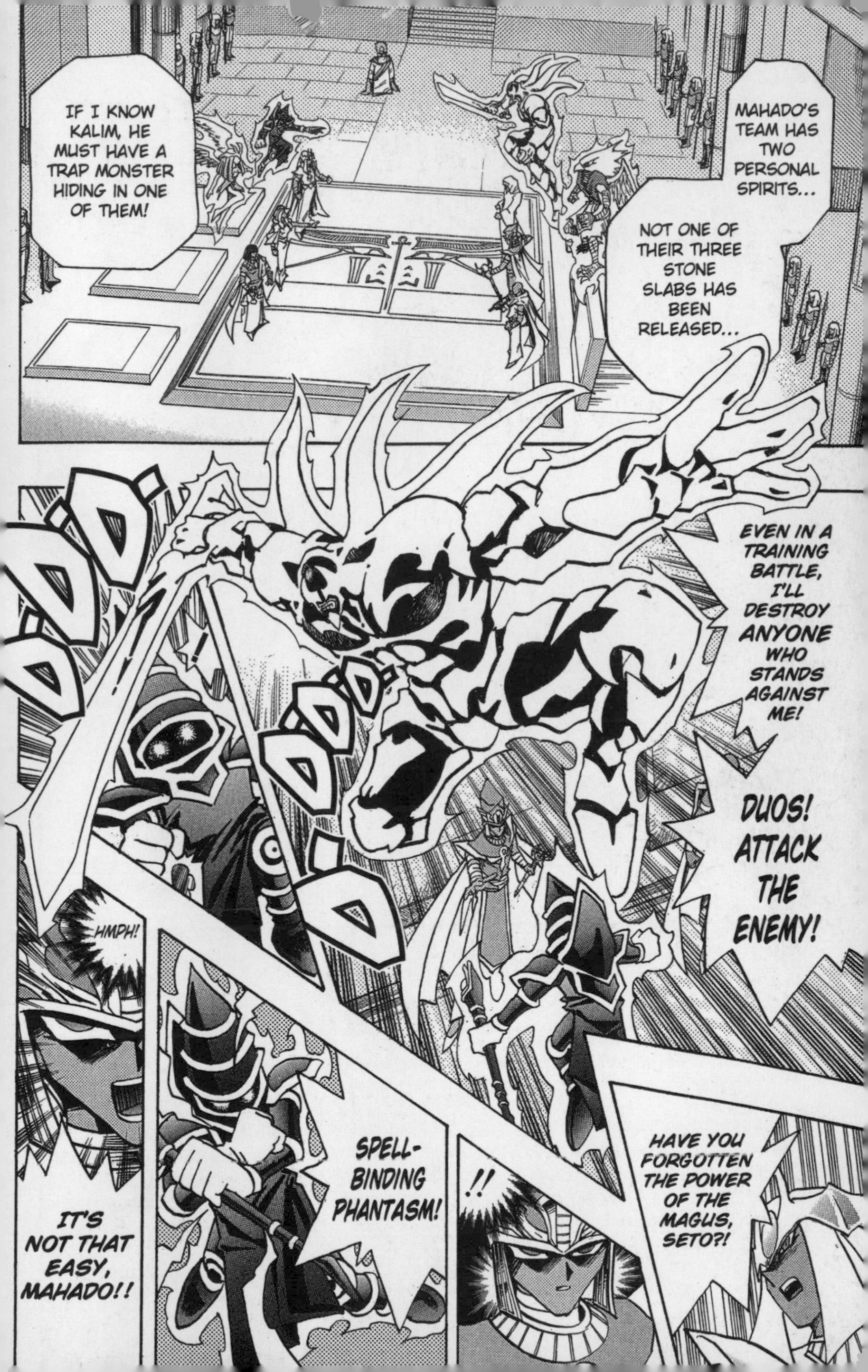
MAHADO'S TEAM HAS TWO PERSONAL SPIRITS...
NOT ONE OF THEIR THREE STONE SLABS HAS BEEN RELEASED...
IF I KNOW KALIM, HE MUST HAVE A TRAP MONSTER HIDING IN ONE OF THEM!
EVEN IN A TRAINING BATTLE, I'LL DESTROY ANYONE WHO STANDS AGAINST ME!
DUOS! ATTACK THE ENEMY!
!
HAVE YOU FORGOTTEN THE POWER OF THE MAGUS, SETO?!
!!
SPELL-BINDING PHANTASM!
HMPH!
IT'S NOT THAT EASY, MAHADO!!

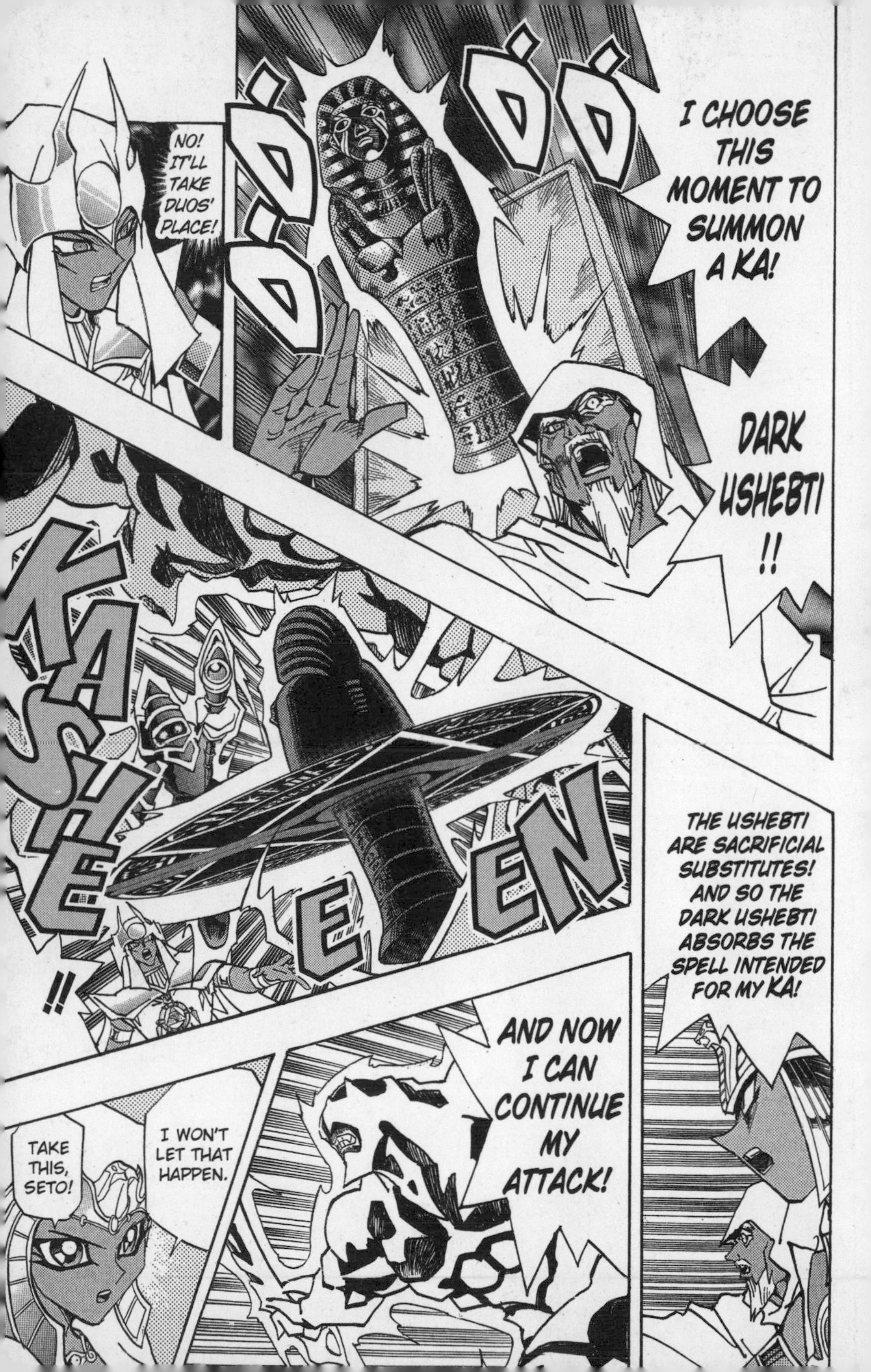
I CHOOSE THIS MOMENT TO SUMMON A KA!
DARK USHEBTI !!
NO! IT'LL TAKE DUOS' PLACE!
THE USHEBTI ARE SACRIFICIAL SUBSTITUTES! AND SO THE DARK USHEBTI ABSORBS THE SPELL INTENDED FOR MY KA!
KASHEEEN !!
AND NOW I CAN CONTINUE MY ATTACK!
I WON'T LET THAT HAPPEN.
TAKE THIS, SETO!

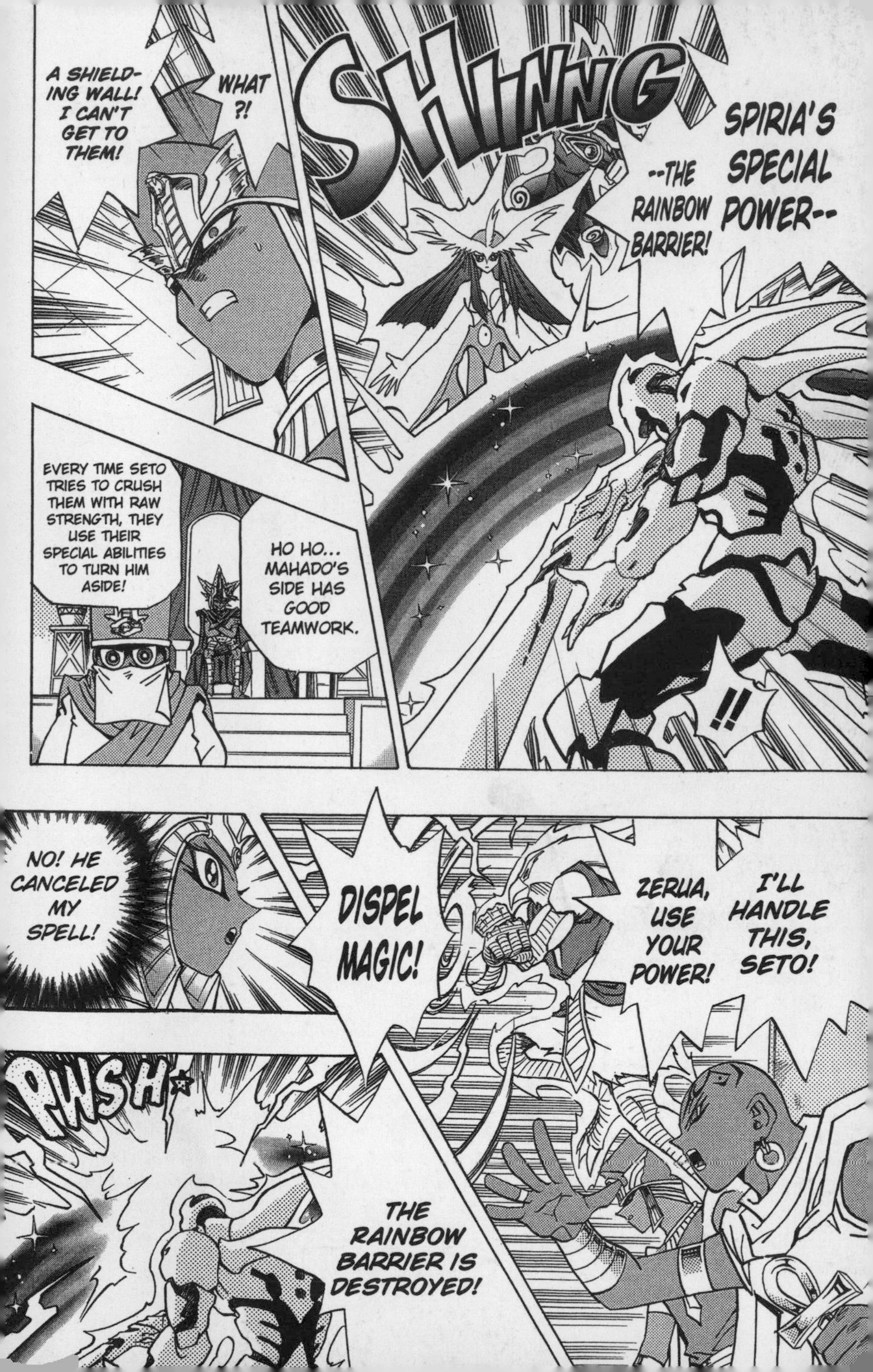

SHIINNG
SPIRIA'S SPECIAL POWER--
--THE RAINBOW BARRIER!
!!
WHAT ?!
A SHIELD-ING WALL! I CAN'T GET TO THEM!
HO HO... MAHADO'S SIDE HAS GOOD TEAMWORK.
EVERY TIME SETO TRIES TO CRUSH THEM WITH RAW STRENGTH, THEY USE THEIR SPECIAL ABILITIES TO TURN HIM ASIDE!
I'LL HANDLE THIS, SETO!
ZERUA, USE YOUR POWER!
DISPEL MAGIC!
NO! HE CANCELED MY SPELL!
THE RAINBOW BARRIER IS DESTROYED!
PWSH

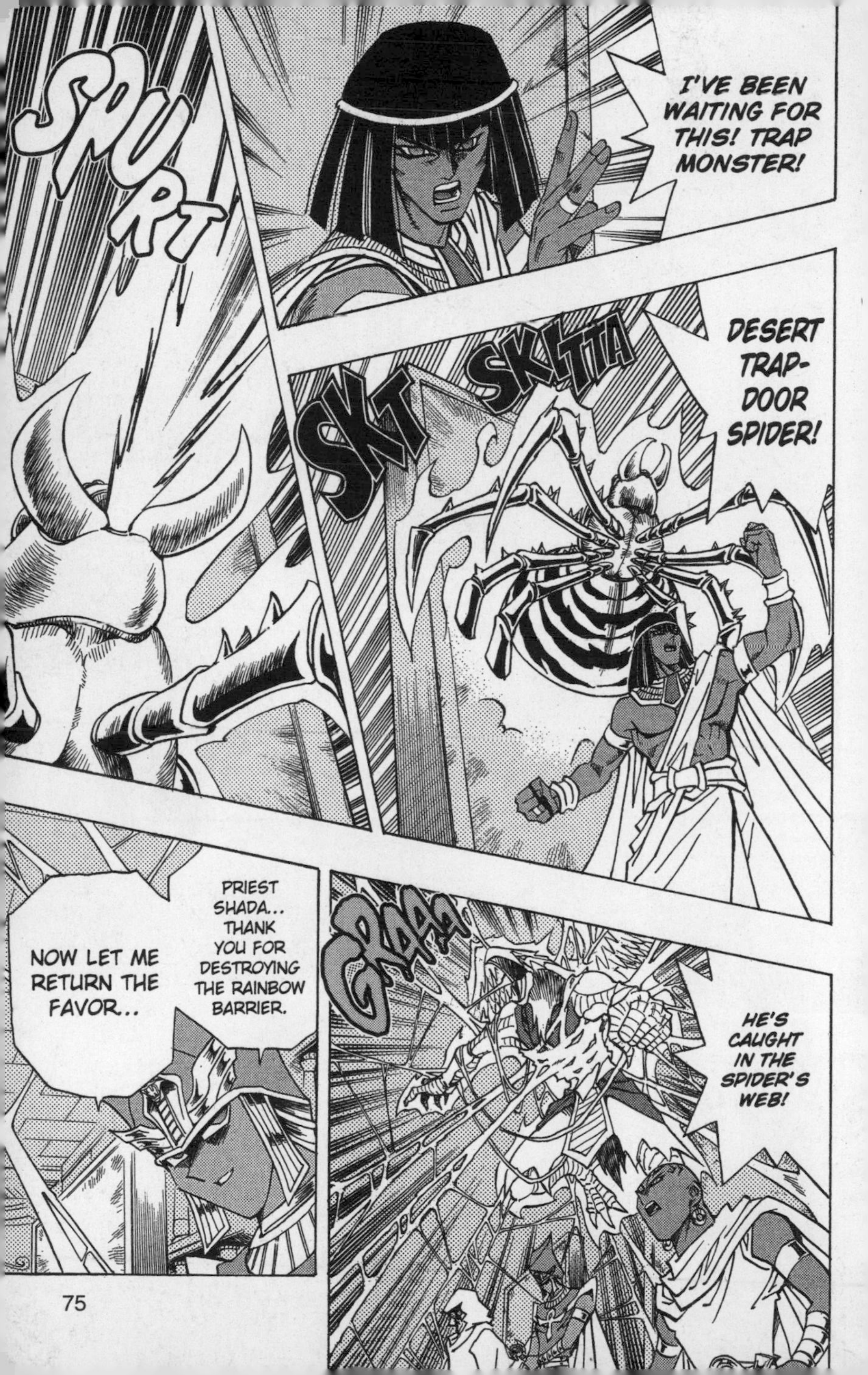
I'VE BEEN WAITING FOR THIS! TRAP MONSTER!
SKT
SKITTA
DESERT TRAP-DOOR SPIDER!
SPURT
GRAA
HE'S CAUGHT IN THE SPIDER'S WEB!
PRIEST SHADA... THANK YOU FOR DESTROYING THE RAINBOW BARRIER.
NOW LET ME RETURN THE FAVOR..

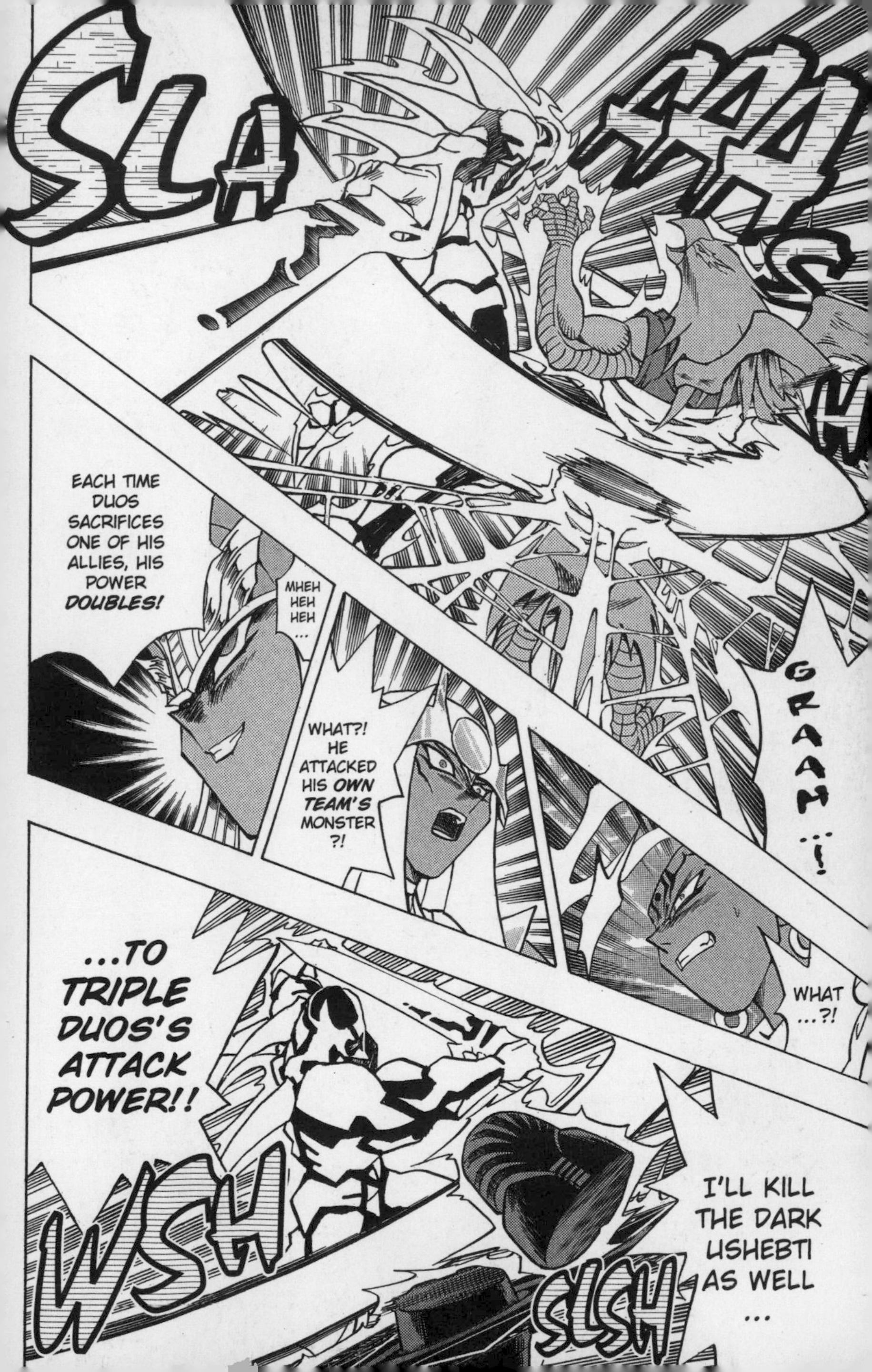
SLAAASH
GRAAH...!
WHAT?! HE ATTACKED HIS OWN TEAM'S MONSTER?!
MHEH HEH HEH...
EACH TIME DUOS SACRIFICES ONE OF HIS ALLIES, HIS POWER DOUBLES!
WHAT...?!
I'LL KILL THE DARK USHEBTI AS WELL...
SLSH
WSH
...TO TRIPLE DUOS'S ATTACK POWER!!

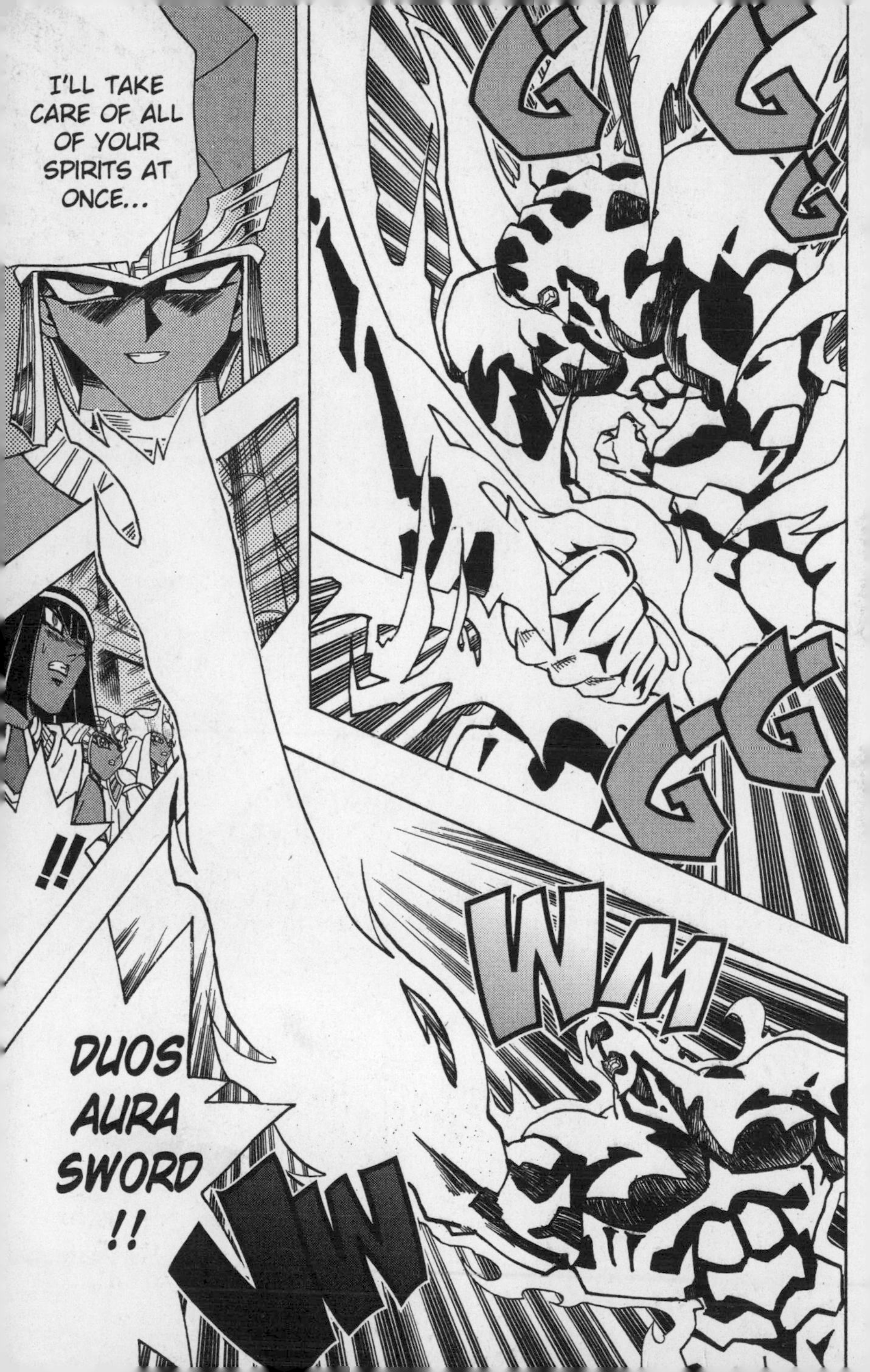
GGG
I'LL TAKE CARE OF ALL OF YOUR SPIRITS AT ONCE...
!!
GG
WM
DUOS AURA SWORD !!
WW

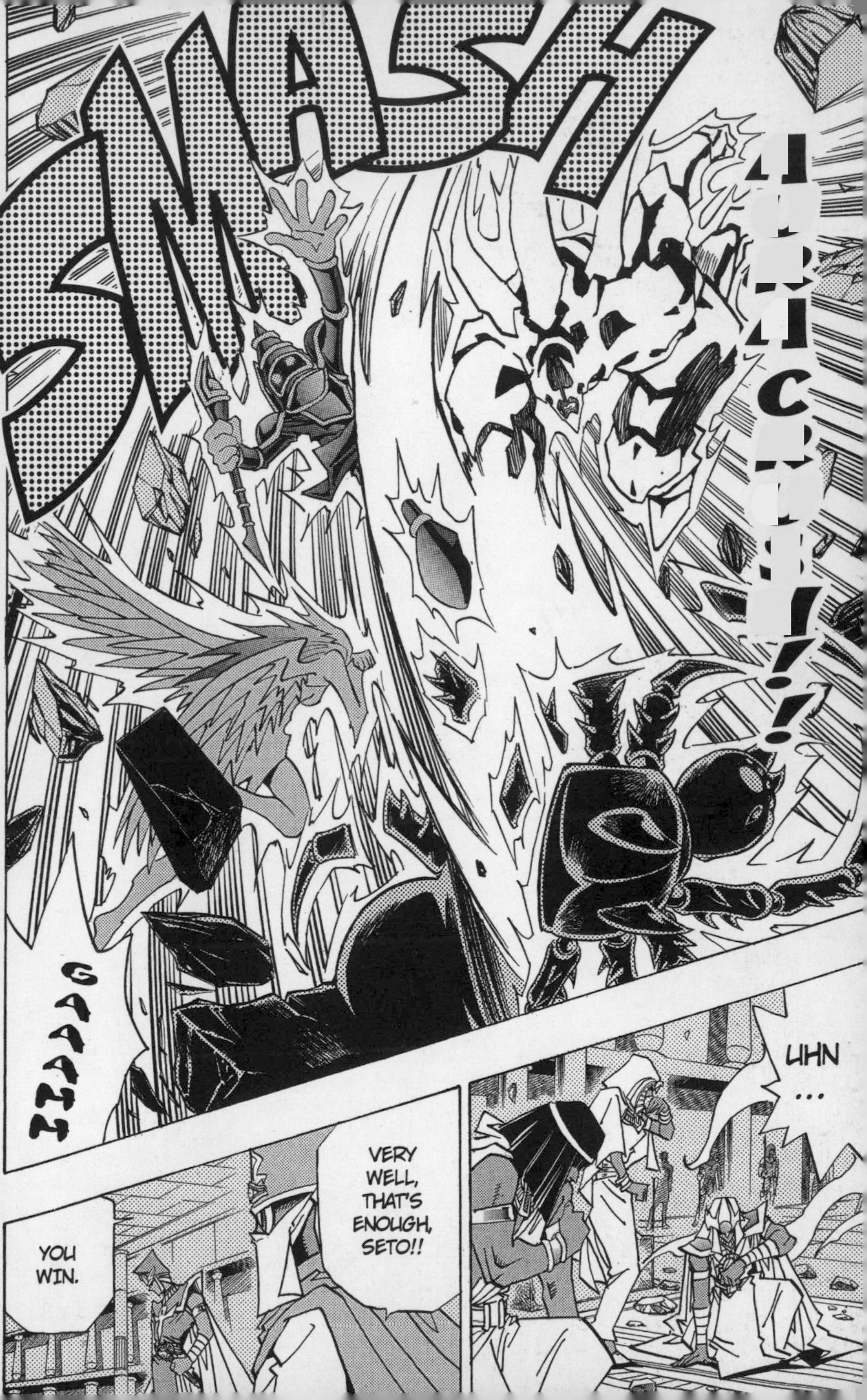
SMASH
GAAAHH
UHN...
VERY WELL, THAT'S ENOUGH, SETO!!
YOU WIN.

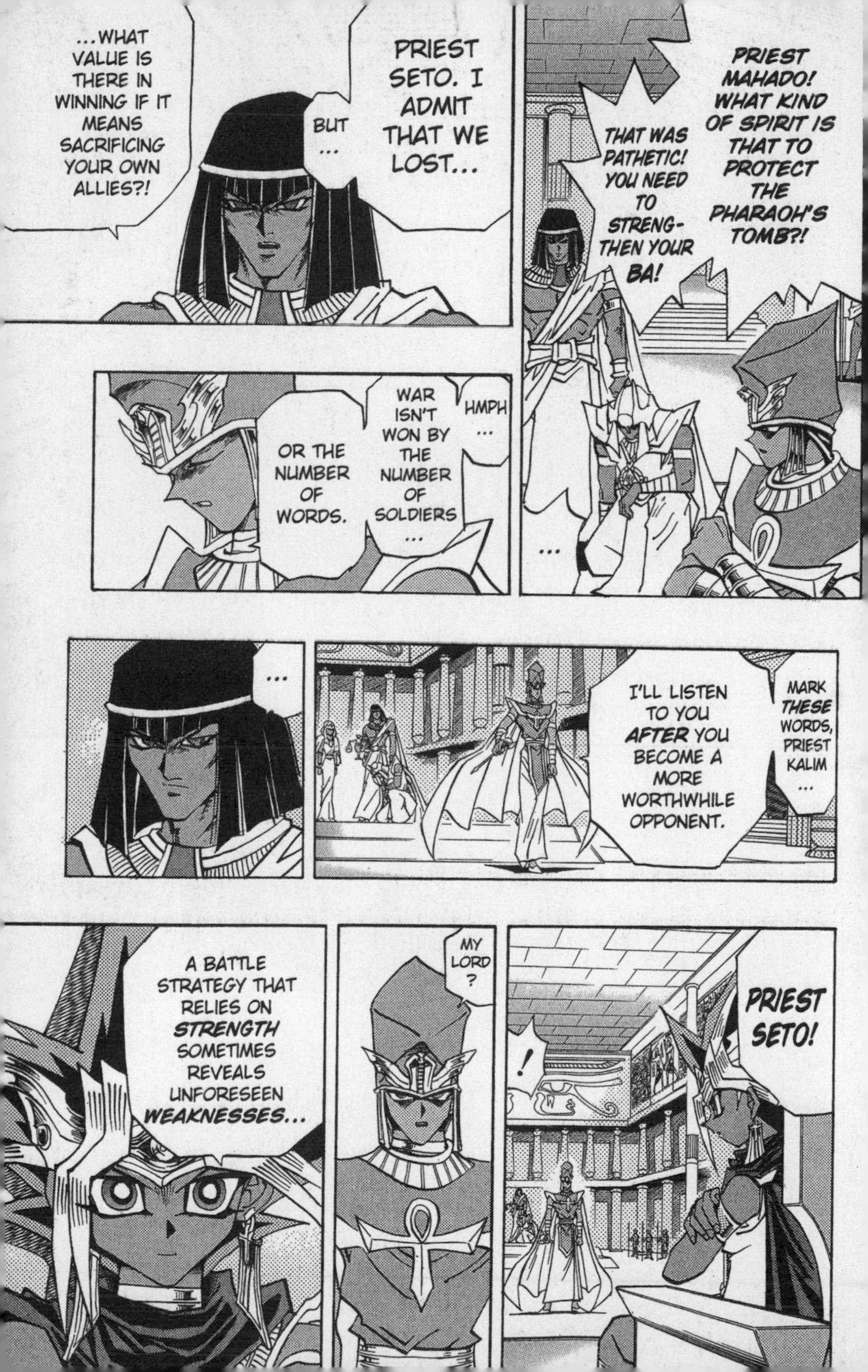
PRIEST MAHADO! WHAT KIND OF SPIRIT IS THAT TO PROTECT THE PHARAOH'S TOMB?!
THAT WAS PATHETIC! YOU NEED TO STRENG-THEN YOUR BA!
...
PRIEST SETO. I ADMIT THAT WE LOST...
BUT ...
...WHAT VALUE IS THERE IN WINNING IF IT MEANS SACRIFICING YOUR OWN ALLIES?!
HMPH ...
WAR ISN'T WON BY THE NUMBER OF SOLDIERS ...
OR THE NUMBER OF WORDS.
MARK THESE WORDS, PRIEST KALIM ...
I'LL LISTEN TO YOU AFTER YOU BECOME A MORE WORTHWHILE OPPONENT.
...
PRIEST SETO!
!
MY LORD ?
A BATTLE STRATEGY THAT RELIES ON STRENGTH SOMETIMES REVEALS UNFORESEEN WEAKNESSES...

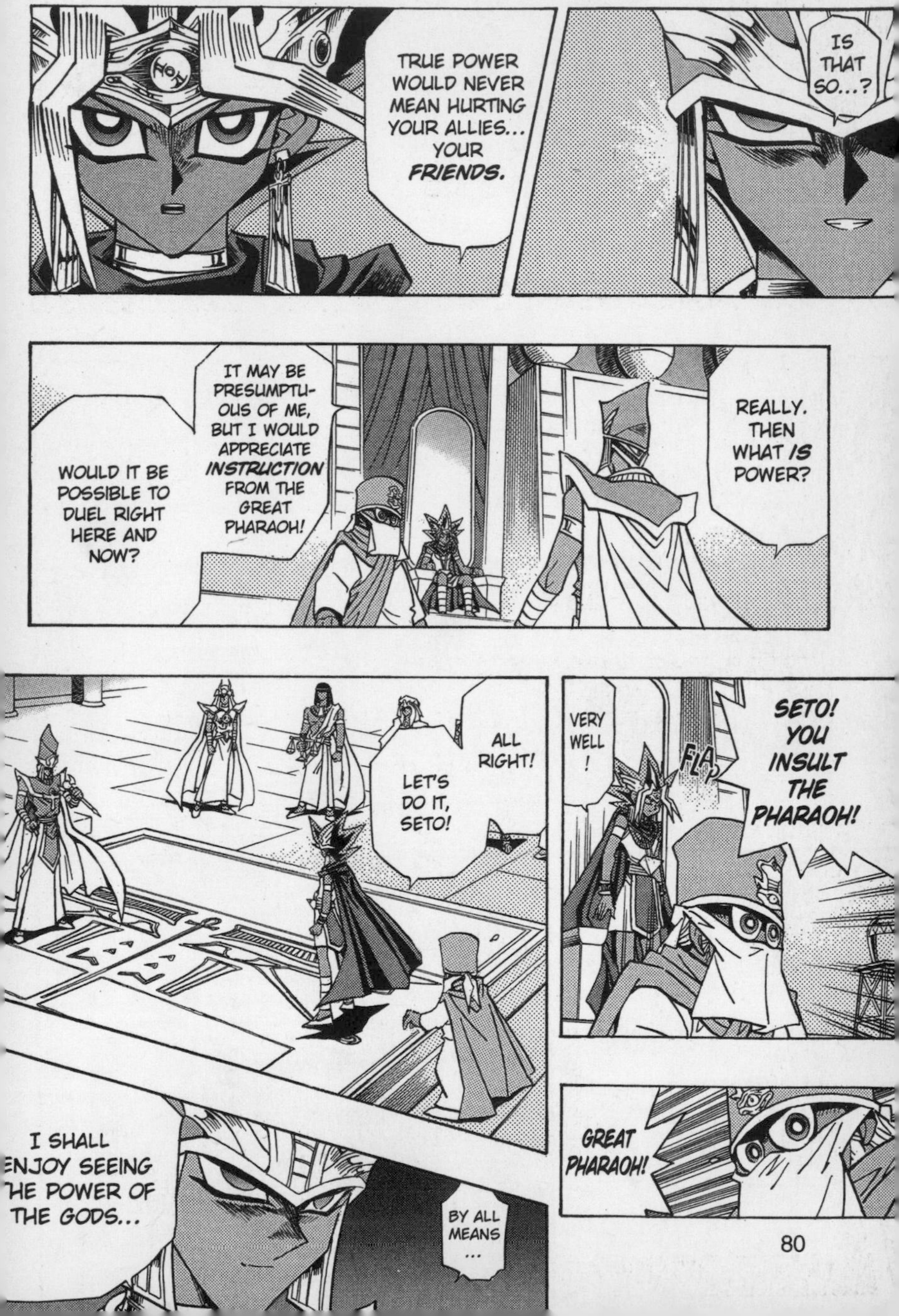
IS THAT SO...?
TRUE POWER WOULD NEVER MEAN HURTING YOUR ALLIES... YOUR *FRIENDS.*
REALLY. THEN WHAT *IS* POWER?
IT MAY BE PRESUMPTUOUS OF ME, BUT I WOULD APPRECIATE *INSTRUCTION* FROM THE GREAT PHARAOH!
WOULD IT BE POSSIBLE TO DUEL RIGHT HERE AND NOW?
SETO! YOU INSULT THE PHARAOH!
FLAP
VERY WELL!
GREAT PHARAOH!
ALL RIGHT!
LET'S DO IT, SETO!
I SHALL ENJOY SEEING THE POWER OF THE GODS...
BY ALL MEANS...

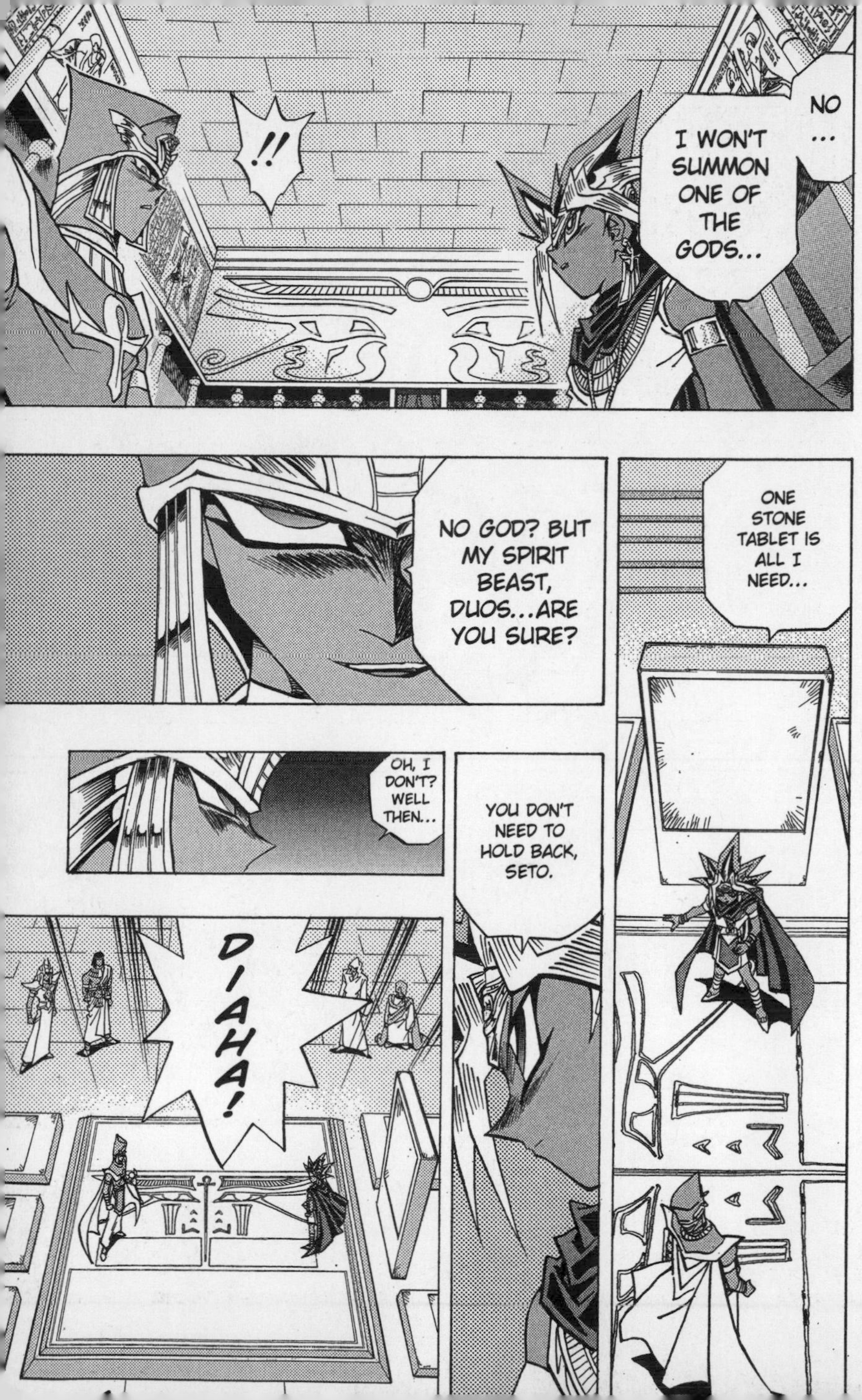
NO ...
I WON'T SUMMON ONE OF THE GODS...
!!
ONE STONE TABLET IS ALL I NEED...
NO GOD? BUT MY SPIRIT BEAST, DUOS...ARE YOU SURE?
YOU DON'T NEED TO HOLD BACK, SETO.
OH, I DON'T? WELL THEN...
DIAHA!

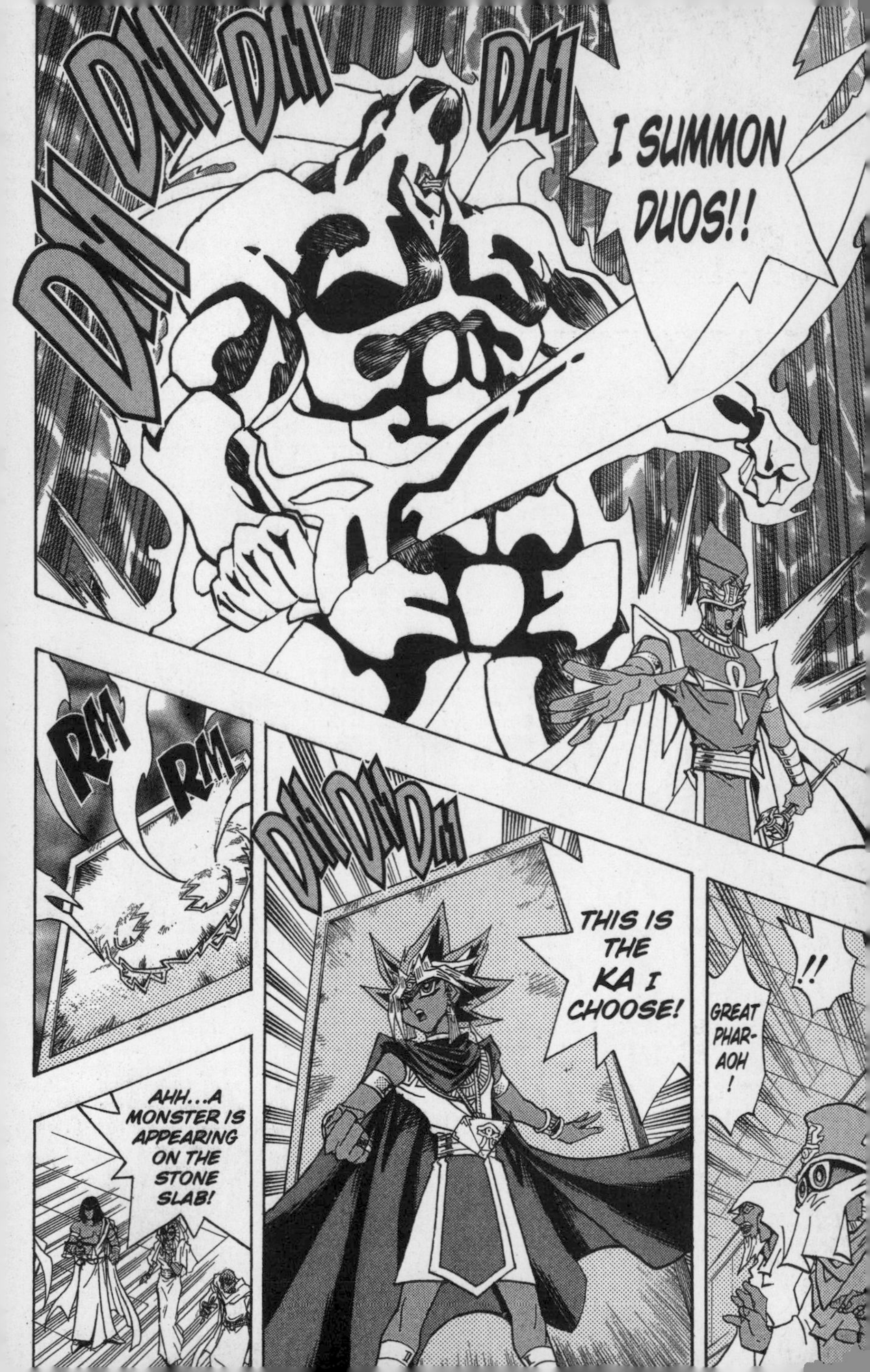
I SUMMON DUOS!!
DM
DM
DM
DM
!!
GREAT PHAR-AOH!
DM DM DM
THIS IS THE KA I CHOOSE!
RM
RM
AHH...A MONSTER IS APPEARING ON THE STONE SLAB!

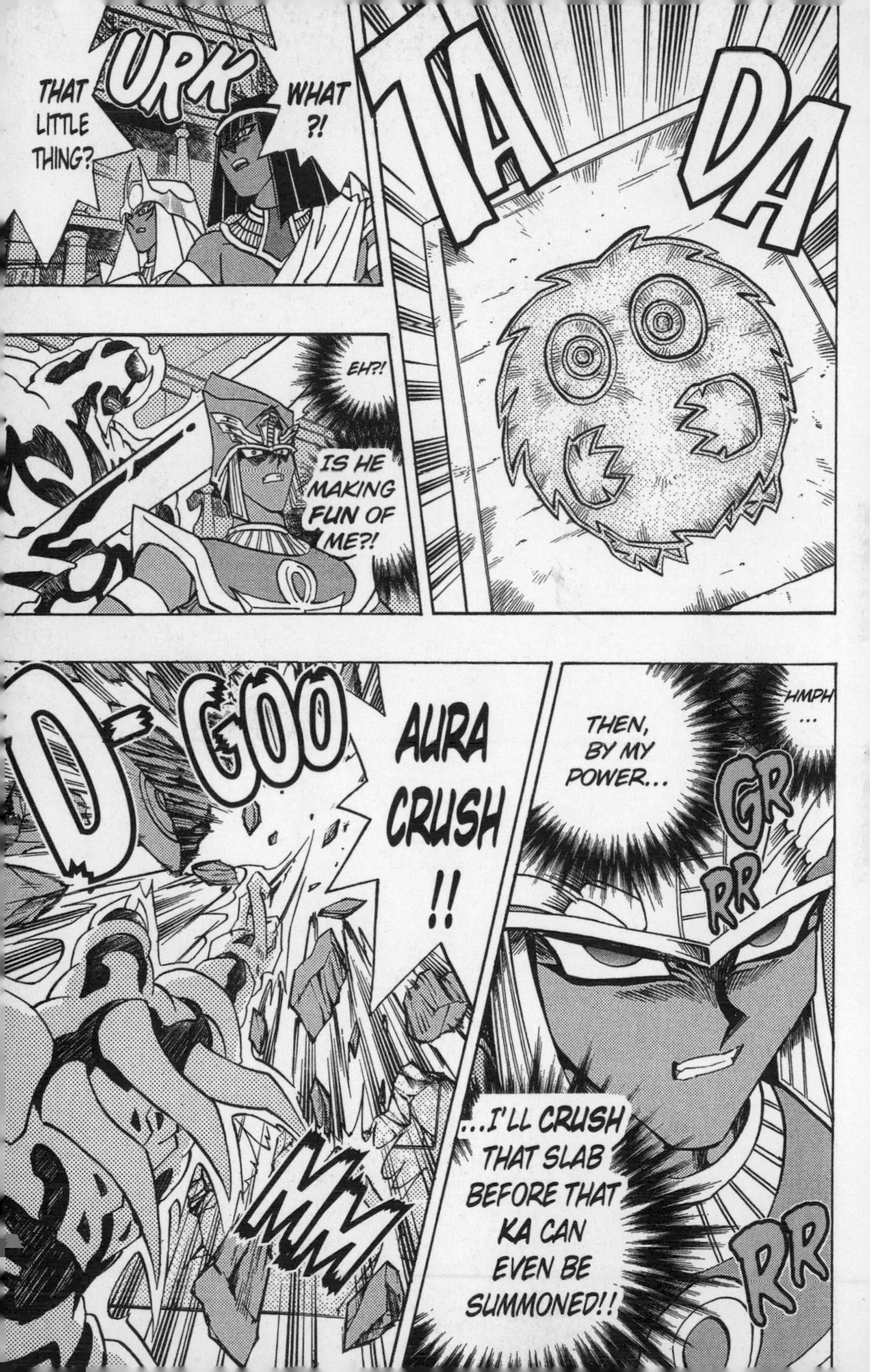
TA
DA
WHAT ?!
URK
THAT LITTLE THING?
EH?!
IS HE MAKING FUN OF ME?!
HMPH ...
THEN, BY MY POWER...
GR RR
...I'LL CRUSH THAT SLAB BEFORE THAT KA CAN EVEN BE SUMMONED!!
RR
AURA CRUSH !!
D-GOO
MM

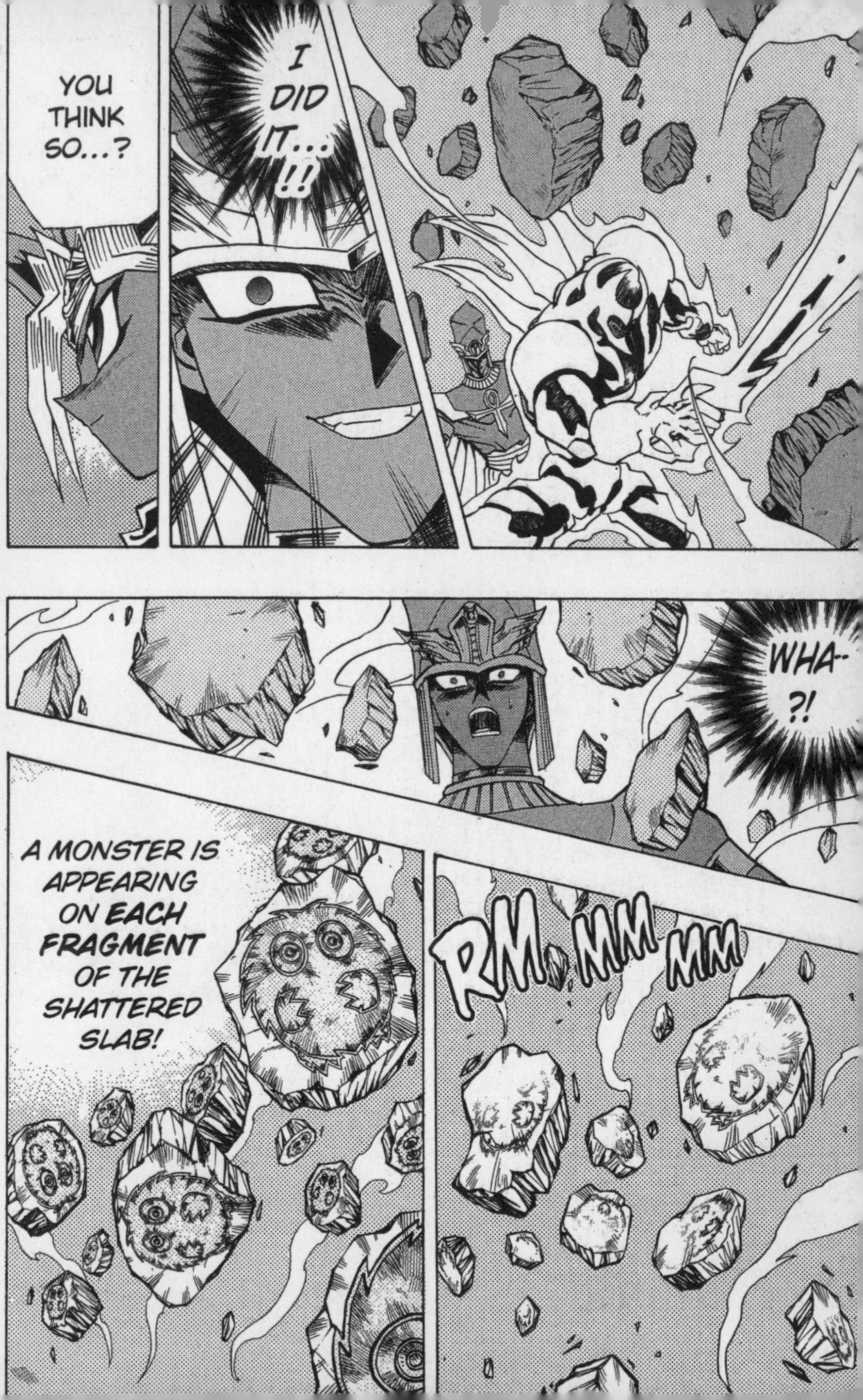
I DID IT...!!
YOU THINK SO...?
WHA-?!
RM MM MM
A MONSTER IS APPEARING ON EACH FRAGMENT OF THE SHATTERED SLAB!

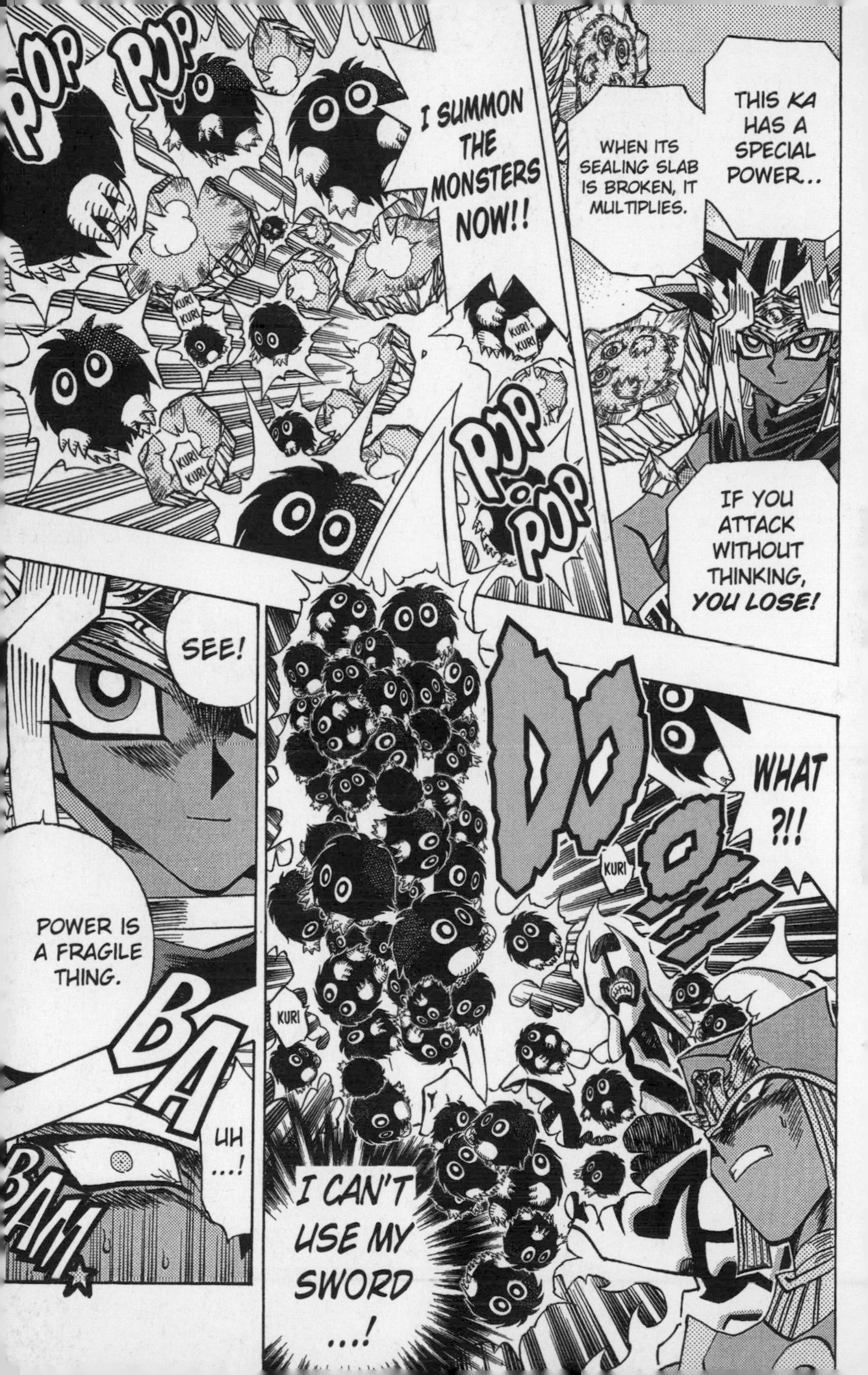
THIS *KA* HAS A SPECIAL POWER...
WHEN ITS SEALING SLAB IS BROKEN, IT MULTIPLIES.
IF YOU ATTACK WITHOUT THINKING, *YOU LOSE!*
POP POP
I SUMMON THE MONSTERS NOW!!
KURI KURI
KURI KURI
KURI KURI
POP POP
WHAT ?!!
KURI
KURI
I CAN'T USE MY SWORD ...!
SEE!
POWER IS A FRAGILE THING.
BA BAM
UH ...!

Duel 14: A Wizards' Battle

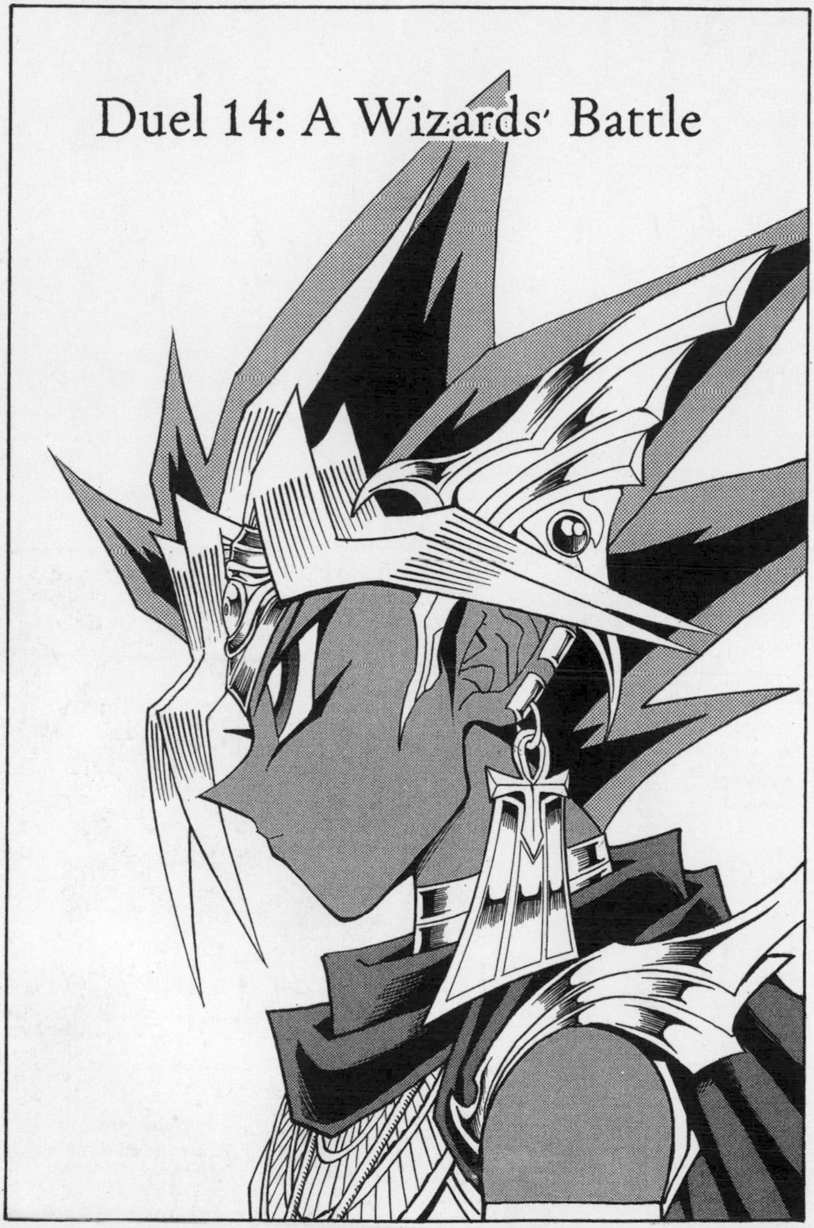

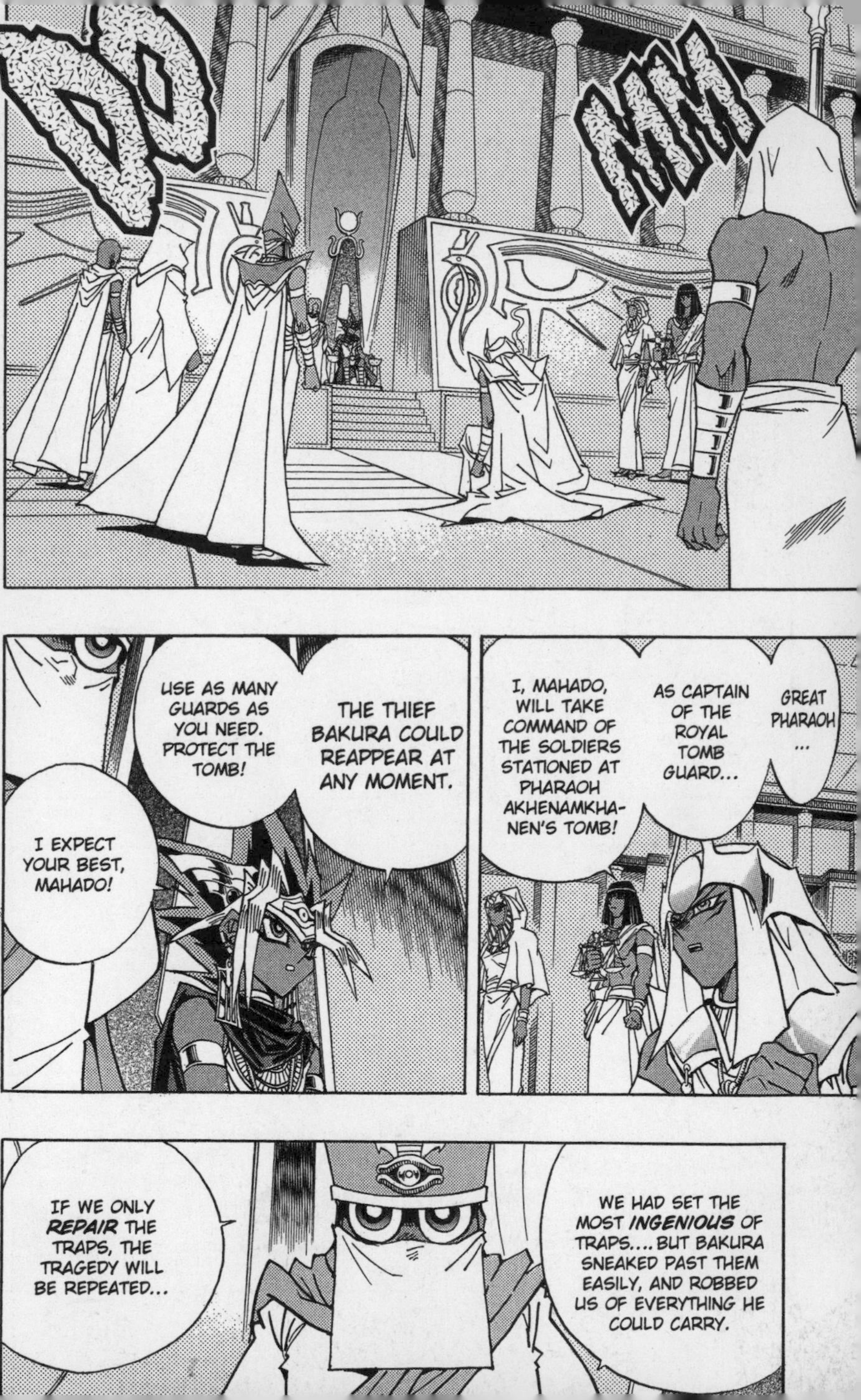
DOMMM
GREAT PHARAOH...
AS CAPTAIN OF THE ROYAL TOMB GUARD...
I, MAHADO, WILL TAKE COMMAND OF THE SOLDIERS STATIONED AT PHARAOH AKHENAMKHANEN'S TOMB!
THE THIEF BAKURA COULD REAPPEAR AT ANY MOMENT.
USE AS MANY GUARDS AS YOU NEED. PROTECT THE TOMB!
I EXPECT YOUR BEST, MAHADO!
WE HAD SET THE MOST *INGENIOUS* OF TRAPS.... BUT BAKURA SNEAKED PAST THEM EASILY, AND ROBBED US OF EVERYTHING HE COULD CARRY.
IF WE ONLY ***REPAIR*** THE TRAPS, THE TRAGEDY WILL BE REPEATED...

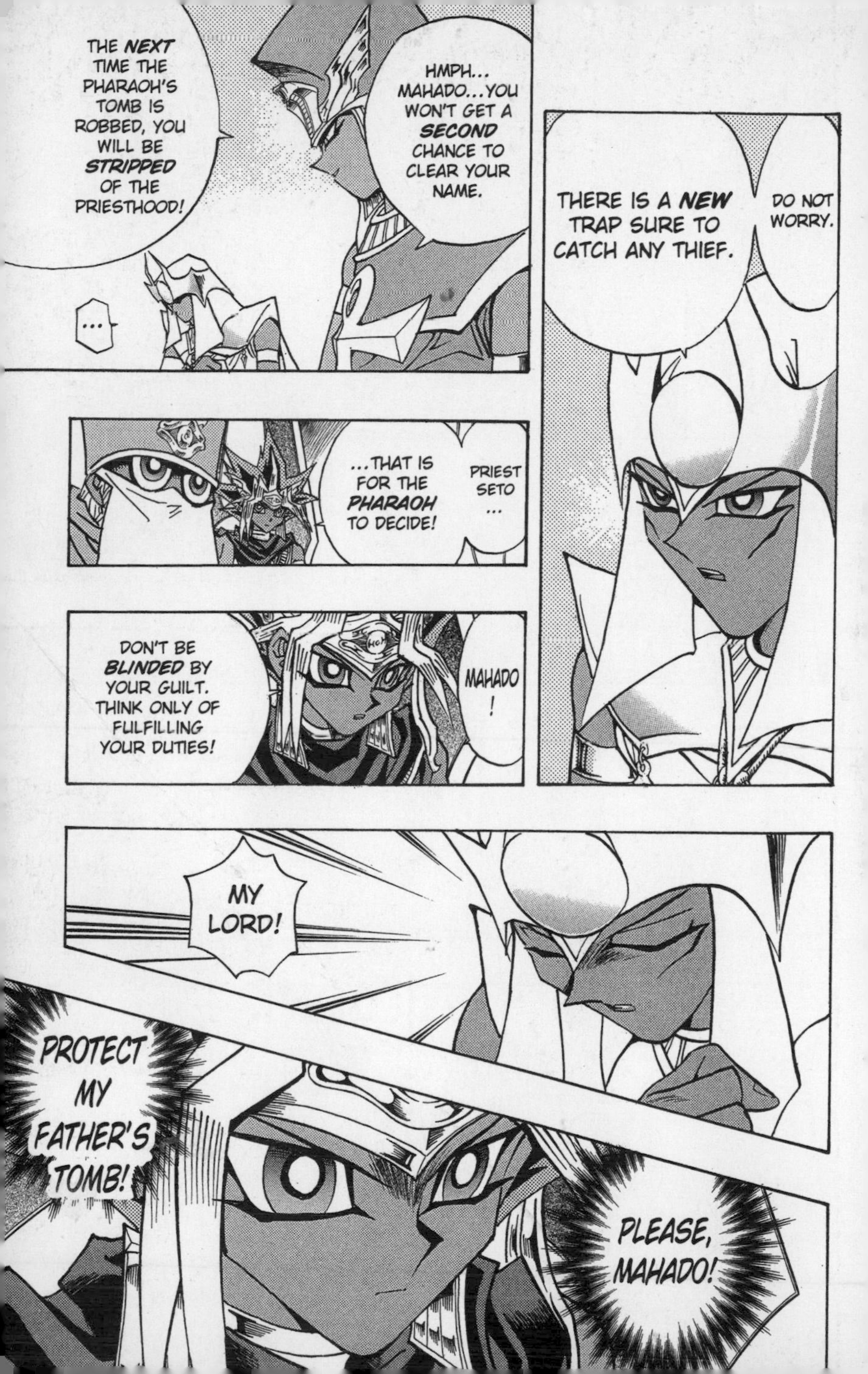
HMPH... MAHADO...YOU WON'T GET A SECOND CHANCE TO CLEAR YOUR NAME.
THE NEXT TIME THE PHARAOH'S TOMB IS ROBBED, YOU WILL BE STRIPPED OF THE PRIESTHOOD!
...
DO NOT WORRY.
THERE IS A NEW TRAP SURE TO CATCH ANY THIEF.
PRIEST SETO ...
...THAT IS FOR THE PHARAOH TO DECIDE!
MAHADO !
DON'T BE BLINDED BY YOUR GUILT. THINK ONLY OF FULFILLING YOUR DUTIES!
MY LORD!
PROTECT MY FATHER'S TOMB!
PLEASE, MAHADO!

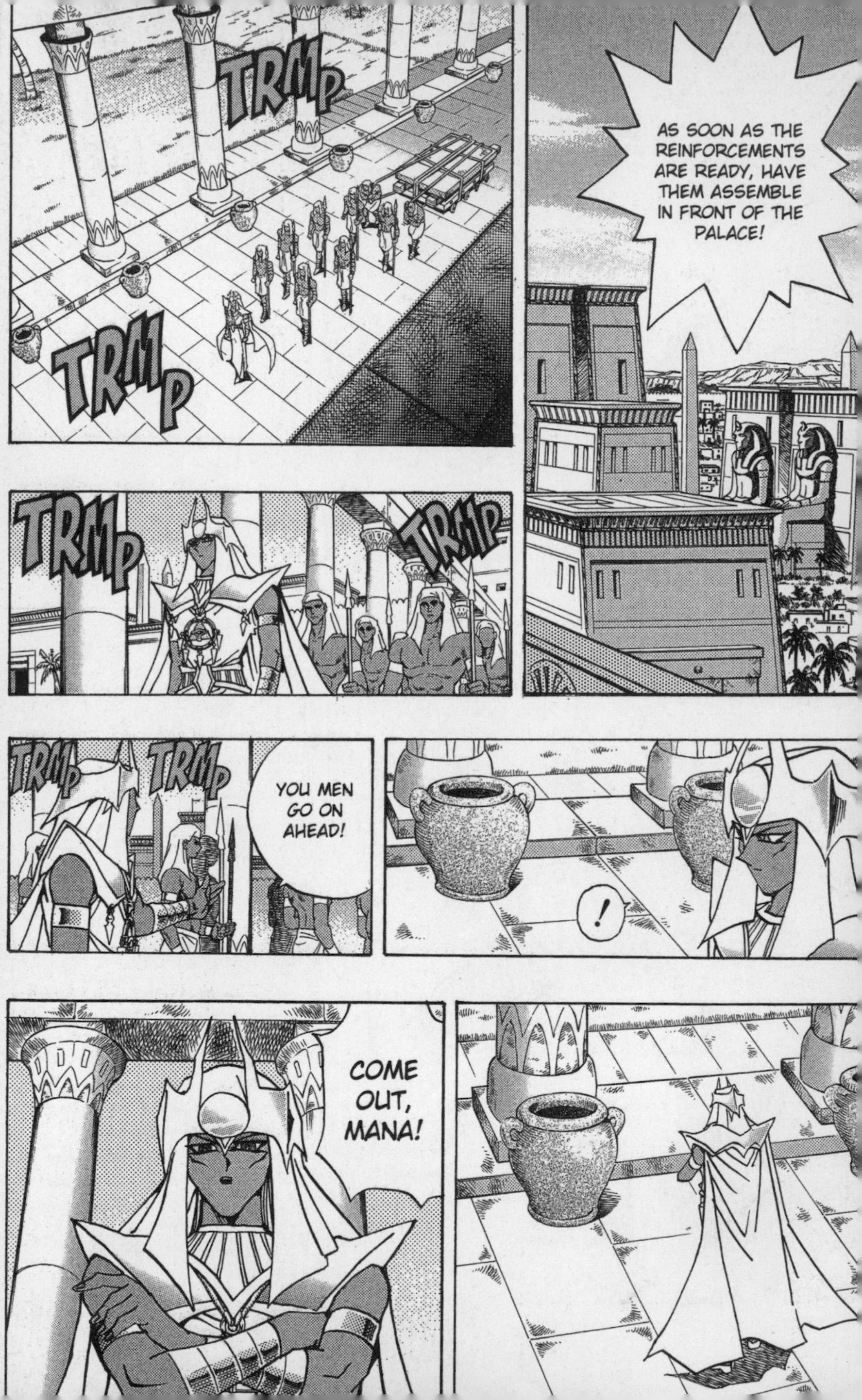
AS SOON AS THE REINFORCEMENTS ARE READY, HAVE THEM ASSEMBLE IN FRONT OF THE PALACE!
TRMP
TRMP
TRMP
TRMP
!
TRMP
TRMP
YOU MEN GO ON AHEAD!
COME OUT, MANA!

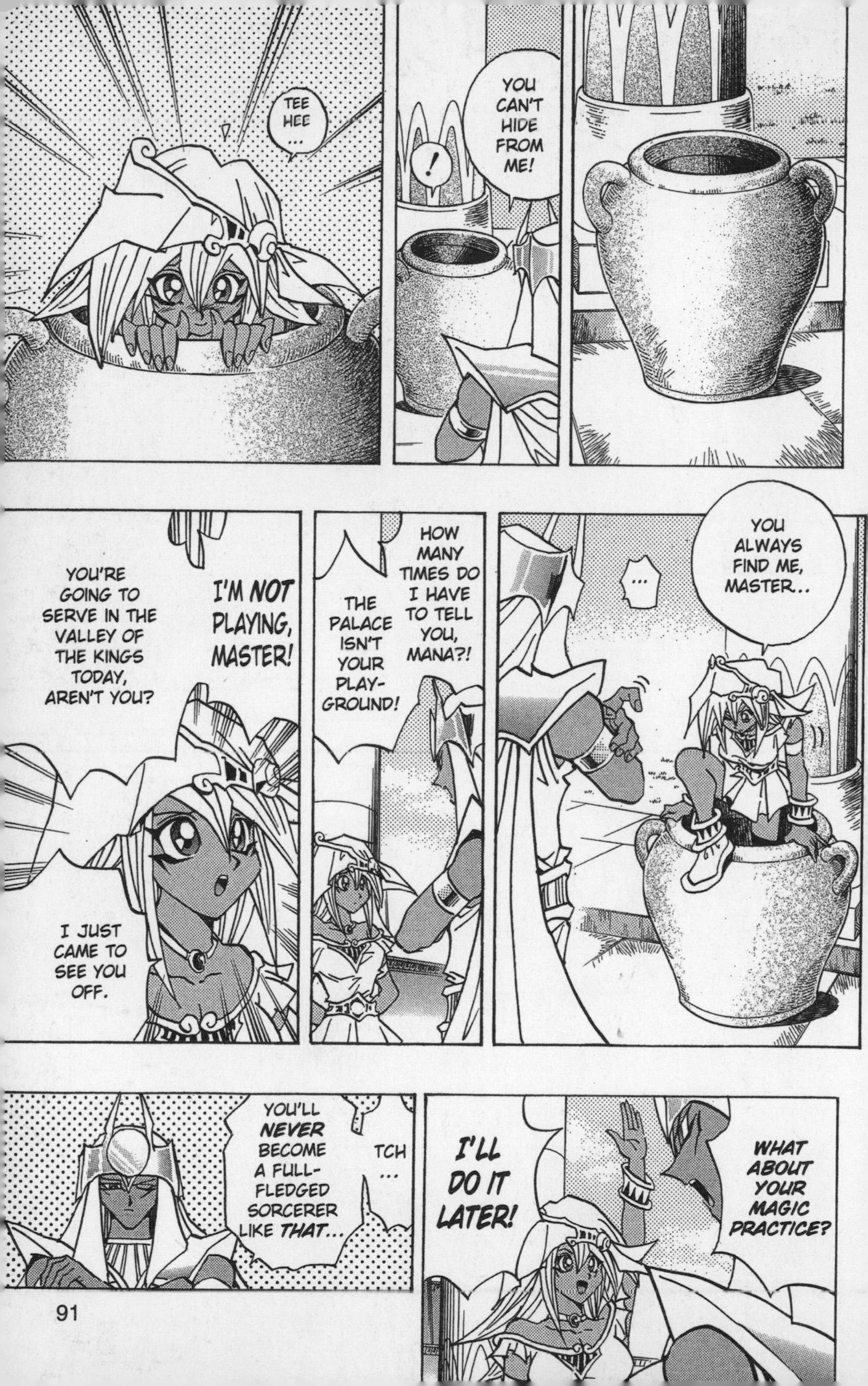
YOU CAN'T HIDE FROM ME!
!
TEE HEE ...
YOU ALWAYS FIND ME, MASTER...
...
HOW MANY TIMES DO I HAVE TO TELL YOU, MANA?!
THE PALACE ISN'T YOUR PLAY-GROUND!
I'M *NOT* PLAYING, MASTER!
YOU'RE GOING TO SERVE IN THE VALLEY OF THE KINGS TODAY, AREN'T YOU?
I JUST CAME TO SEE YOU OFF.
WHAT ABOUT YOUR MAGIC PRACTICE?
I'LL DO IT LATER!
TCH ...
YOU'LL *NEVER* BECOME A FULL-FLEDGED SORCERER LIKE *THAT*...

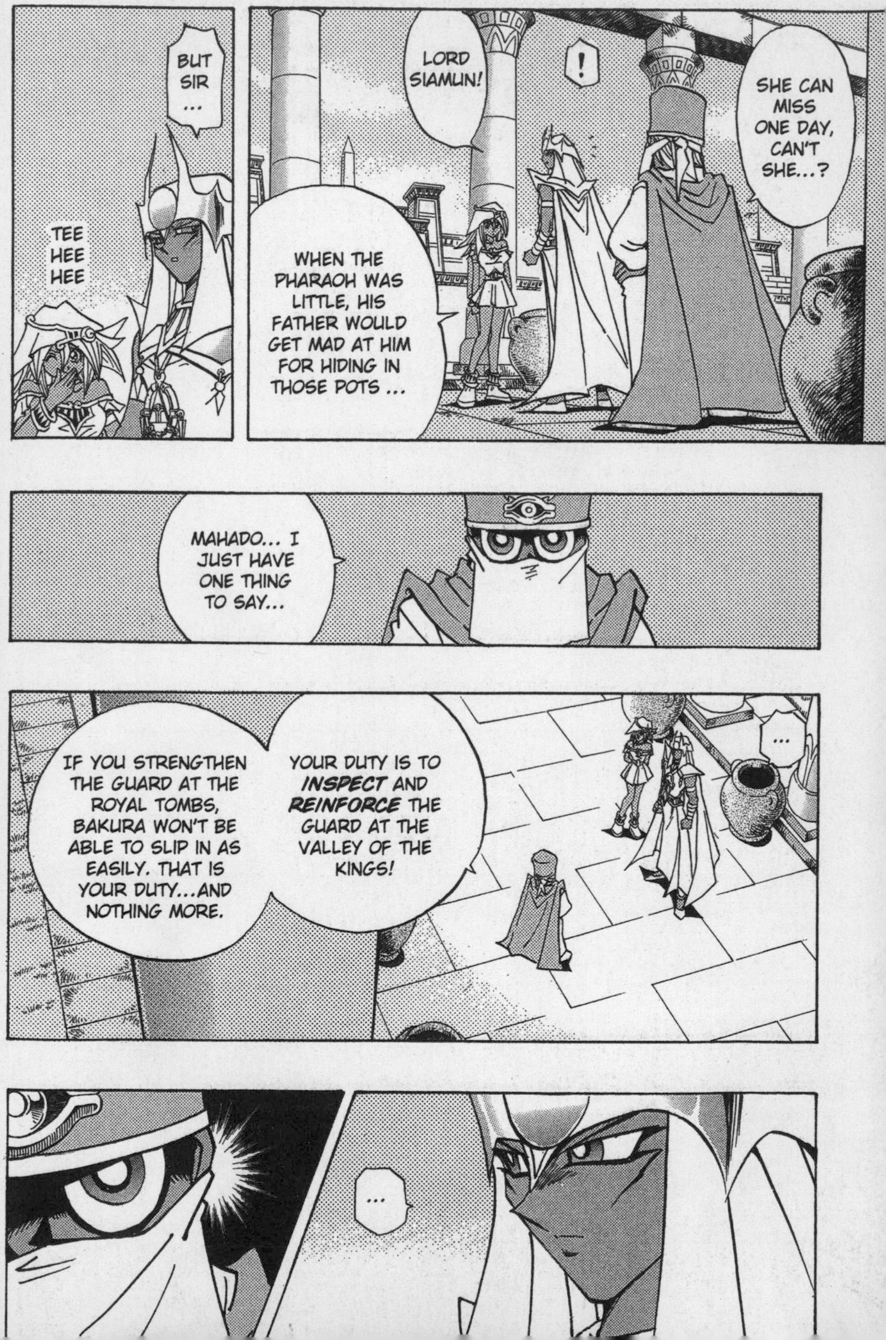
SHE CAN MISS ONE DAY, CAN'T SHE...?
!
LORD SIAMUN!
WHEN THE PHARAOH WAS LITTLE, HIS FATHER WOULD GET MAD AT HIM FOR HIDING IN THOSE POTS ...
BUT SIR ...
TEE HEE HEE
MAHADO... I JUST HAVE ONE THING TO SAY...
...
YOUR DUTY IS TO *INSPECT* AND *REINFORCE* THE GUARD AT THE VALLEY OF THE KINGS!
IF YOU STRENGTHEN THE GUARD AT THE ROYAL TOMBS, BAKURA WON'T BE ABLE TO SLIP IN AS EASILY. THAT IS YOUR DUTY...AND NOTHING MORE.
...

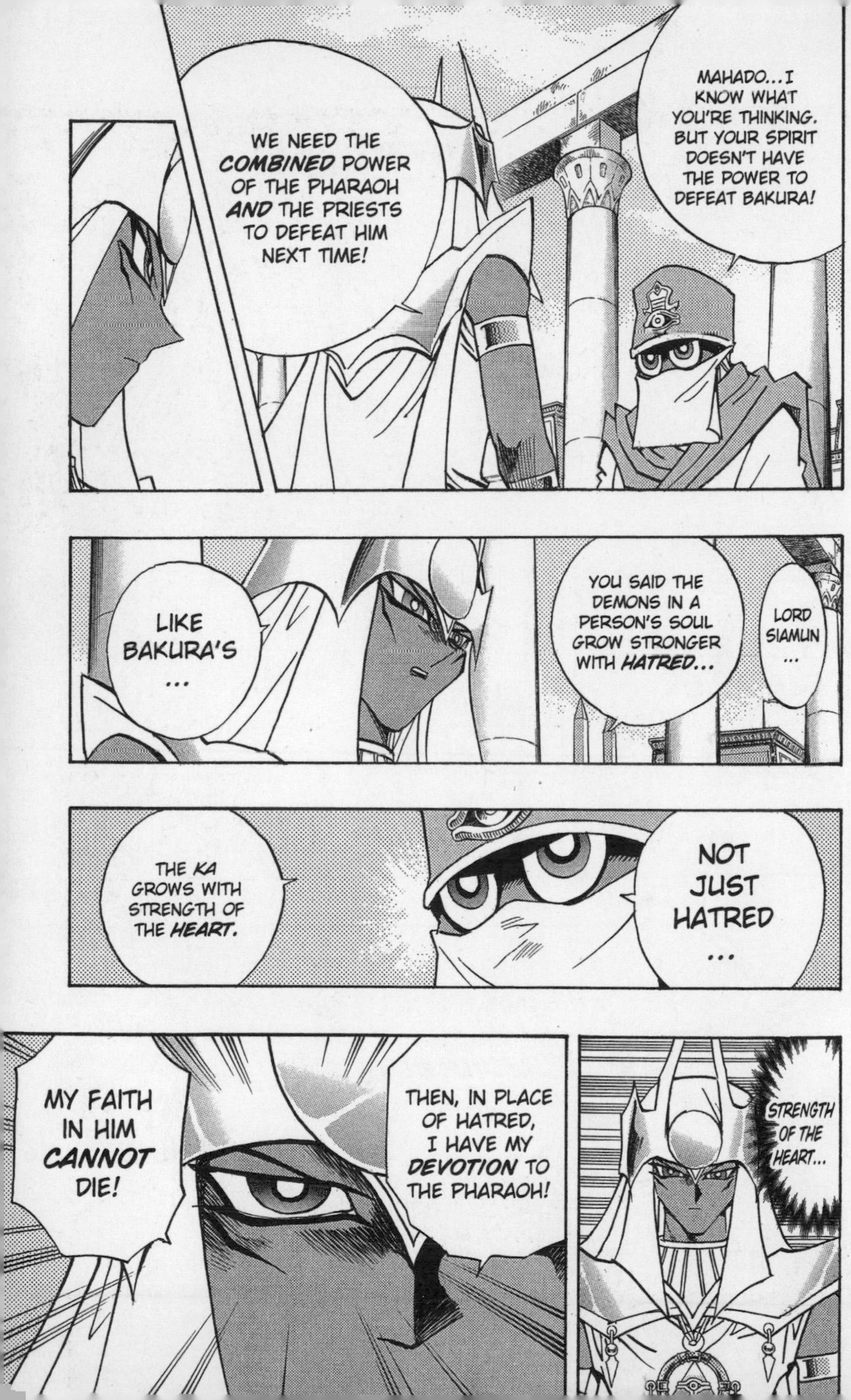
MAHADO...I KNOW WHAT YOU'RE THINKING. BUT YOUR SPIRIT DOESN'T HAVE THE POWER TO DEFEAT BAKURA!
WE NEED THE *COMBINED* POWER OF THE PHARAOH *AND* THE PRIESTS TO DEFEAT HIM NEXT TIME!
LORD SIAMUN ...
YOU SAID THE DEMONS IN A PERSON'S SOUL GROW STRONGER WITH *HATRED...*
LIKE BAKURA'S ...
NOT JUST HATRED ...
THE *KA* GROWS WITH STRENGTH OF THE *HEART.*
STRENGTH OF THE HEART...
THEN, IN PLACE OF HATRED, I HAVE MY *DEVOTION* TO THE PHARAOH!
MY FAITH IN HIM *CANNOT* DIE!

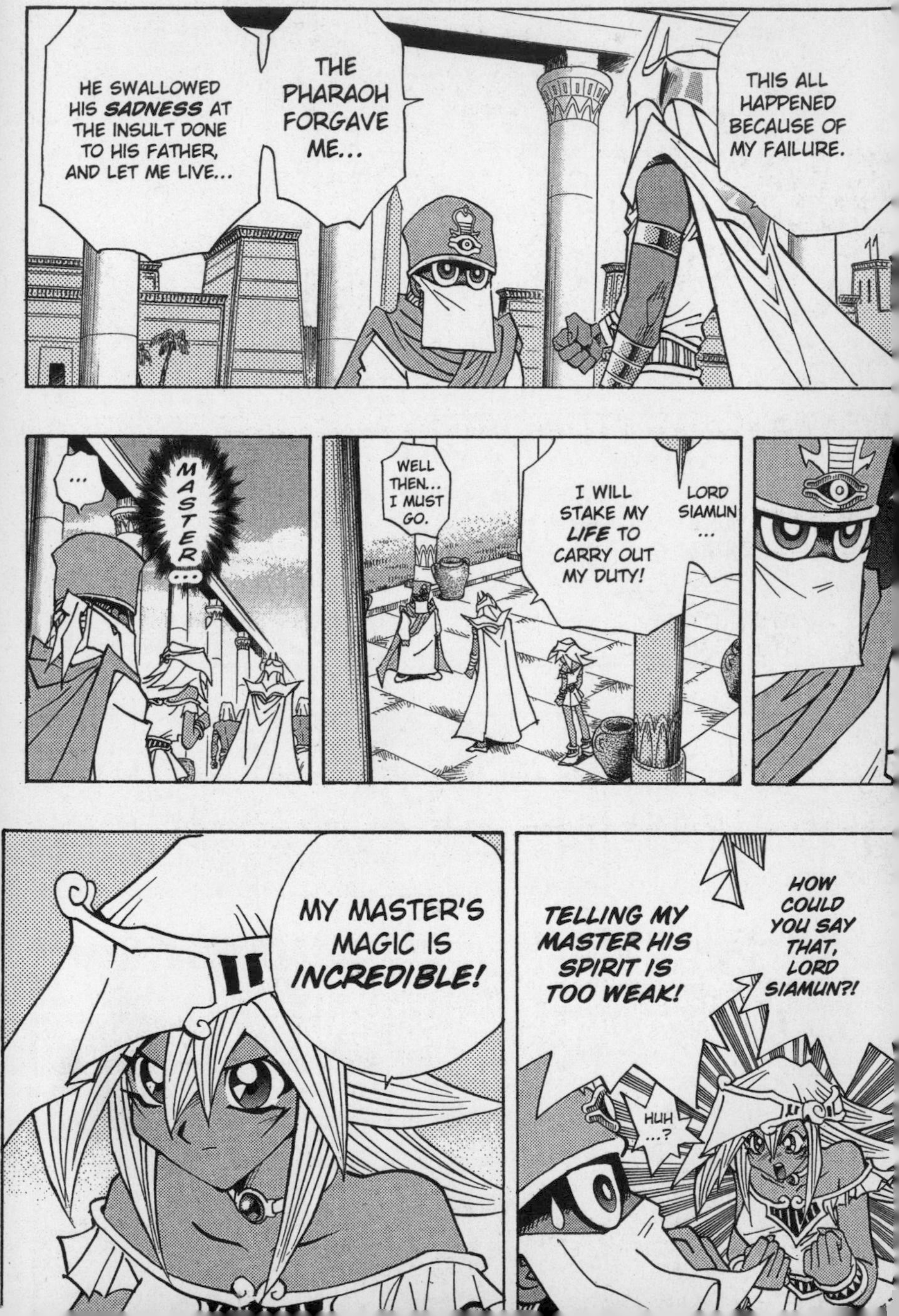
THIS ALL HAPPENED BECAUSE OF MY FAILURE.
THE PHARAOH FORGAVE ME...
HE SWALLOWED HIS SADNESS AT THE INSULT DONE TO HIS FATHER, AND LET ME LIVE...
LORD SIAMUN...
I WILL STAKE MY LIFE TO CARRY OUT MY DUTY!
WELL THEN... I MUST GO.
MASTER...
...
HOW COULD YOU SAY THAT, LORD SIAMUN?!
TELLING MY MASTER HIS SPIRIT IS TOO WEAK!
HUH...?
MY MASTER'S MAGIC IS INCREDIBLE!

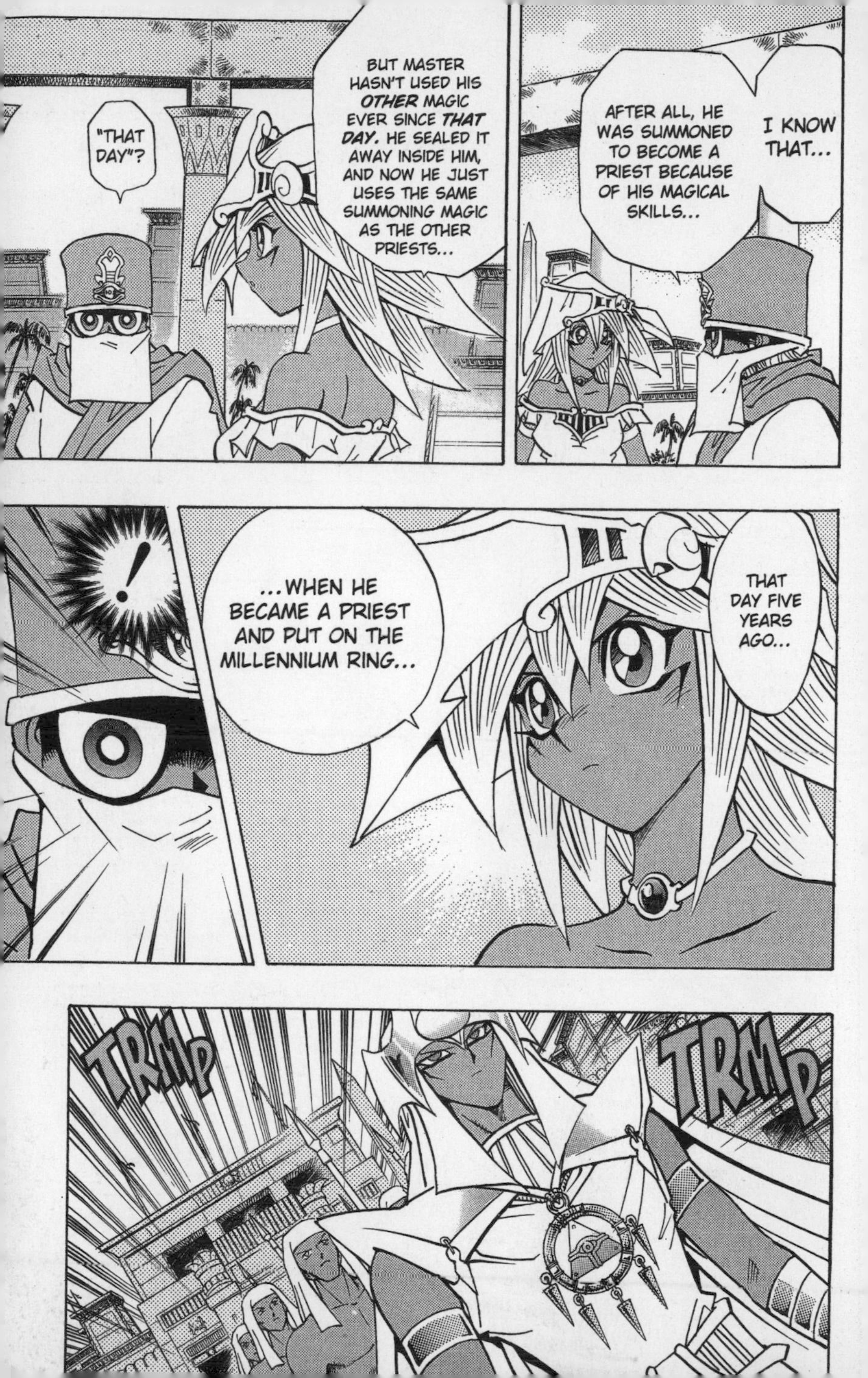
I KNOW THAT...
AFTER ALL, HE WAS SUMMONED TO BECOME A PRIEST BECAUSE OF HIS MAGICAL SKILLS...
BUT MASTER HASN'T USED HIS *OTHER* MAGIC EVER SINCE ***THAT DAY.*** HE SEALED IT AWAY INSIDE HIM, AND NOW HE JUST USES THE SAME SUMMONING MAGIC AS THE OTHER PRIESTS...
"THAT DAY"?
THAT DAY FIVE YEARS AGO...
...WHEN HE BECAME A PRIEST AND PUT ON THE MILLENNIUM RING...
!
TRMP
TRMP

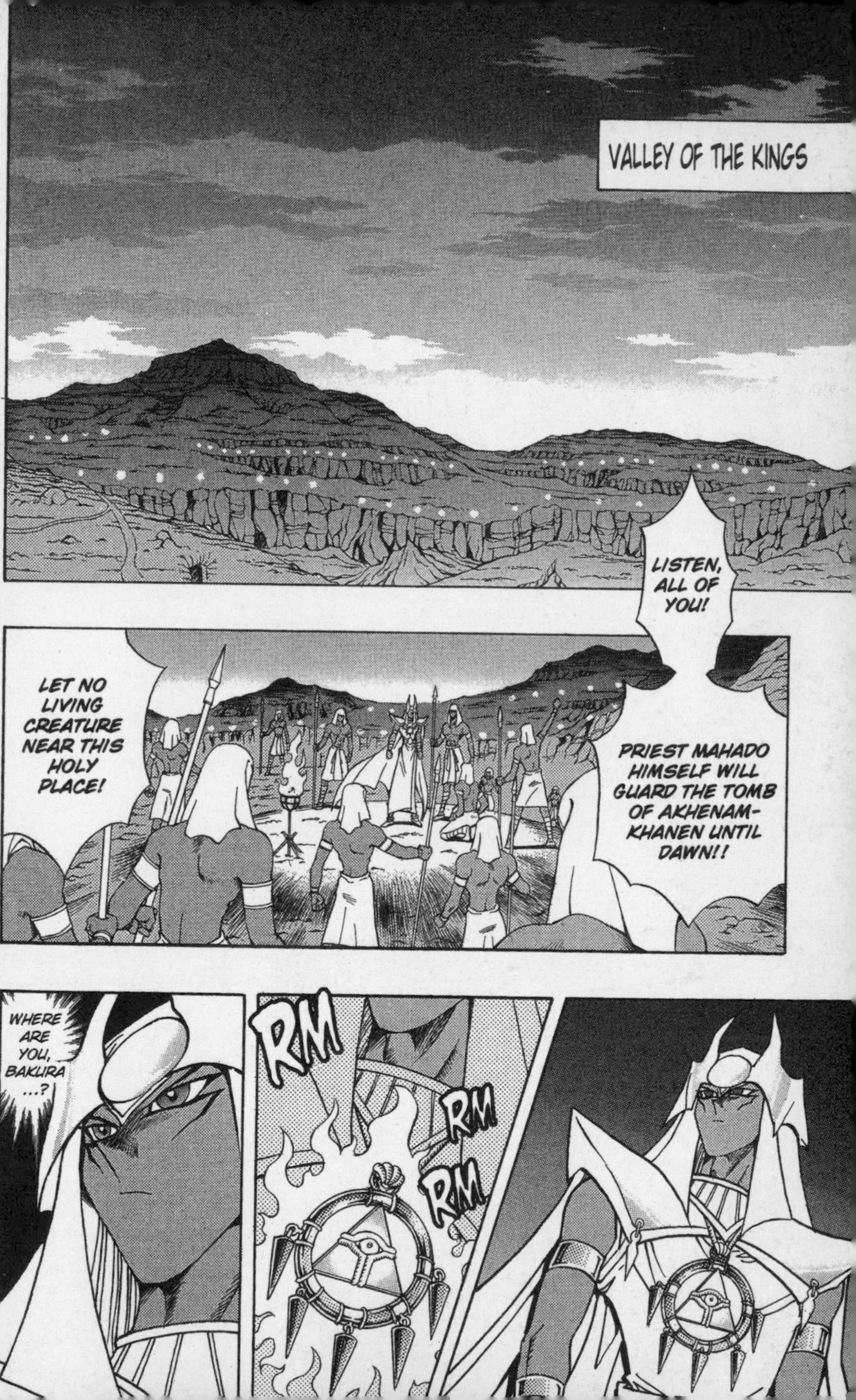
VALLEY OF THE KINGS
LISTEN, ALL OF YOU!
PRIEST MAHADO HIMSELF WILL GUARD THE TOMB OF AKHENAM-KHANEN UNTIL DAWN!!
LET NO LIVING CREATURE NEAR THIS HOLY PLACE!
RM
RM
RM
WHERE ARE YOU, BAKURA ...?

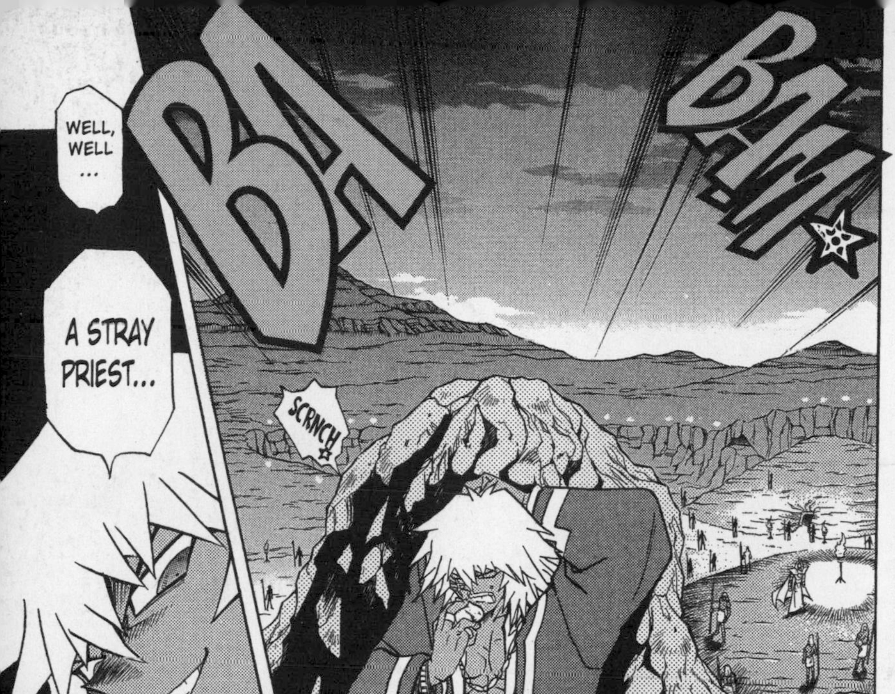
BA
BAM
WELL, WELL ...
A STRAY PRIEST...
SCRNCH
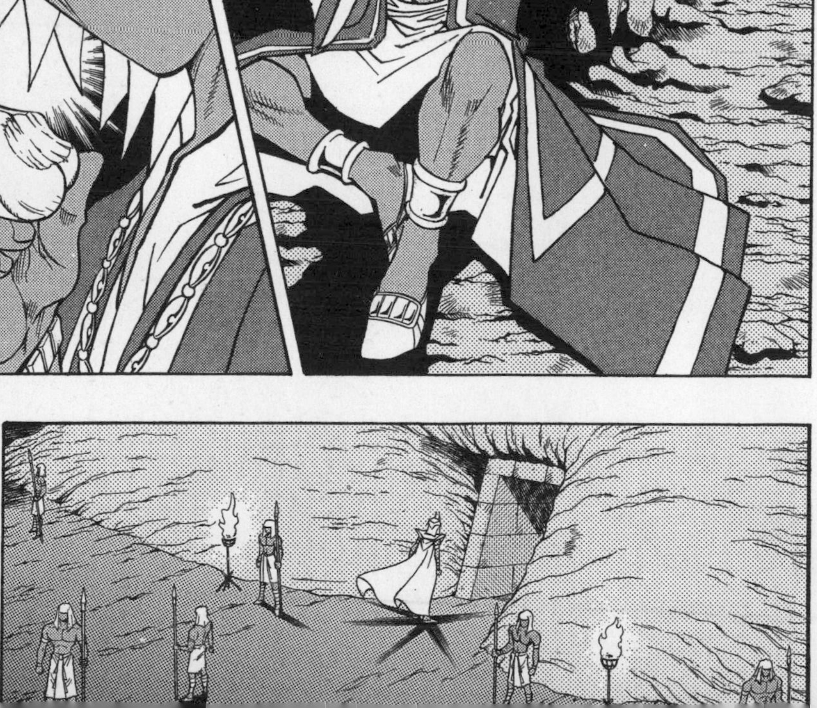

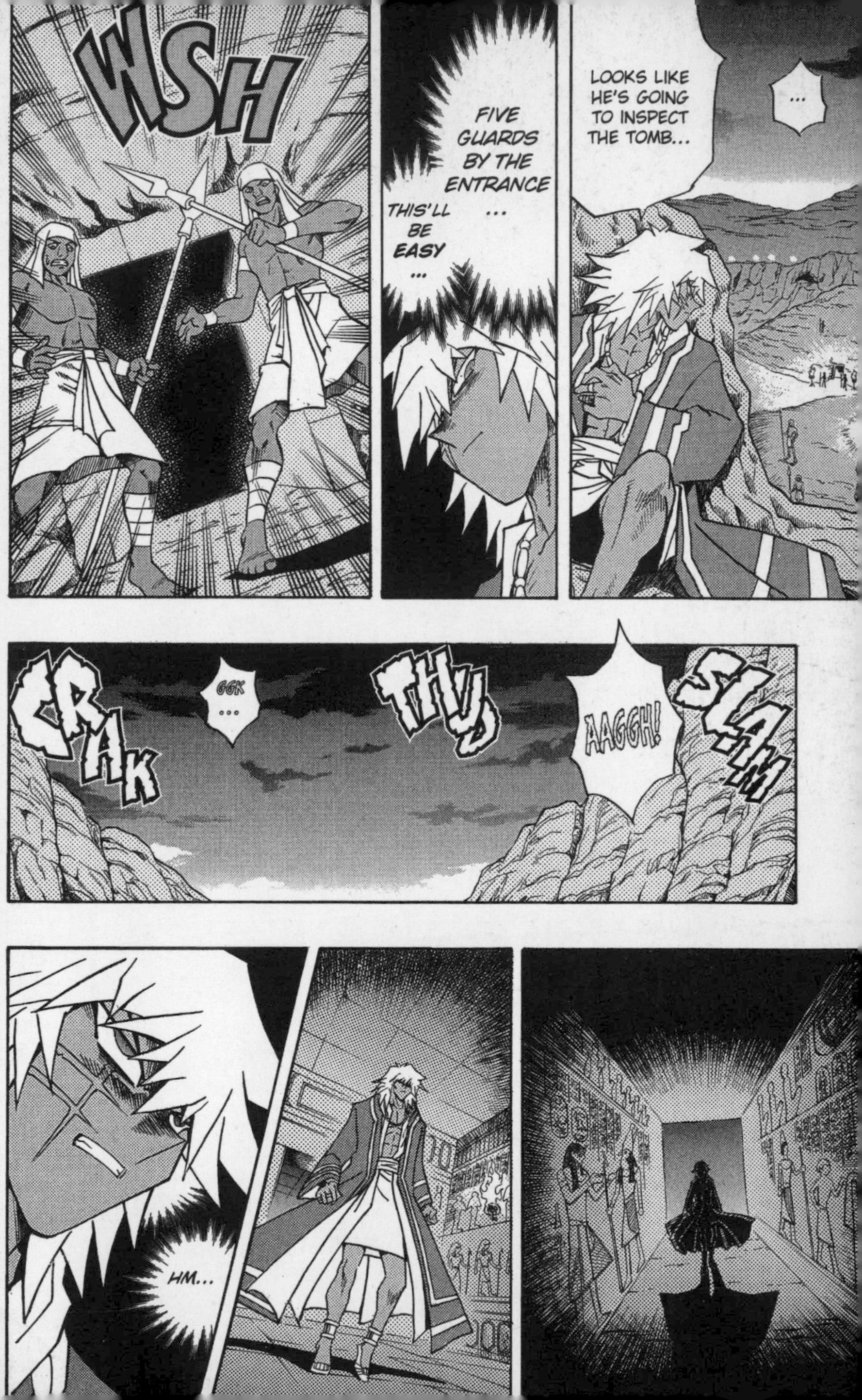
...
LOOKS LIKE HE'S GOING TO INSPECT THE TOMB...
FIVE GUARDS BY THE ENTRANCE...
THIS'LL BE EASY...
WSH
SLAM
AAGGH!
THUD
GGK...
CRAK
HM...

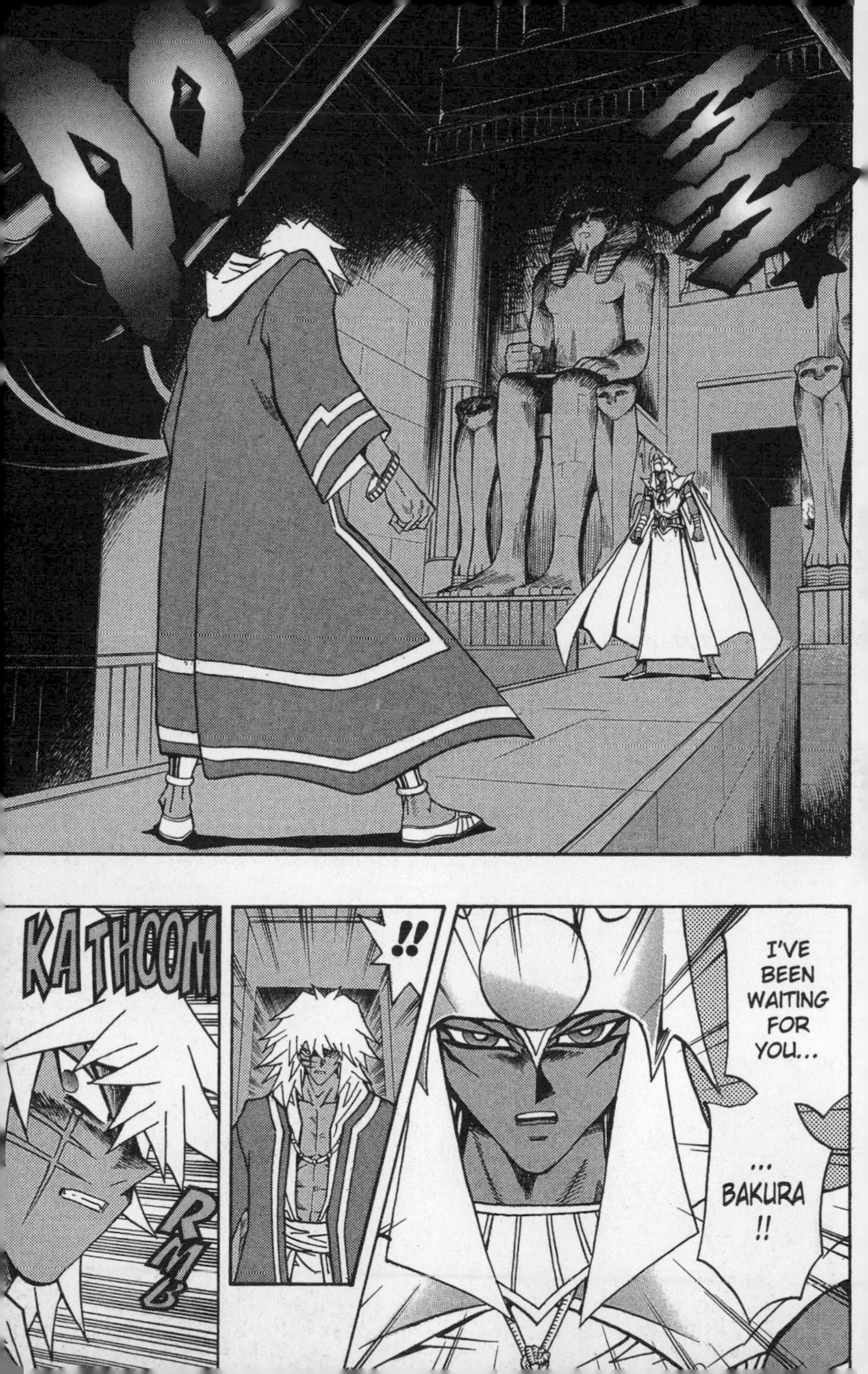
I'VE BEEN WAITING FOR YOU...
... BAKURA !!
!!
KA THOOM
RMB

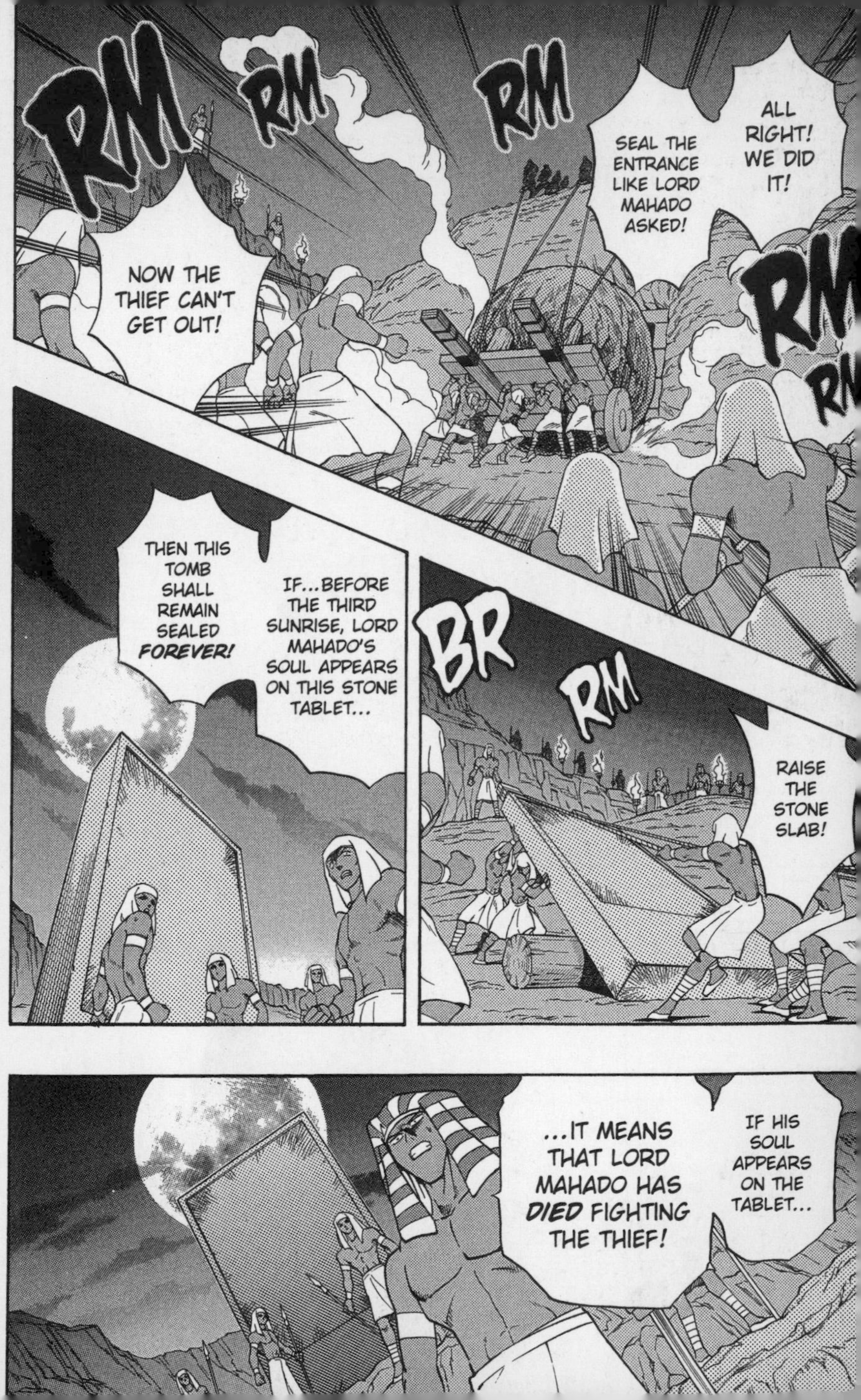
RM RM RM
ALL RIGHT! WE DID IT!
SEAL THE ENTRANCE LIKE LORD MAHADO ASKED!
NOW THE THIEF CAN'T GET OUT!
BR RM
RAISE THE STONE SLAB!
IF...BEFORE THE THIRD SUNRISE, LORD MAHADO'S SOUL APPEARS ON THIS STONE TABLET...
THEN THIS TOMB SHALL REMAIN SEALED *FOREVER!*
IF HIS SOUL APPEARS ON THE TABLET...
...IT MEANS THAT LORD MAHADO HAS *DIED* FIGHTING THE THIEF!

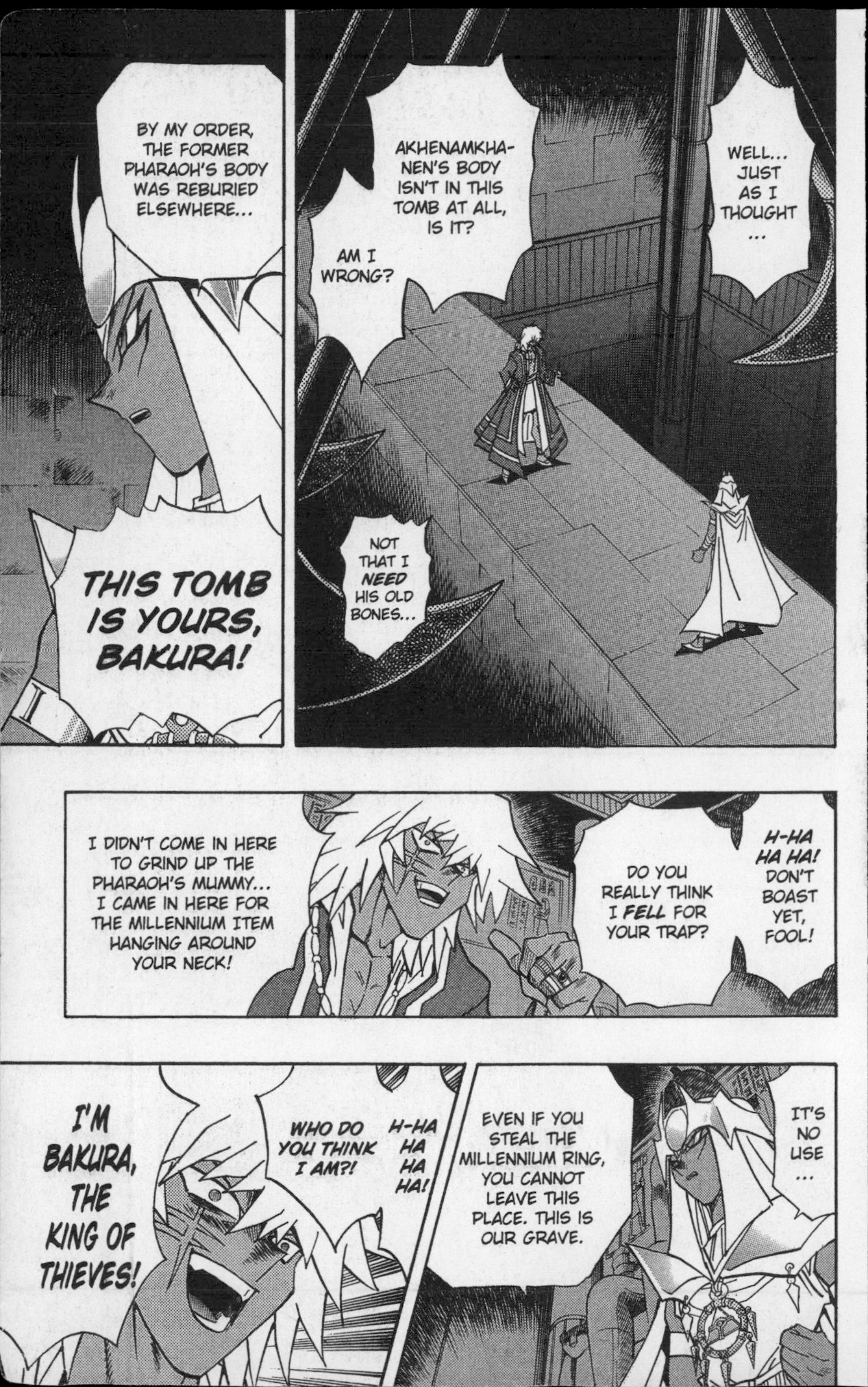
WELL... JUST AS I THOUGHT ...
AKHENAMKHA-NEN'S BODY ISN'T IN THIS TOMB AT ALL, IS IT?
AM I WRONG?
NOT THAT I *NEED* HIS OLD BONES...
BY MY ORDER, THE FORMER PHARAOH'S BODY WAS REBURIED ELSEWHERE...
THIS TOMB IS YOURS, BAKURA!
H-HA HA HA! DON'T BOAST YET, FOOL!
DO YOU REALLY THINK I *FELL* FOR YOUR TRAP?
I DIDN'T COME IN HERE TO GRIND UP THE PHARAOH'S MUMMY... I CAME IN HERE FOR THE MILLENNIUM ITEM HANGING AROUND YOUR NECK!
IT'S NO USE ...
EVEN IF YOU STEAL THE MILLENNIUM RING, YOU CANNOT LEAVE THIS PLACE. THIS IS OUR GRAVE.
H-HA HA HA HA!
WHO DO YOU THINK I AM?!
I'M BAKURA, THE KING OF THIEVES!

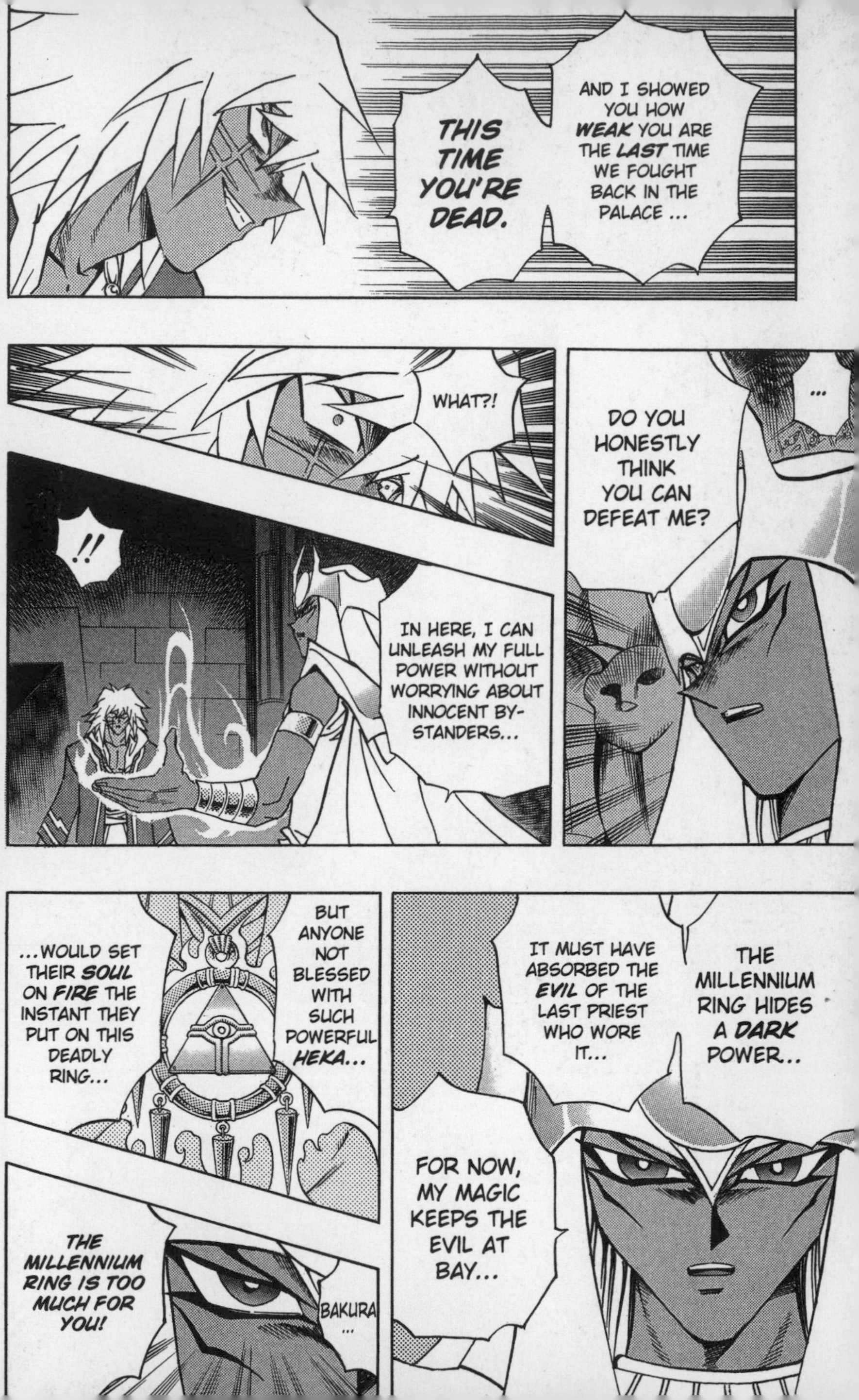
AND I SHOWED YOU HOW *WEAK* YOU ARE THE *LAST* TIME WE FOUGHT BACK IN THE PALACE ...
THIS TIME YOU'RE DEAD.
...
DO YOU HONESTLY THINK YOU CAN DEFEAT ME?
WHAT?!
!!
IN HERE, I CAN UNLEASH MY FULL POWER WITHOUT WORRYING ABOUT INNOCENT BY-STANDERS...
THE MILLENNIUM RING HIDES A *DARK* POWER...
IT MUST HAVE ABSORBED THE *EVIL* OF THE LAST PRIEST WHO WORE IT...
FOR NOW, MY MAGIC KEEPS THE EVIL AT BAY...
BUT ANYONE NOT BLESSED WITH SUCH POWERFUL *HEKA*...
...WOULD SET THEIR *SOUL* ON *FIRE* THE INSTANT THEY PUT ON THIS DEADLY RING...
BAKURA ...
THE MILLENNIUM RING IS TOO MUCH FOR YOU!

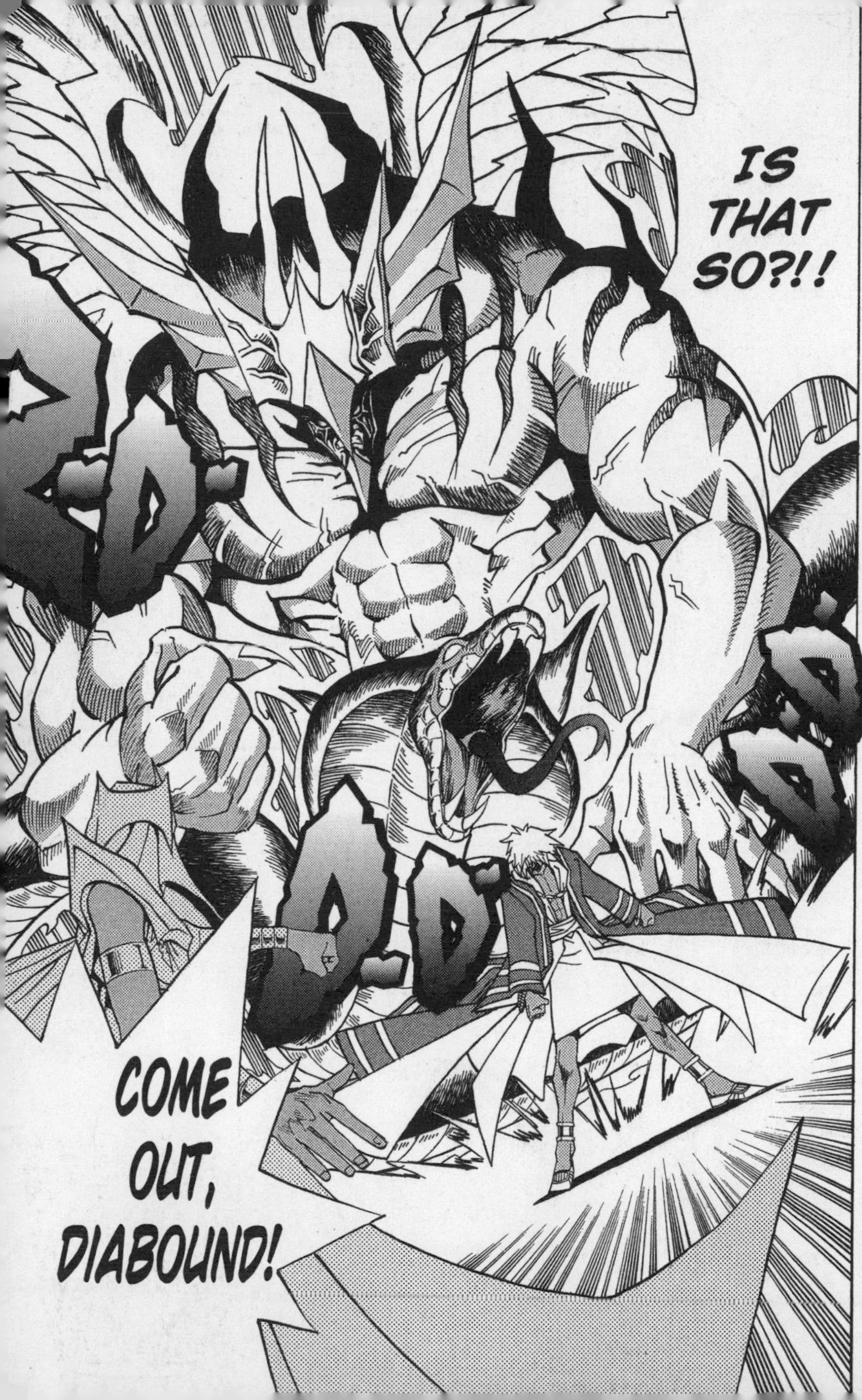
IS THAT SO?!!
COME OUT, DIABOUND!

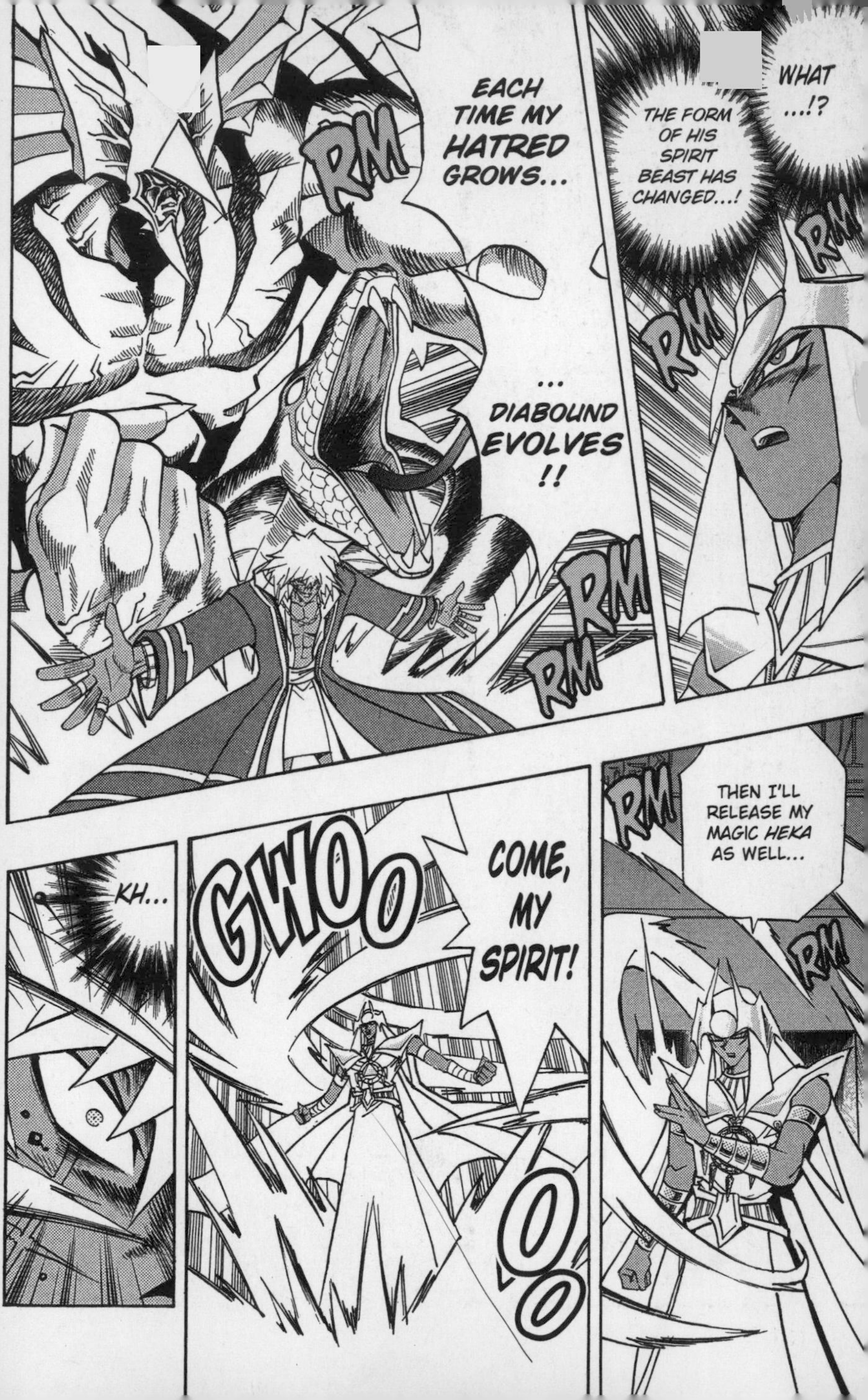
WHAT ...!?
THE FORM OF HIS SPIRIT BEAST HAS CHANGED...!
RM
RM
EACH TIME MY HATRED GROWS...
RM
... DIABOUND EVOLVES !!
RM
RM
RM
THEN I'LL RELEASE MY MAGIC HEKA AS WELL...
RM
RM
COME, MY SPIRIT!
GWOO
OO
KH...

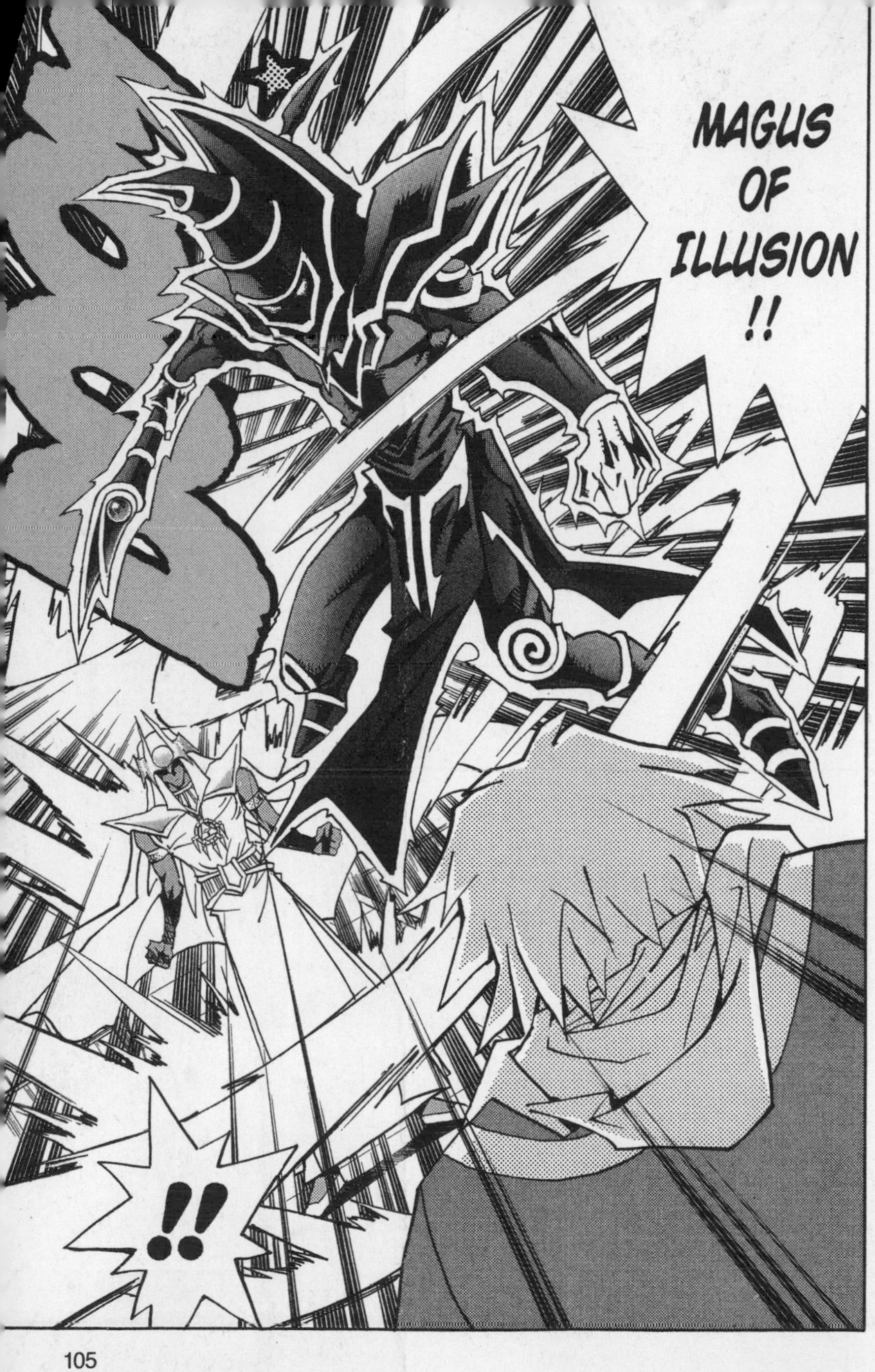
MAGUS OF ILLUSION !!
!!

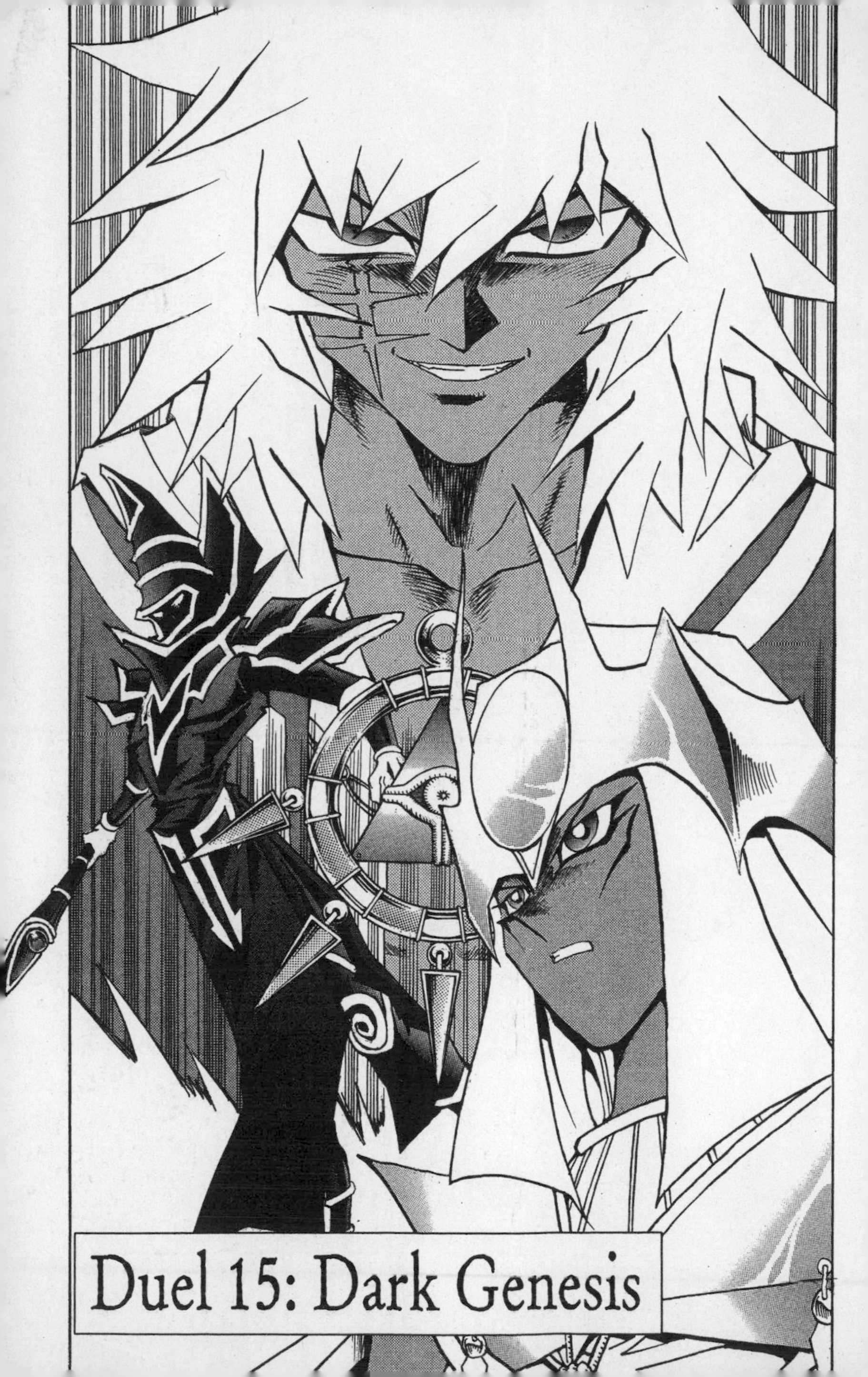
Duel 15: Dark Genesis

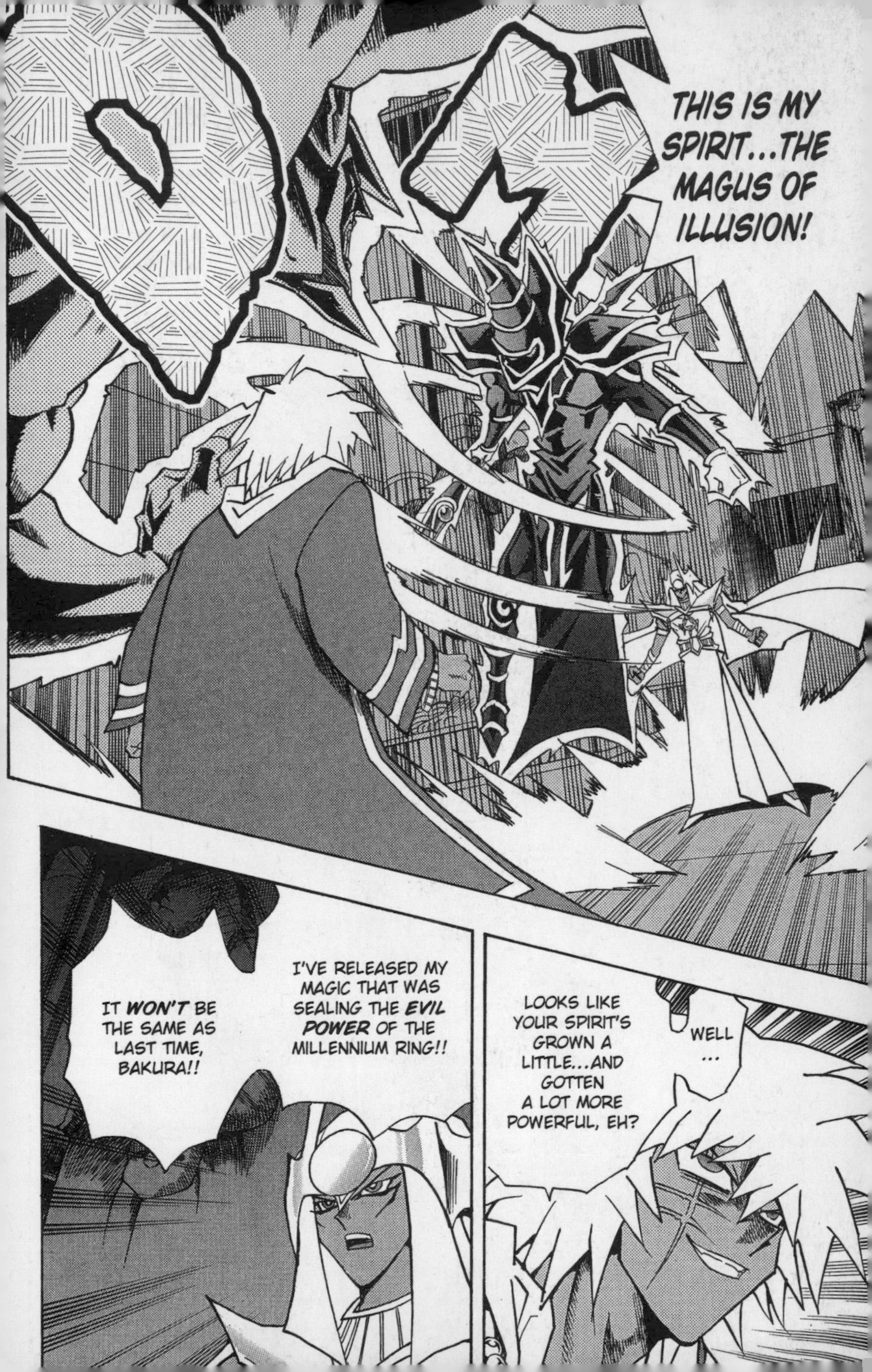
THIS IS MY SPIRIT...THE MAGUS OF ILLUSION!
WELL ...
LOOKS LIKE YOUR SPIRIT'S GROWN A LITTLE...AND GOTTEN A LOT MORE POWERFUL, EH?
I'VE RELEASED MY MAGIC THAT WAS SEALING THE *EVIL POWER* OF THE MILLENNIUM RING!!
IT *WON'T* BE THE SAME AS LAST TIME, BAKURA!!

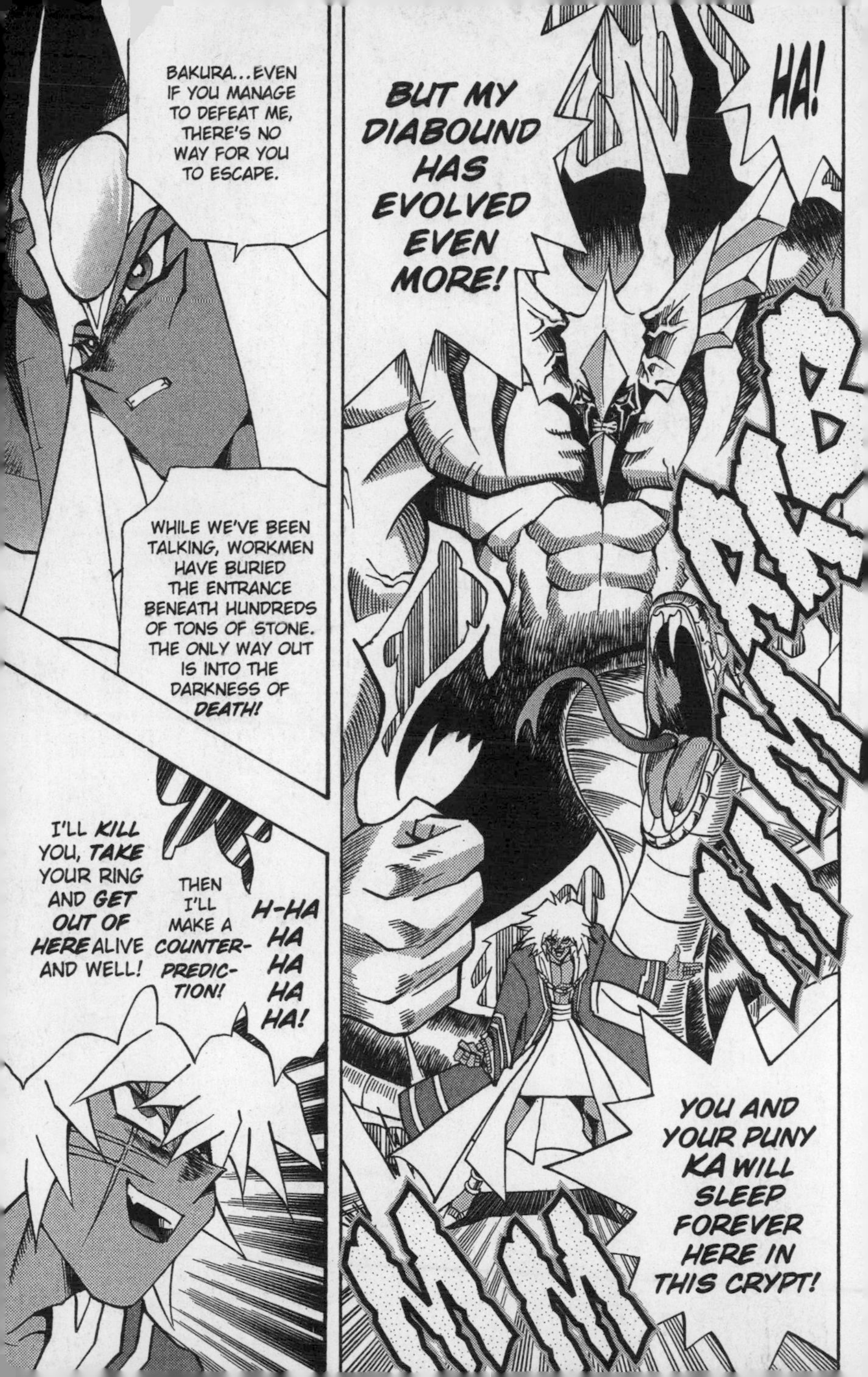
HA!
BUT MY DIABOUND HAS EVOLVED EVEN MORE!
YOU AND YOUR PUNY KA WILL SLEEP FOREVER HERE IN THIS CRYPT!
BAKURA...EVEN IF YOU MANAGE TO DEFEAT ME, THERE'S NO WAY FOR YOU TO ESCAPE.
WHILE WE'VE BEEN TALKING, WORKMEN HAVE BURIED THE ENTRANCE BENEATH HUNDREDS OF TONS OF STONE. THE ONLY WAY OUT IS INTO THE DARKNESS OF *DEATH!*
H-HA HA HA HA HA!
THEN I'LL MAKE A *COUNTER-PREDICTION!*
I'LL *KILL* YOU, *TAKE* YOUR RING AND *GET OUT OF HERE* ALIVE AND WELL!

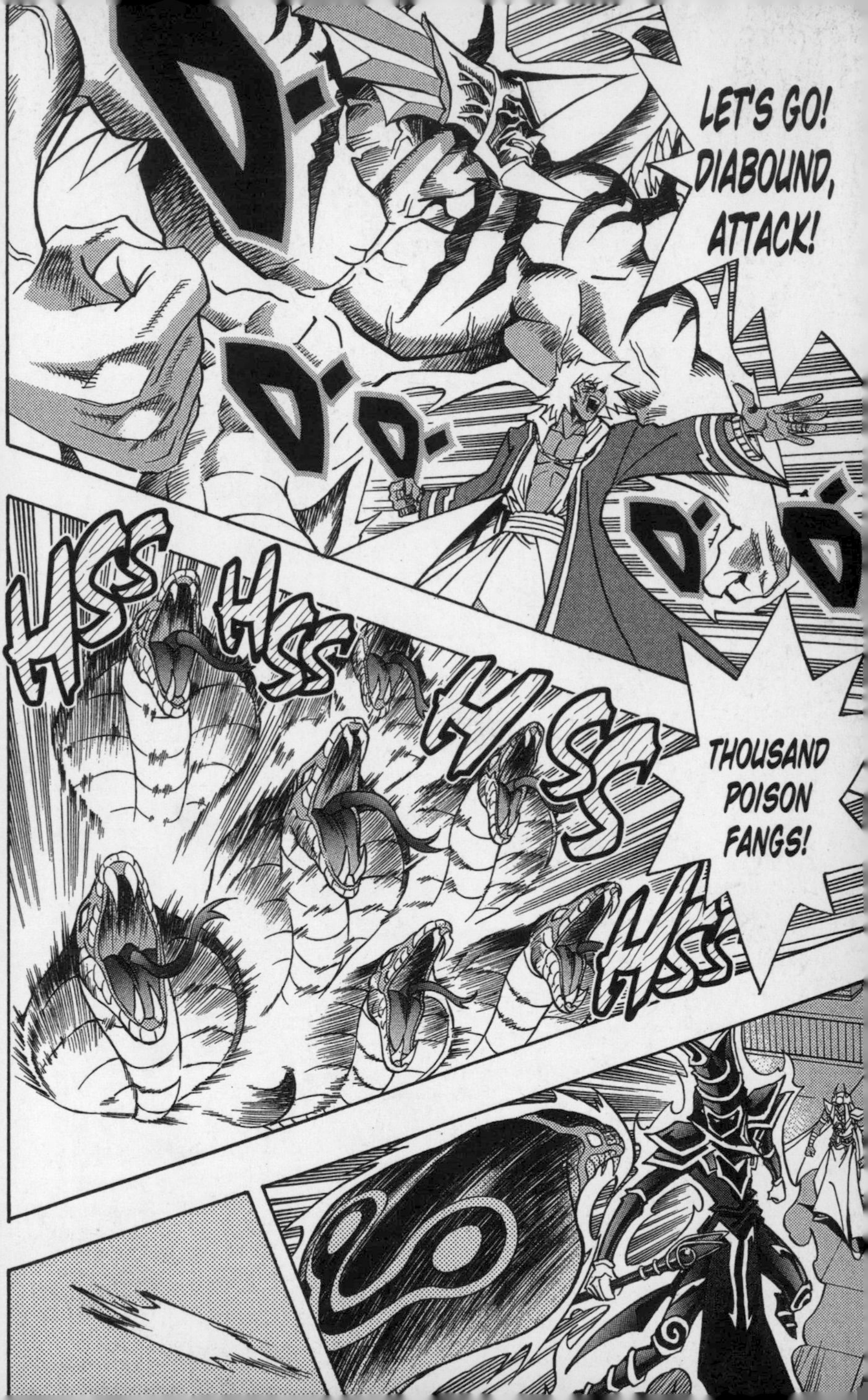
LET'S GO! DIABOUND, ATTACK!
THOUSAND POISON FANGS!
HSS HSS HSS HSS

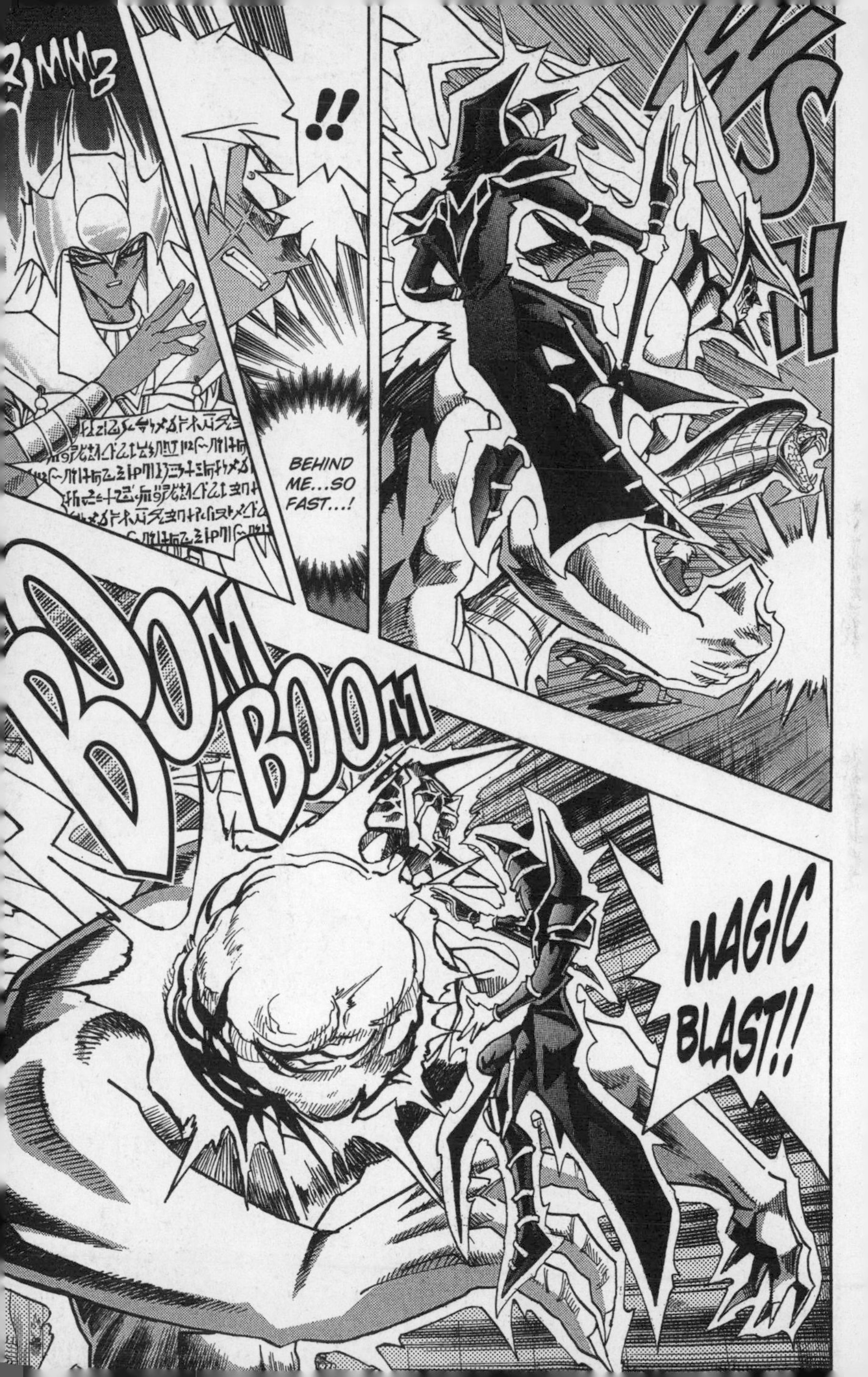
!!
BEHIND ME...SO FAST...!
MAGIC BLAST!!
BOOM BOOM

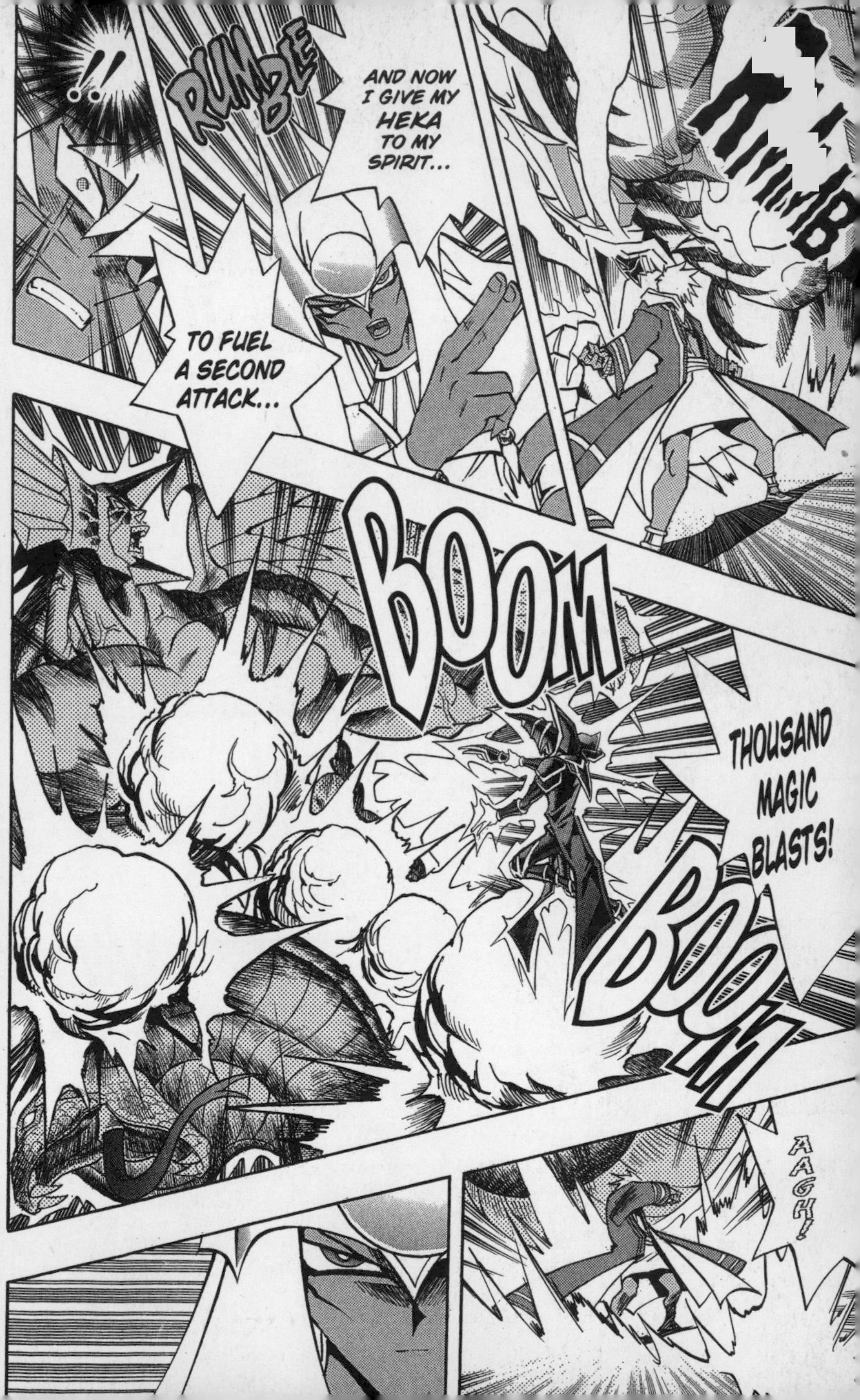
AND NOW I GIVE MY HEKA TO MY SPIRIT...
TO FUEL A SECOND ATTACK...
!!
RUMBLE
BOOM
THOUSAND MAGIC BLASTS!
BOOM
AAGH!

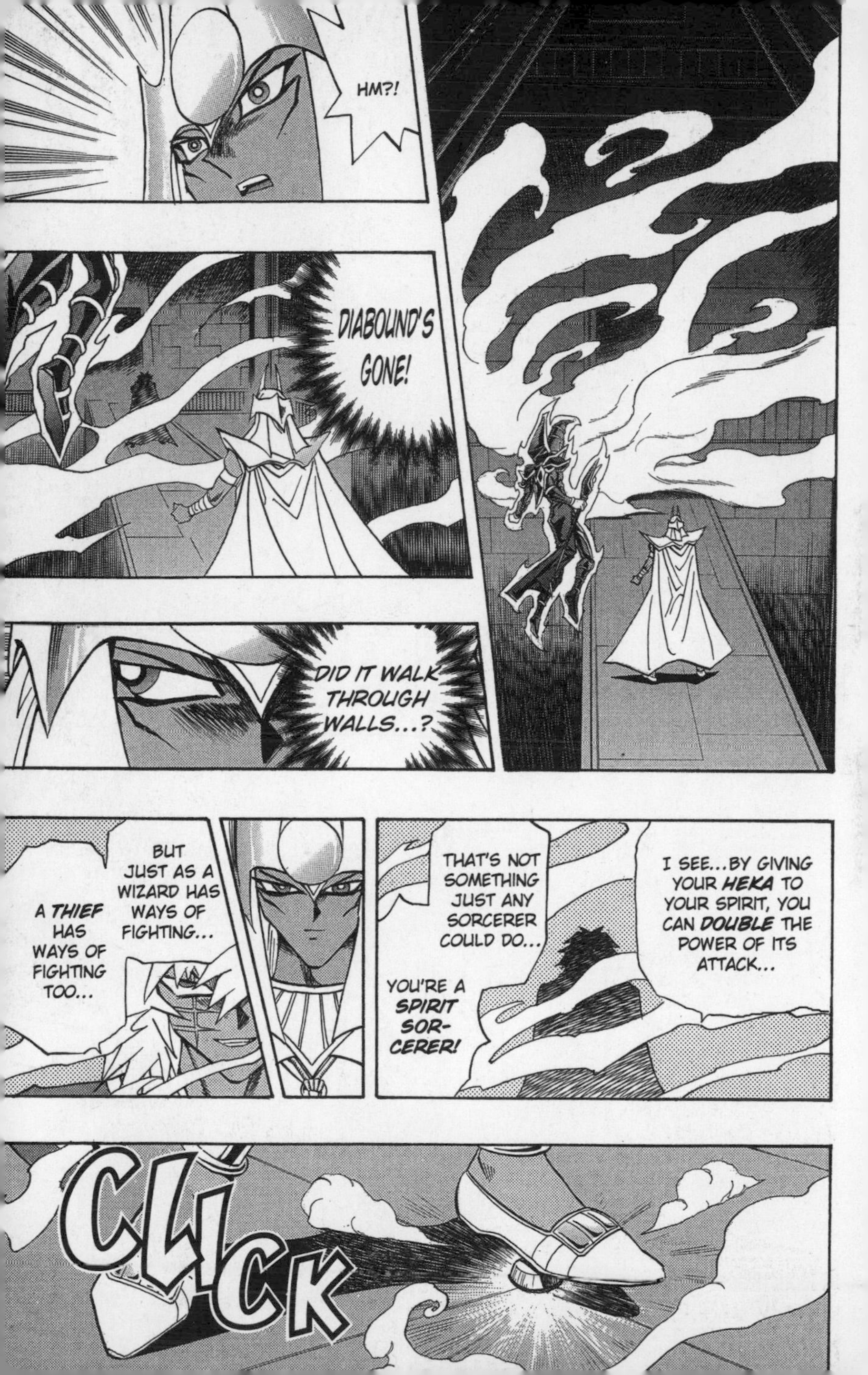
HM?!
DIABOUND'S GONE!
DID IT WALK THROUGH WALLS...?
I SEE...BY GIVING YOUR *HEKA* TO YOUR SPIRIT, YOU CAN *DOUBLE* THE POWER OF ITS ATTACK...
THAT'S NOT SOMETHING JUST ANY SORCERER COULD DO...
YOU'RE A *SPIRIT SOR-CERER!*
BUT JUST AS A WIZARD HAS WAYS OF FIGHTING...
A *THIEF* HAS WAYS OF FIGHTING TOO...
CLICK

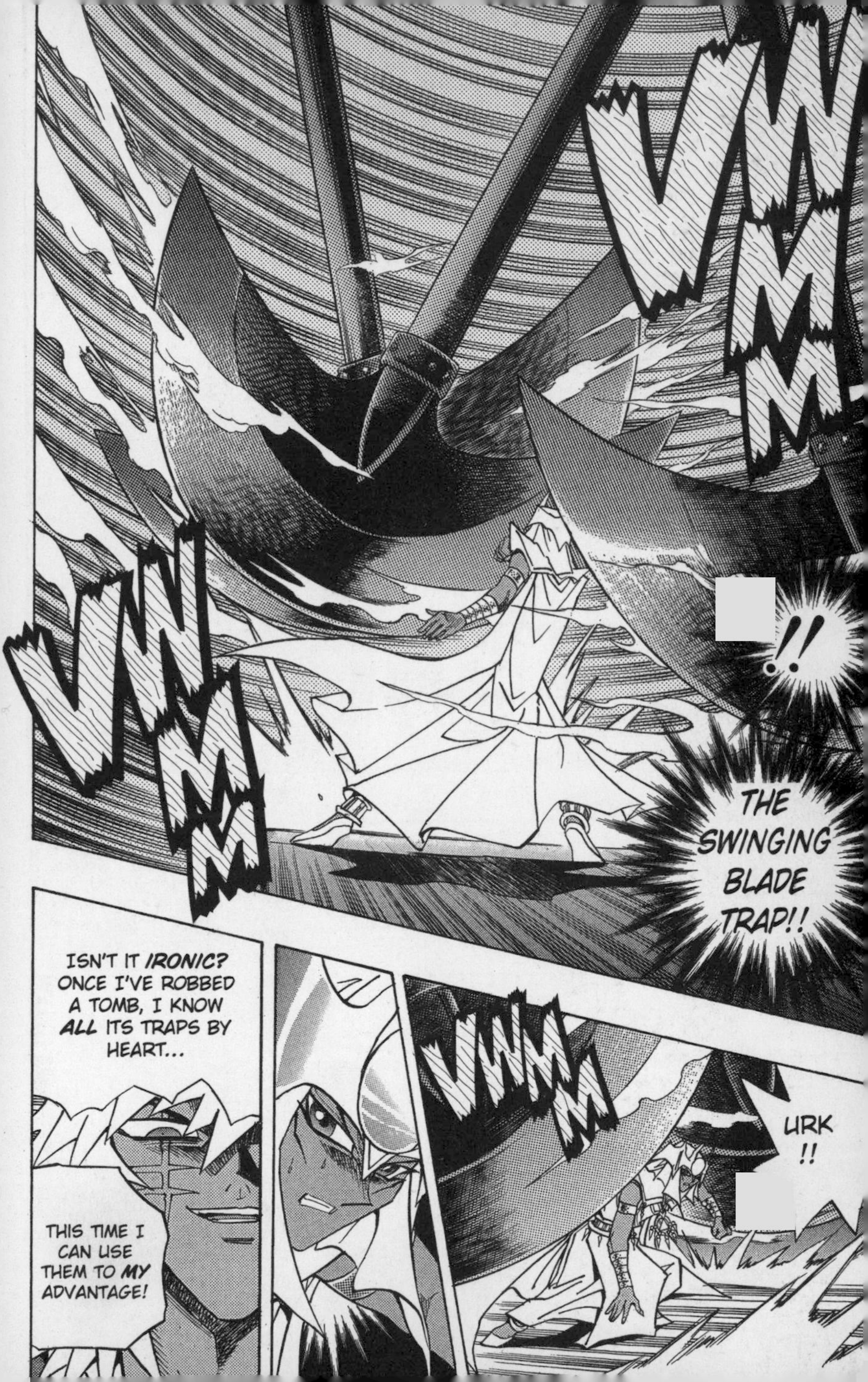
VWMMM
!!
VWMMM
THE SWINGING BLADE TRAP!!
VWM
URK !!
ISN'T IT *IRONIC?* ONCE I'VE ROBBED A TOMB, I KNOW ***ALL*** ITS TRAPS BY HEART...
THIS TIME I CAN USE THEM TO ***MY*** ADVANTAGE!

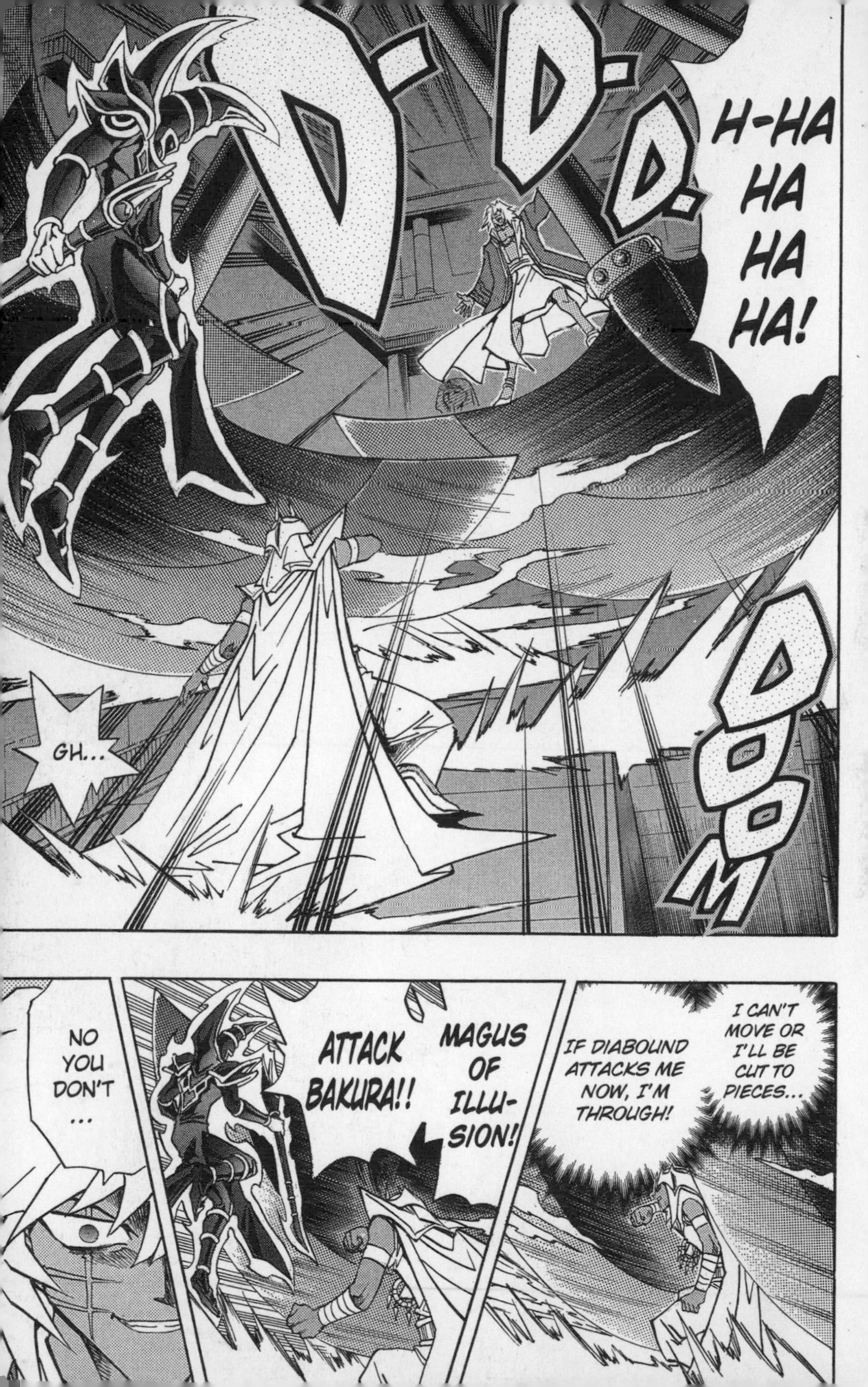
H-HA HA HA HA!
D D D
DOOOM
GH...
I CAN'T MOVE OR I'LL BE CUT TO PIECES...
IF DIABOUND ATTACKS ME NOW, I'M THROUGH!
MAGUS OF ILLU-SION!
ATTACK BAKURA!!
NO YOU DON'T ...

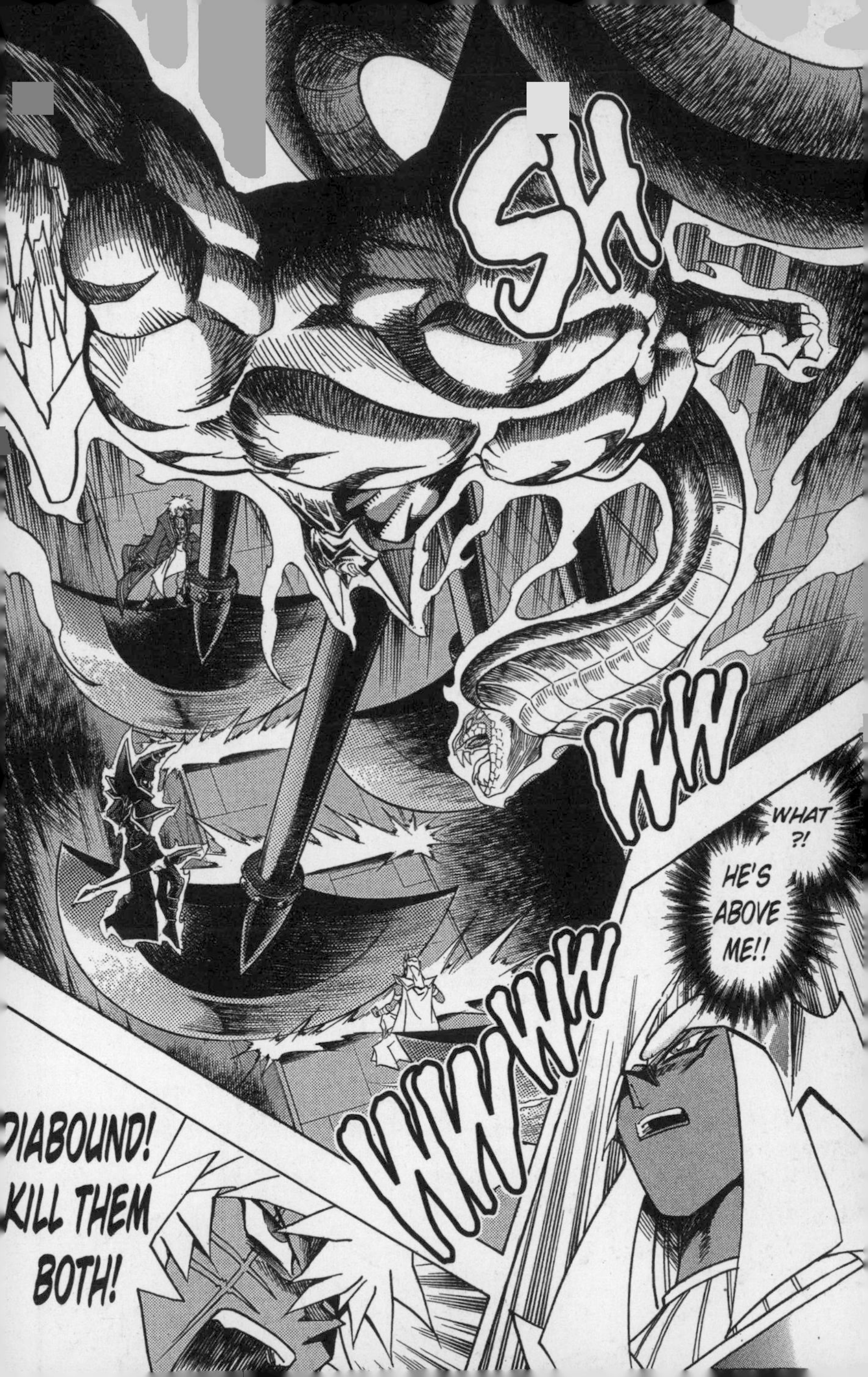
SH
WW
WHAT?!
HE'S ABOVE ME!!
WWWWW
DIABOUND! KILL THEM BOTH!

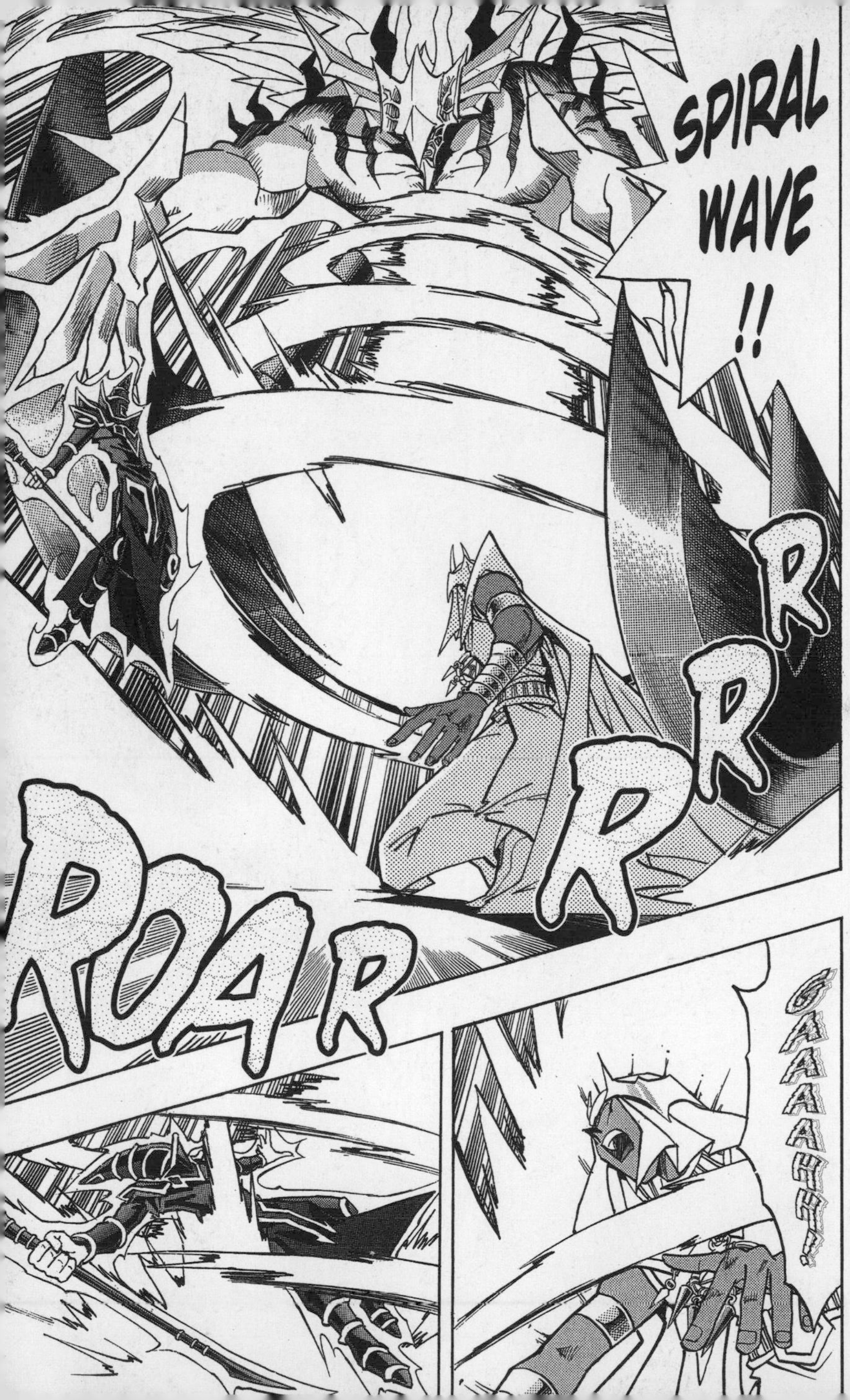
SPIRAL WAVE !!
RRRRROAR
GAAAAHH!?

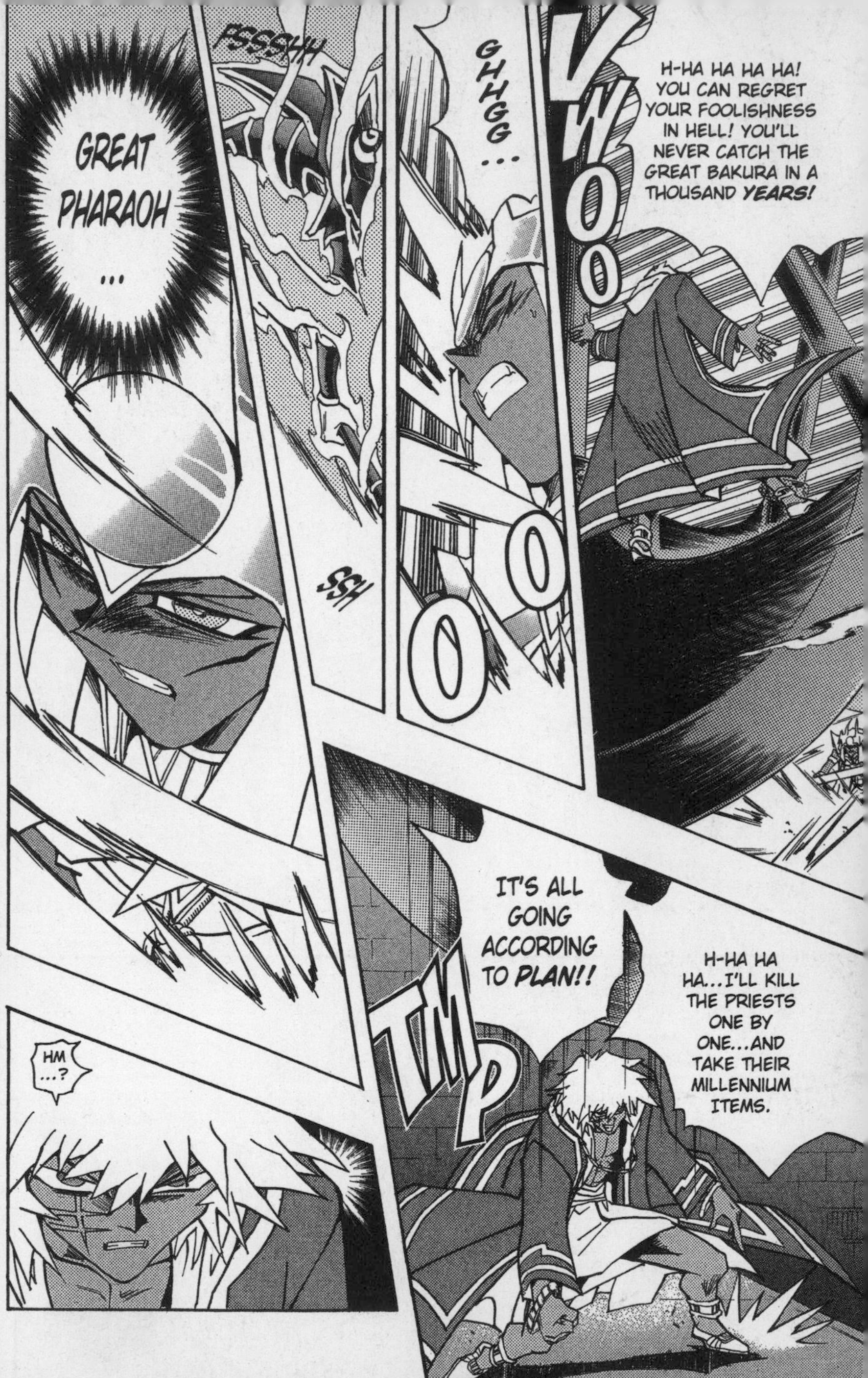
H-HA HA HA HA! YOU CAN REGRET YOUR FOOLISHNESS IN HELL! YOU'LL NEVER CATCH THE GREAT BAKURA IN A THOUSAND YEARS!
WOOOOOO
GHHGG...
FSSSHH
SSH
GREAT PHARAOH...
H-HA HA HA...I'LL KILL THE PRIESTS ONE BY ONE...AND TAKE THEIR MILLENNIUM ITEMS.
IT'S ALL GOING ACCORDING TO PLAN!!
TMP
HM...?

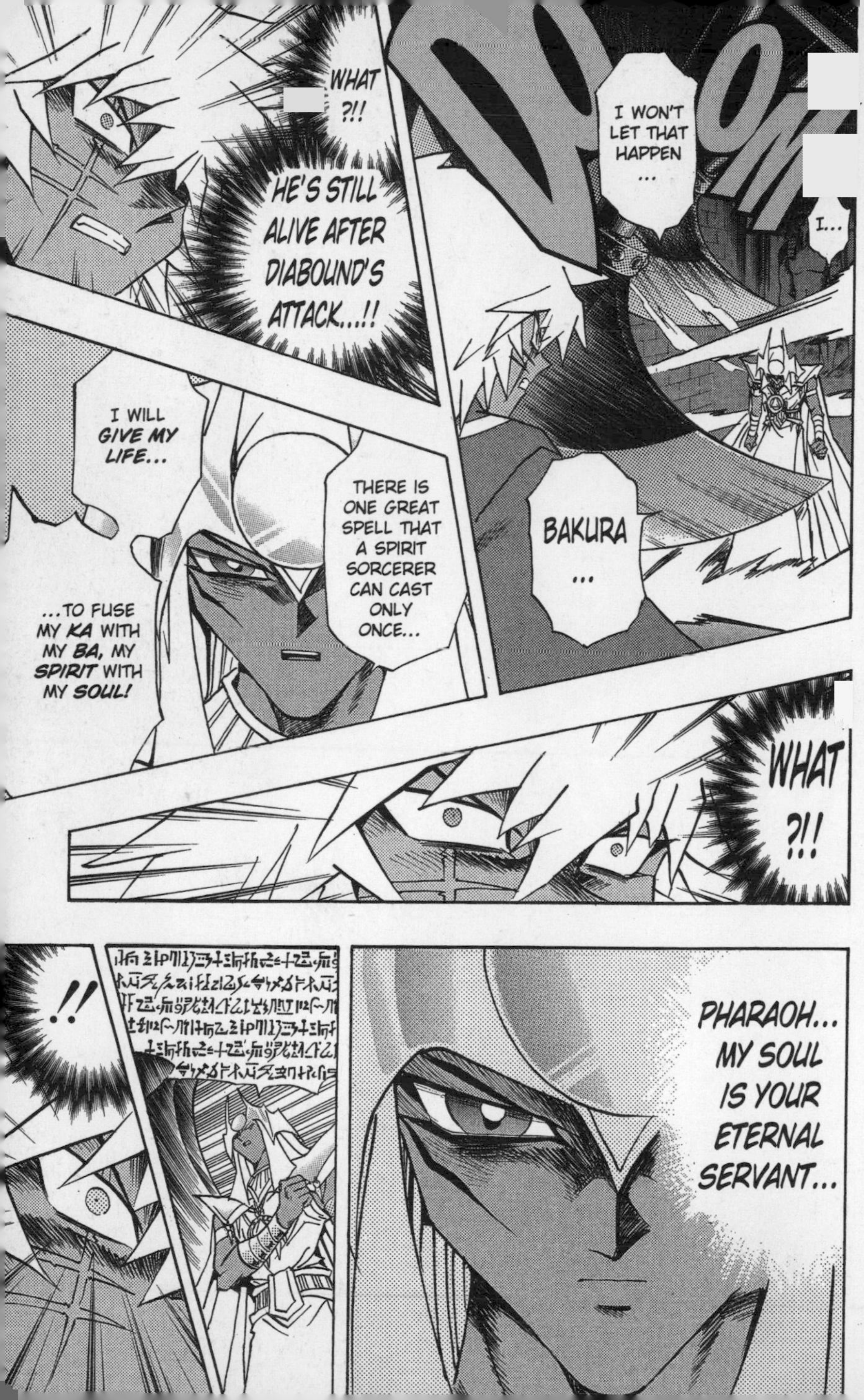
I WON'T LET THAT HAPPEN ...
I...
BAKURA ...
WHAT ?!!
HE'S STILL ALIVE AFTER DIABOUND'S ATTACK...!!
THERE IS ONE GREAT SPELL THAT A SPIRIT SORCERER CAN CAST ONLY ONCE...
I WILL GIVE MY LIFE...
...TO FUSE MY KA WITH MY BA, MY SPIRIT WITH MY SOUL!
WHAT ?!!
PHARAOH... MY SOUL IS YOUR ETERNAL SERVANT...
!!

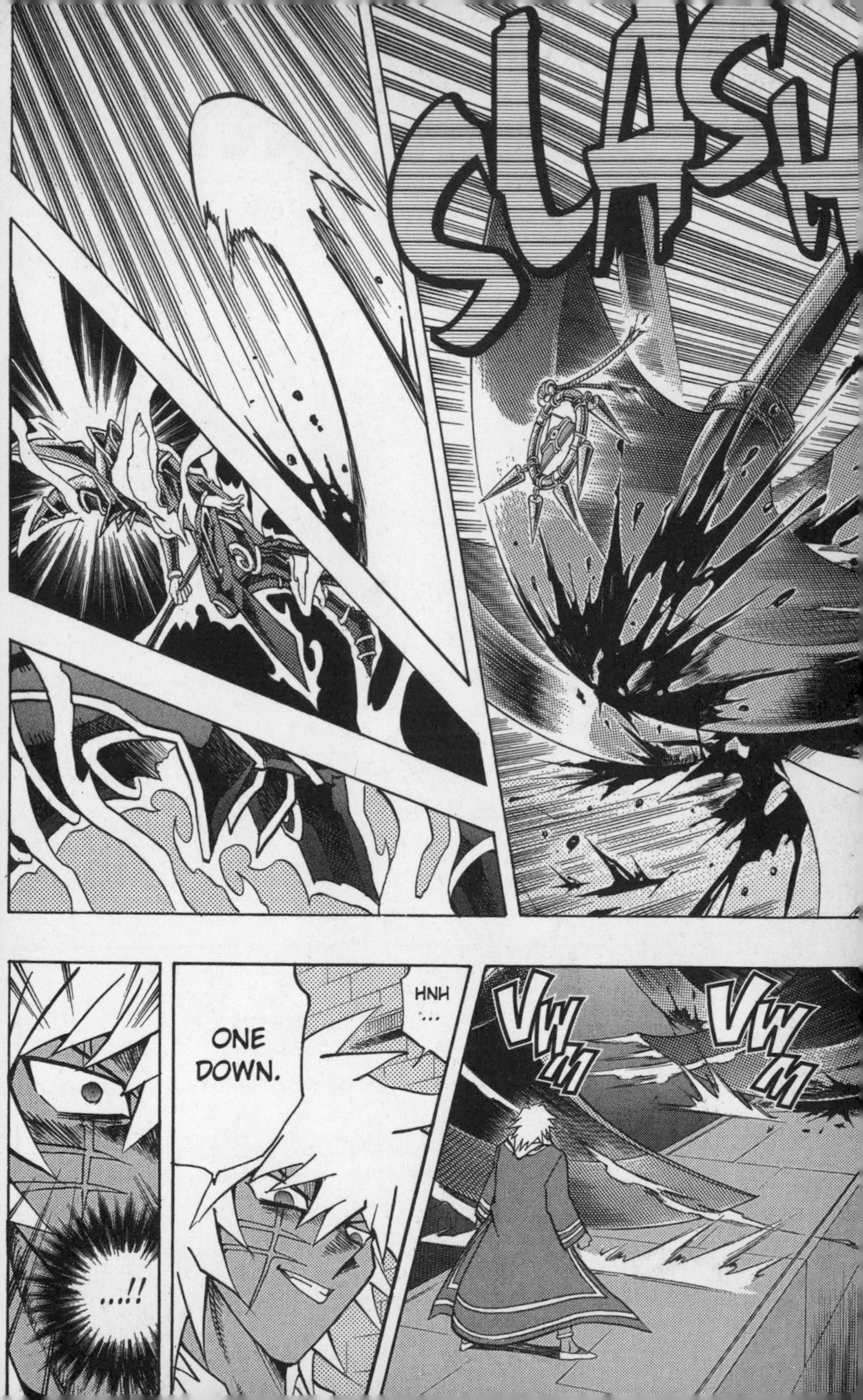
SLASH
VWM
VWM
HNH...
ONE DOWN.
....!!

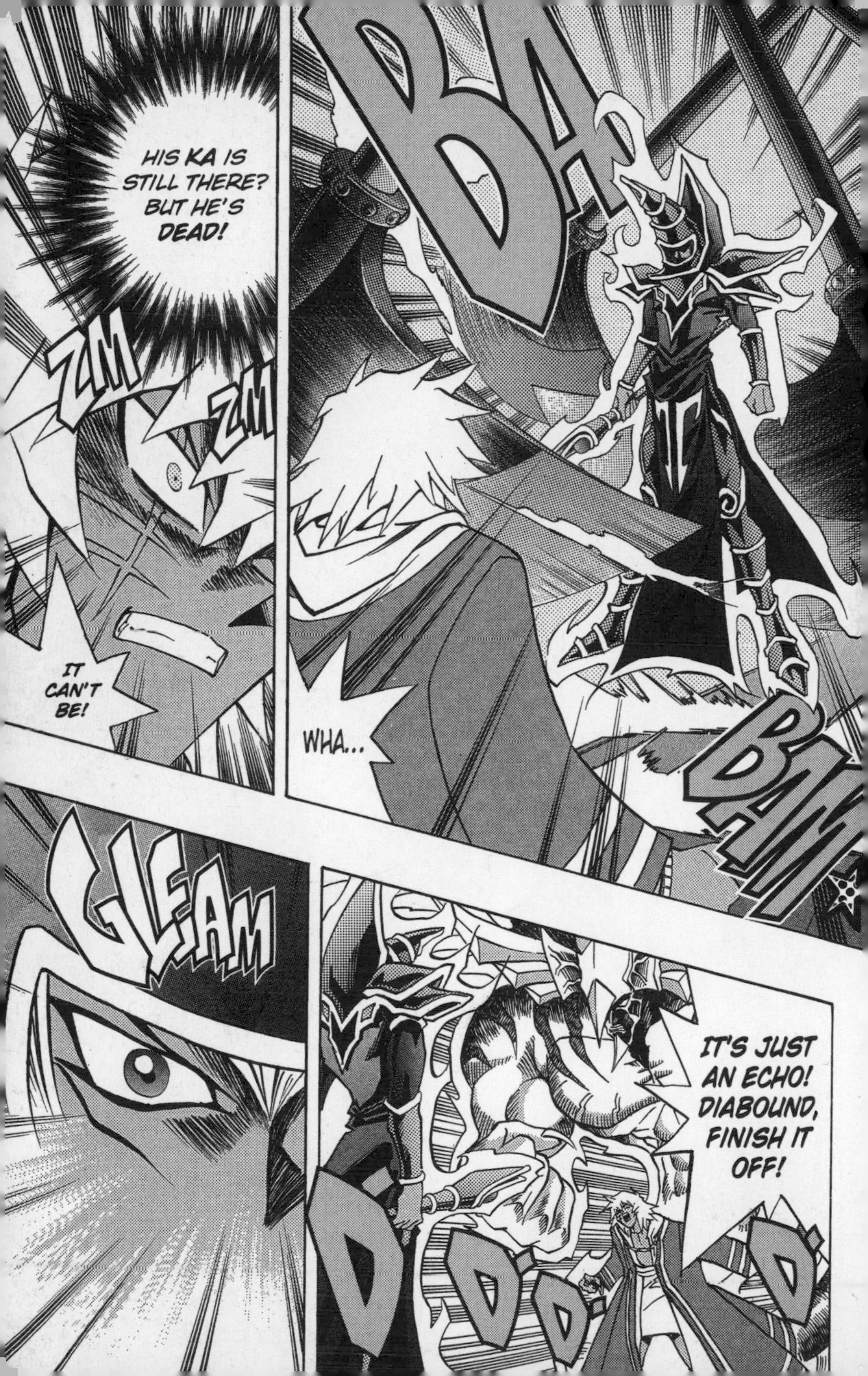
WHA...
BAM
HIS KA IS STILL THERE? BUT HE'S DEAD!
ZM
ZM
IT CAN'T BE!
IT'S JUST AN ECHO! DIABOUND, FINISH IT OFF!
GLEAM

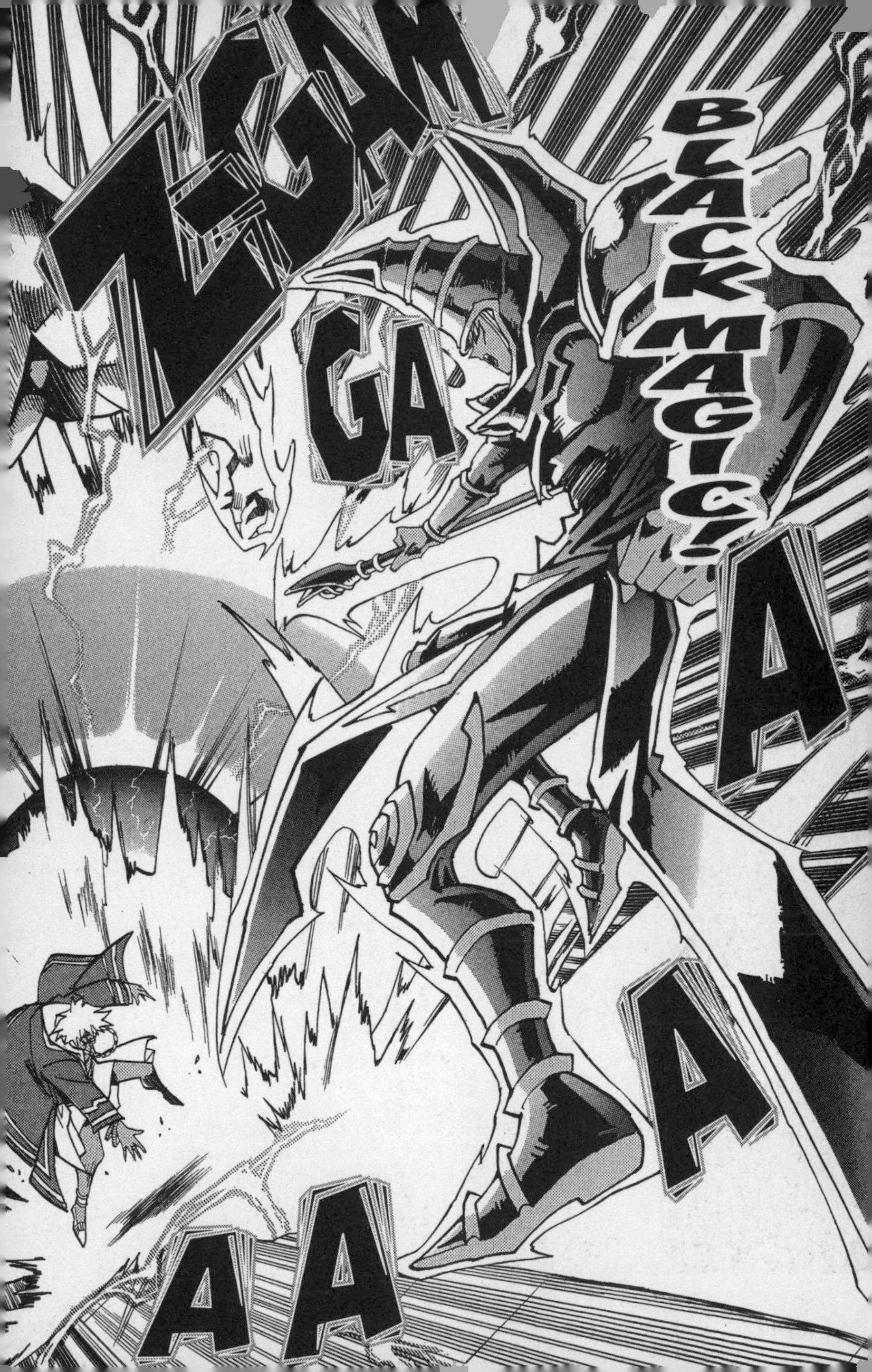
BLACK MAGIC!
ZGAAAAA

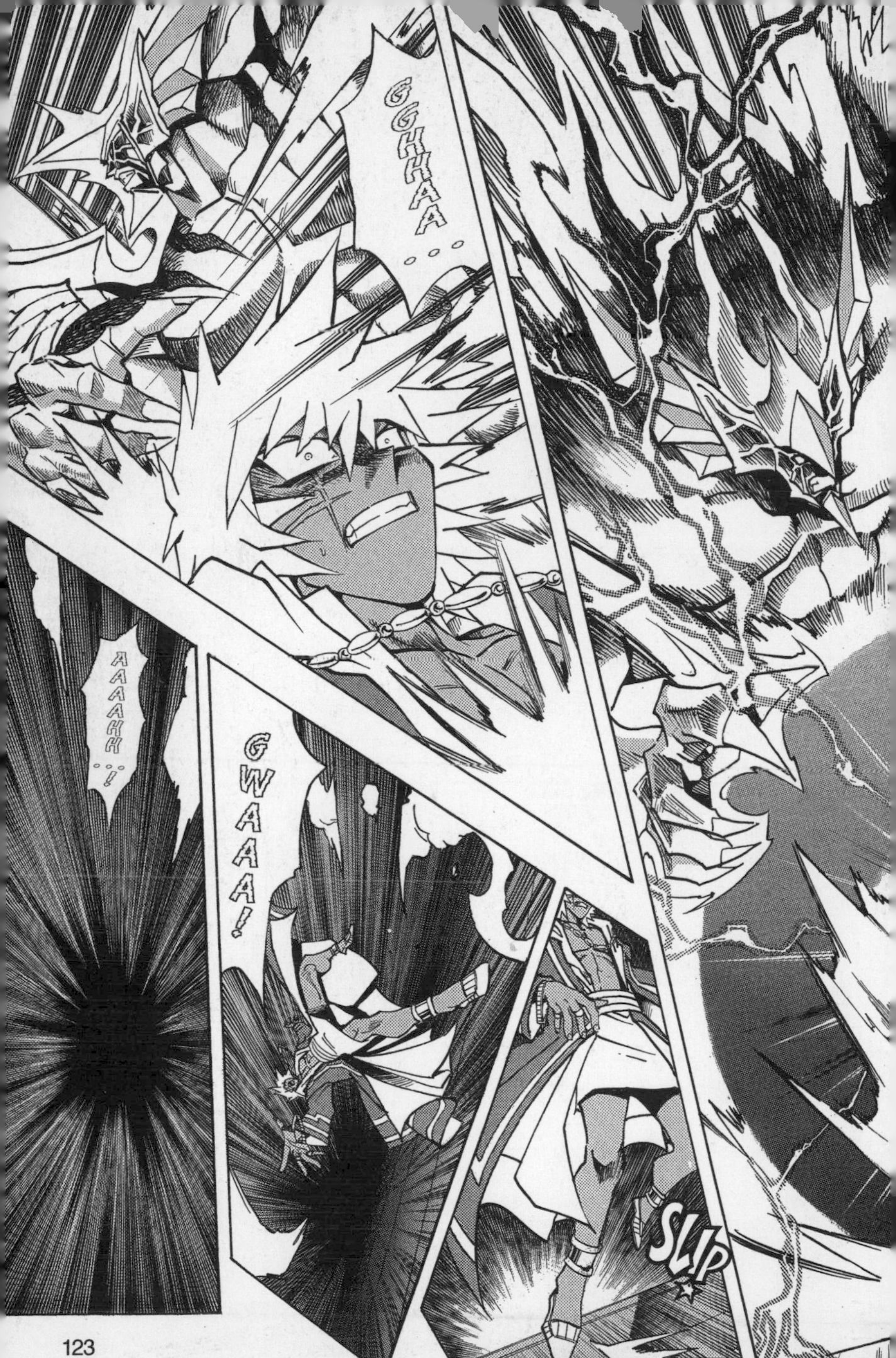
GGHHAAA...
SLIP
GWAAAA!
AAAAHH...!

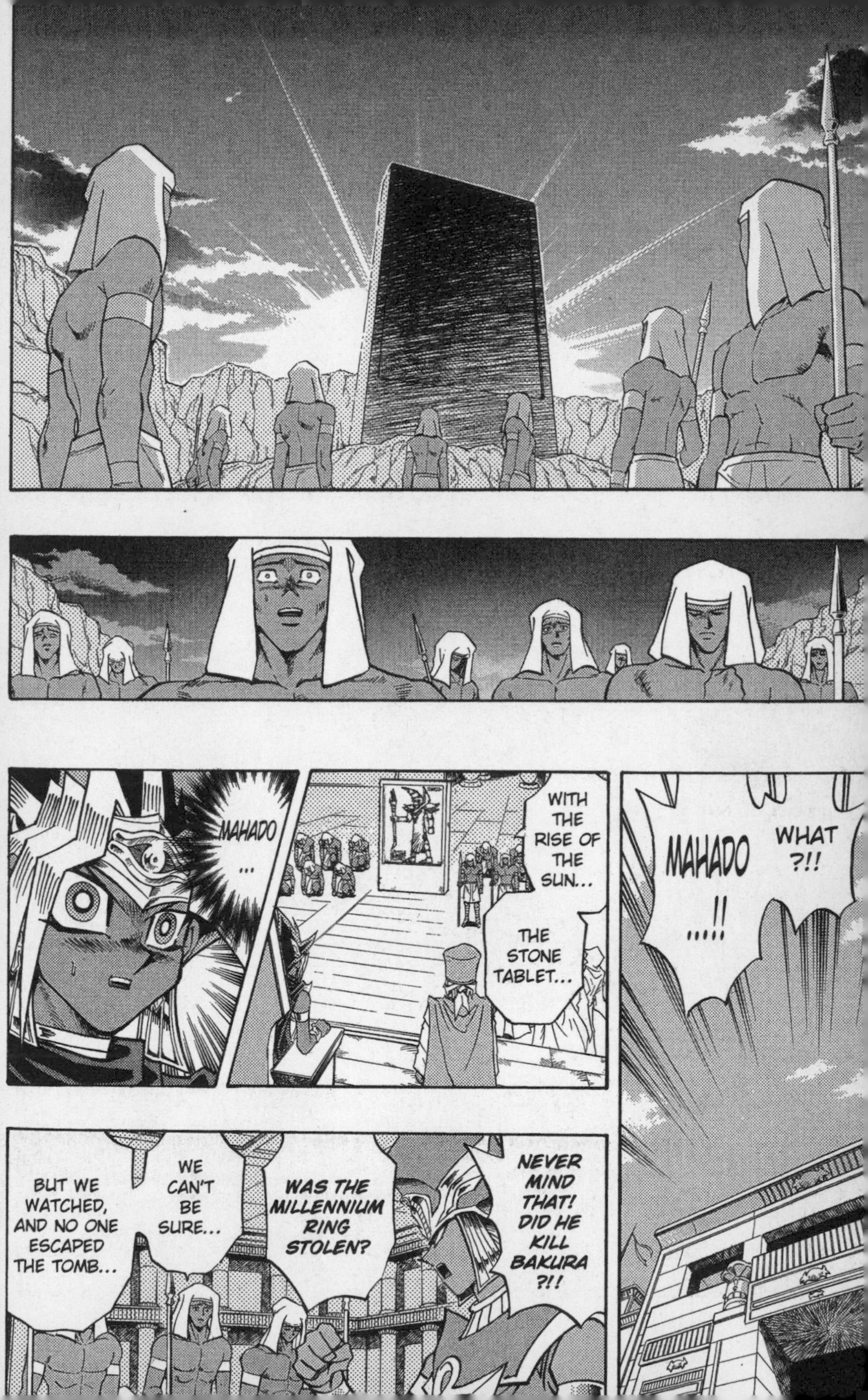
WHAT?!!
MAHADO ....!!
WITH THE RISE OF THE SUN...
THE STONE TABLET...
MAHADO ...
NEVER MIND THAT! DID HE KILL BAKURA?!!
WAS THE MILLENNIUM RING STOLEN?
WE CAN'T BE SURE...
BUT WE WATCHED, AND NO ONE ESCAPED THE TOMB...

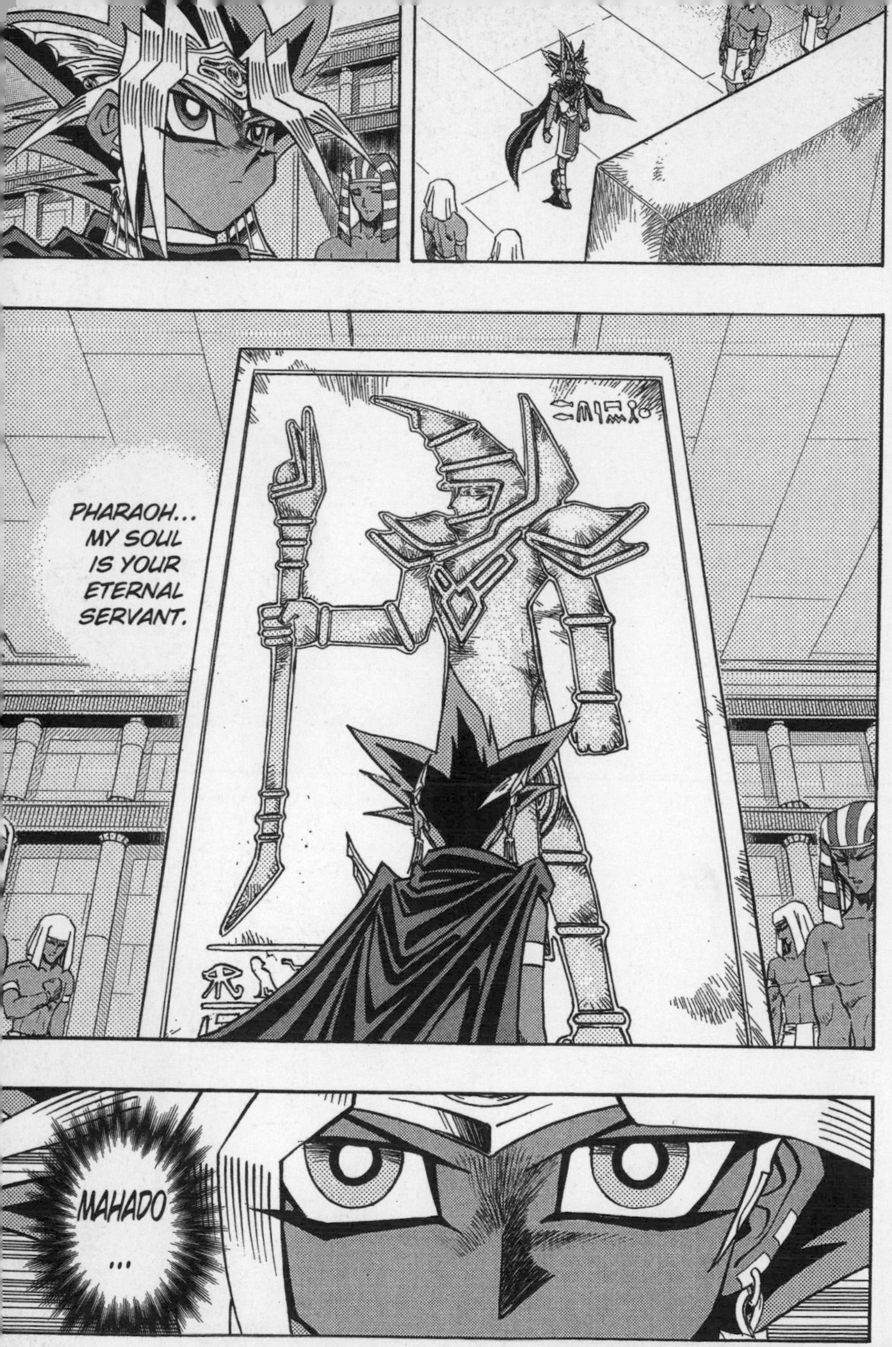
PHARAOH... MY SOUL IS YOUR ETERNAL SERVANT.
MAHADO ...

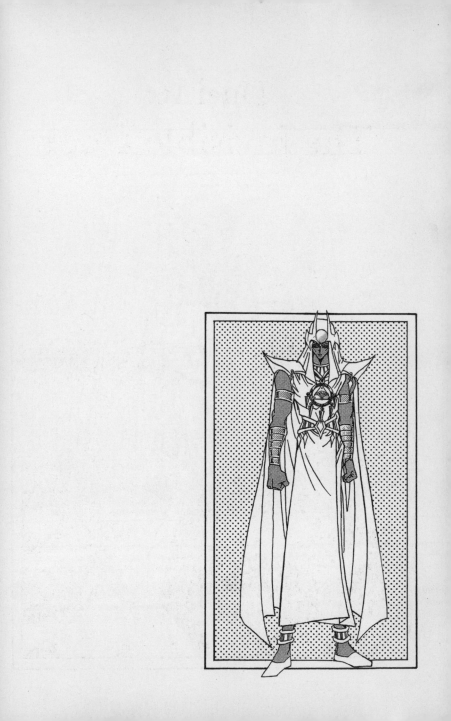

Duel 16: The Invisible Door

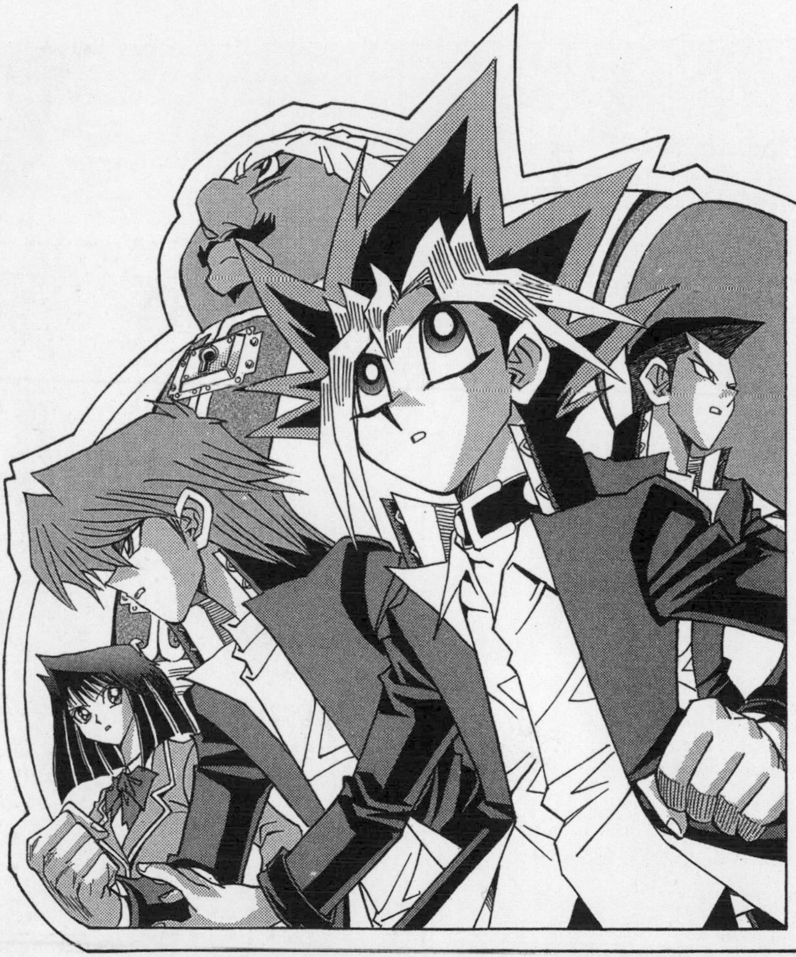

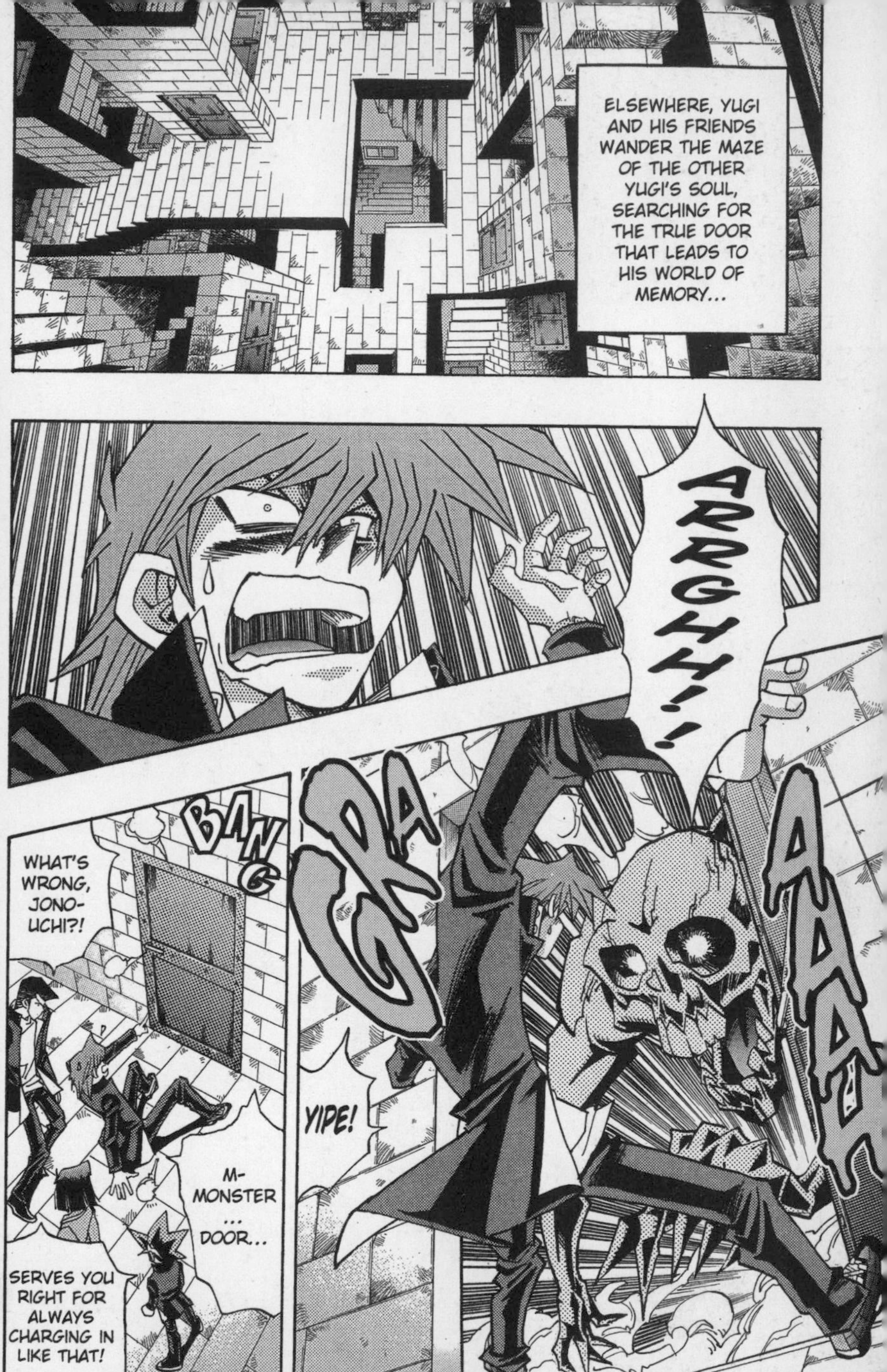
ELSEWHERE, YUGI AND HIS FRIENDS WANDER THE MAZE OF THE OTHER YUGI'S SOUL, SEARCHING FOR THE TRUE DOOR THAT LEADS TO HIS WORLD OF MEMORY...
ARRGHH!!
CRA
AAA
YIPE!
BANG
WHAT'S WRONG, JONO-UCHI?!
M-MONSTER ... DOOR...
SERVES YOU RIGHT FOR ALWAYS CHARGING IN LIKE THAT!

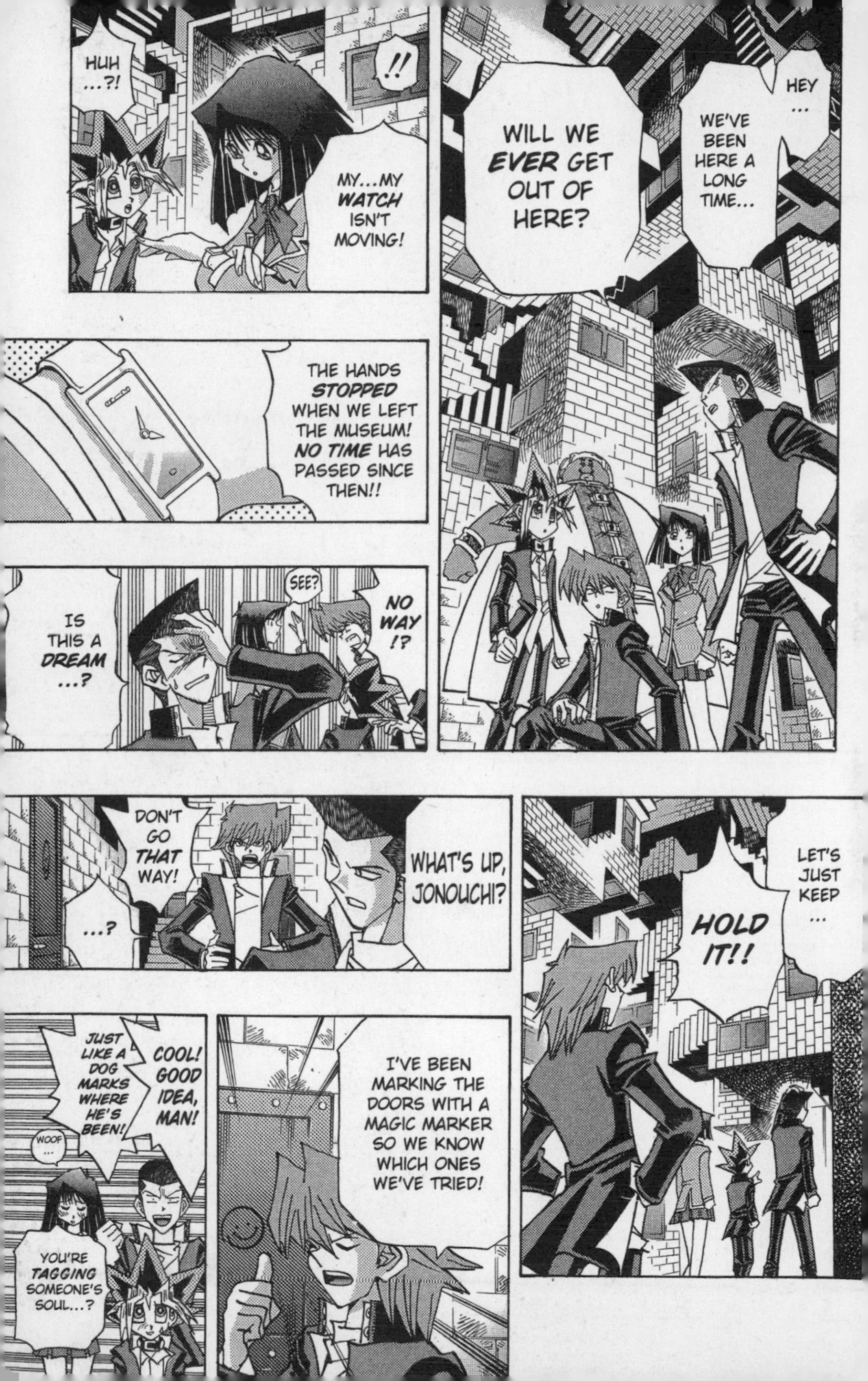
HEY ...
WE'VE BEEN HERE A LONG TIME...
WILL WE EVER GET OUT OF HERE?
!!
MY...MY WATCH ISN'T MOVING!
HUH ...?!
THE HANDS STOPPED WHEN WE LEFT THE MUSEUM! NO TIME HAS PASSED SINCE THEN!!
NO WAY !?
SEE?
IS THIS A DREAM ...?
LET'S JUST KEEP ...
HOLD IT!!
WHAT'S UP, JONOUCHI?
DON'T GO THAT WAY!
...?
I'VE BEEN MARKING THE DOORS WITH A MAGIC MARKER SO WE KNOW WHICH ONES WE'VE TRIED!
COOL! GOOD IDEA, MAN!
JUST LIKE A DOG MARKS WHERE HE'S BEEN!
WOOF ...
YOU'RE TAGGING SOMEONE'S SOUL...?

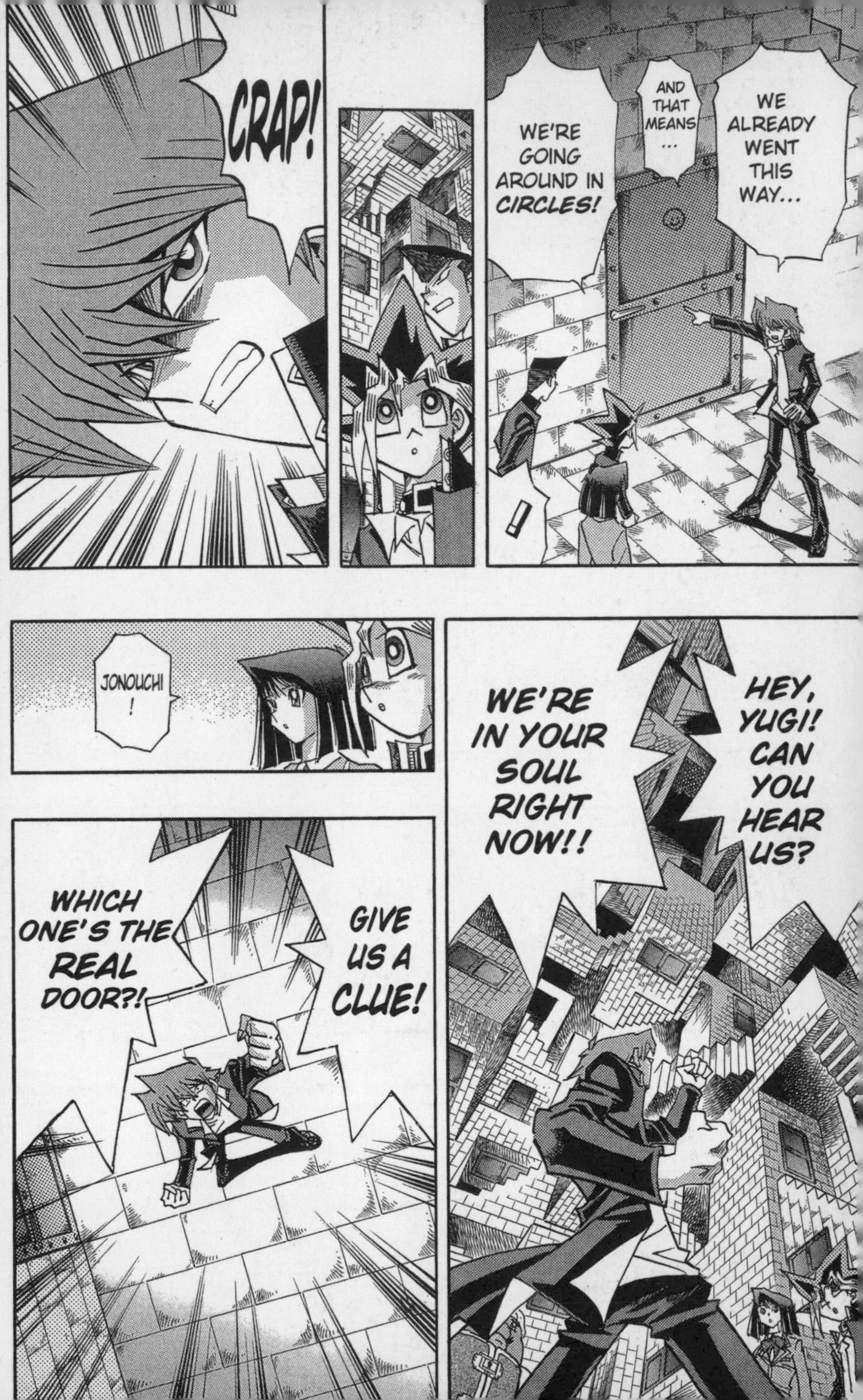
WE ALREADY WENT THIS WAY...
AND THAT MEANS...
WE'RE GOING AROUND IN CIRCLES!
!
CRAP!
HEY, YUGI! CAN YOU HEAR US?
WE'RE IN YOUR SOUL RIGHT NOW!!
JONOUCHI!
GIVE US A CLUE!
WHICH ONE'S THE REAL DOOR?!

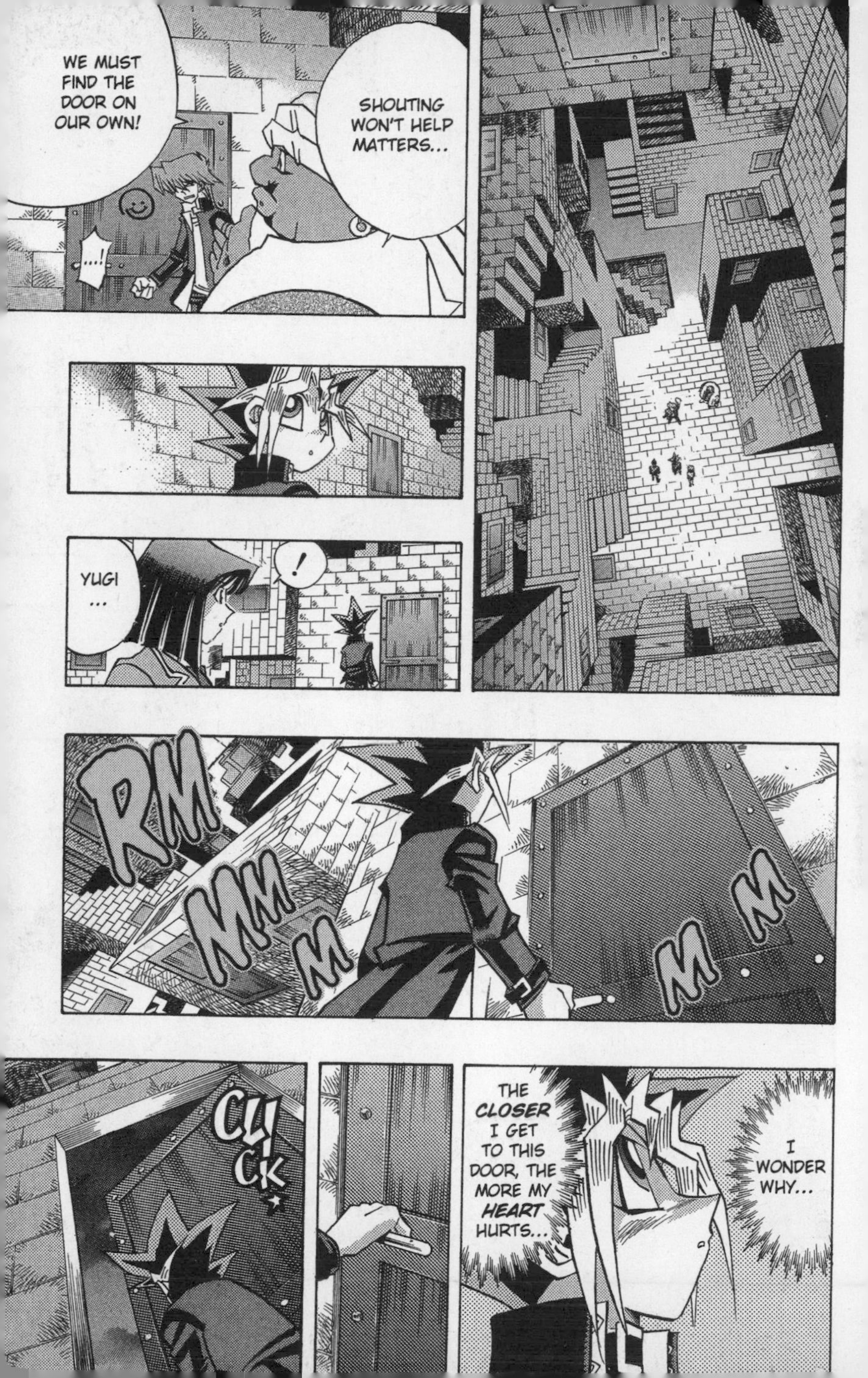
SHOUTING WON'T HELP MATTERS...
WE MUST FIND THE DOOR ON OUR OWN!
...!
!
YUGI ...
RMMMMMMM
THE CLOSER I GET TO THIS DOOR, THE MORE MY HEART HURTS...
I WONDER WHY...
CLICK

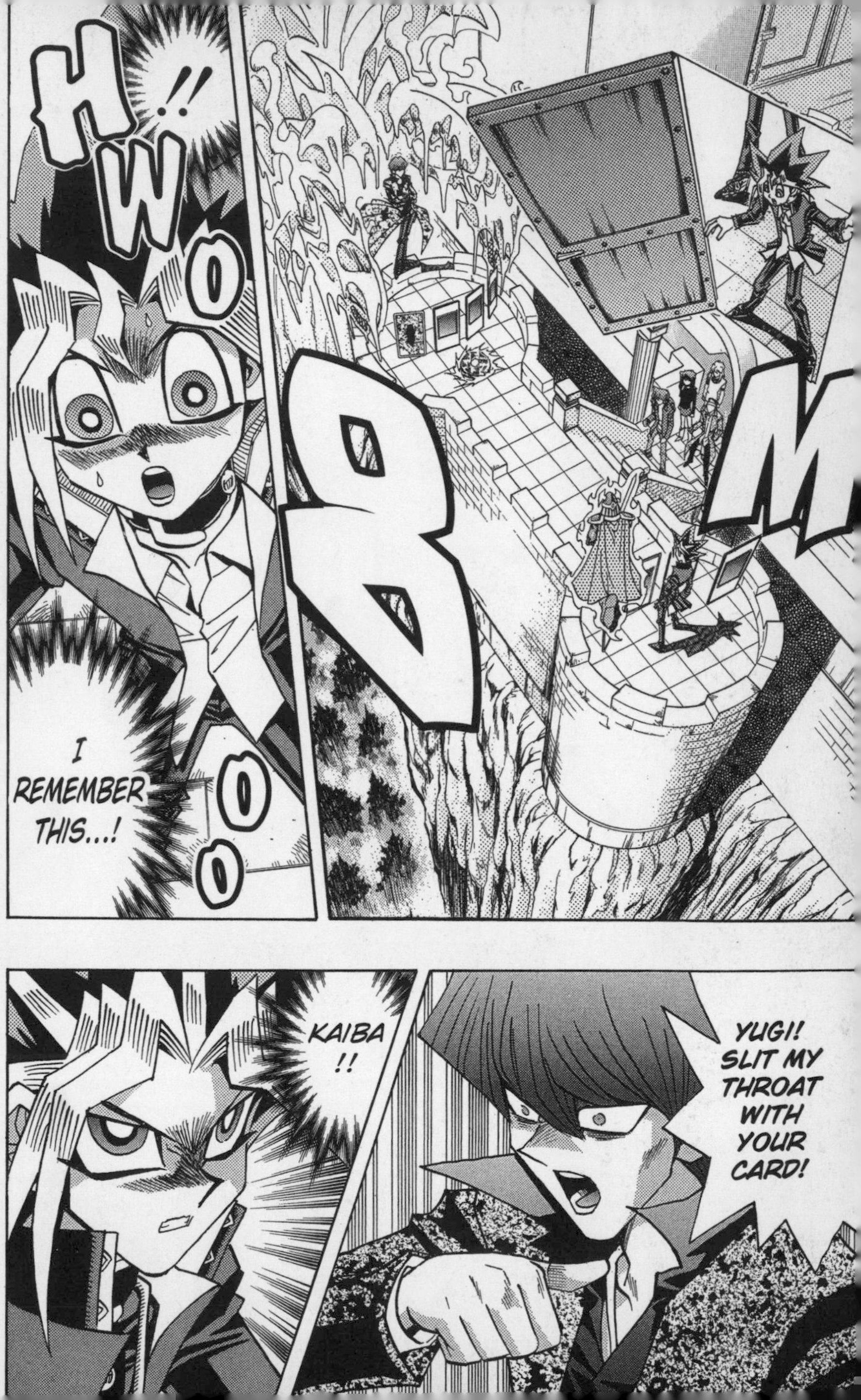
I REMEMBER THIS...!
YUGI! SLIT MY THROAT WITH YOUR CARD!
KAIBA!!

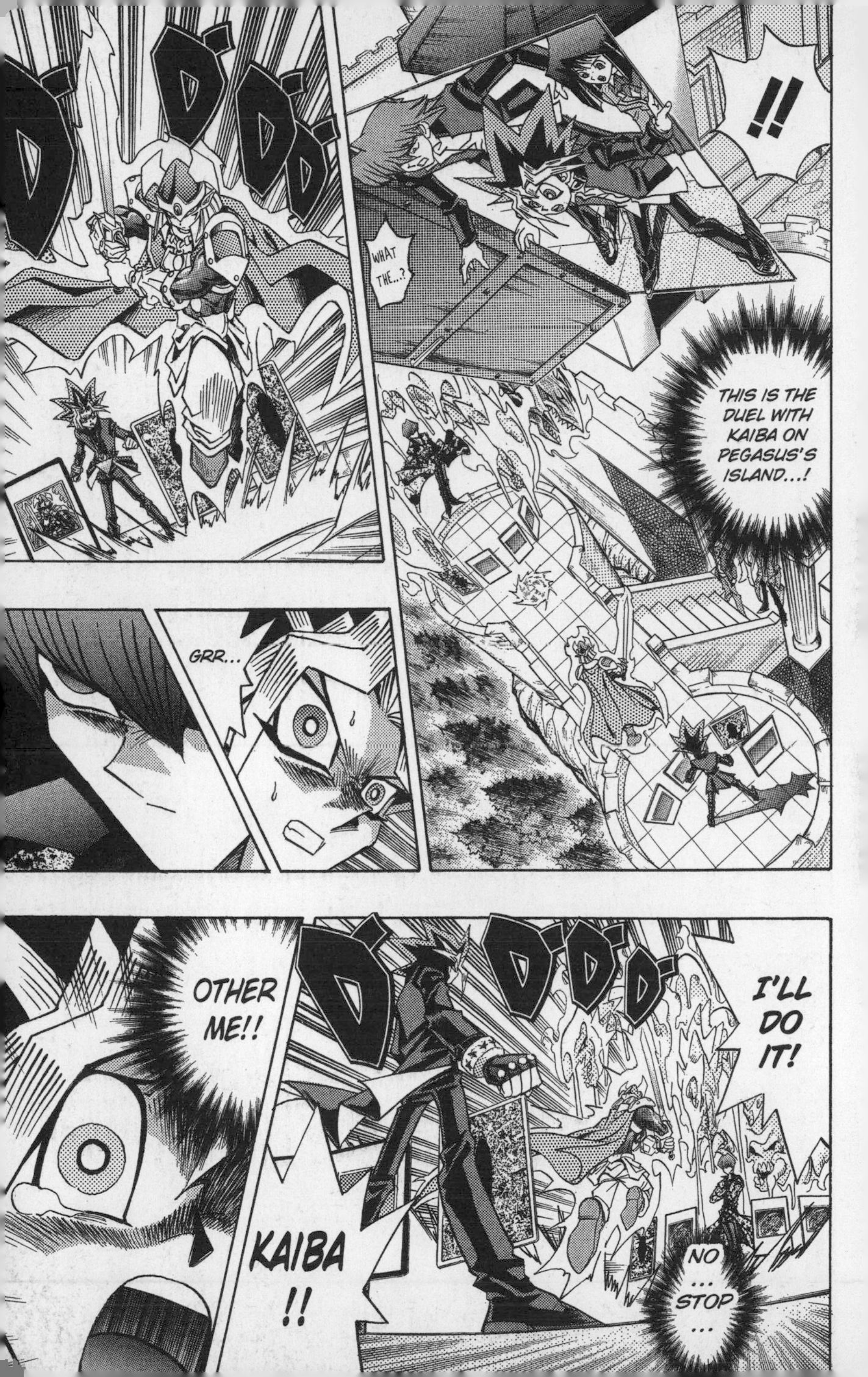
!!
WHAT THE...?
THIS IS THE DUEL WITH KAIBA ON PEGASUS'S ISLAND...!
DDDD
GRR...
I'LL DO IT!
DDDD
NO ... STOP ...
OTHER ME!!
KAIBA !!

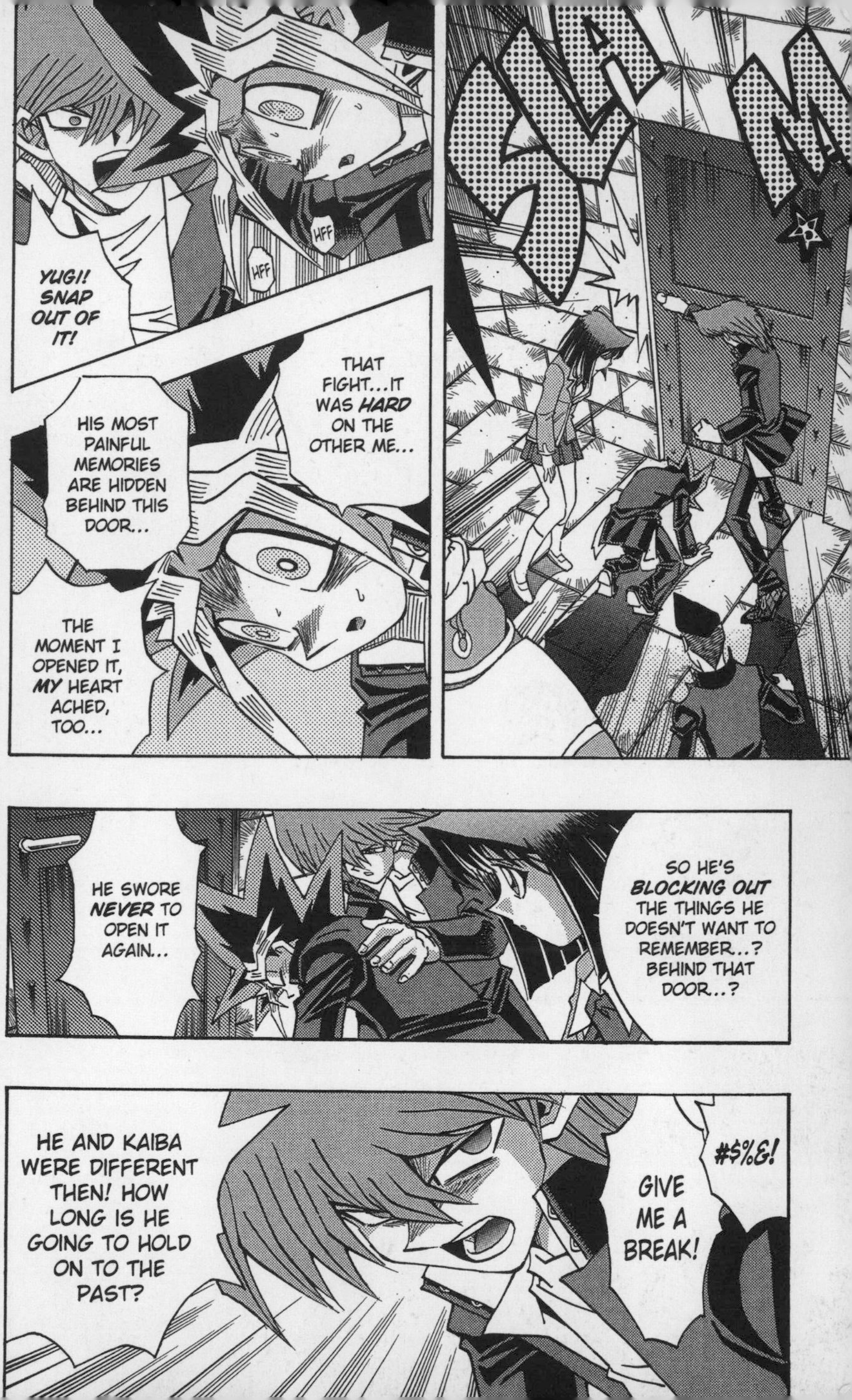
SLAM
YUGI! SNAP OUT OF IT!
HFF
HFF
THAT FIGHT...IT WAS **HARD** ON THE OTHER ME...
HIS MOST PAINFUL MEMORIES ARE HIDDEN BEHIND THIS DOOR...
THE MOMENT I OPENED IT, **MY** HEART ACHED, TOO...
SO HE'S **BLOCKING OUT** THE THINGS HE DOESN'T WANT TO REMEMBER..? BEHIND THAT DOOR..?
HE SWORE **NEVER** TO OPEN IT AGAIN...
#$%&!
GIVE ME A BREAK!
HE AND KAIBA WERE DIFFERENT THEN! HOW LONG IS HE GOING TO HOLD ON TO THE PAST?

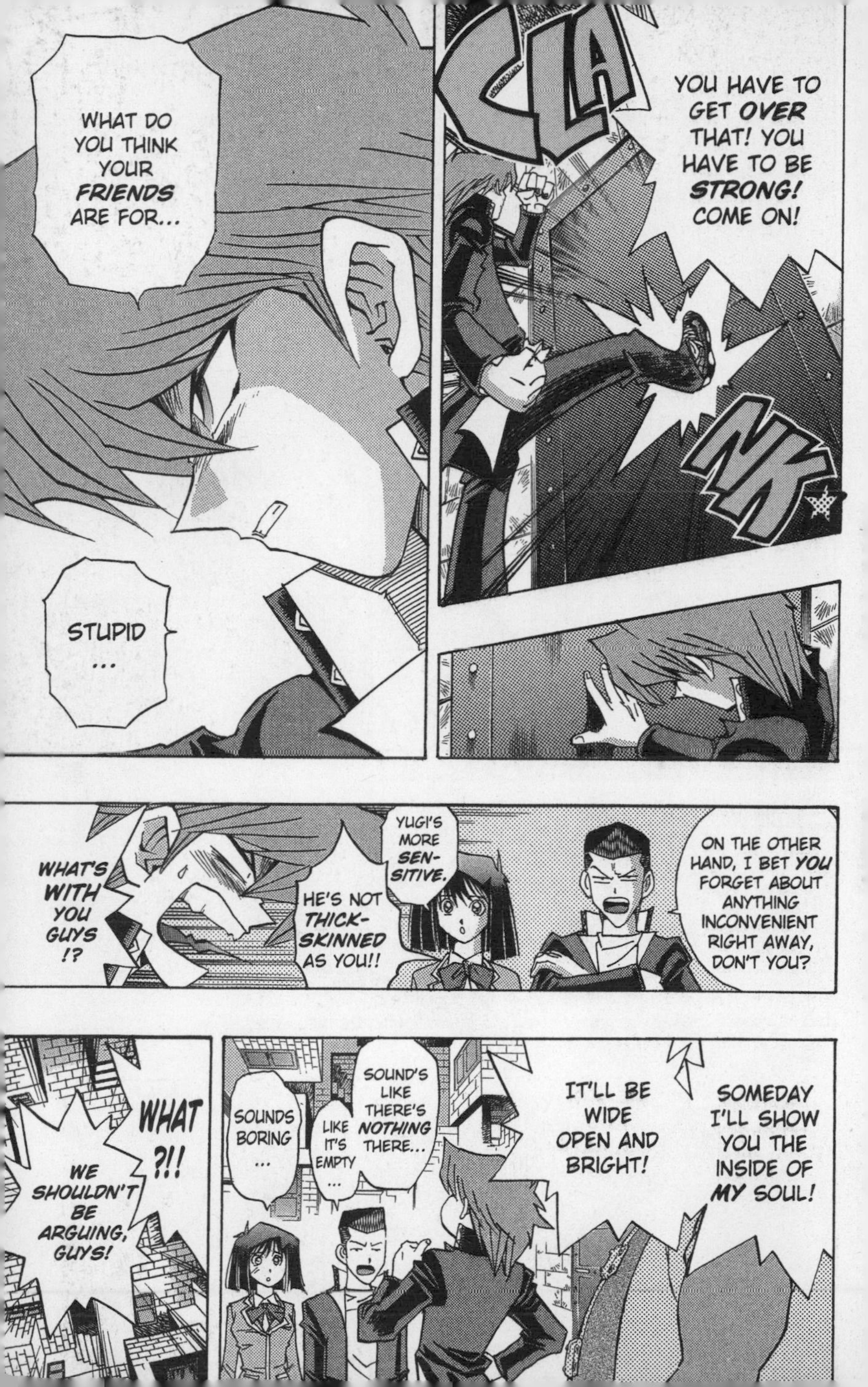
YOU HAVE TO GET OVER THAT! YOU HAVE TO BE STRONG! COME ON!
CLA
NK
WHAT DO YOU THINK YOUR FRIENDS ARE FOR...
STUPID ...
ON THE OTHER HAND, I BET YOU FORGET ABOUT ANYTHING INCONVENIENT RIGHT AWAY, DON'T YOU?
YUGI'S MORE SEN-SITIVE.
HE'S NOT THICK-SKINNED AS YOU!!
WHAT'S WITH YOU GUYS !?
SOMEDAY I'LL SHOW YOU THE INSIDE OF MY SOUL!
IT'LL BE WIDE OPEN AND BRIGHT!
SOUND'S LIKE THERE'S NOTHING THERE...
LIKE IT'S EMPTY ...
SOUNDS BORING ...
WHAT ?!!
WE SHOULDN'T BE ARGUING, GUYS!

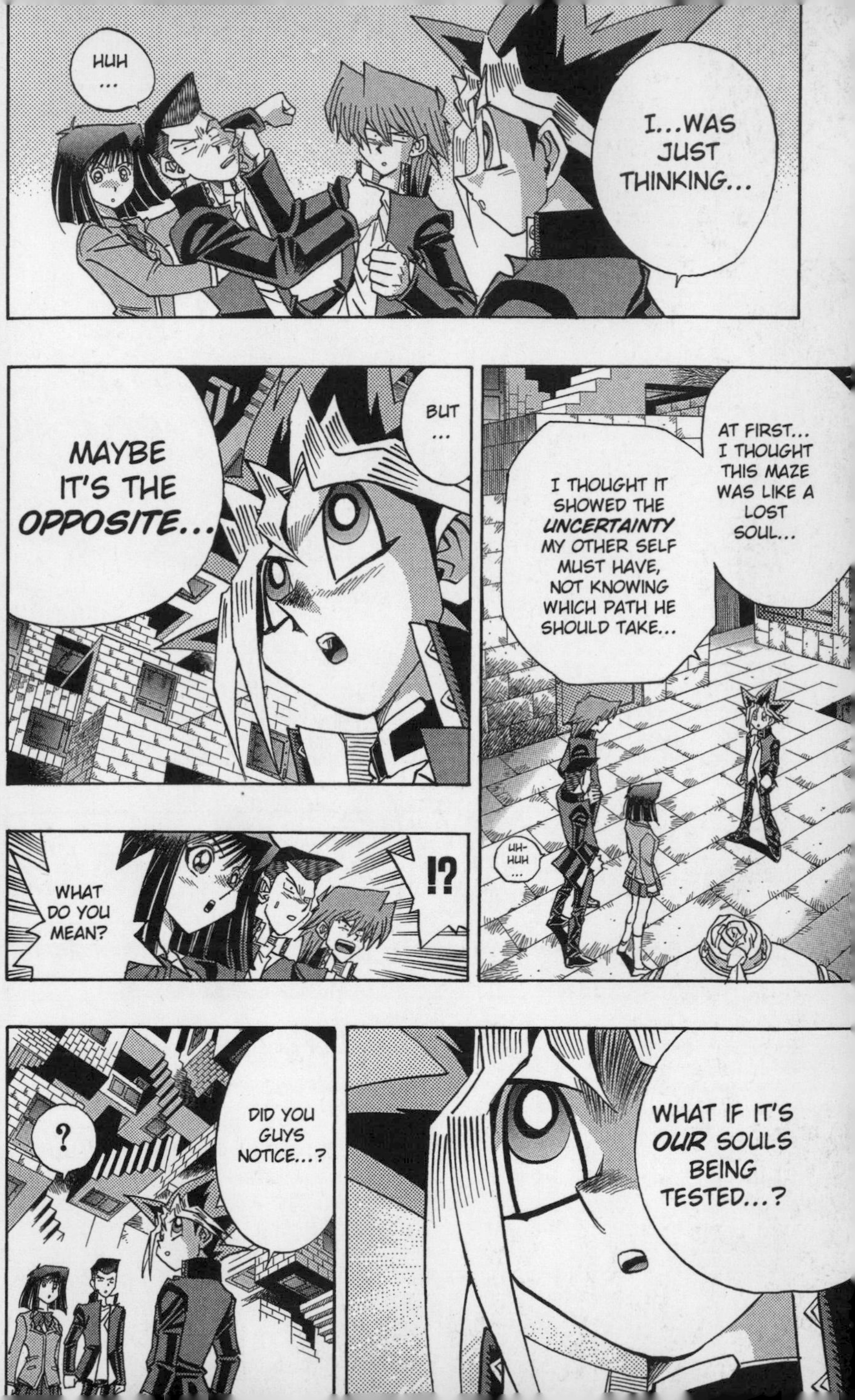
I...WAS JUST THINKING...
HUH ...
AT FIRST... I THOUGHT THIS MAZE WAS LIKE A LOST SOUL...
I THOUGHT IT SHOWED THE UNCERTAINTY MY OTHER SELF MUST HAVE, NOT KNOWING WHICH PATH HE SHOULD TAKE...
UH-HUH ...
BUT ...
MAYBE IT'S THE OPPOSITE...
!?
WHAT DO YOU MEAN?
WHAT IF IT'S OUR SOULS BEING TESTED...?
DID YOU GUYS NOTICE...?
?

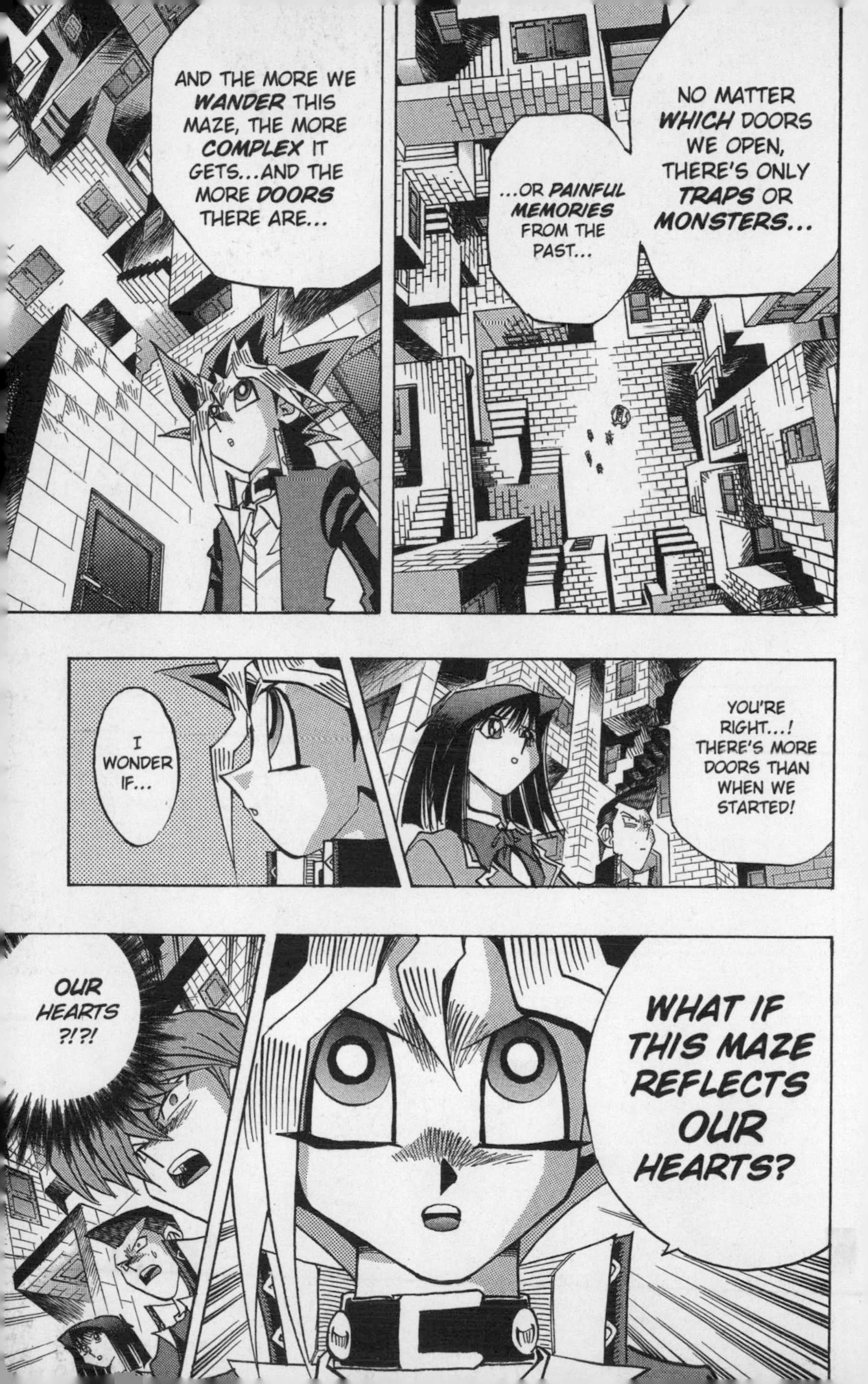
NO MATTER WHICH DOORS WE OPEN, THERE'S ONLY TRAPS OR MONSTERS...
...OR PAINFUL MEMORIES FROM THE PAST...
AND THE MORE WE WANDER THIS MAZE, THE MORE COMPLEX IT GETS...AND THE MORE DOORS THERE ARE...
YOU'RE RIGHT...! THERE'S MORE DOORS THAN WHEN WE STARTED!
I WONDER IF...
WHAT IF THIS MAZE REFLECTS OUR HEARTS?
OUR HEARTS ?!?!

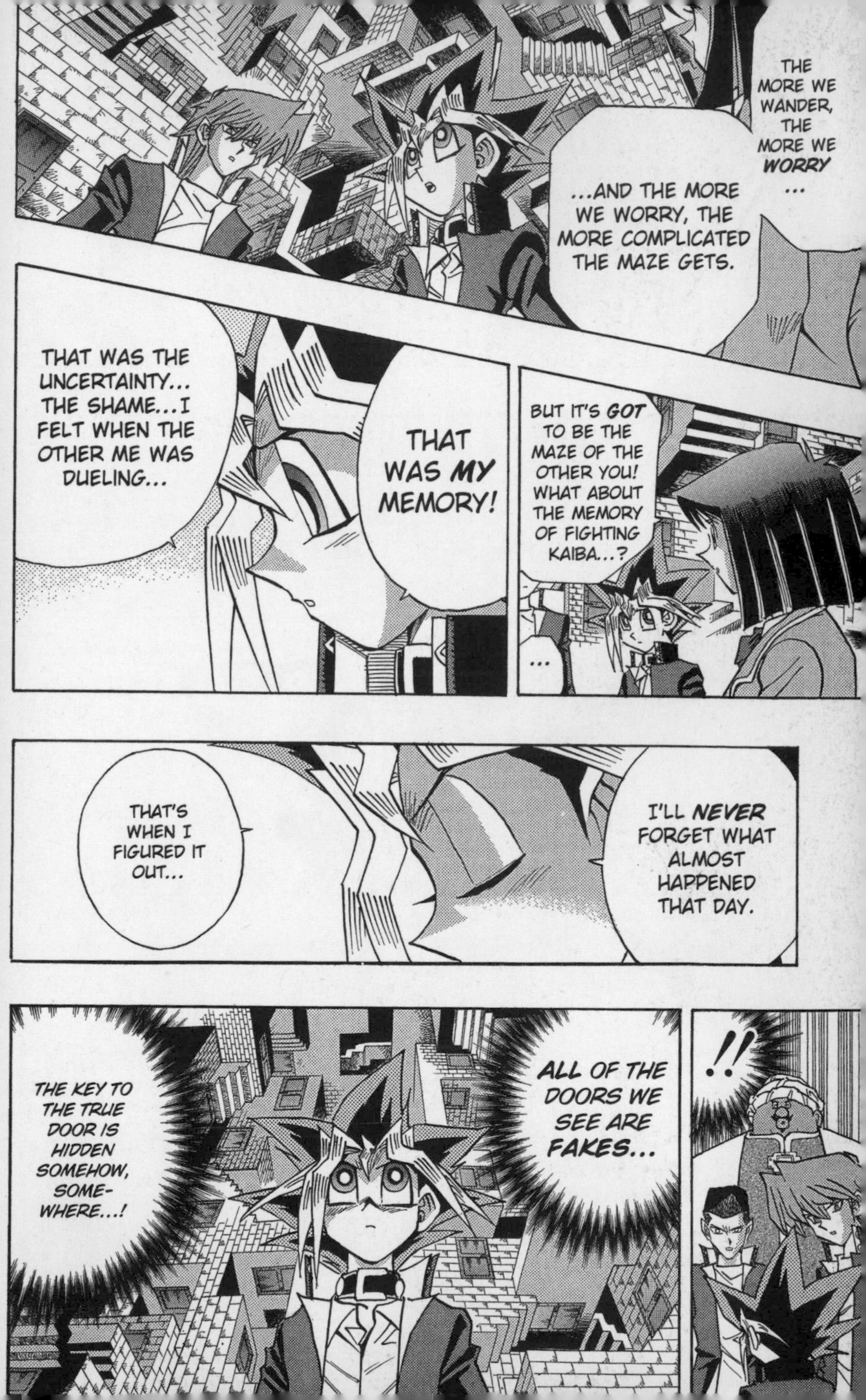
THE MORE WE WANDER, THE MORE WE WORRY...
...AND THE MORE WE WORRY, THE MORE COMPLICATED THE MAZE GETS.
BUT IT'S GOT TO BE THE MAZE OF THE OTHER YOU! WHAT ABOUT THE MEMORY OF FIGHTING KAIBA...?
...
THAT WAS MY MEMORY!
THAT WAS THE UNCERTAINTY... THE SHAME...I FELT WHEN THE OTHER ME WAS DUELING...
I'LL NEVER FORGET WHAT ALMOST HAPPENED THAT DAY.
THAT'S WHEN I FIGURED IT OUT...
!!
ALL OF THE DOORS WE SEE ARE FAKES...
THE KEY TO THE TRUE DOOR IS HIDDEN SOMEHOW, SOME-WHERE...!

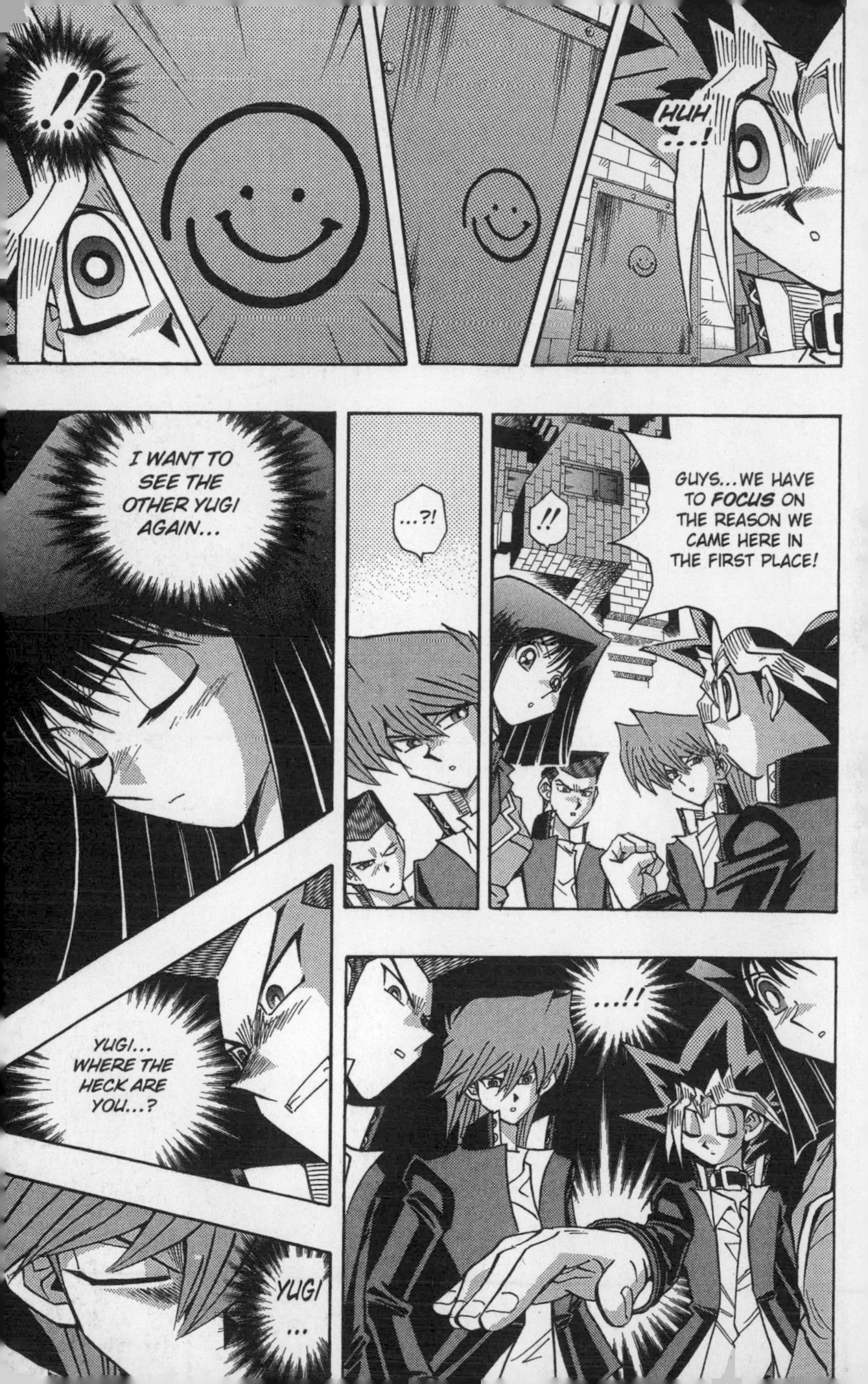
HUH ...!
!!
GUYS... WE HAVE TO FOCUS ON THE REASON WE CAME HERE IN THE FIRST PLACE!
!!
...?!
...!!
I WANT TO SEE THE OTHER YUGI AGAIN...
YUGI... WHERE THE HECK ARE YOU...?
YUGI ...

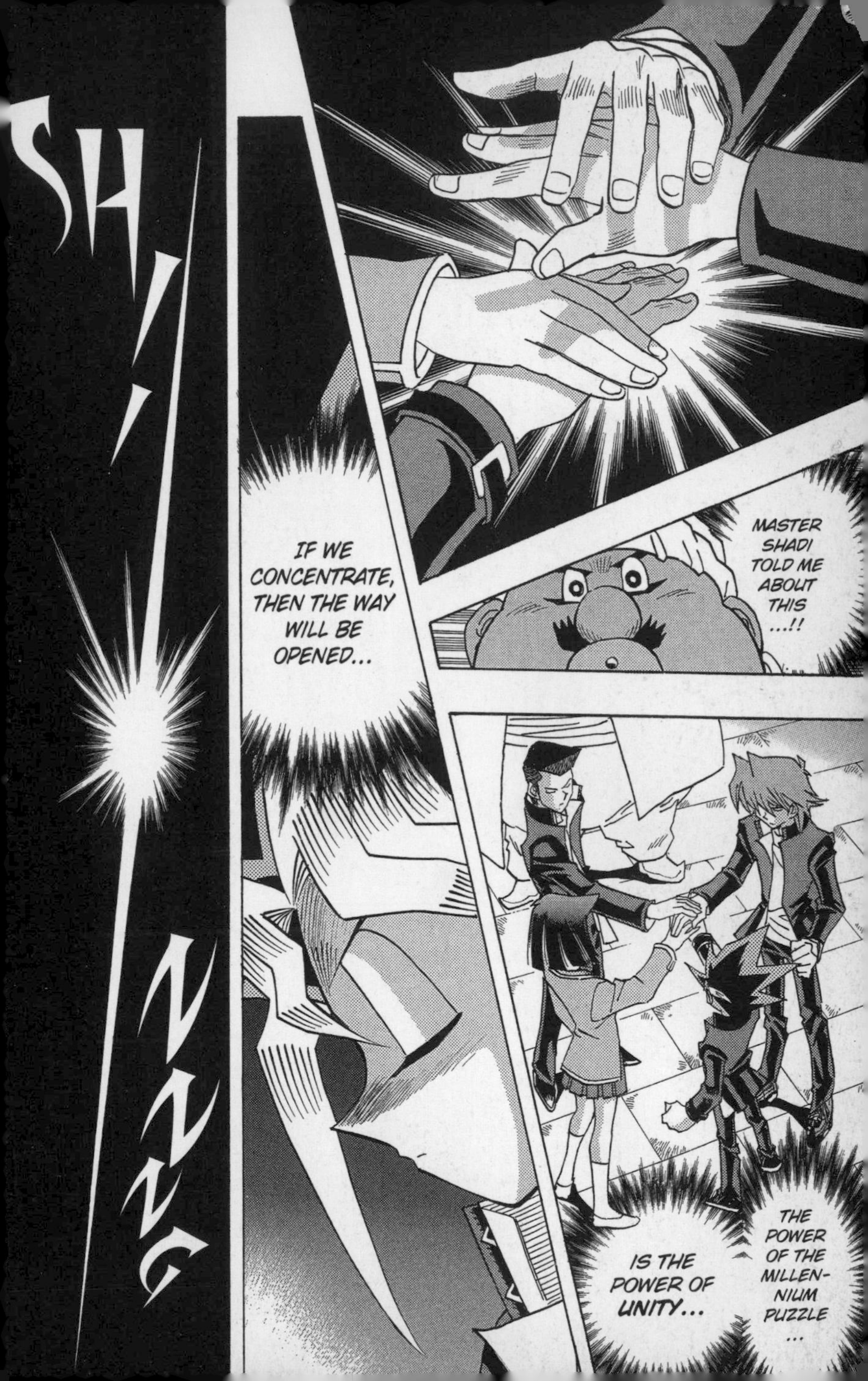
MASTER SHADI TOLD ME ABOUT THIS ...!!
IF WE CONCENTRATE, THEN THE WAY WILL BE OPENED...
THE POWER OF THE MILLEN-NIUM PUZZLE ...
IS THE POWER OF UNITY...
SHIIIINNNG

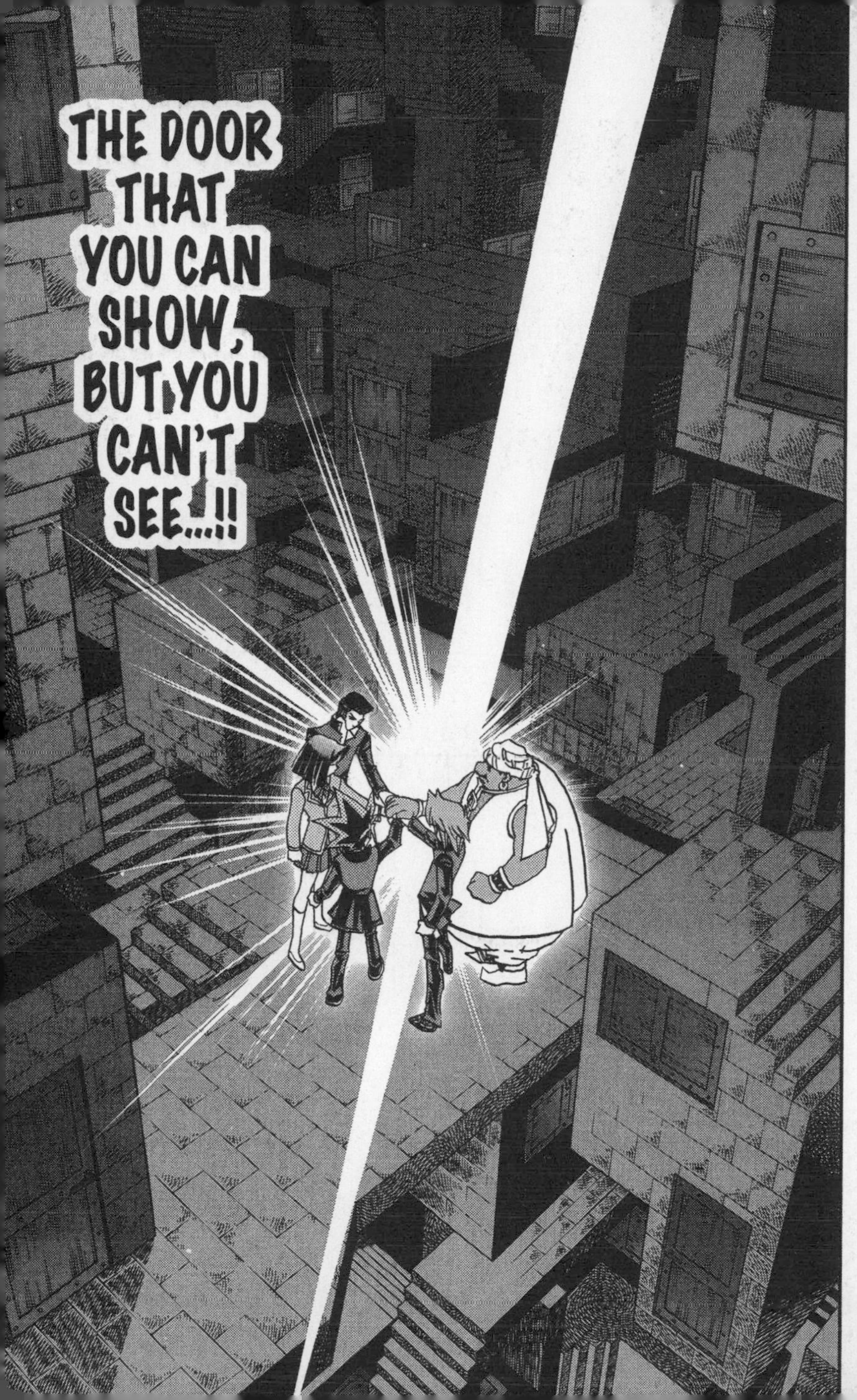
THE DOOR THAT YOU CAN SHOW, BUT YOU CAN'T SEE...!!

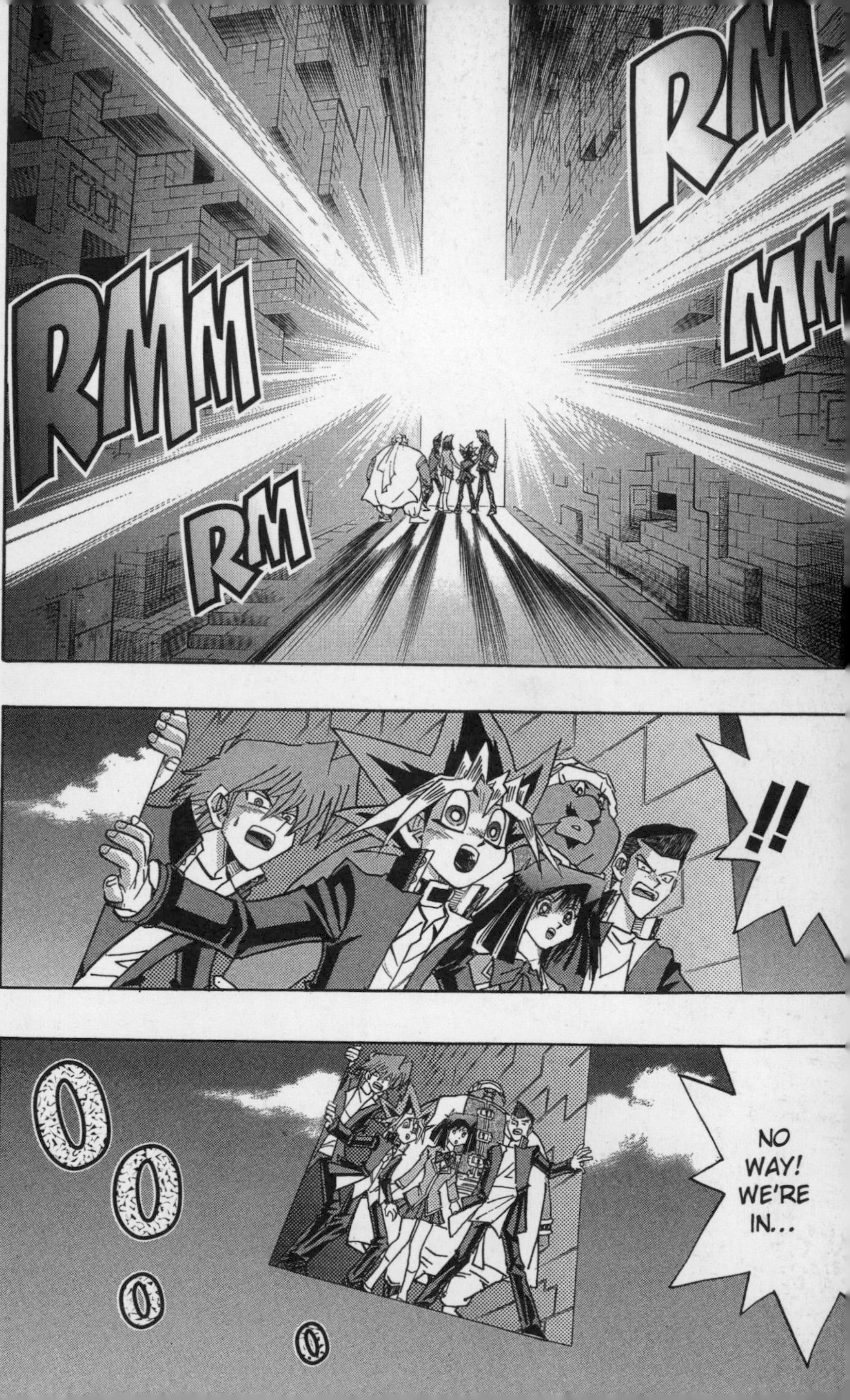

RM
MM
RMM
RM
!!
NO WAY! WE'RE IN...

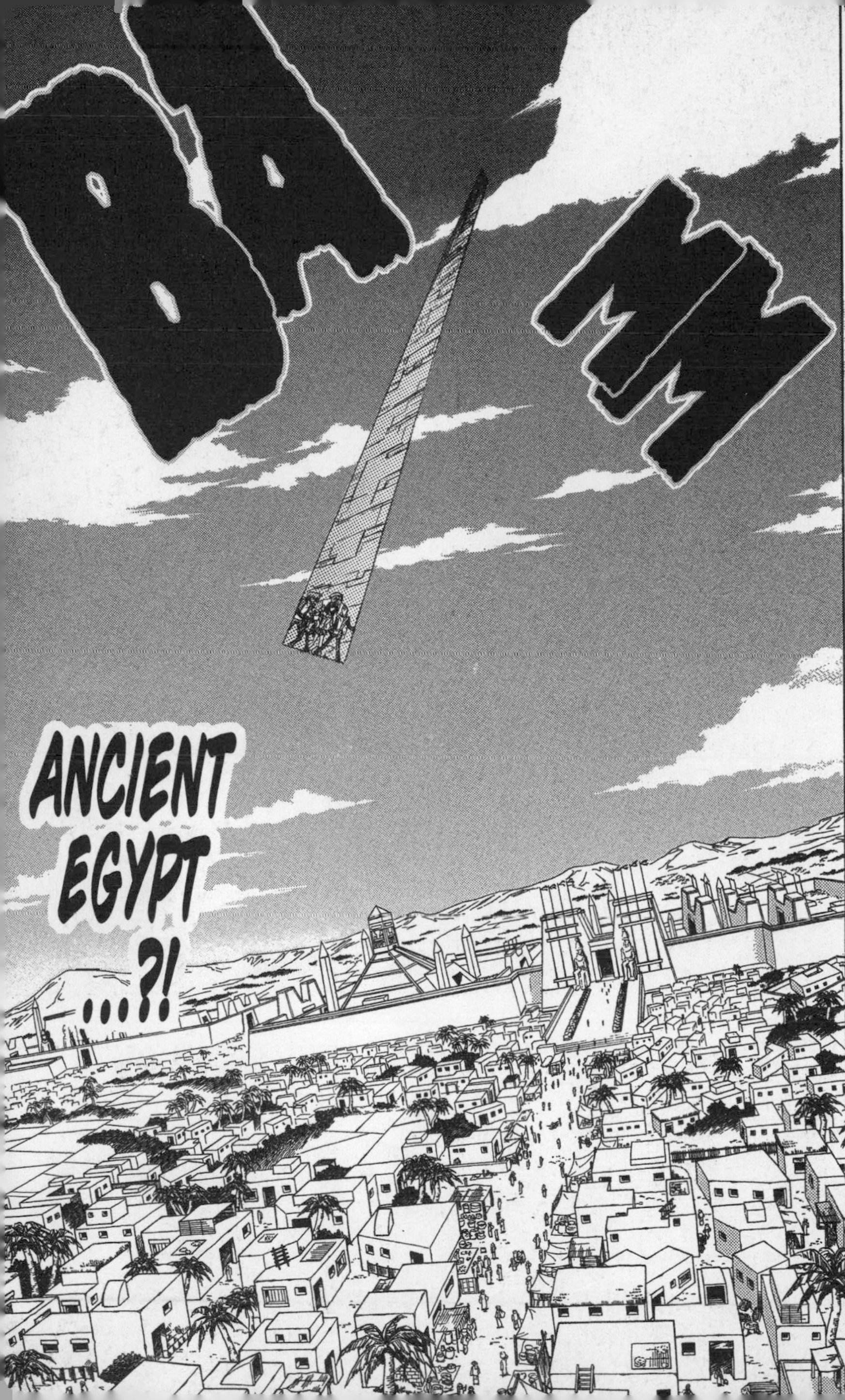
BAMM
ANCIENT EGYPT ...?!

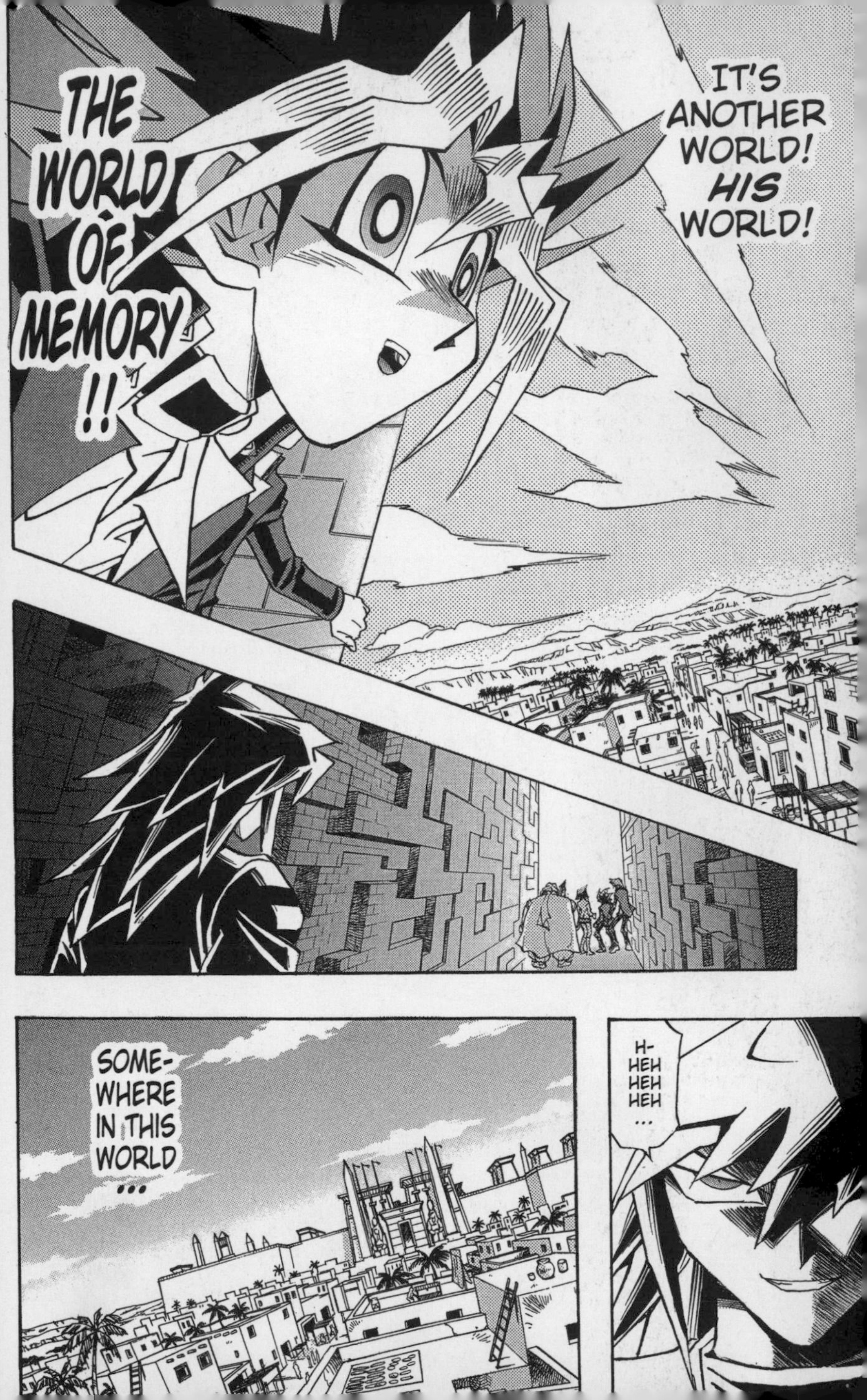
IT'S ANOTHER WORLD! HIS WORLD!
THE WORLD OF MEMORY!!
H-HEH HEH HEH...
SOME-WHERE IN THIS WORLD...

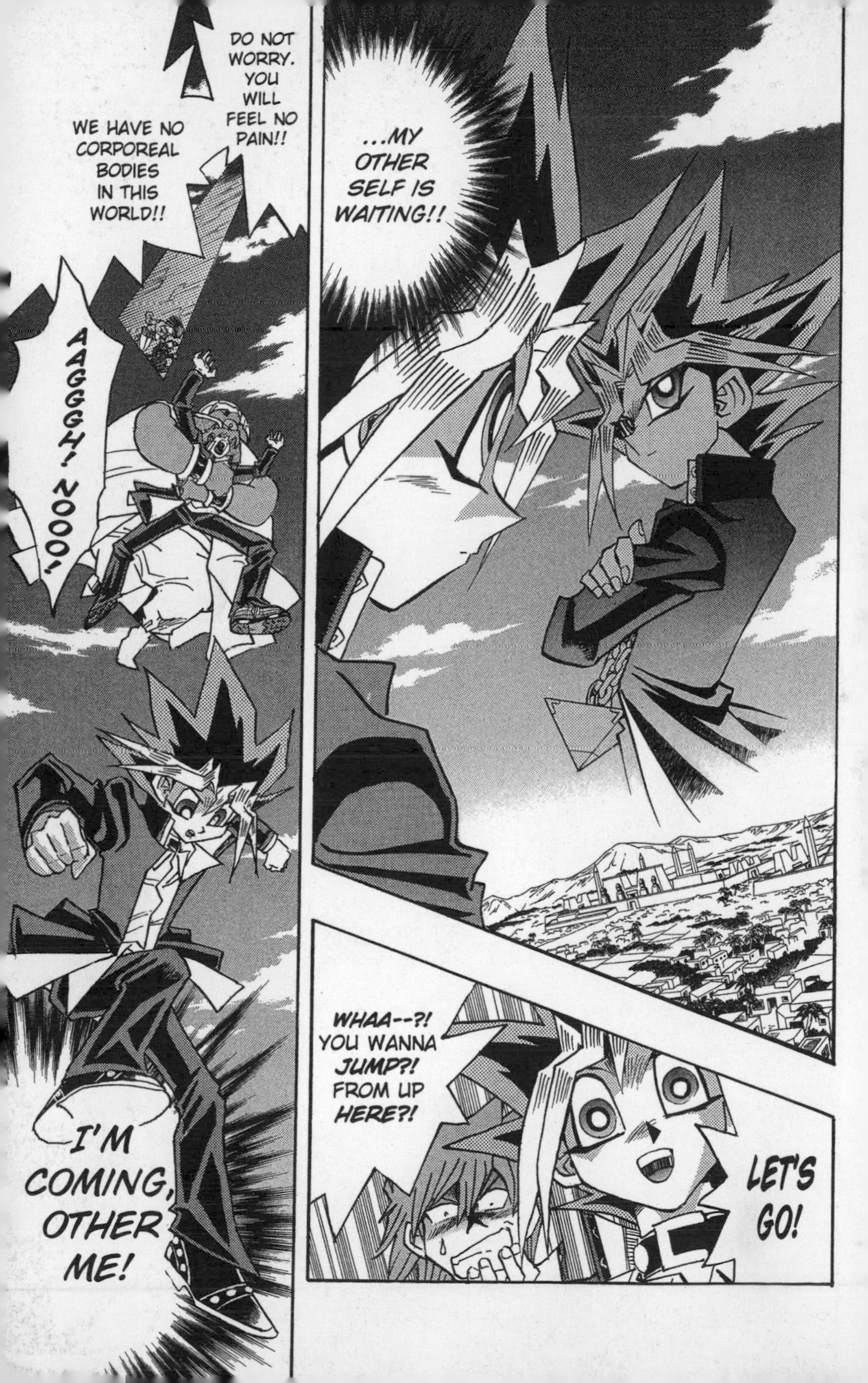
...MY OTHER SELF IS WAITING!!
LET'S GO!
WHAA--?! YOU WANNA JUMP?! FROM UP HERE?!
DO NOT WORRY. YOU WILL FEEL NO PAIN!!
WE HAVE NO CORPOREAL BODIES IN THIS WORLD!!
AAGGGH! NOOO!
I'M COMING, OTHER ME!

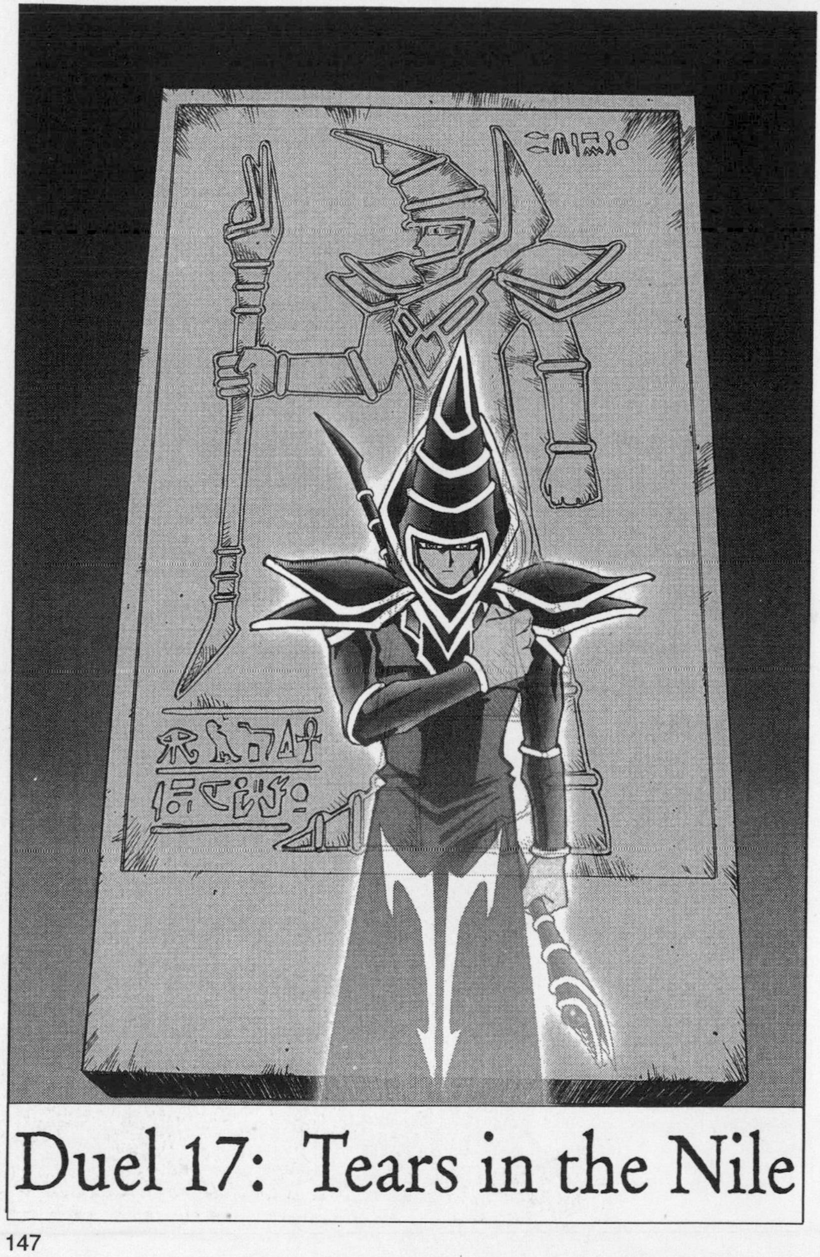

Duel 17: Tears in the Nile

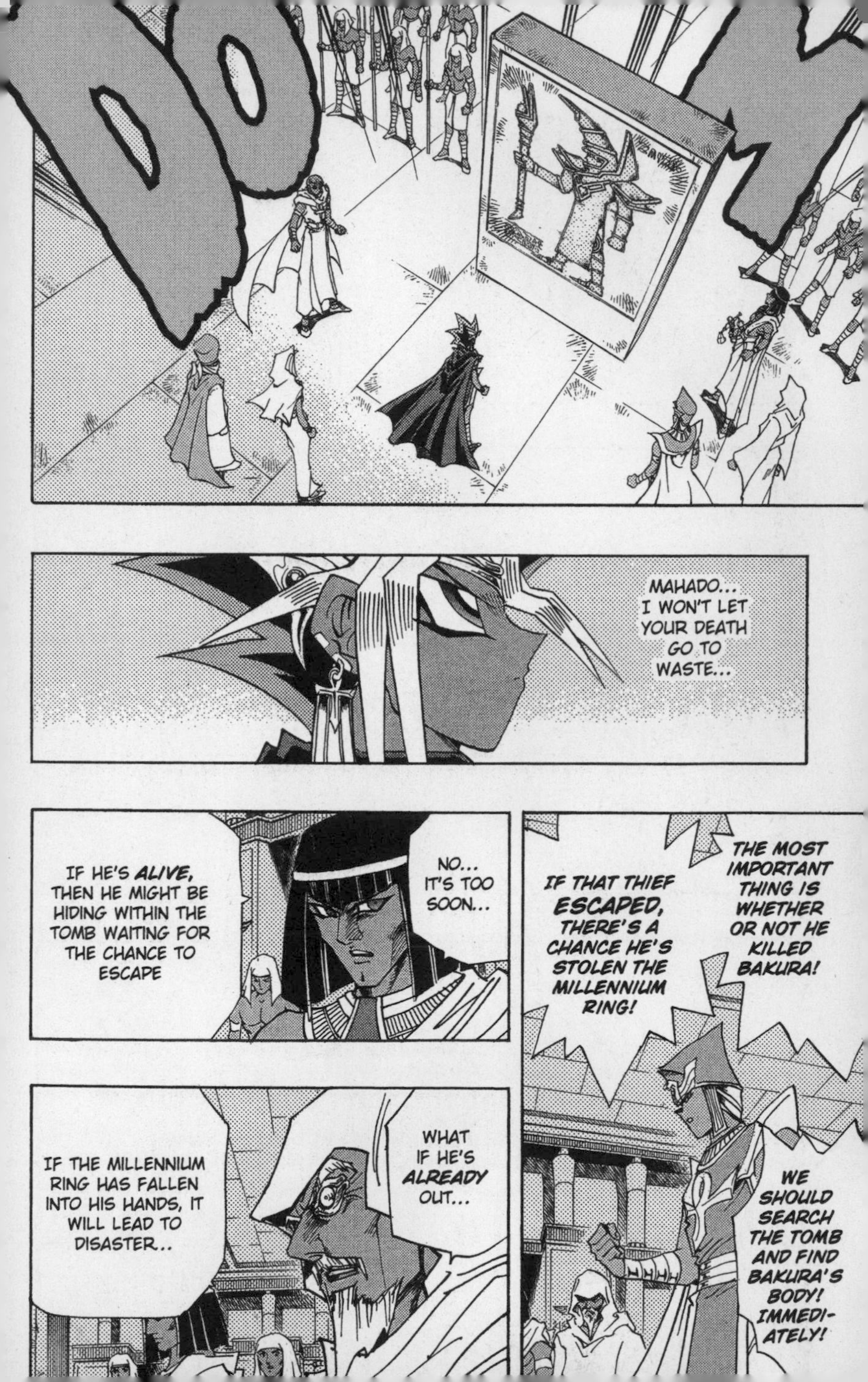
MAHADO... I WON'T LET YOUR DEATH GO TO WASTE...
THE MOST IMPORTANT THING IS WHETHER OR NOT HE KILLED BAKURA!
IF THAT THIEF ESCAPED, THERE'S A CHANCE HE'S STOLEN THE MILLENNIUM RING!
WE SHOULD SEARCH THE TOMB AND FIND BAKURA'S BODY! IMMEDI-ATELY!
NO... IT'S TOO SOON...
IF HE'S ALIVE, THEN HE MIGHT BE HIDING WITHIN THE TOMB WAITING FOR THE CHANCE TO ESCAPE
WHAT IF HE'S ALREADY OUT...
IF THE MILLENNIUM RING HAS FALLEN INTO HIS HANDS, IT WILL LEAD TO DISASTER...

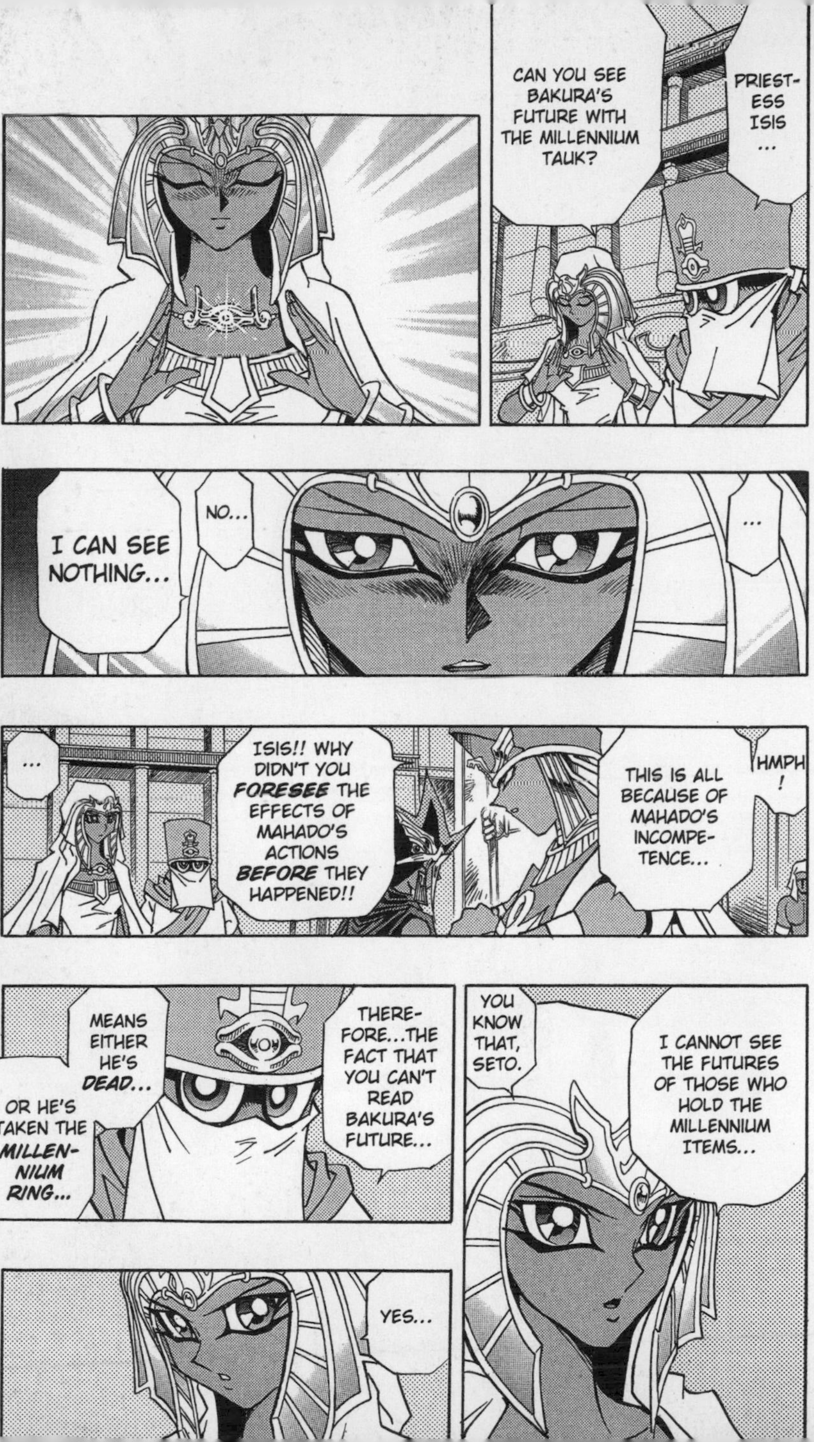
PRIEST-ESS ISIS...
CAN YOU SEE BAKURA'S FUTURE WITH THE MILLENNIUM TAUK?
...
NO...
I CAN SEE NOTHING...
HMPH!
THIS IS ALL BECAUSE OF MAHADO'S INCOMPETENCE...
ISIS!! WHY DIDN'T YOU FORESEE THE EFFECTS OF MAHADO'S ACTIONS BEFORE THEY HAPPENED!!
...
I CANNOT SEE THE FUTURES OF THOSE WHO HOLD THE MILLENNIUM ITEMS...
YOU KNOW THAT, SETO.
THERE-FORE...THE FACT THAT YOU CAN'T READ BAKURA'S FUTURE...
MEANS EITHER HE'S DEAD...
OR HE'S TAKEN THE MILLEN-NIUM RING...
YES...

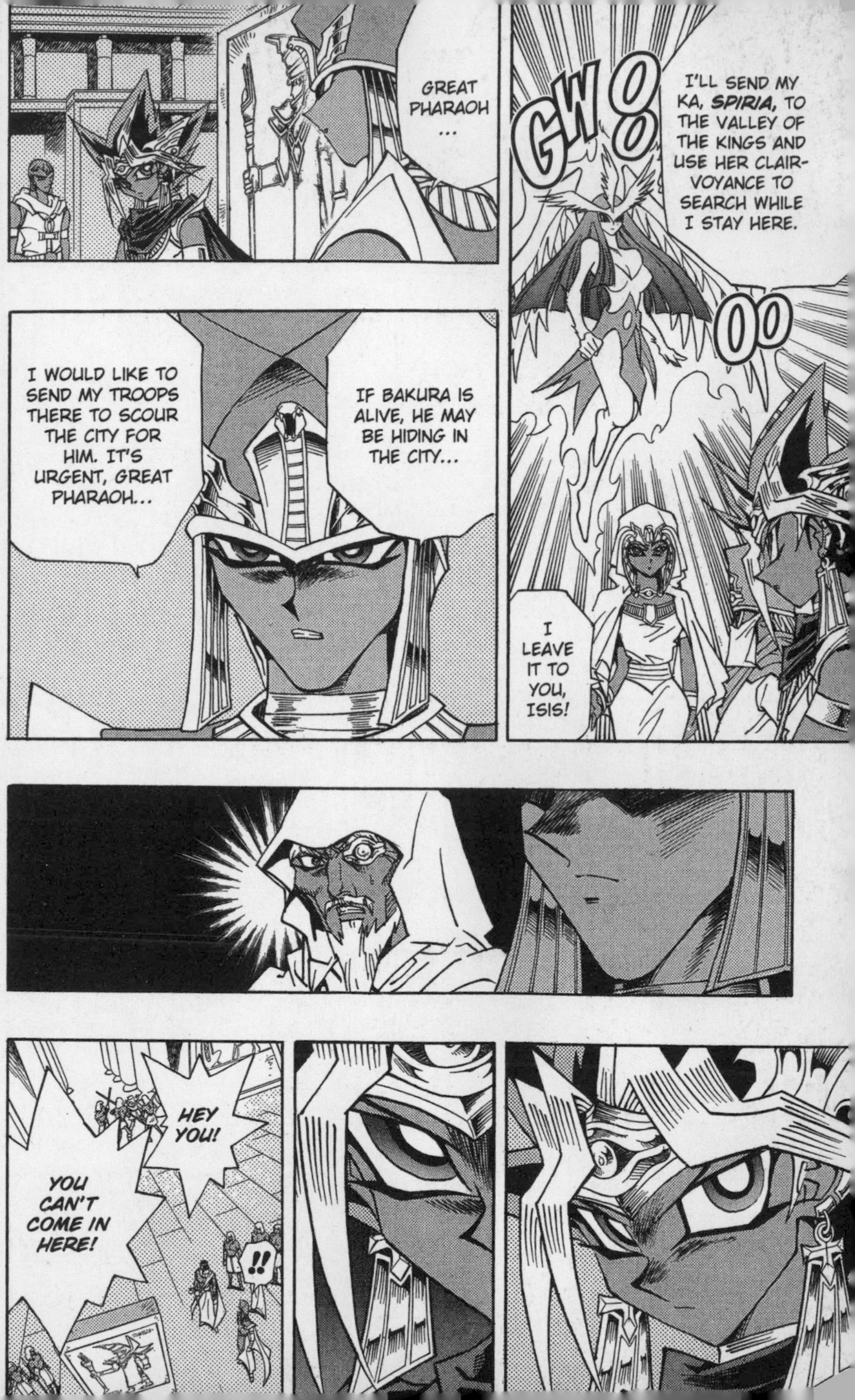
GWO
I'LL SEND MY KA, SPIRIA, TO THE VALLEY OF THE KINGS AND USE HER CLAIR-VOYANCE TO SEARCH WHILE I STAY HERE.
OO
I LEAVE IT TO YOU, ISIS!
GREAT PHARAOH ...
IF BAKURA IS ALIVE, HE MAY BE HIDING IN THE CITY...
I WOULD LIKE TO SEND MY TROOPS THERE TO SCOUR THE CITY FOR HIM. IT'S URGENT, GREAT PHARAOH...
HEY YOU!
YOU CAN'T COME IN HERE!
!!

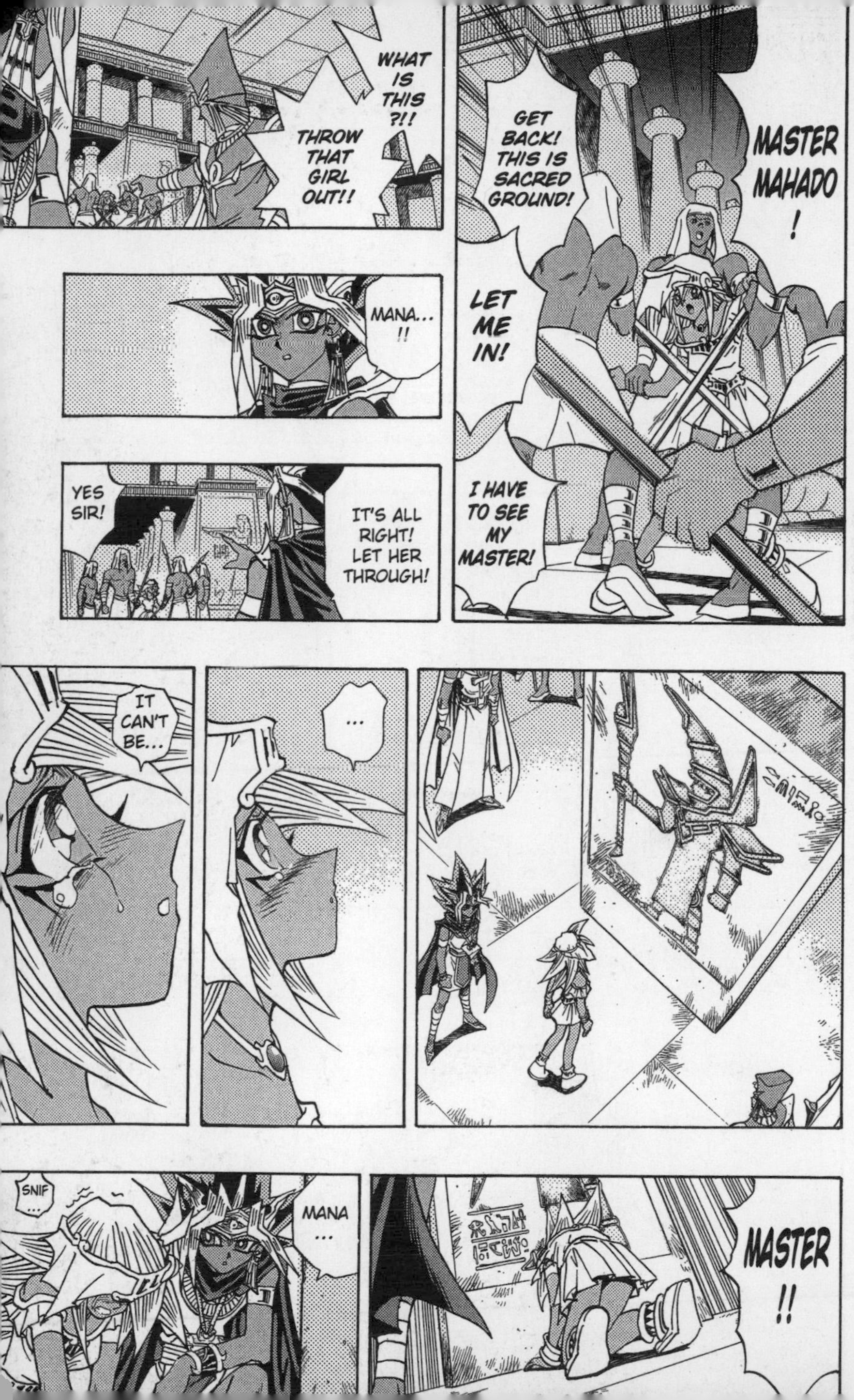
MASTER MAHADO!
GET BACK! THIS IS SACRED GROUND!
LET ME IN!
I HAVE TO SEE MY MASTER!
WHAT IS THIS?!!
THROW THAT GIRL OUT!!
MANA...!!
IT'S ALL RIGHT! LET HER THROUGH!
YES SIR!
...
IT CAN'T BE...
MASTER!!
MANA...
SNIF...

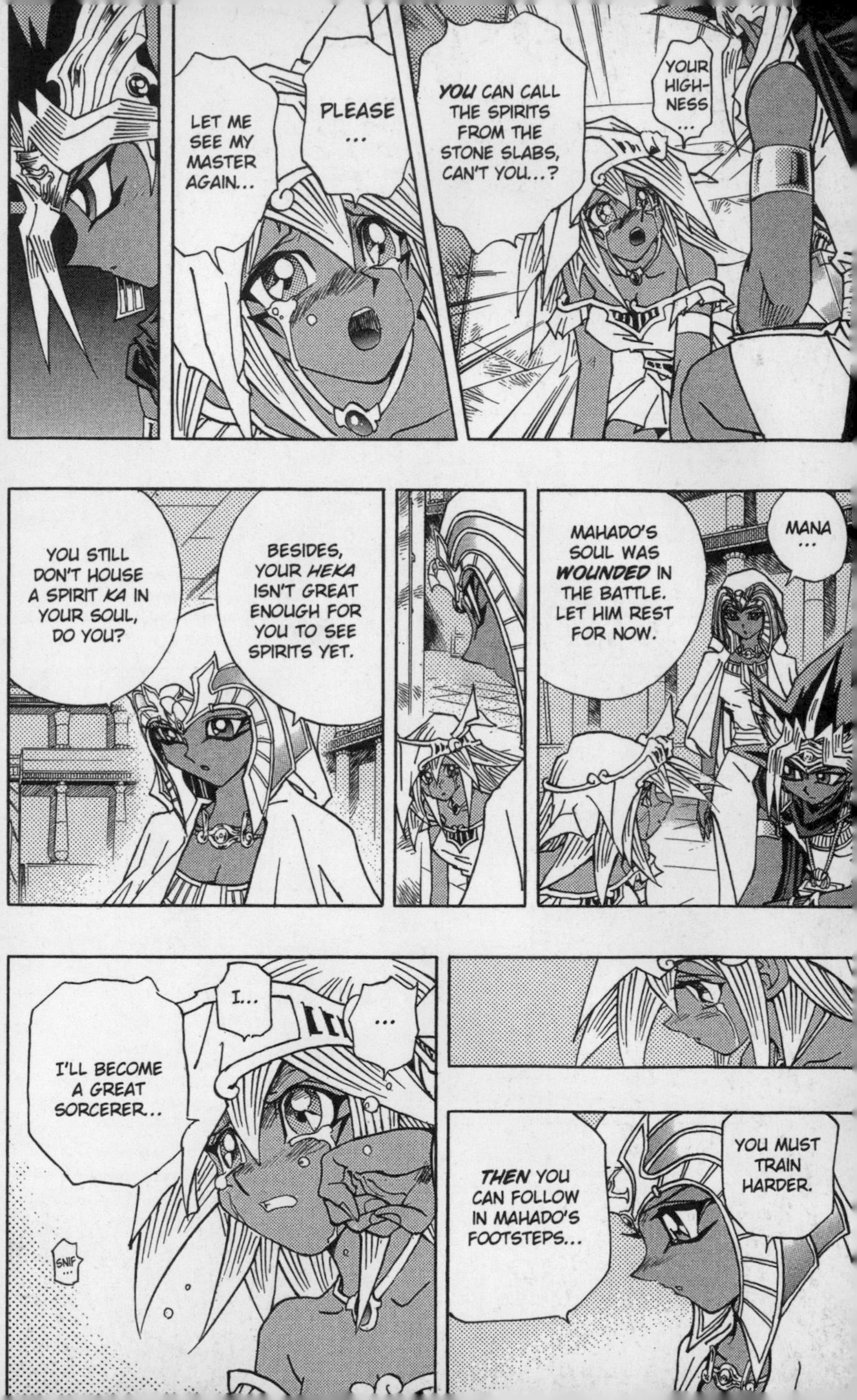
YOUR HIGH-NESS ...
YOU CAN CALL THE SPIRITS FROM THE STONE SLABS, CAN'T YOU...?
PLEASE ...
LET ME SEE MY MASTER AGAIN...
MANA ...
MAHADO'S SOUL WAS WOUNDED IN THE BATTLE. LET HIM REST FOR NOW.
YOU STILL DON'T HOUSE A SPIRIT KA IN YOUR SOUL, DO YOU?
BESIDES, YOUR HEKA ISN'T GREAT ENOUGH FOR YOU TO SEE SPIRITS YET.
YOU MUST TRAIN HARDER.
THEN YOU CAN FOLLOW IN MAHADO'S FOOTSTEPS...
...
I...
I'LL BECOME A GREAT SORCERER...
SNIF ...

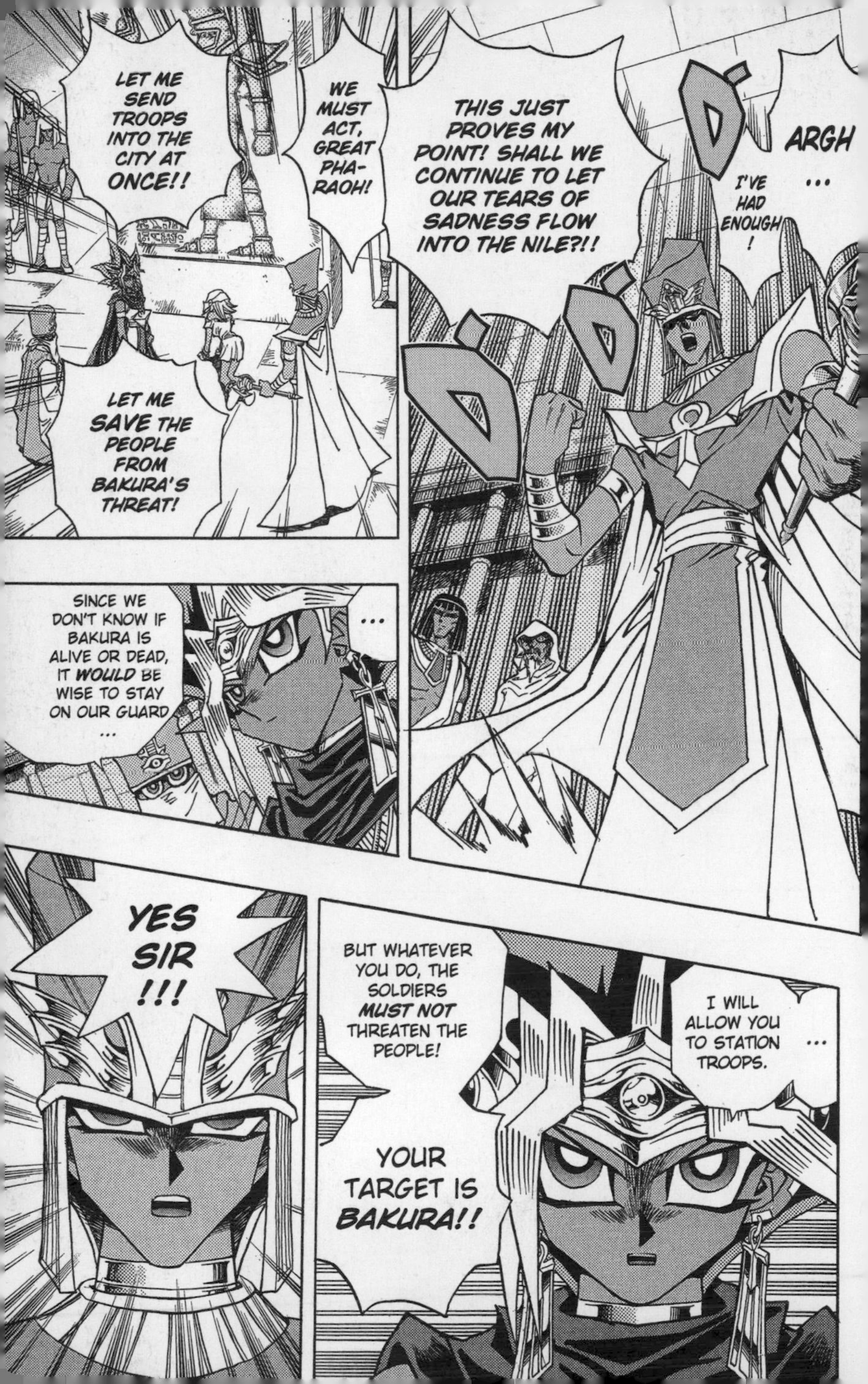
ARGH ...
I'VE HAD ENOUGH!
THIS JUST PROVES MY POINT! SHALL WE CONTINUE TO LET OUR TEARS OF SADNESS FLOW INTO THE NILE?!!
WE MUST ACT, GREAT PHA-RAOH!
LET ME SEND TROOPS INTO THE CITY AT ONCE!!
LET ME SAVE THE PEOPLE FROM BAKURA'S THREAT!
...
SINCE WE DON'T KNOW IF BAKURA IS ALIVE OR DEAD, IT WOULD BE WISE TO STAY ON OUR GUARD ...
I WILL ALLOW YOU TO STATION TROOPS. ...
BUT WHATEVER YOU DO, THE SOLDIERS MUST NOT THREATEN THE PEOPLE!
YOUR TARGET IS BAKURA!!
YES SIR!!!

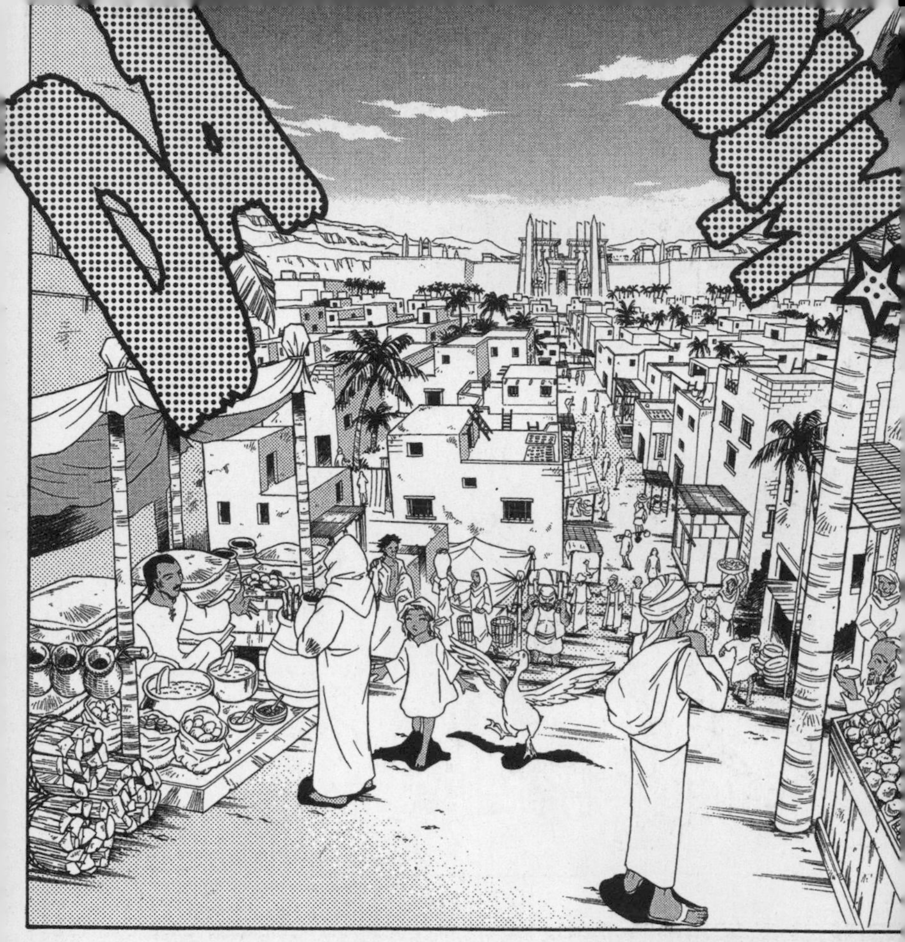

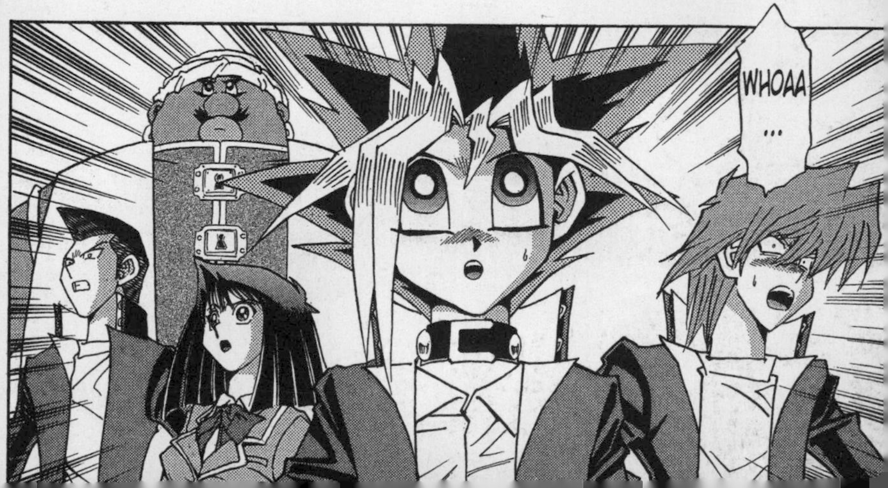
WHOAA ...

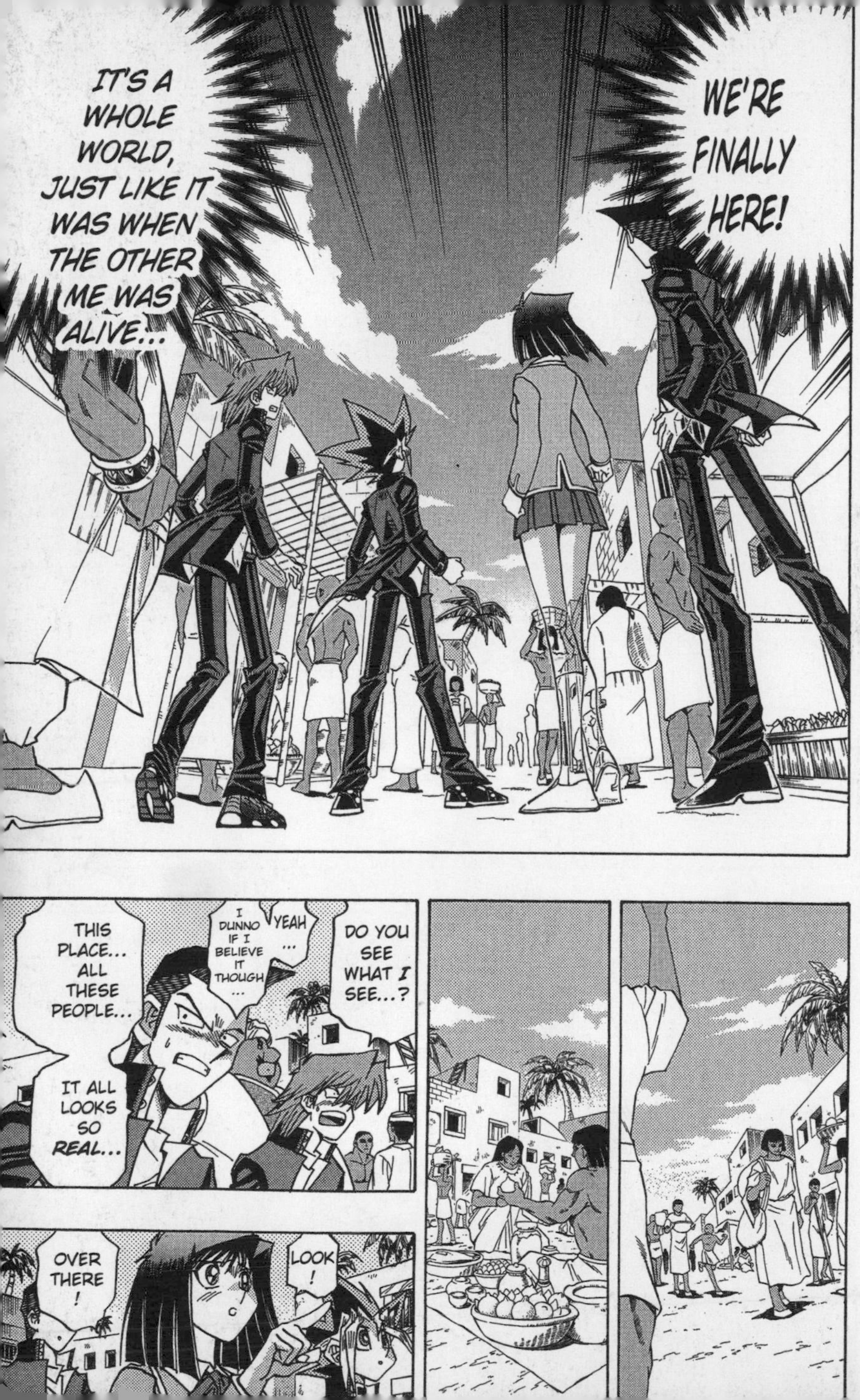

WE'RE FINALLY HERE!
IT'S A WHOLE WORLD, JUST LIKE IT WAS WHEN THE OTHER ME WAS ALIVE...
DO YOU SEE WHAT *I* SEE...?
YEAH...
I DUNNO IF I BELIEVE IT THOUGH...
THIS PLACE... ALL THESE PEOPLE...
IT ALL LOOKS SO *REAL*...
LOOK!
OVER THERE!

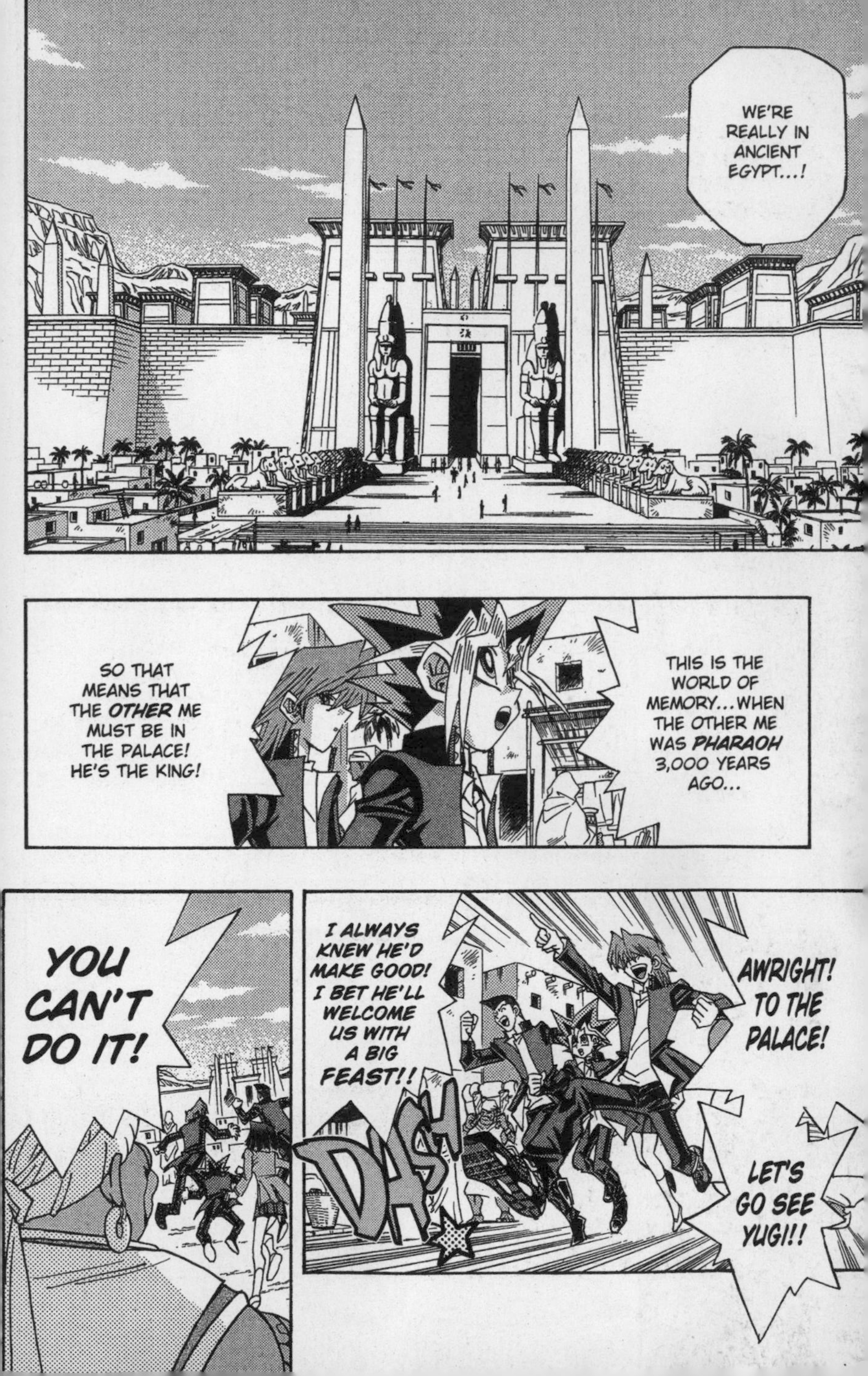
WE'RE REALLY IN ANCIENT EGYPT...!
THIS IS THE WORLD OF MEMORY...WHEN THE OTHER ME WAS PHARAOH 3,000 YEARS AGO...
SO THAT MEANS THAT THE OTHER ME MUST BE IN THE PALACE! HE'S THE KING!
AWRIGHT! TO THE PALACE!
I ALWAYS KNEW HE'D MAKE GOOD! I BET HE'LL WELCOME US WITH A BIG FEAST!!
DASH
LET'S GO SEE YUGI!!
YOU CAN'T DO IT!

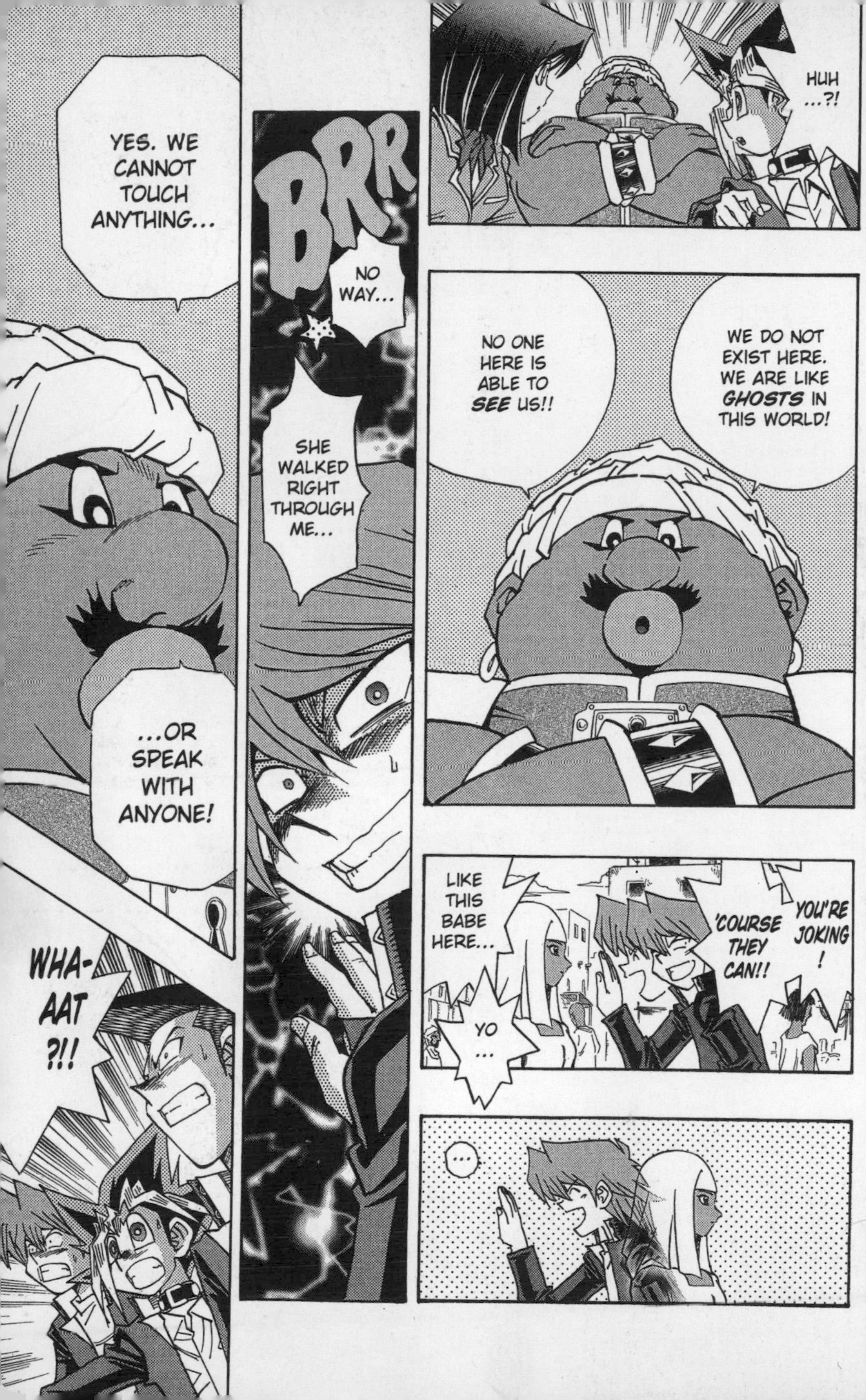
HUH ...?!
WE DO NOT EXIST HERE. WE ARE LIKE *GHOSTS* IN THIS WORLD!
NO ONE HERE IS ABLE TO *SEE* US!!
YOU'RE JOKING!
'COURSE THEY CAN!!
LIKE THIS BABE HERE...
YO ...
...
BRR
NO WAY...
SHE WALKED RIGHT THROUGH ME...
YES. WE CANNOT TOUCH ANYTHING...
...OR SPEAK WITH ANYONE!
WHA-AAT ?!!

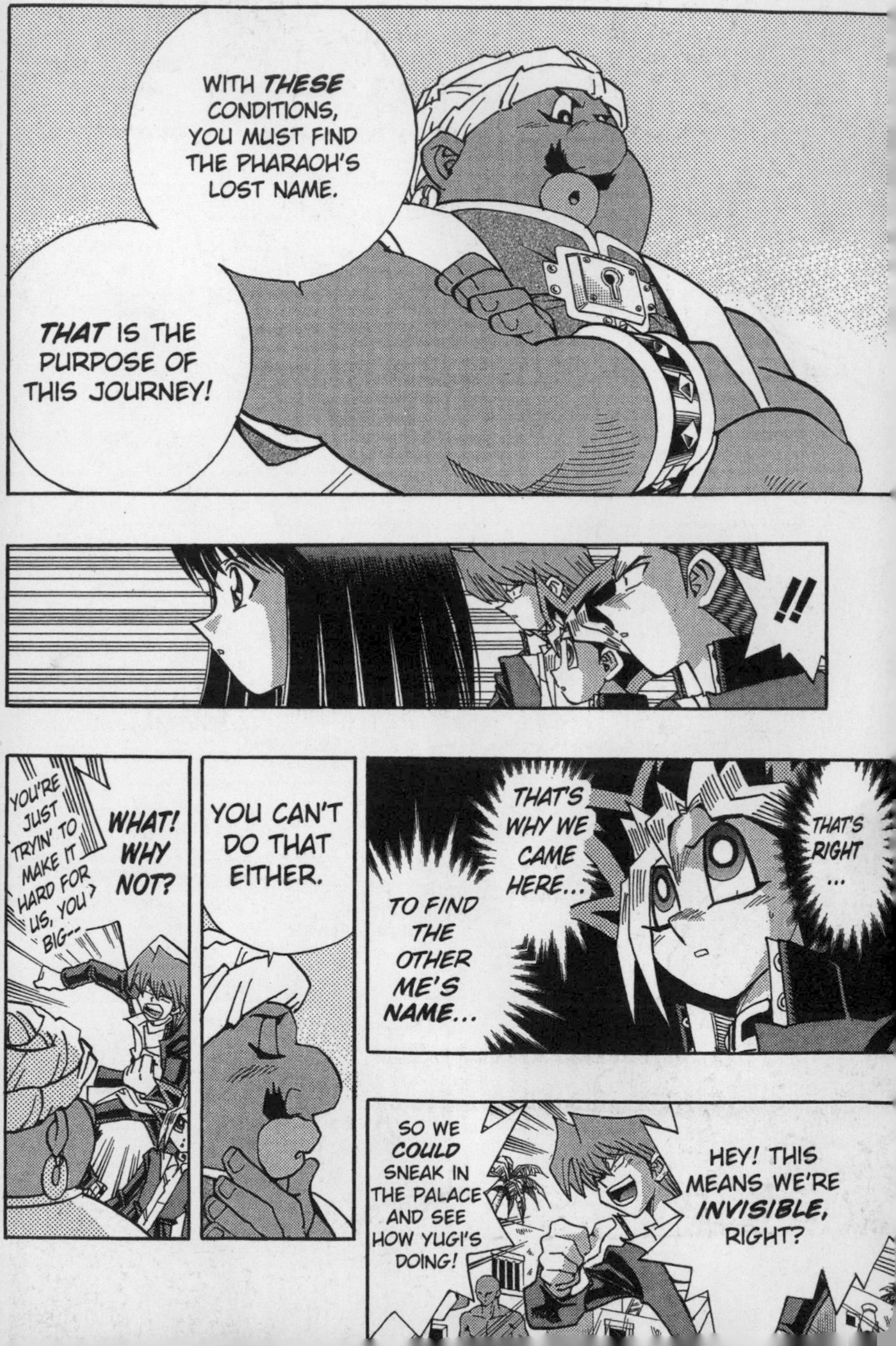
WITH *THESE* CONDITIONS, YOU MUST FIND THE PHARAOH'S LOST NAME.
THAT IS THE PURPOSE OF THIS JOURNEY!
!!
THAT'S RIGHT ...
THAT'S WHY WE CAME HERE...
TO FIND THE OTHER ME'S NAME...
HEY! THIS MEANS WE'RE *INVISIBLE*, RIGHT?
SO WE *COULD* SNEAK IN THE PALACE AND SEE HOW YUGI'S DOING!
YOU CAN'T DO THAT EITHER.
WHAT! WHY NOT?
YOU'RE JUST TRYIN' TO MAKE IT HARD FOR US, YOU BIG--

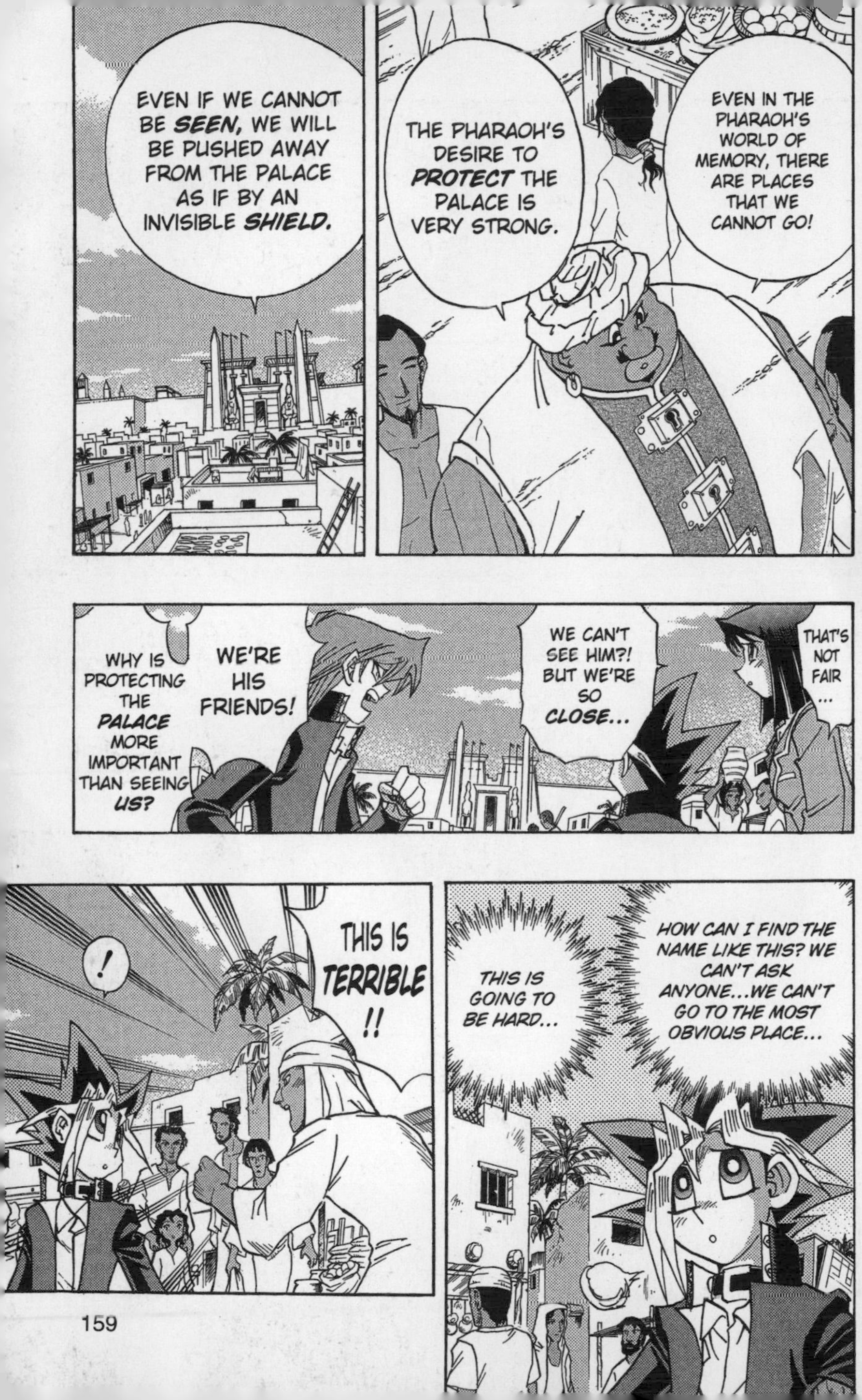
EVEN IN THE PHARAOH'S WORLD OF MEMORY, THERE ARE PLACES THAT WE CANNOT GO!
THE PHARAOH'S DESIRE TO PROTECT THE PALACE IS VERY STRONG.
EVEN IF WE CANNOT BE SEEN, WE WILL BE PUSHED AWAY FROM THE PALACE AS IF BY AN INVISIBLE SHIELD.
THAT'S NOT FAIR ...
WE CAN'T SEE HIM?! BUT WE'RE SO CLOSE...
WE'RE HIS FRIENDS!
WHY IS PROTECTING THE PALACE MORE IMPORTANT THAN SEEING US?
HOW CAN I FIND THE NAME LIKE THIS? WE CAN'T ASK ANYONE...WE CAN'T GO TO THE MOST OBVIOUS PLACE...
THIS IS GOING TO BE HARD...
THIS IS TERRIBLE !!
!

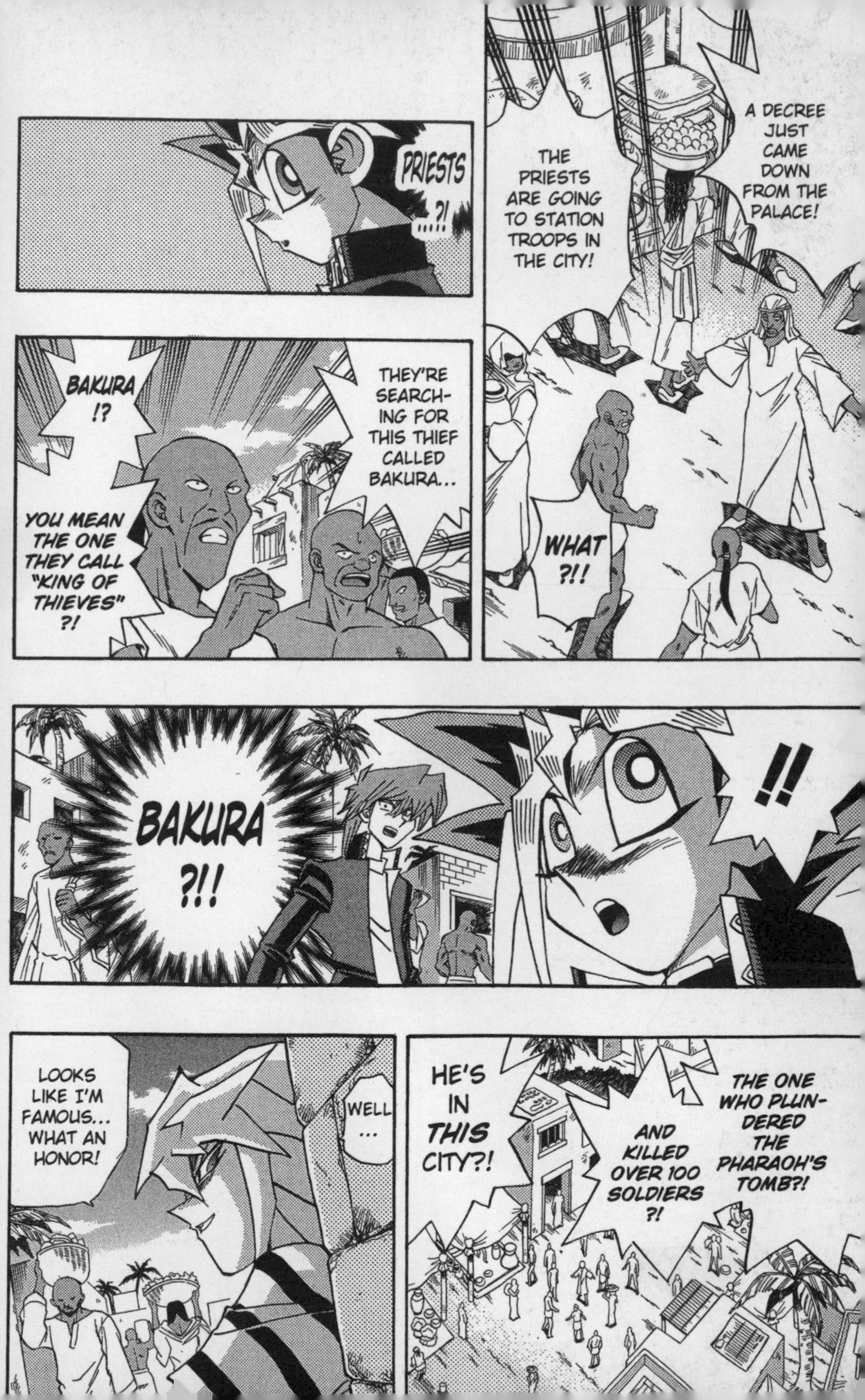
A DECREE JUST CAME DOWN FROM THE PALACE!
THE PRIESTS ARE GOING TO STATION TROOPS IN THE CITY!
WHAT ?!!
PRIESTS ...?!
THEY'RE SEARCH-ING FOR THIS THIEF CALLED BAKURA...
BAKURA !?
YOU MEAN THE ONE THEY CALL "KING OF THIEVES" ?!
!!
BAKURA ?!!
THE ONE WHO PLUN-DERED THE PHARAOH'S TOMB?!
AND KILLED OVER 100 SOLDIERS ?!
HE'S IN THIS CITY?!
WELL ...
LOOKS LIKE I'M FAMOUS... WHAT AN HONOR!

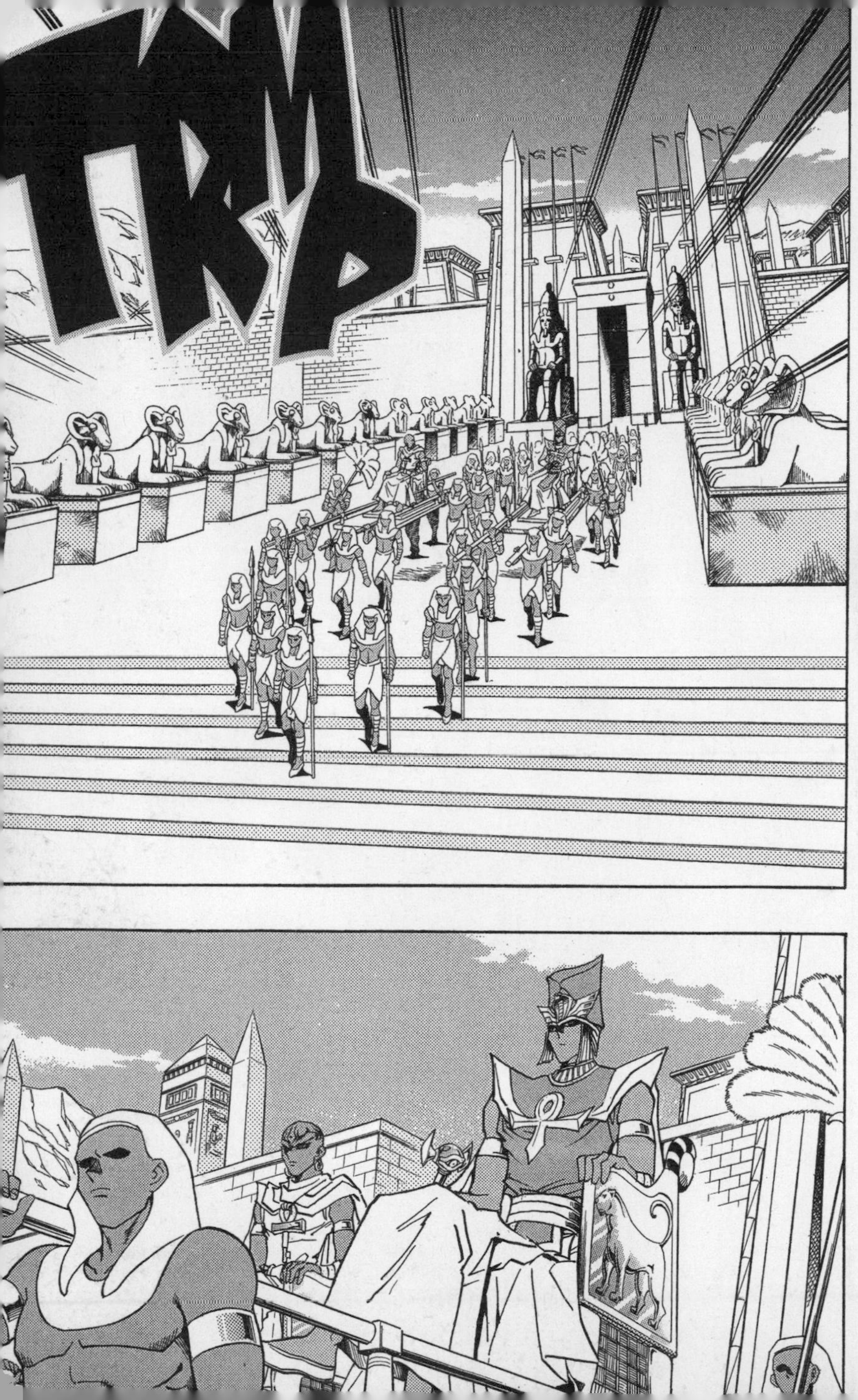
TRUD

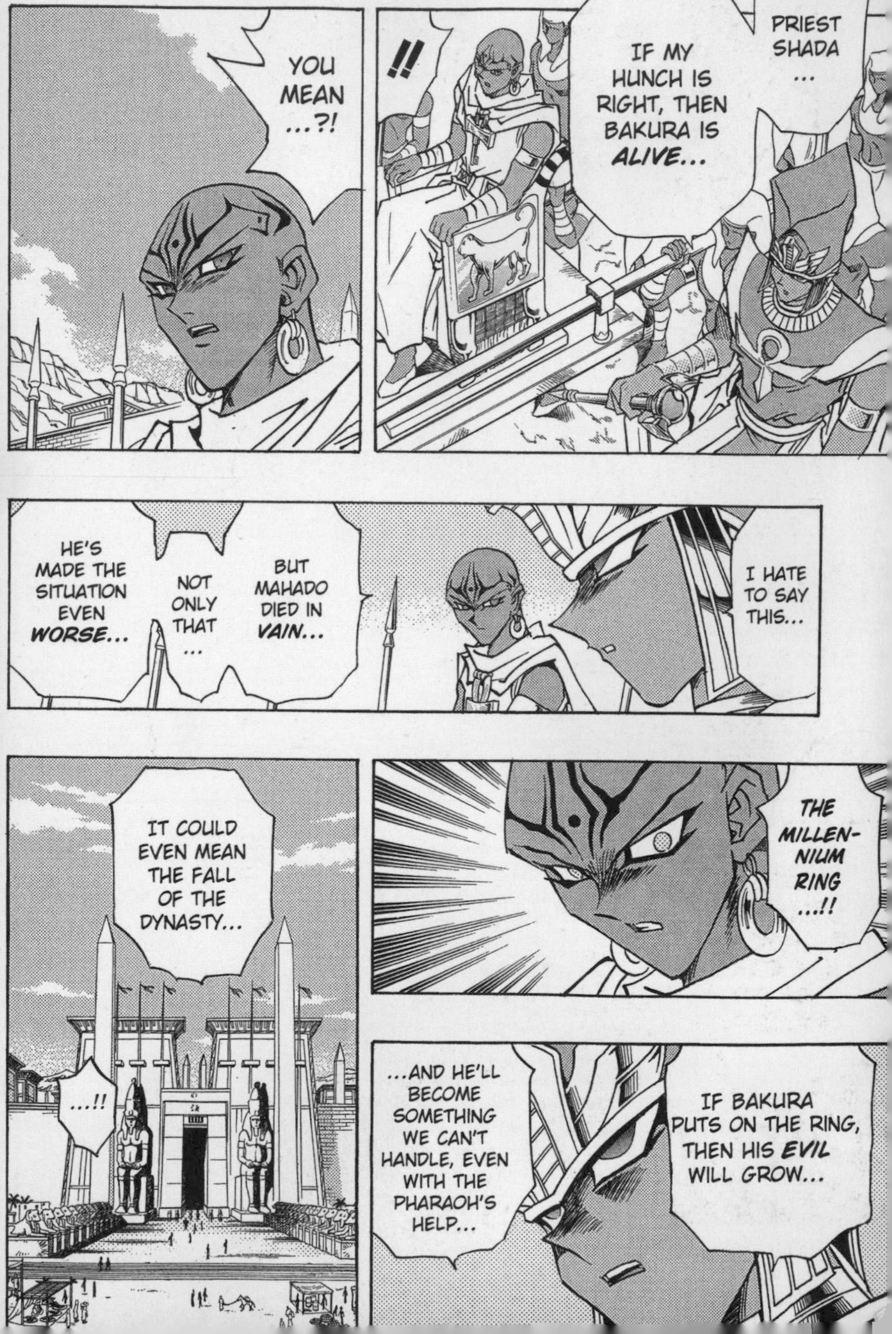
PRIEST SHADA ...
IF MY HUNCH IS RIGHT, THEN BAKURA IS *ALIVE*...
!!
YOU MEAN ...?!
I HATE TO SAY THIS...
BUT MAHADO DIED IN *VAIN*...
NOT ONLY THAT ...
HE'S MADE THE SITUATION EVEN *WORSE*...
THE MILLEN-NIUM RING ...!!
IF BAKURA PUTS ON THE RING, THEN HIS *EVIL* WILL GROW...
...AND HE'LL BECOME SOMETHING WE CAN'T HANDLE, EVEN WITH THE PHARAOH'S HELP...
IT COULD EVEN MEAN THE FALL OF THE DYNASTY...
...!!

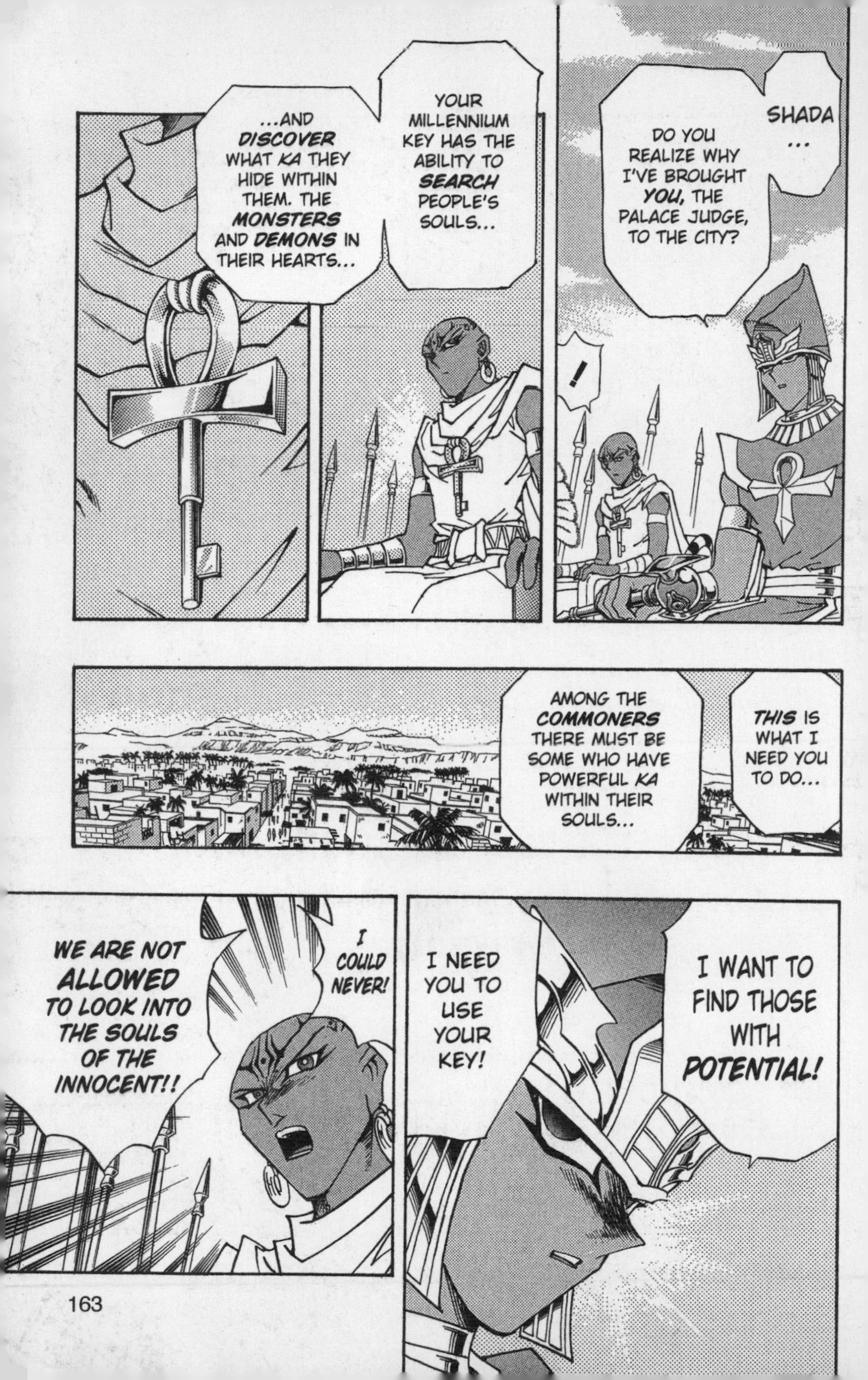
SHADA ...
DO YOU REALIZE WHY I'VE BROUGHT YOU, THE PALACE JUDGE, TO THE CITY?
!
YOUR MILLENNIUM KEY HAS THE ABILITY TO SEARCH PEOPLE'S SOULS...
...AND DISCOVER WHAT KA THEY HIDE WITHIN THEM. THE MONSTERS AND DEMONS IN THEIR HEARTS...
THIS IS WHAT I NEED YOU TO DO...
AMONG THE COMMONERS THERE MUST BE SOME WHO HAVE POWERFUL KA WITHIN THEIR SOULS...
I WANT TO FIND THOSE WITH POTENTIAL!
I NEED YOU TO USE YOUR KEY!
I COULD NEVER!
WE ARE NOT ALLOWED TO LOOK INTO THE SOULS OF THE INNOCENT!!

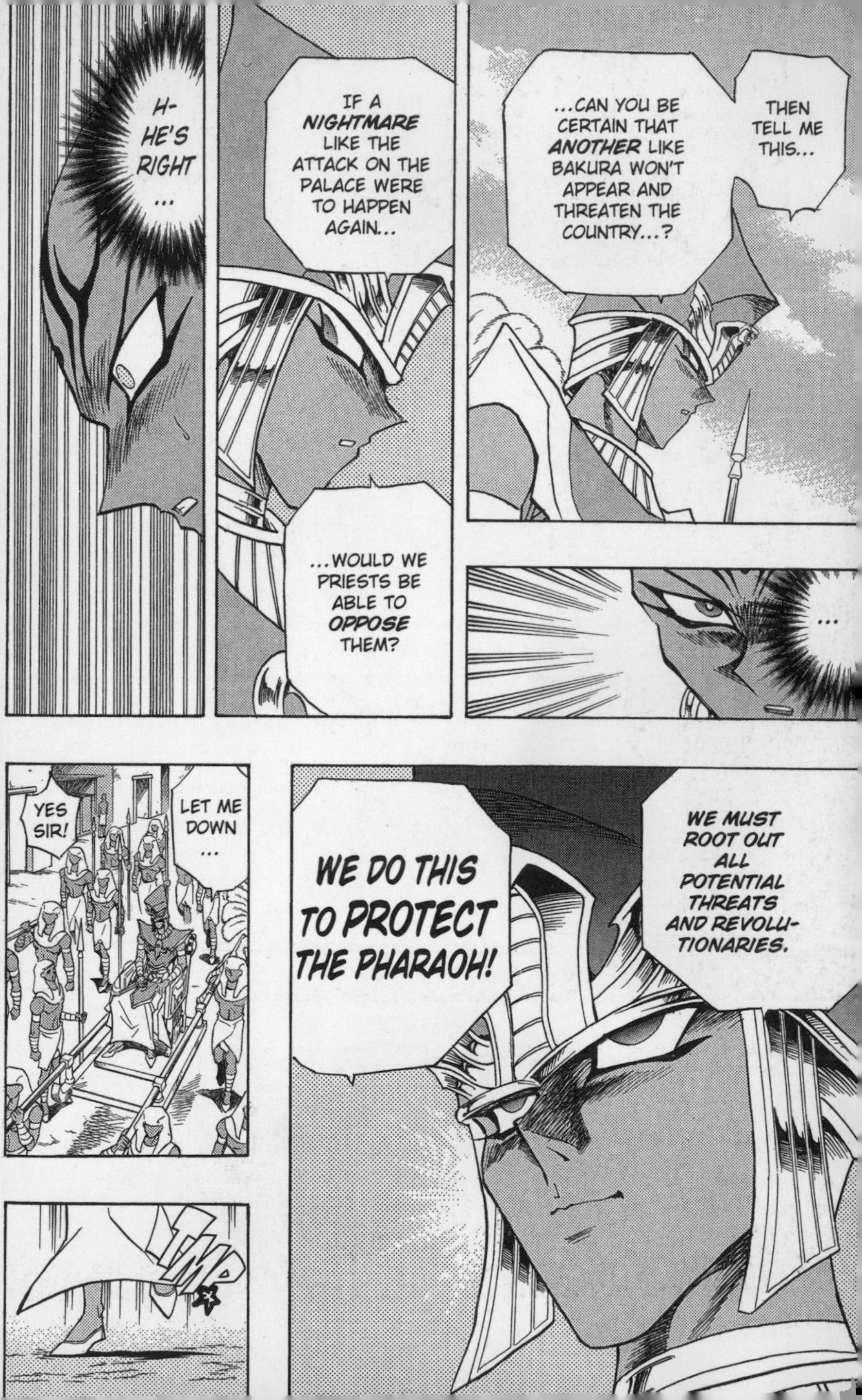
THEN TELL ME THIS...
...CAN YOU BE CERTAIN THAT ANOTHER LIKE BAKURA WON'T APPEAR AND THREATEN THE COUNTRY...?
...
IF A NIGHTMARE LIKE THE ATTACK ON THE PALACE WERE TO HAPPEN AGAIN...
...WOULD WE PRIESTS BE ABLE TO OPPOSE THEM?
H-HE'S RIGHT...
WE MUST ROOT OUT ALL POTENTIAL THREATS AND REVOLU-TIONARIES.
WE DO THIS TO PROTECT THE PHARAOH!
LET ME DOWN...
YES SIR!

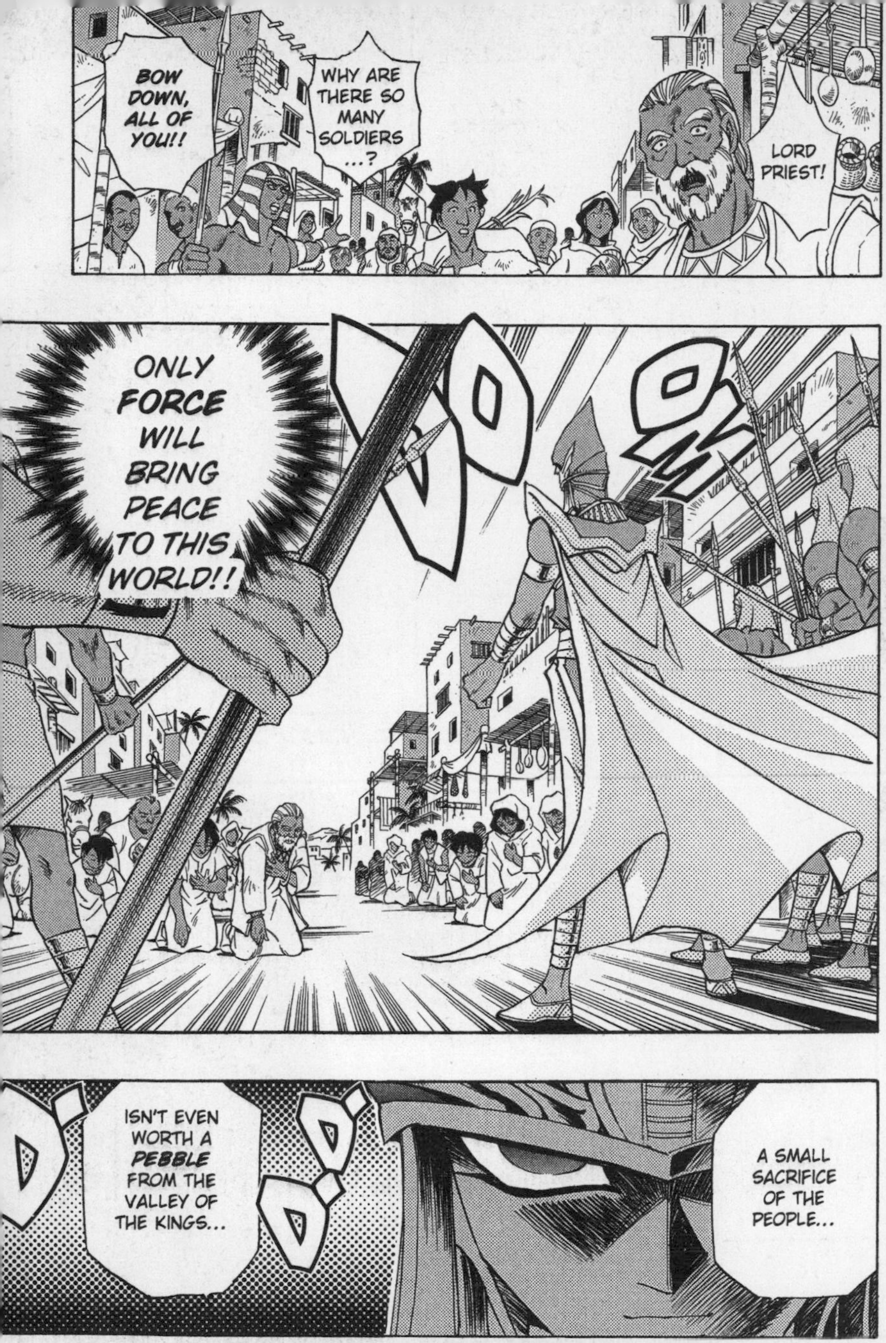
LORD PRIEST!
WHY ARE THERE SO MANY SOLDIERS ...?
BOW DOWN, ALL OF YOU!!
ONLY FORCE WILL BRING PEACE TO THIS WORLD!!
A SMALL SACRIFICE OF THE PEOPLE...
ISN'T EVEN WORTH A PEBBLE FROM THE VALLEY OF THE KINGS...

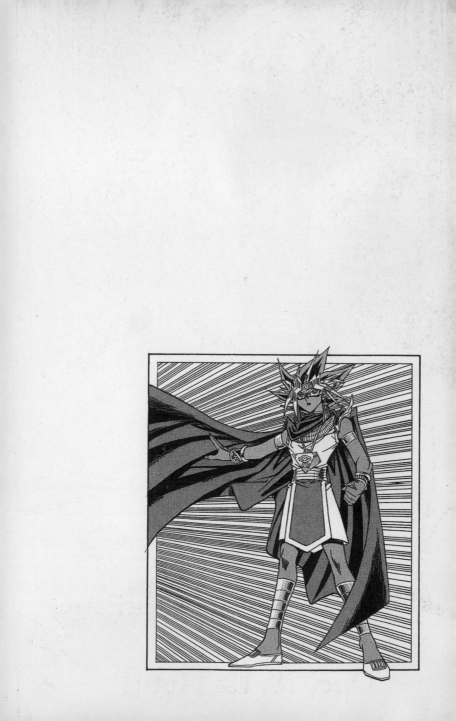

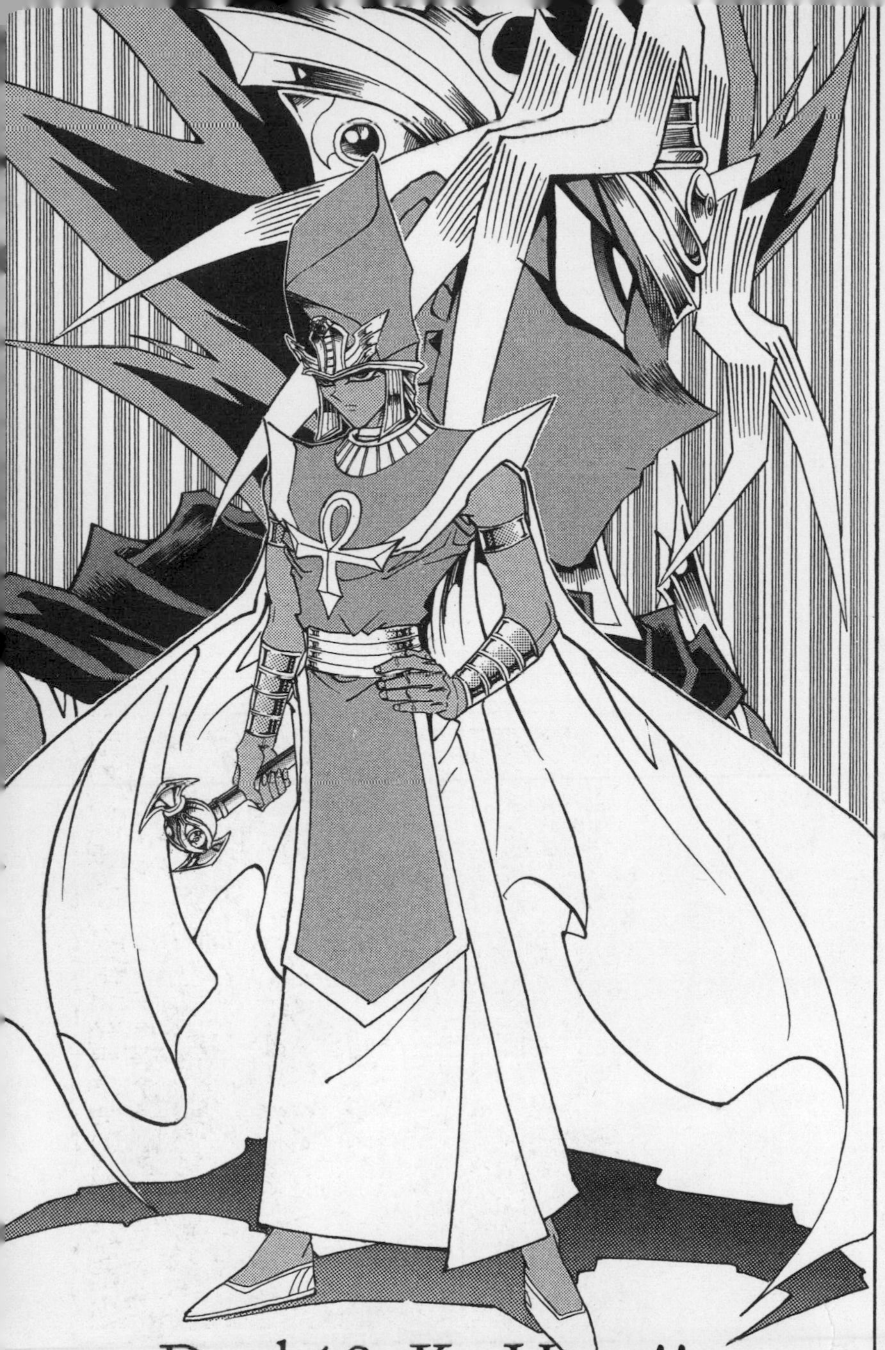

Duel 18: Ka Hunt!!

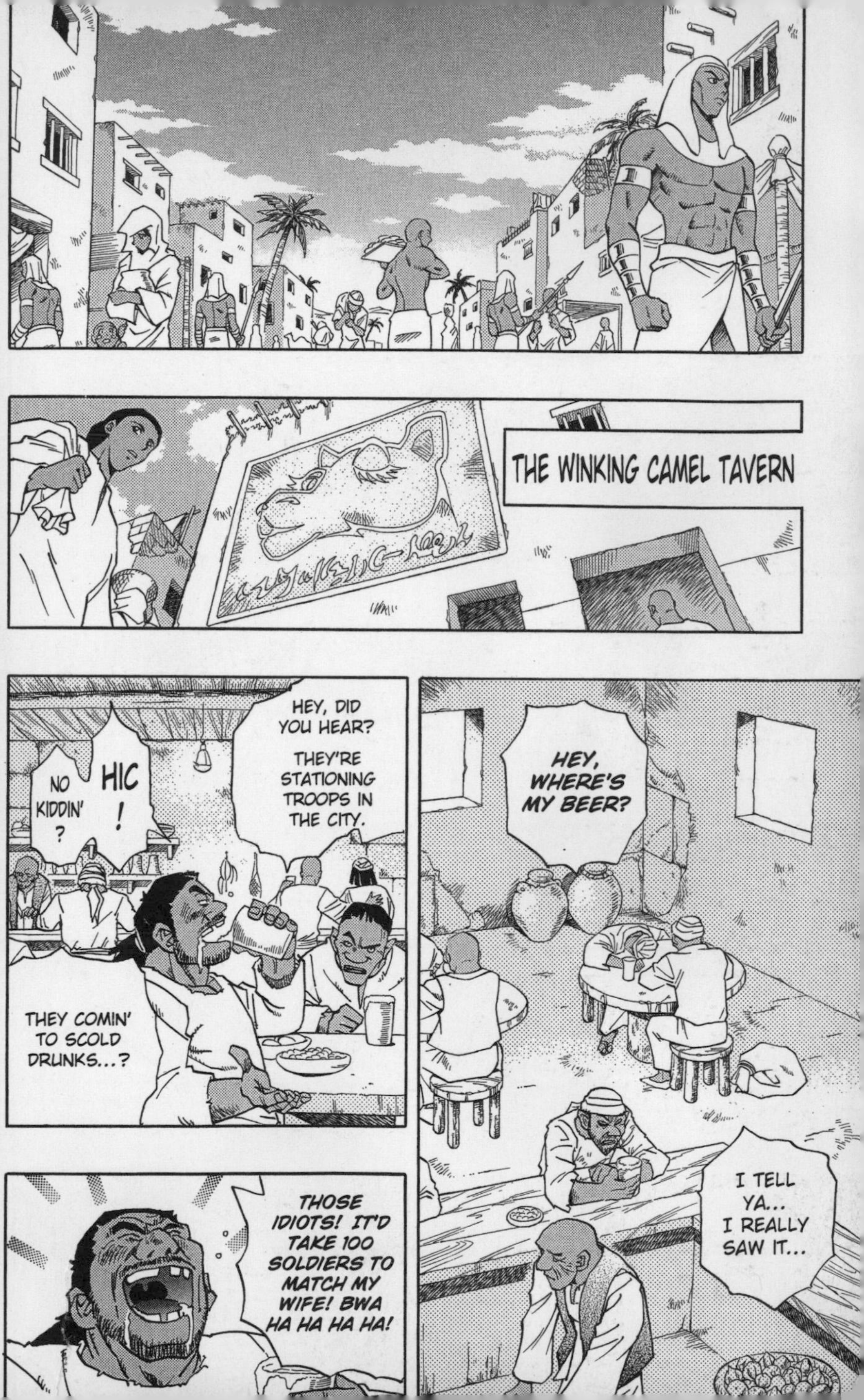
THE WINKING CAMEL TAVERN
HEY, WHERE'S MY BEER?
I TELL YA... I REALLY SAW IT...
HEY, DID YOU HEAR?
THEY'RE STATIONING TROOPS IN THE CITY.
HIC!
NO KIDDIN'?
THEY COMIN' TO SCOLD DRUNKS...?
THOSE IDIOTS! IT'D TAKE 100 SOLDIERS TO MATCH MY WIFE! BWA HA HA HA HA!

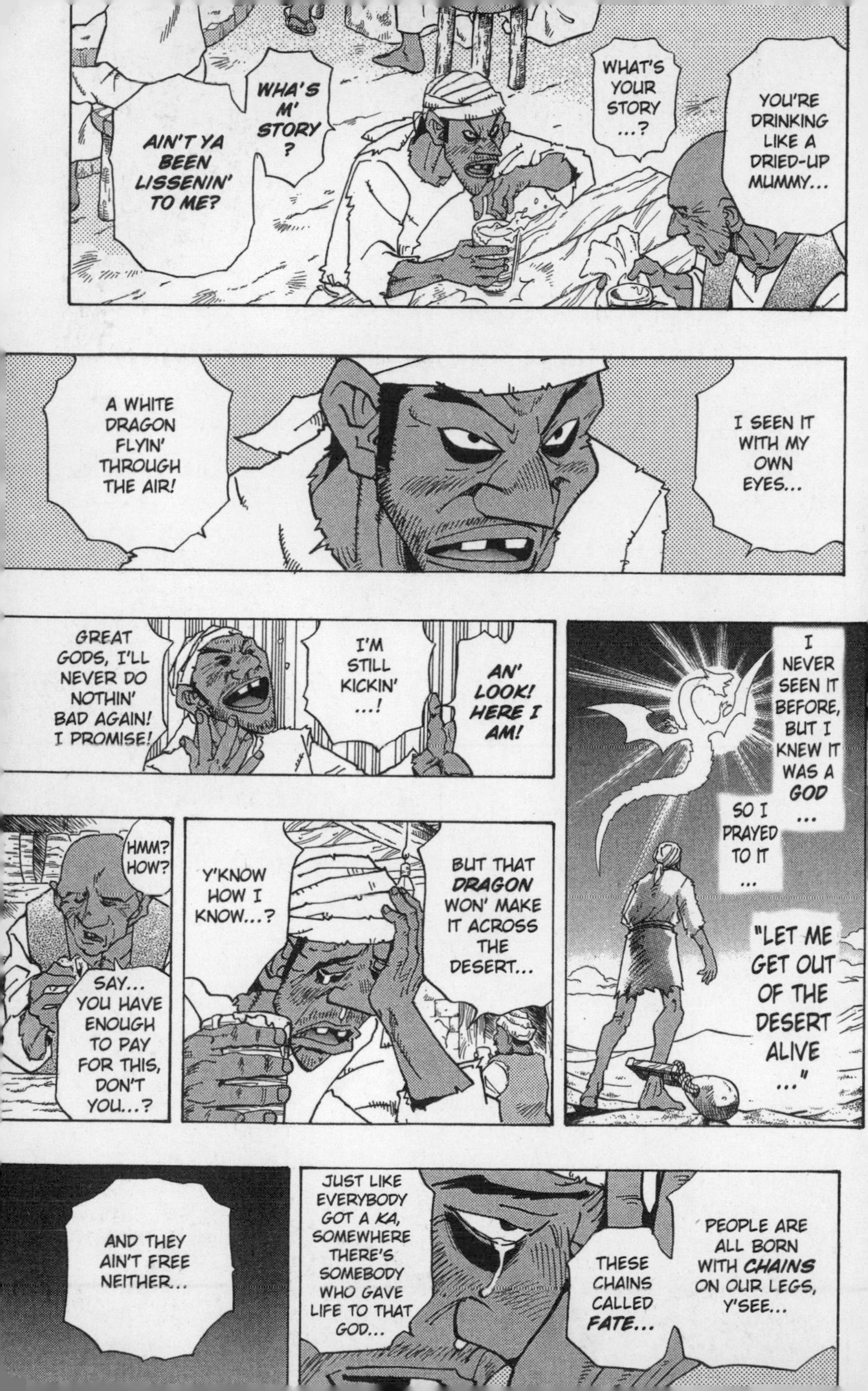
YOU'RE DRINKING LIKE A DRIED-UP MUMMY...
WHAT'S YOUR STORY ...?
WHA'S M' STORY ?
AIN'T YA BEEN LISSENIN' TO ME?
I SEEN IT WITH MY OWN EYES...
A WHITE DRAGON FLYIN' THROUGH THE AIR!
I NEVER SEEN IT BEFORE, BUT I KNEW IT WAS A GOD ...
SO I PRAYED TO IT ...
"LET ME GET OUT OF THE DESERT ALIVE ..."
AN' LOOK! HERE I AM!
I'M STILL KICKIN' ...!
GREAT GODS, I'LL NEVER DO NOTHIN' BAD AGAIN! I PROMISE!
BUT THAT DRAGON WON' MAKE IT ACROSS THE DESERT...
Y'KNOW HOW I KNOW...?
HMM? HOW?
SAY... YOU HAVE ENOUGH TO PAY FOR THIS, DON'T YOU...?
PEOPLE ARE ALL BORN WITH CHAINS ON OUR LEGS, Y'SEE...
THESE CHAINS CALLED FATE...
JUST LIKE EVERYBODY GOT A KA, SOMEWHERE THERE'S SOMEBODY WHO GAVE LIFE TO THAT GOD...
AND THEY AIN'T FREE NEITHER...

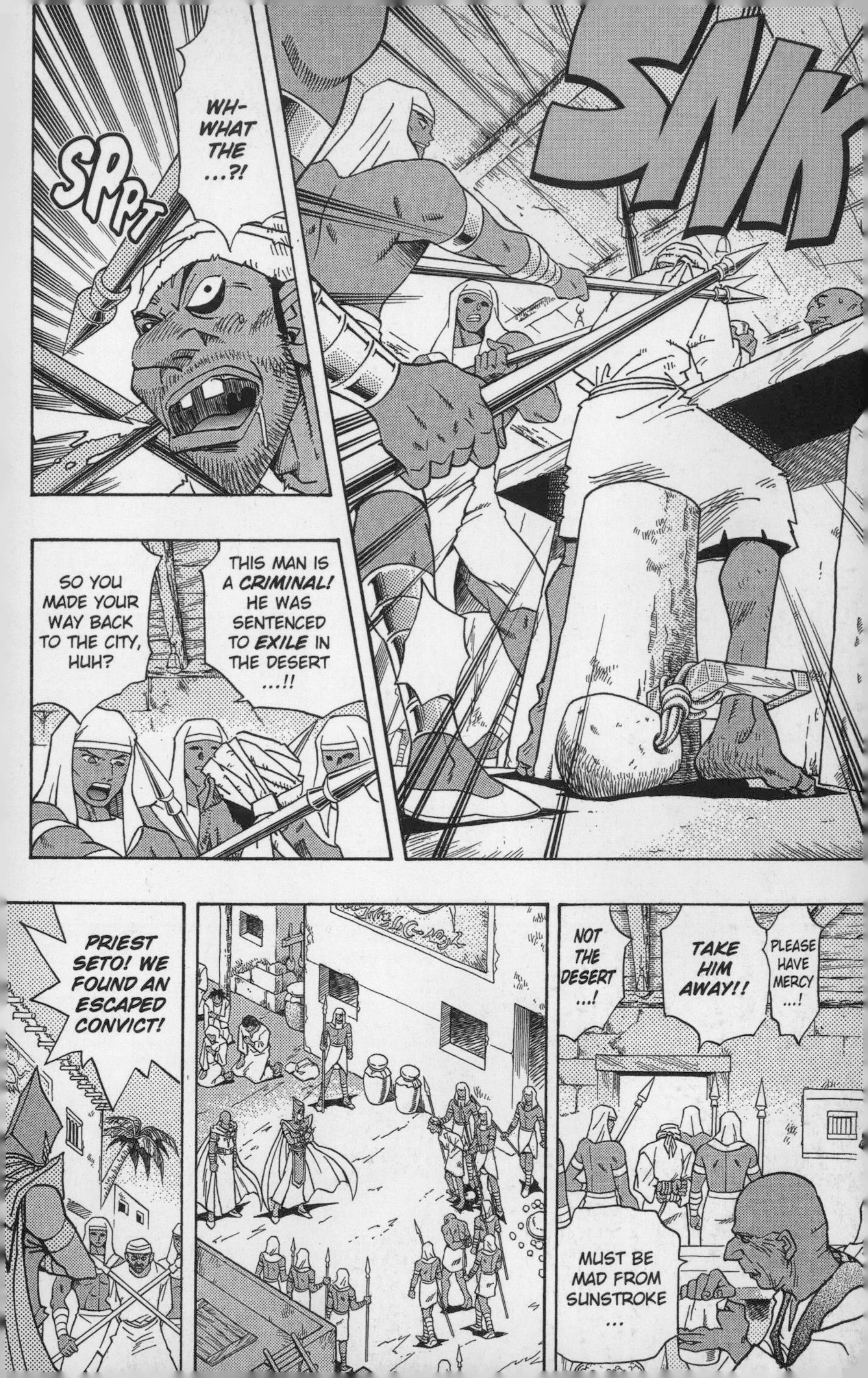
SNK
SPPT
WH- WHAT THE ...?!
THIS MAN IS A CRIMINAL! HE WAS SENTENCED TO EXILE IN THE DESERT ...!!
SO YOU MADE YOUR WAY BACK TO THE CITY, HUH?
PLEASE HAVE MERCY ...!
TAKE HIM AWAY!!
NOT THE DESERT ...!
MUST BE MAD FROM SUNSTROKE ...
PRIEST SETO! WE FOUND AN ESCAPED CONVICT!

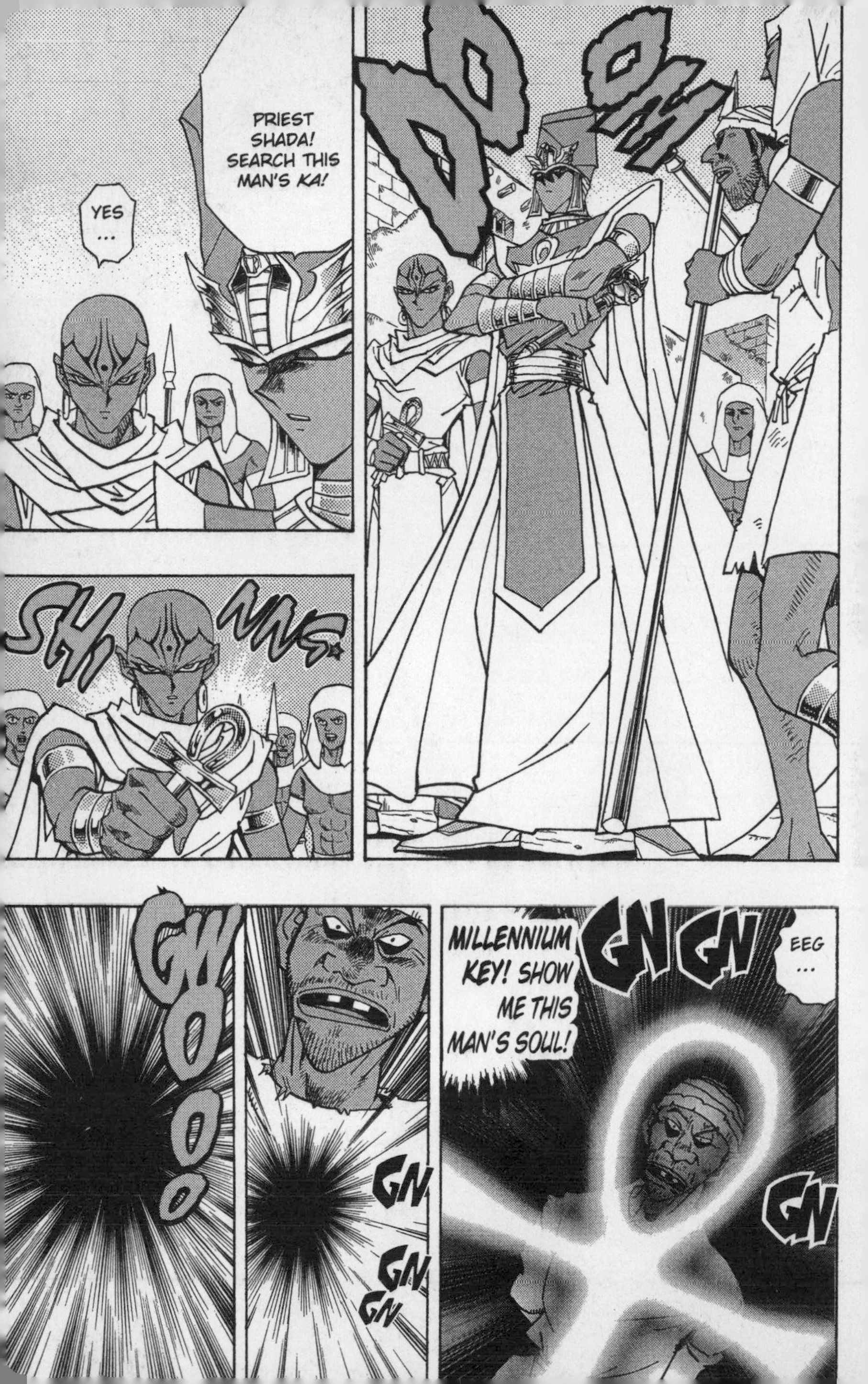
DOOM
PRIEST SHADA! SEARCH THIS MAN'S KA!
YES ...
SHING
EEG ...
GNGN
MILLENNIUM KEY! SHOW ME THIS MAN'S SOUL!
GN
GN
GN
GN
GWOOOO

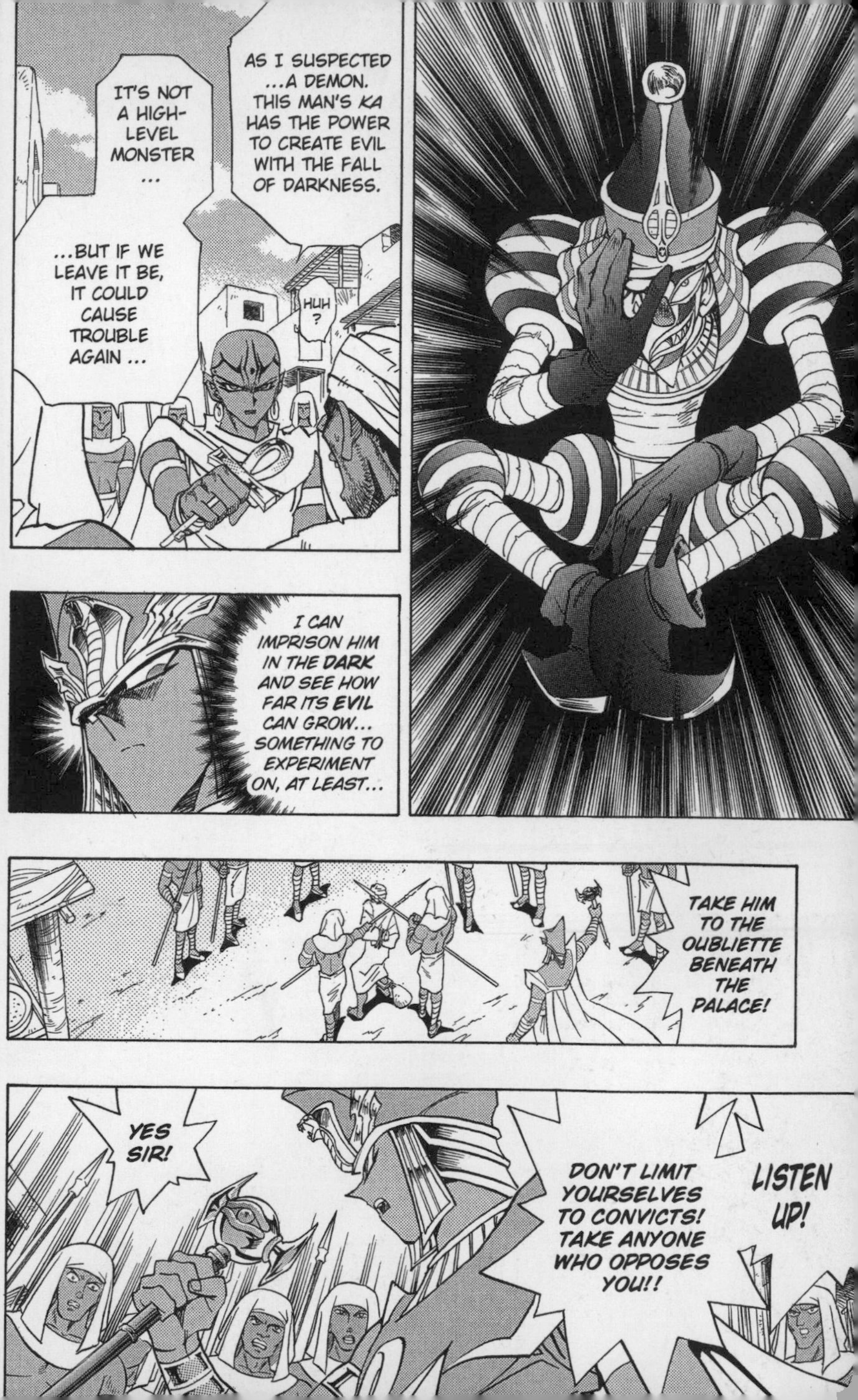
AS I SUSPECTED ...A DEMON. THIS MAN'S *KA* HAS THE POWER TO CREATE EVIL WITH THE FALL OF DARKNESS.
IT'S NOT A HIGH-LEVEL MONSTER ...
HUH ?
...BUT IF WE LEAVE IT BE, IT COULD CAUSE TROUBLE AGAIN ...
I CAN IMPRISON HIM IN THE DARK AND SEE HOW FAR ITS EVIL CAN GROW... SOMETHING TO EXPERIMENT ON, AT LEAST...
TAKE HIM TO THE OUBLIETTE BENEATH THE PALACE!
LISTEN UP!
DON'T LIMIT YOURSELVES TO CONVICTS! TAKE ANYONE WHO OPPOSES YOU!!
YES SIR!

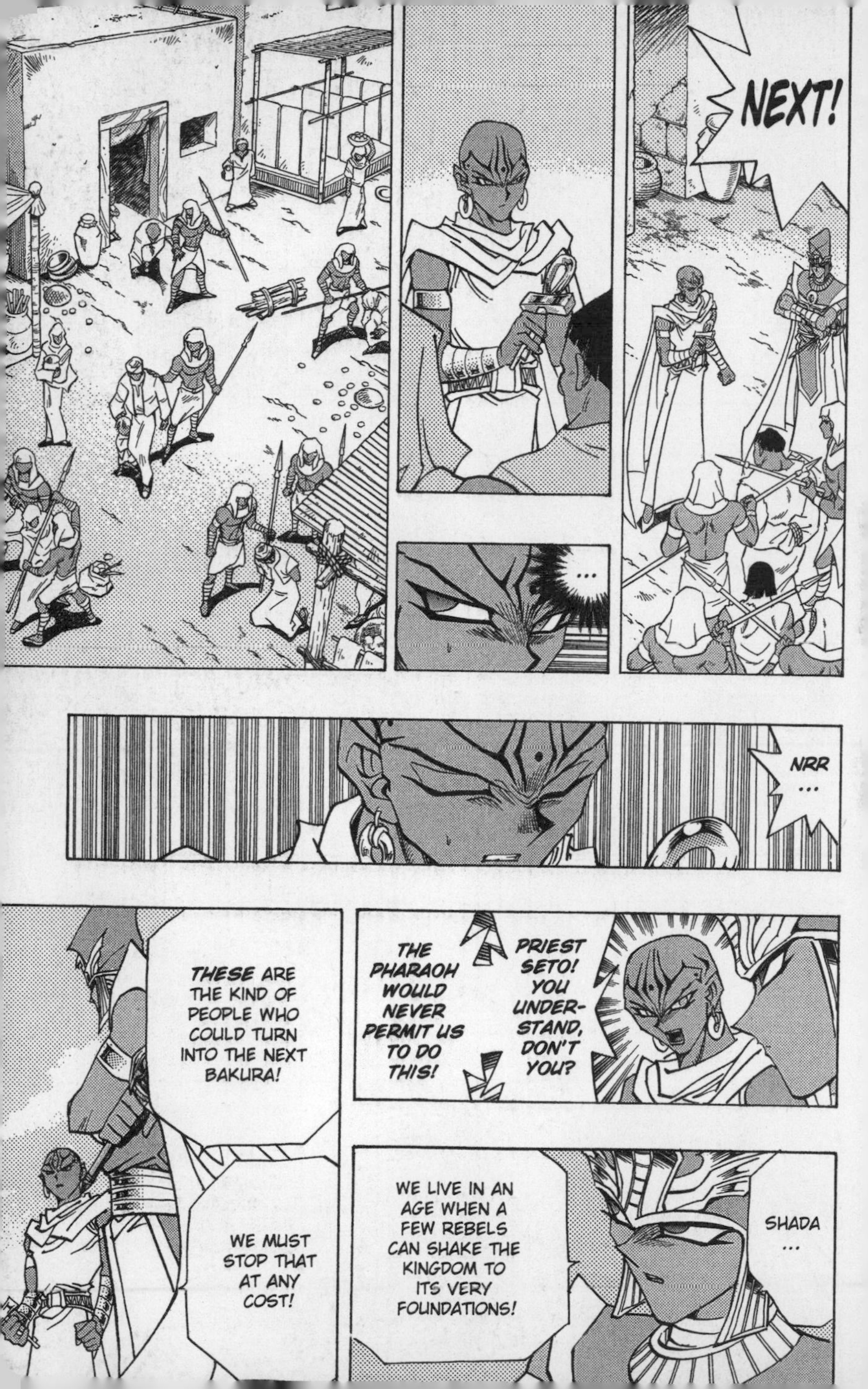
NEXT!
...
NRR ...
PRIEST SETO! YOU UNDERSTAND, DON'T YOU?
THE PHARAOH WOULD NEVER PERMIT US TO DO THIS!
SHADA ...
WE LIVE IN AN AGE WHEN A FEW REBELS CAN SHAKE THE KINGDOM TO ITS VERY FOUNDATIONS!
THESE ARE THE KIND OF PEOPLE WHO COULD TURN INTO THE NEXT BAKURA!
WE MUST STOP THAT AT ANY COST!

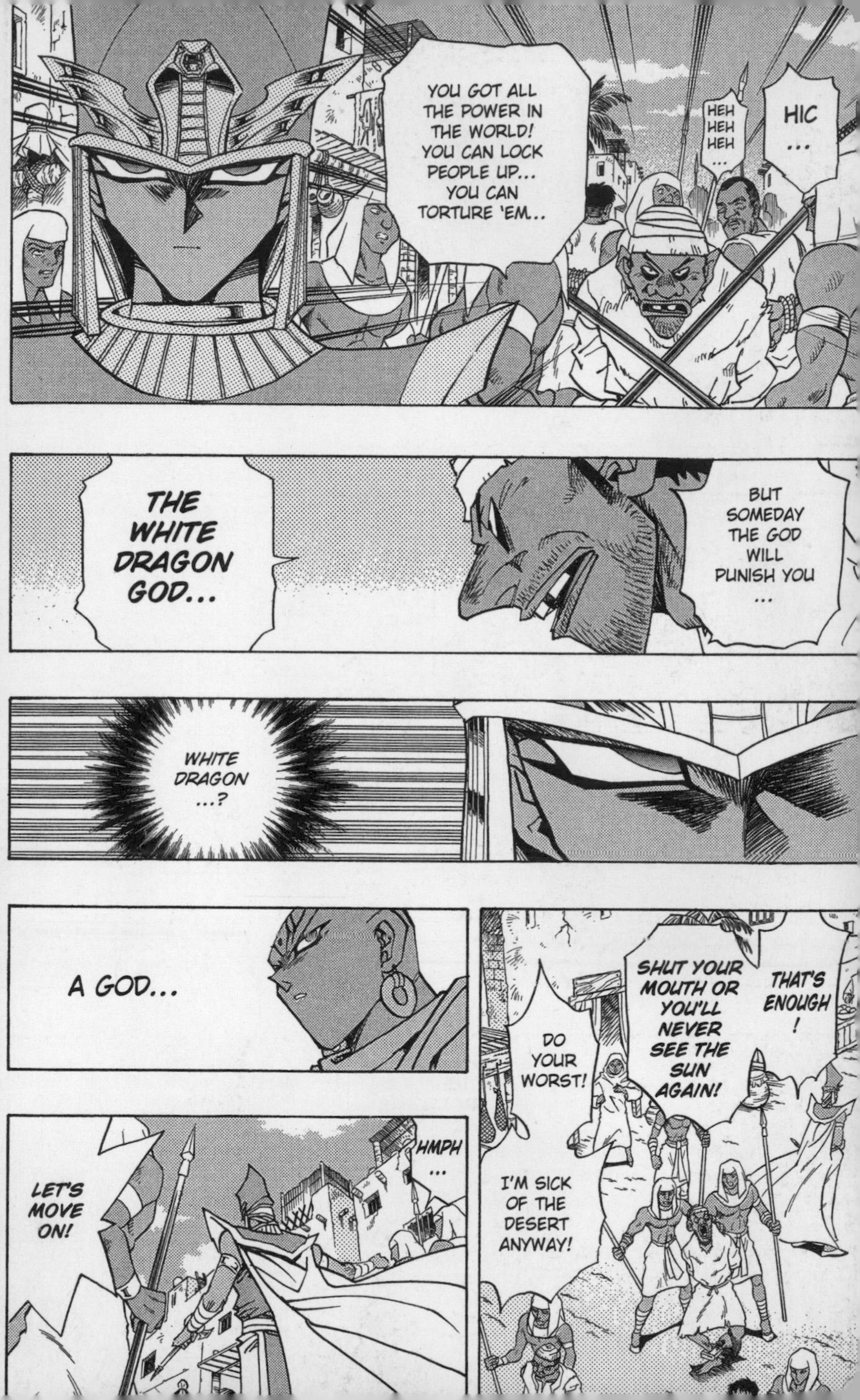
HIC ...
HEH HEH HEH ...
YOU GOT ALL THE POWER IN THE WORLD! YOU CAN LOCK PEOPLE UP... YOU CAN TORTURE 'EM...
BUT SOMEDAY THE GOD WILL PUNISH YOU ...
THE WHITE DRAGON GOD...
WHITE DRAGON ...?
THAT'S ENOUGH!
SHUT YOUR MOUTH OR YOU'LL NEVER SEE THE SUN AGAIN!
DO YOUR WORST!
I'M SICK OF THE DESERT ANYWAY!
A GOD...
HMPH ...
LET'S MOVE ON!

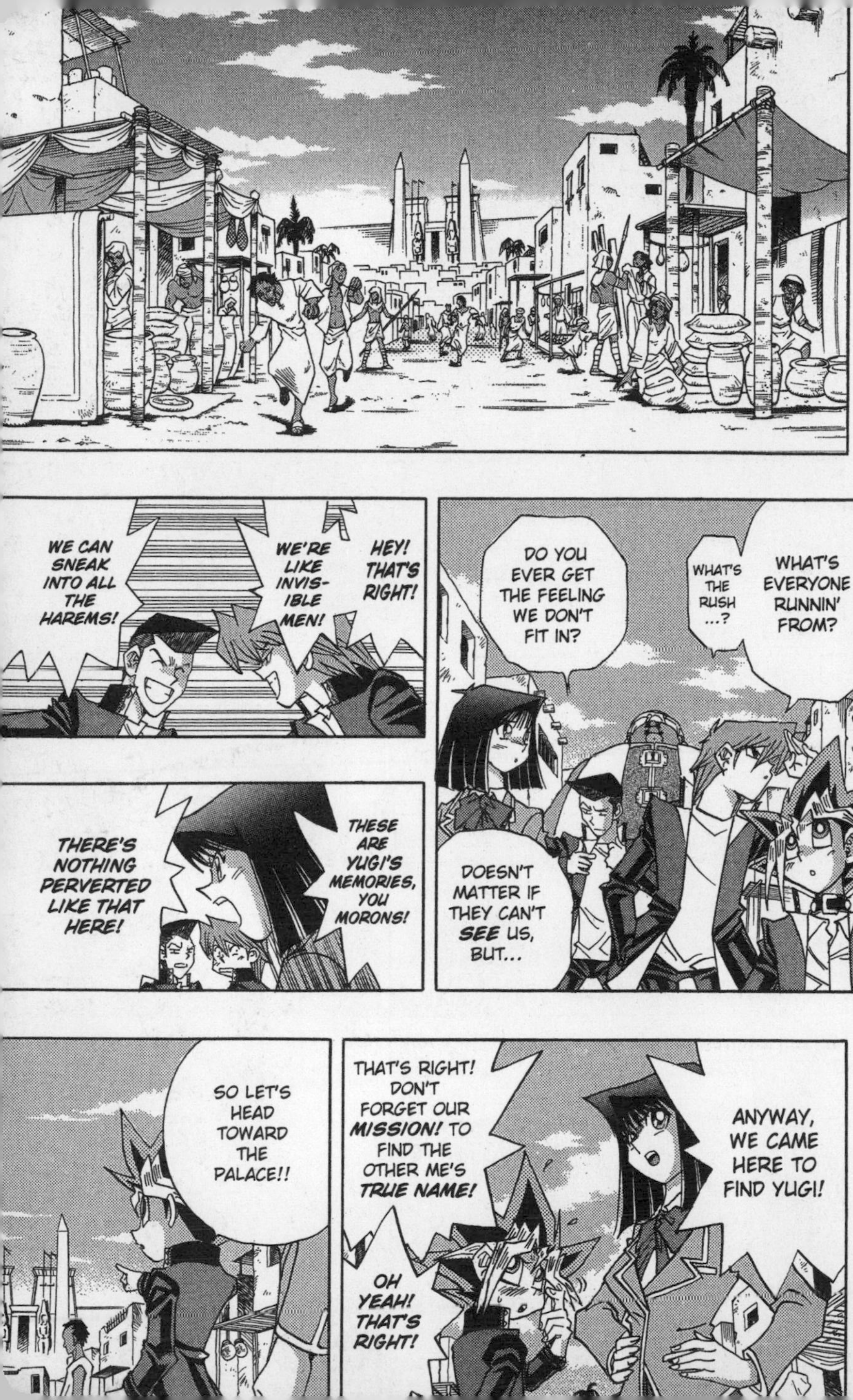
WHAT'S EVERYONE RUNNIN' FROM?
WHAT'S THE RUSH ...?
DO YOU EVER GET THE FEELING WE DON'T FIT IN?
DOESN'T MATTER IF THEY CAN'T SEE US, BUT...
HEY! THAT'S RIGHT!
WE'RE LIKE INVISIBLE MEN!
WE CAN SNEAK INTO ALL THE HAREMS!
THESE ARE YUGI'S MEMORIES, YOU MORONS!
THERE'S NOTHING PERVERTED LIKE THAT HERE!
ANYWAY, WE CAME HERE TO FIND YUGI!
THAT'S RIGHT! DON'T FORGET OUR MISSION! TO FIND THE OTHER ME'S TRUE NAME!
OH YEAH! THAT'S RIGHT!
SO LET'S HEAD TOWARD THE PALACE!!

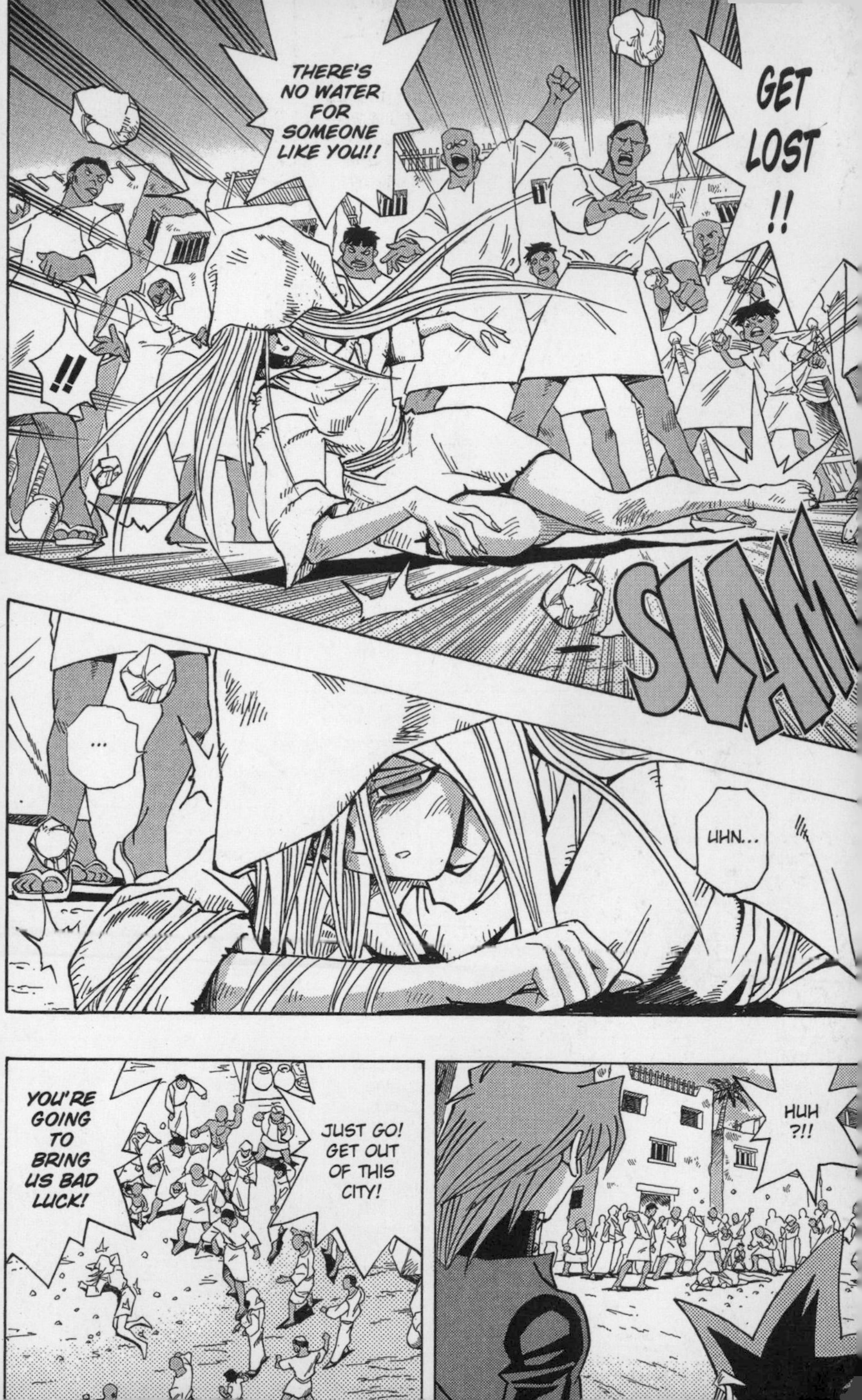
GET LOST !!
THERE'S NO WATER FOR SOMEONE LIKE YOU!!
!!
SLAM
UHN...
...
HUH ?!!
JUST GO! GET OUT OF THIS CITY!
YOU'RE GOING TO BRING US BAD LUCK!

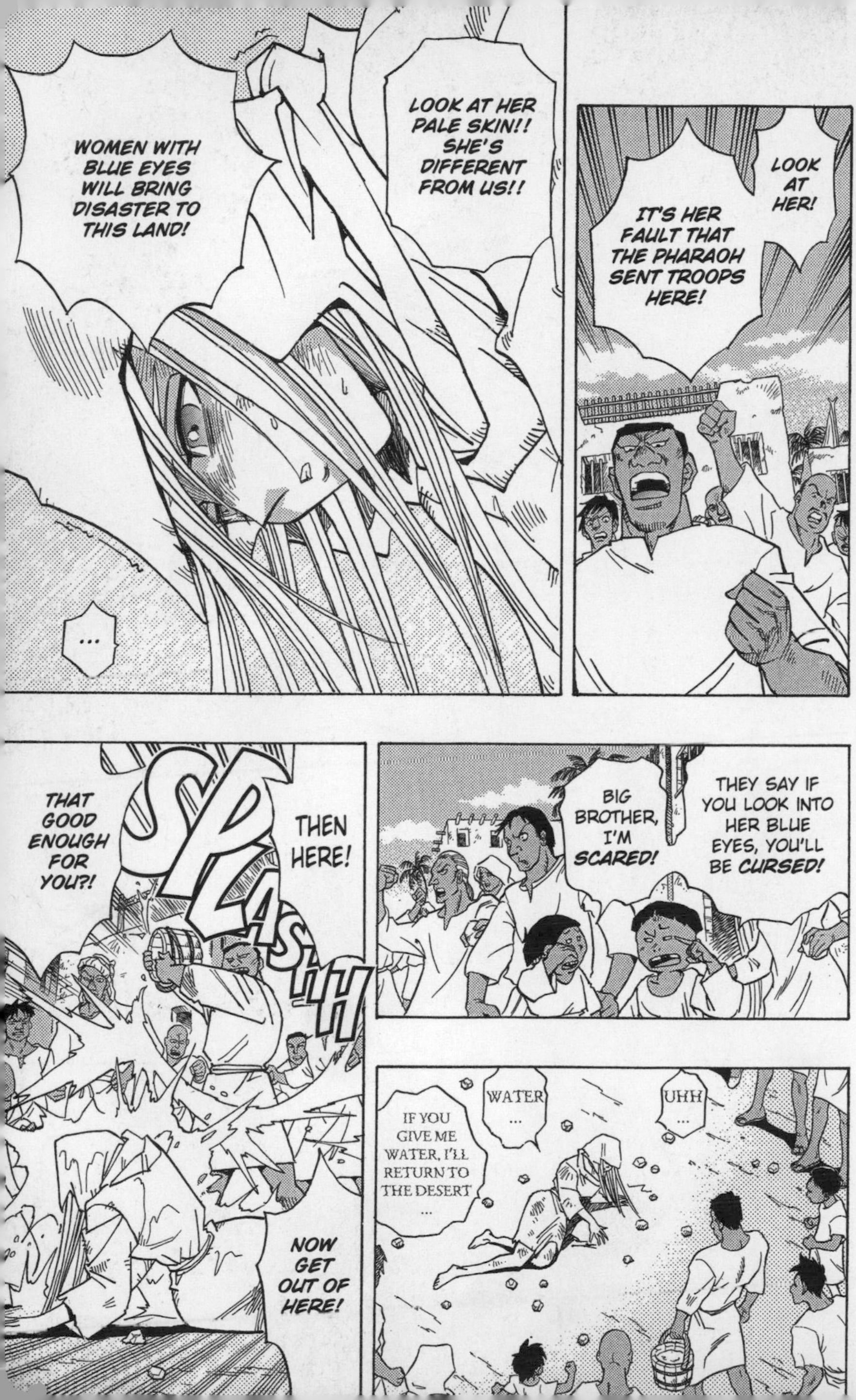
LOOK AT HER!
IT'S HER FAULT THAT THE PHARAOH SENT TROOPS HERE!
LOOK AT HER PALE SKIN!! SHE'S DIFFERENT FROM US!!
WOMEN WITH BLUE EYES WILL BRING DISASTER TO THIS LAND!
...
THEY SAY IF YOU LOOK INTO HER BLUE EYES, YOU'LL BE CURSED!
BIG BROTHER, I'M SCARED!
UHH ...
WATER ...
IF YOU GIVE ME WATER, I'LL RETURN TO THE DESERT ...
THEN HERE!
THAT GOOD ENOUGH FOR YOU?!
SPLASH
NOW GET OUT OF HERE!

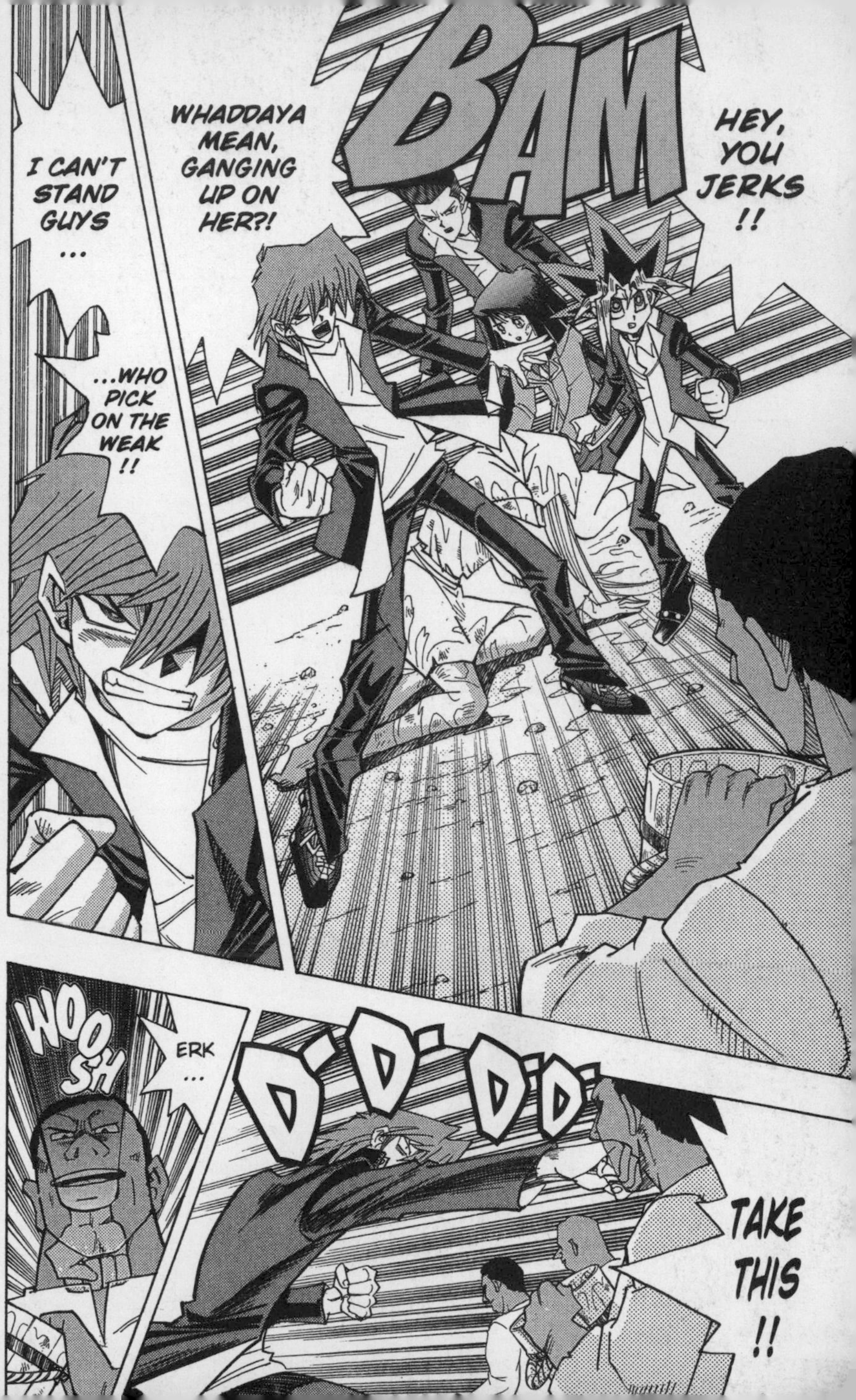
BAM
HEY, YOU JERKS !!
WHADDAYA MEAN, GANGING UP ON HER?!
I CAN'T STAND GUYS ...
...WHO PICK ON THE WEAK !!
TAKE THIS !!
D-D-D-D
ERK ...
WOOSH

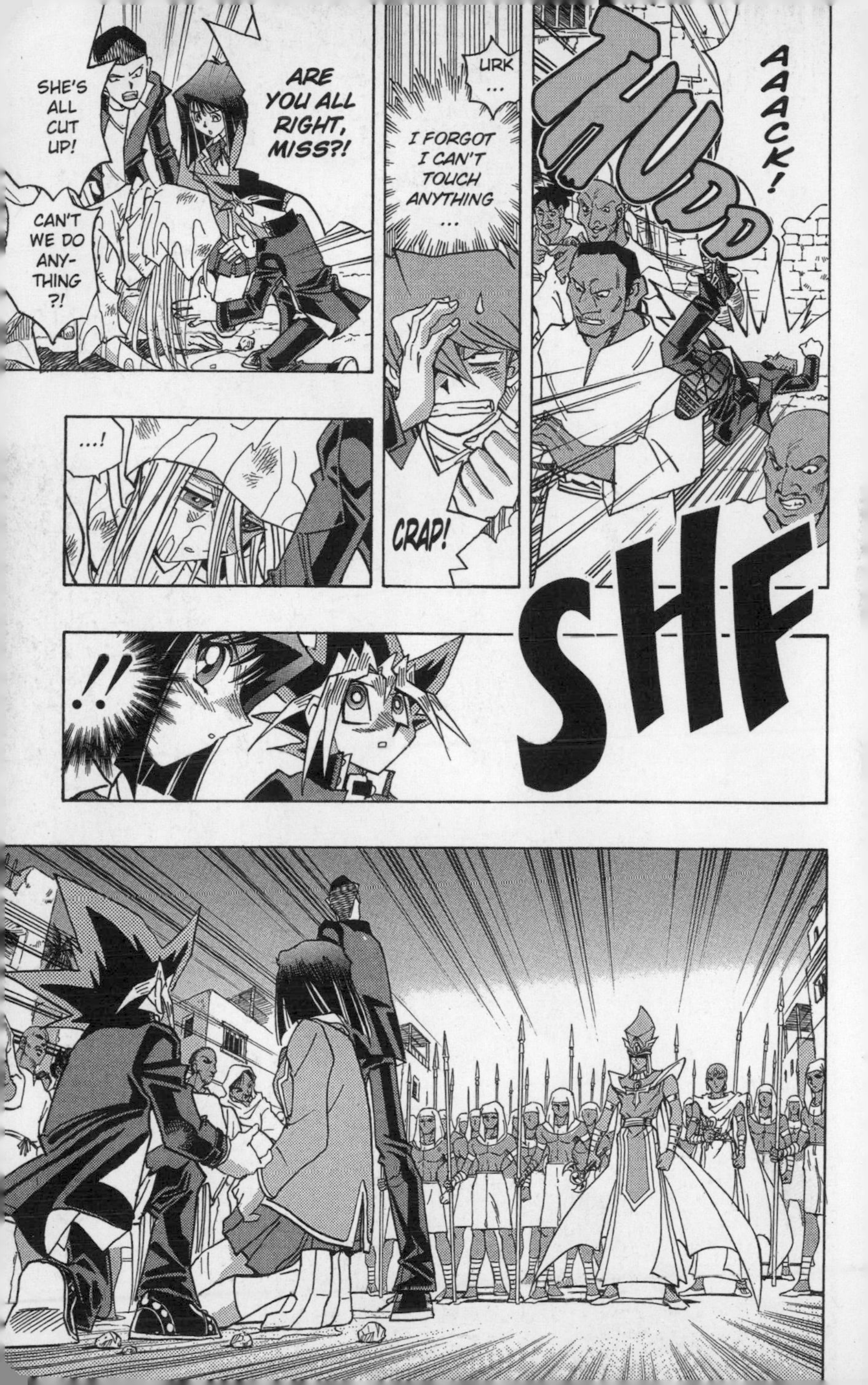
THUDD
AAAACK!
URK...
I FORGOT I CAN'T TOUCH ANYTHING...
CRAP!
ARE YOU ALL RIGHT, MISS?!
SHE'S ALL CUT UP!
CAN'T WE DO ANYTHING?!
...!
SHF
!!

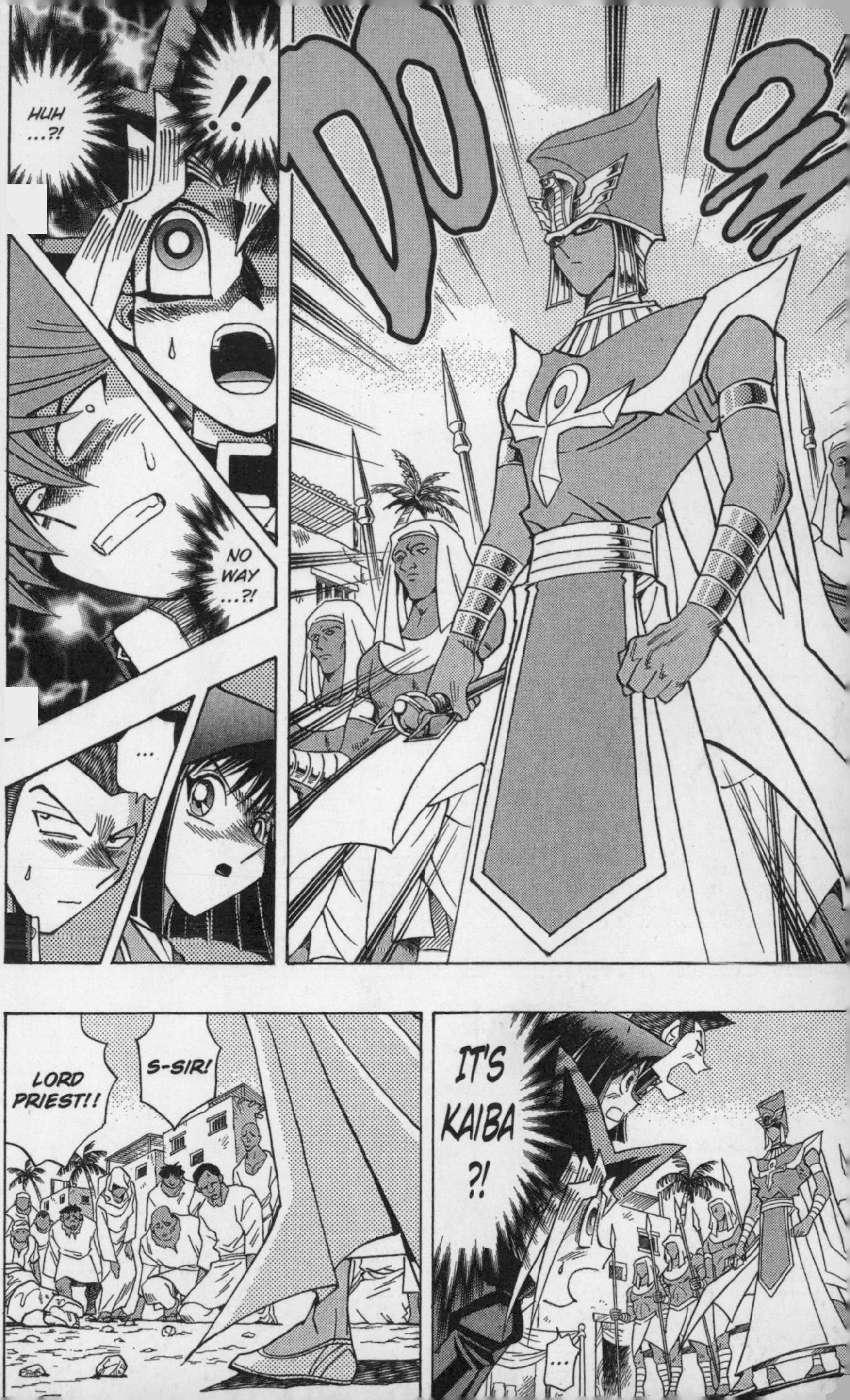
DOOOM
!!
HUH...?!
NO WAY...?!
...
IT'S KAIBA?!
...
S-SIR!
LORD PRIEST!!

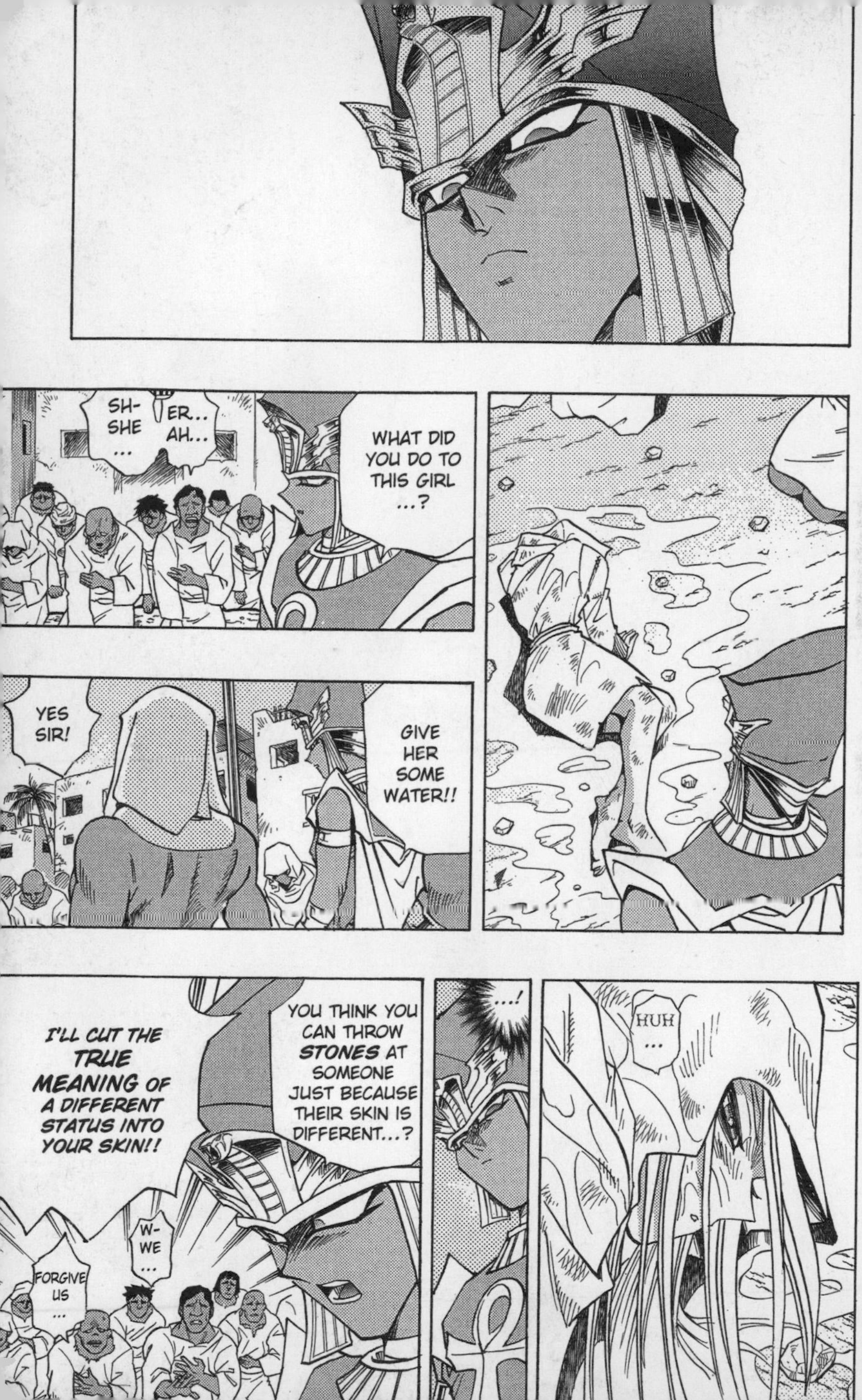
WHAT DID YOU DO TO THIS GIRL ...?
ER... AH...
SH- SHE ...
GIVE HER SOME WATER!!
YES SIR!
HUH ...
...!
YOU THINK YOU CAN THROW STONES AT SOMEONE JUST BECAUSE THEIR SKIN IS DIFFERENT...?
I'LL CUT THE TRUE MEANING OF A DIFFERENT STATUS INTO YOUR SKIN!!
W- WE ...
FORGIVE US ...

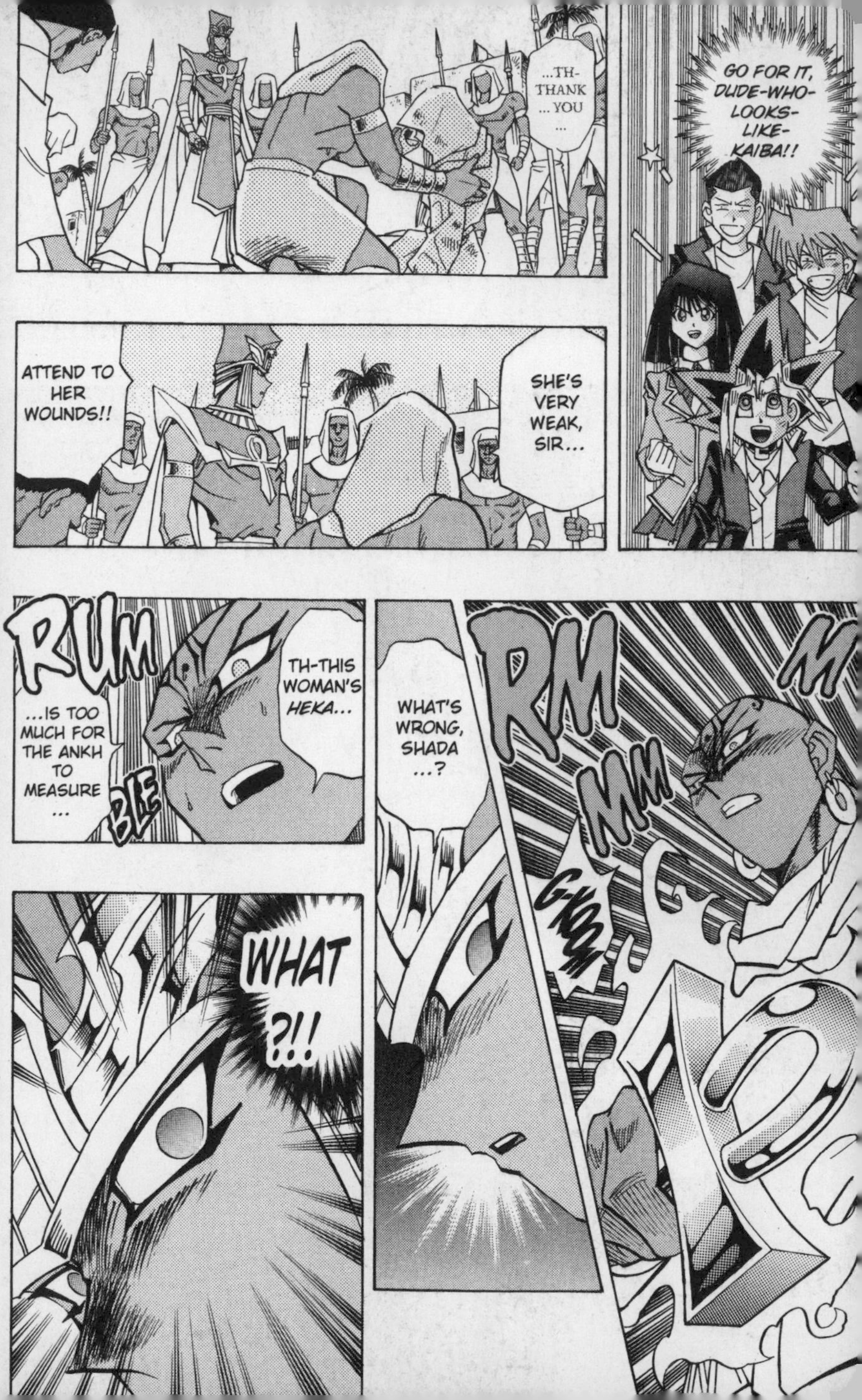
GO FOR IT, DUDE-WHO-LOOKS-LIKE-KAIBA!!
...TH-THANK ...YOU ...
SHE'S VERY WEAK, SIR...
ATTEND TO HER WOUNDS!!
RM
MM
MM
WHAT'S WRONG, SHADA ...?
TH-THIS WOMAN'S HEKA...
...IS TOO MUCH FOR THE ANKH TO MEASURE ...
RUM
BLE
WHAT ?!!

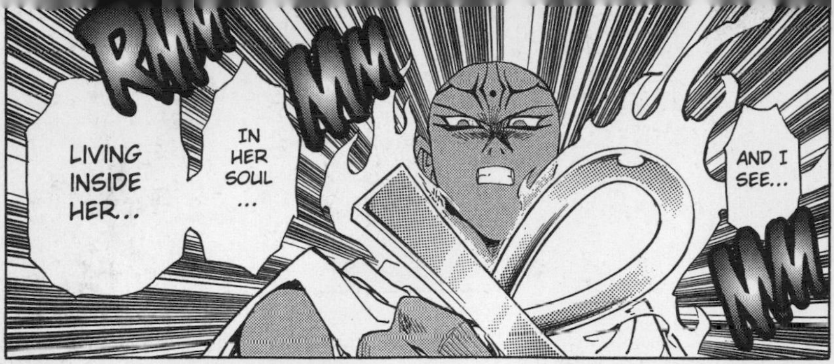
AND I SEE...
MM
MM
RMM
IN HER SOUL ...
LIVING INSIDE HER...

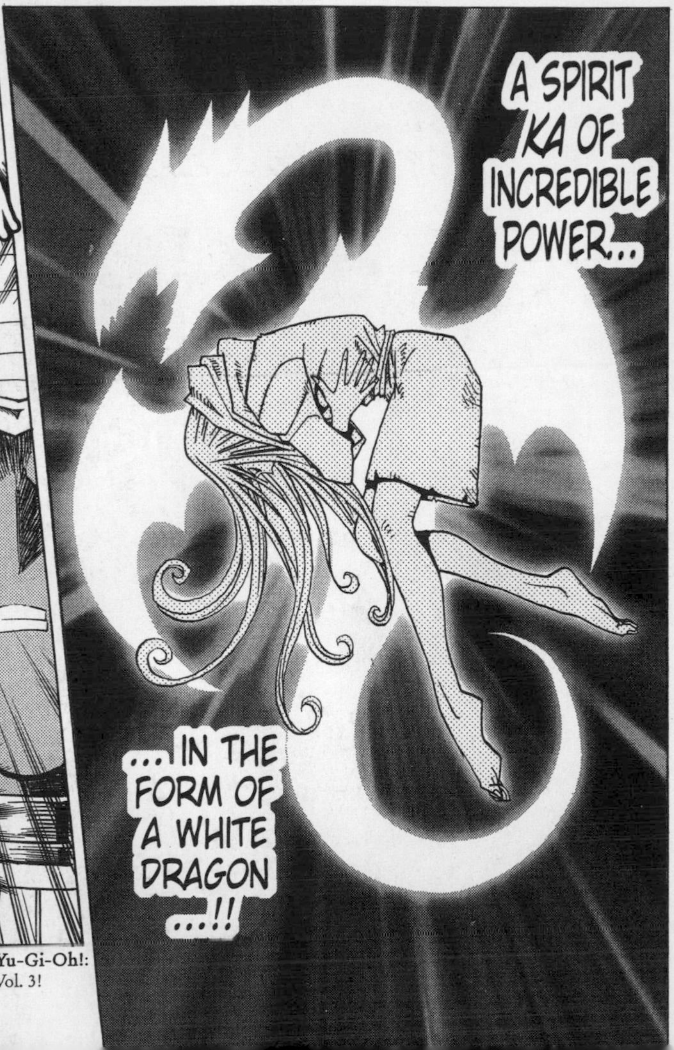
A SPIRIT KA OF INCREDIBLE POWER...
... IN THE FORM OF A WHITE DRAGON ...!!

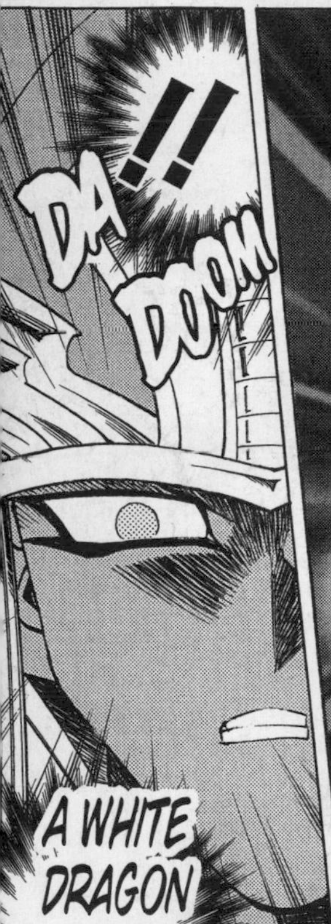
DA!!
DOOM
A WHITE DRAGON ...!!

To Be Continued in **Yu-Gi-Oh!: Millennium World** Vol. 3!

IN THE NEXT VOLUME...

BAKURA'S BACK! The mad tomb robber returns to finish what he started...and this time, the entire city is his target! As Yu-Gi-Oh challenges Bakura to a rematch, Yugi and his friends can only watch helplessly...or is there something they can do after all? Can Slifer the Sky Dragon defeat Diabound? What is the secret of the foreign girl whose soul contains the spirit of the White Dragon? For the sake of Egypt, Bakura must be destroyed!!

AVAILABLE NOW!

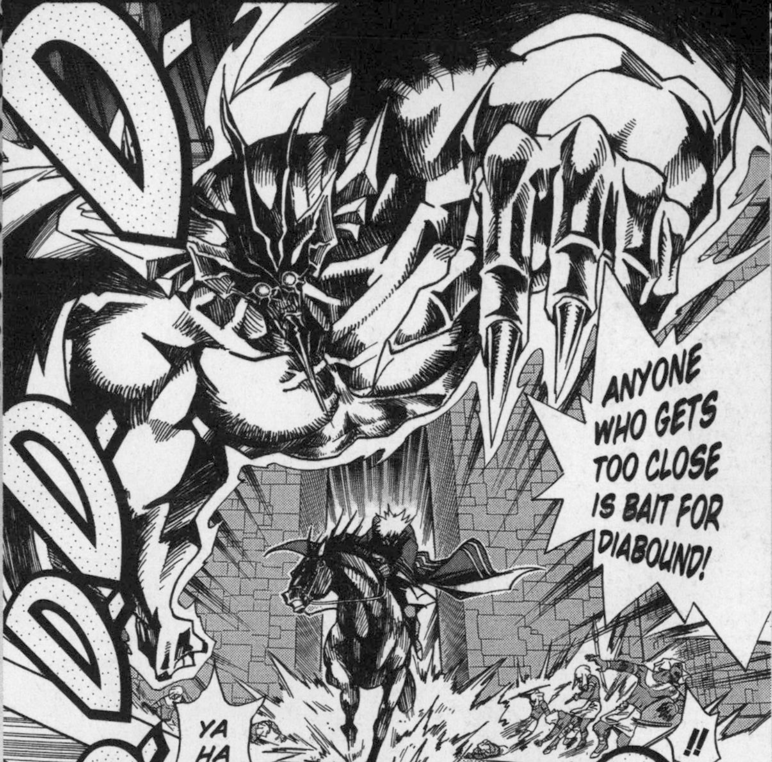
ANYONE WHO GETS TOO CLOSE IS BAIT FOR DIABOUND!
!!
YA HA HA HA HA HA!

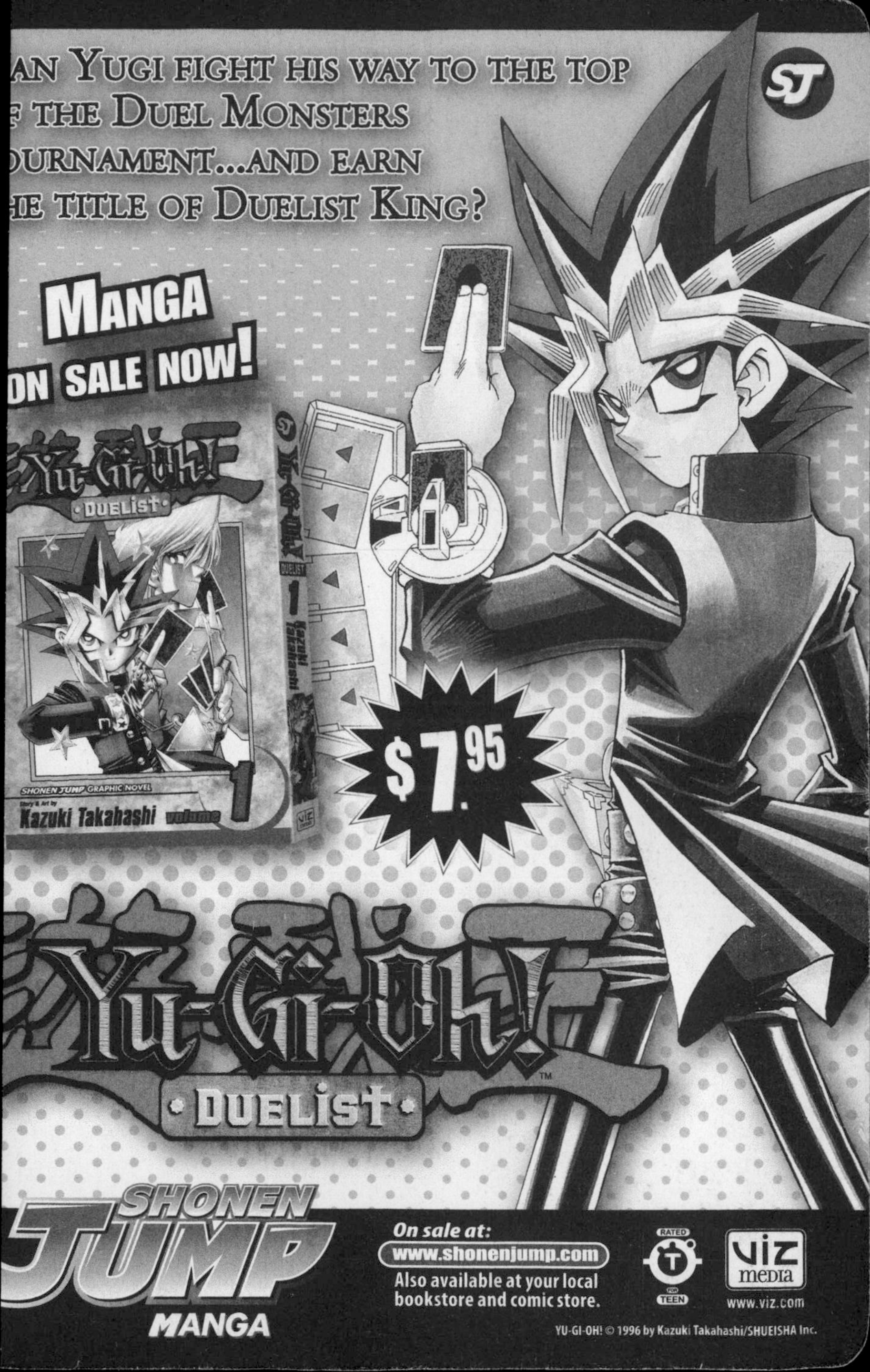
AN YUGI FIGHT HIS WAY TO THE TOP
F THE DUEL MONSTERS
OURNAMENT...AND EARN
HE TITLE OF DUELIST KING?
SJ
MANGA
ON SALE NOW!
YU-GI-OH! DUELIST
SHONEN JUMP GRAPHIC NOVEL
Story & Art by
Kazuki Takahashi volume 1
$7.95
YU-GI-OH! ™
• DUELIST •
SHONEN JUMP
MANGA
On sale at:
www.shonenjump.com
Also available at your local
bookstore and comic store.
RATED T FOR TEEN
VIZ media
www.viz.com
YU-GI-OH! © 1996 by Kazuki Takahashi/SHUEISHA Inc.

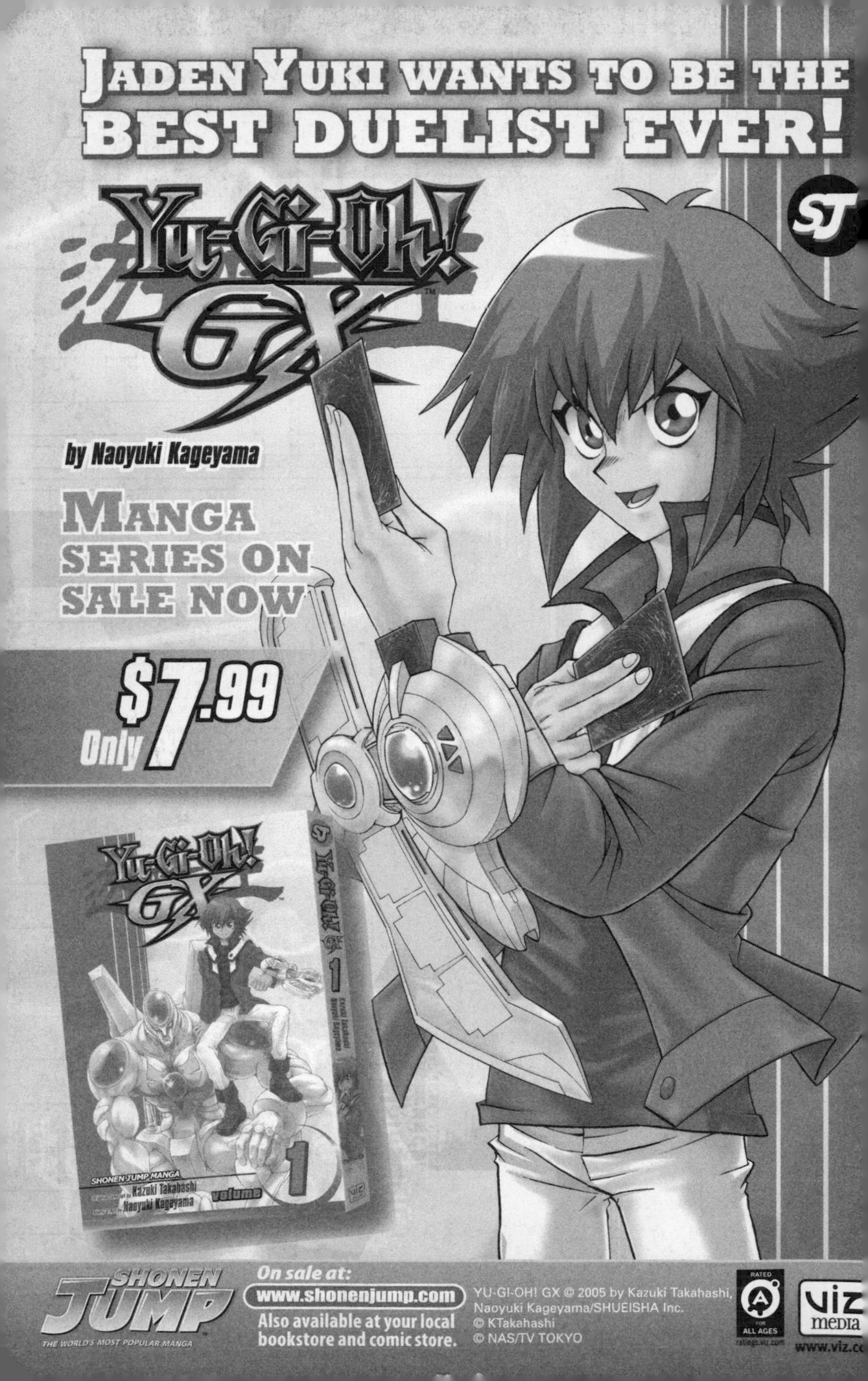

JADEN YUKI WANTS TO BE THE
BEST DUELIST EVER!
SJ
YU-GI-OH! GX
by Naoyuki Kageyama
MANGA SERIES ON SALE NOW
Only $7.99
YU-GI-OH! GX
SHONEN JUMP MANGA
Kazuki Takahashi
Naoyuki Kageyama
volume 1
SHONEN JUMP
THE WORLD'S MOST POPULAR MANGA
On sale at:
www.shonenjump.com
Also available at your local bookstore and comic store.
YU-GI-OH! GX © 2005 by Kazuki Takahashi, Naoyuki Kageyama/SHUEISHA Inc.
© KTakahashi
© NAS/TV TOKYO
RATED A FOR ALL AGES
ratings.viz.com
VIZ media

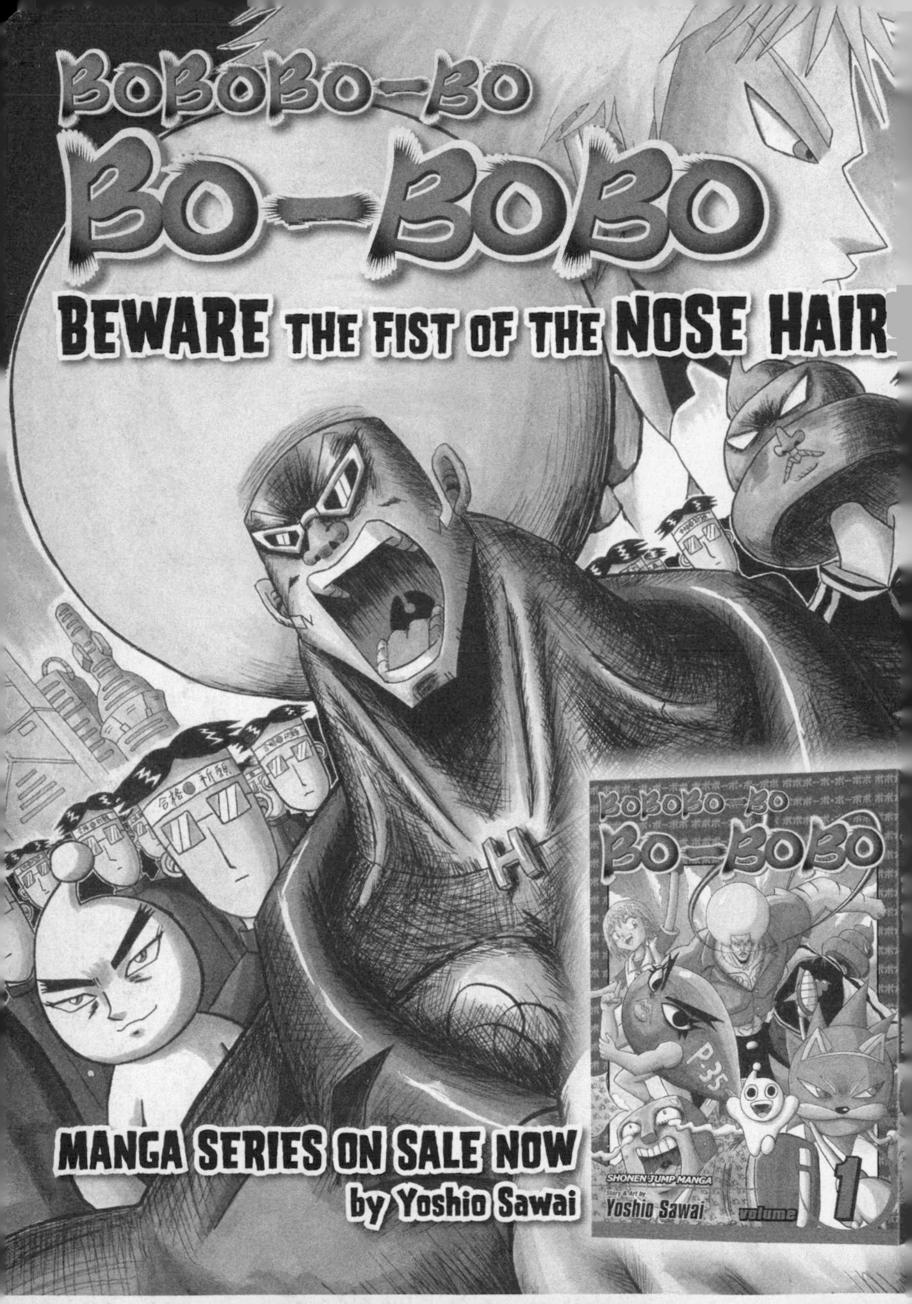
BOBOBO-BO
BO-BOBO
BEWARE THE FIST OF THE NOSE HAIR
MANGA SERIES ON SALE NOW
by Yoshio Sawai
BOBOBO-BO
BO-BOBO
SHONEN JUMP MANGA
Story & Art by
Yoshio Sawai
volume 1

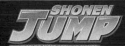

SHONEN JUMP

THE WORLD'S MOST POPULAR MANGA

BLEACH

STORY AND ART BY
TITE KUBO

ONE PIECE

STORY AND ART BY
EIICHIRO ODA

STORY AND ART BY
HIROYUKI ASADA

JUMP INTO THE ACTION BY TELLING US WHAT YOU LOVE (AND WHAT YOU DON'T)

LET YOUR VOICE BE HEARD!

SHONENJUMP.VIZ.COM/MANGASURVEY

HELP US MAKE MORE OF THE WORLD'S MOST POPULAR MANGA!

www.viz.com